DISCARD

Trade and Empire

The British Customs Service
in Colonial America
1660–1775

Trade and Empire

The British Customs Service in Colonial America

1660–1775

Thomas C. Barrow

Harvard University Press
Cambridge, Massachusetts
1967

Library of Congress Catalog Card Number 67-11666

Printed in the United States of America

To my Mother and my Father

Preface

FOR a century, from its inception in 1673 to its collapse in 1775, the colonial customs service was the principal agency of enforcement for English commercial laws and regulations. As such, it was centrally involved in both the creation and execution of policy. And it is on that aspect of the customs service — its contribution to the creation and execution of colonial policy — that this study is concentrated.

Certain handicaps are involved in any attempt to recreate the history of the customs service. Many of the official records were lost or destroyed during the hectic days of the Revolution. Most of the remainder were consumed in a fire in the Plantation Wing of the London Customs House in 1814. Consequently there exists today no convenient, unified source of information on the service. However, the Customs Department itself was a branch of the English Treasury, and the Treasury Papers survive in profusion, many customs house documents among them. Other items may be located in the Colonial Office Papers and in other official series, while such private collections as the papers of the Duke of Newcastle offer further information. The gaps are numerous, the results not entirely satisfactory, but at least the broad outlines of the story can be established.

To the directors and staff of the various libraries and historical societies I have visited I am most grateful, with particular thanks to Kenneth Timings and Noel Blakiston of the Public Record Office and to R. C. Jarvis of the King's Beam House, London, all of whom were more than generous with their time and patience. To the History Department of Harvard University, the American Philosophical Society, and the Society of Colonial Dames, I am grateful for their financial assistance with this project. And for the generous financial support provided by the Research Council of the University of Missouri I am particularly appreciative. My thanks also to Stanley N. Katz for both his friendship and help along the way and to David Ransome for his voluntary, time-consuming labors.

vii

Preface

In any study covering such an extended period there are certain to be errors, and I can only hope that they have been kept to a minimum. If they have it is partly the contribution of Neil Stout and L. Kinvin Wroth, both of whom read an early version of the manuscript and made helpful suggestions. William Paxton has spent considerable time at various stages of this study, saving me from many stylistic errors. And to Bernard Bailyn, who supervised the original work from which this study comes, I owe a special debt. Finally to my wife, who made the whole project worthwhile, I owe the most of all.

T. C. B.

Columbia, Missouri
March 1966

Contents

Trade and Empire

The British Customs Service
in Colonial America
1660–1775

Abbreviations

Introduction

A Theory of Empire

. . . whereby to make this little Northerne corner of the world, to be in a short time the richest Storehouse and Staple for marchandize in all Europe.[1]

HISTORIANS refer to the "Old Colonial System" but in fact there was little that was systematic about the organization of the First British Empire. Based largely on a patchwork mosaic of measures adopted through expediency or accident, the imperial structure had little coherence or uniformity. If there was any organizing principle at all behind the resultant arrangements it was to be found, not in consciously defined systems, but rather in the unconscious assumptions with which the average Englishman of two or three centuries ago approached the day-to-day problems of empire. If asked to justify the existence of the empire, Englishmen generally in the days of William of Orange or of George III would have replied in much the same way, the similarities of their answers arising from a fundamental theory of empire implicitly held, if not always explicitly stated, by the majority of Englishmen. Mercantilism, it has been pointed out, never achieved the unified, coherent expression that might have been expected. The term itself was not in popular use until the colonial period was near its close.[2] Yet for all its lack of formal contemporary definition, mercantilism was a doctrine — or, more accurately, a series of assumptions — of pervasive influence.

Modern analysts have reduced the complex elements of the mercantilist theories to one primary item — the balance of international trade. According to mercantilist dogma, "there existed only a fixed amount of trade in the world, and . . . it behooved each nation to compete as fiercely and successfully as possible for as large a share of that amount as it could secure."[3] This fundamental conviction influenced all the other

I

items in the mercantilist's arsenal of economic beliefs. Bullionism was an early, somewhat naïve expression of the trade balance conception; the later elaborate paraphernalia of duties and bounties, of import restrictions and export encouragements, grew naturally out of the same principle. In this respect, mercantilism was a doctrine of international economic warfare.

So far as the colonies were concerned, the heart of the mercantilist program was found in the commercial system outlined in the various Navigation Acts. Ideally, the colonies and the mother country together would form complementary units, each supplying the other's needs, thus creating the self-sufficiency that would better equip the mother country to engage in the international commercial competition. In pursuit of this imperial self-sufficiency the mother country necessarily was entitled to regulate the economic activities of her colonists. The simplicity of this concept, with its implication of a natural harmony of interests between colonies and mother country, should not obscure the fact that this "theory relegated the Colonies to a position of permanent subordination in the economic evolution of the Empire."[4] The colonists were dependents, not partners; subordinates, not equals. If there was one central, unifying idea behind the organization of the First British Empire, it was the unquestioned commercial supremacy of the mother country.

As to the Navigation Acts themselves, historians have disagreed not only on the attitude of the American colonists toward these regulations but also as to their effectiveness. For George Bancroft, ardent disciple of free trade, the Navigation Acts were the major source of friction between the colonists and England: "The commercial liberties of rising states were shackled by paper chains, and the principles of natural justice subjected to the fears and covetousness of English shopkeepers."[5] According to George Louis Beer, the commercial system offered benefits to both the mother country and the colonists: "The system as a whole was thus based on the idea of the mutual reciprocity of the economic interests of mother country and colony." As to the operation of the commercial regulations, which Bancroft had found ineffectual prior to 1763, Beer argued that despite minor weaknesses the effectiveness of the system "as a whole was not seriously impaired."[6] The latest word on the Navigation Acts has been offered by Oliver M. Dickerson, who states succinctly that the Navigation System "worked" and that the trouble arose only "with the change of policy beginning in 1764, where the dominant motive was not regulation and development, but regulation for the sake of revenue and political exploitation."[7]

The treatment of the Navigation Acts in particular, and the "Old Colonial System" in general, by the various historians suggests a fundamental point of disagreement: did or did not the Americans oppose the regulatory principles involved in the English commercial laws? Or, to put the question another way, did the American colonists willingly accept their theoretical position as economic and political subordinates? Here, of course, care must be taken to differentiate between the theory and the reality of the "Old Colonial System." The Navigation Acts might have been objectionable to the colonists in principle, but if the regulations were not in fact enforced, the Americans would have little reason for complaint.[8]

Discussion of the attitude of the colonists toward the English system raises another question: if the Americans did object to the controls over their commercial activities, were the means of enforcement available to the English adequate for the coercion of a recalcitrant colonial society? The system of commercial regulations could have been effective either through the voluntary cooperation of the colonists or through the ability of the English government to impose its wishes in spite of opposition. If the evidence suggests that the colonists did oppose the restrictive principles of the Navigation System, the effectiveness of enforcement then becomes the principal question. It is on this dual problem of the attitude of the colonists and the effectiveness of the commercial regulations that the history of the British customs service in America is centered.

I

Origins of the Colonial Service

THE colonial customs service was called into being through the desire of the English government to achieve enforcement of the Navigation Acts in the American colonies. The purpose of the Navigation Laws themselves was neatly summarized in the preface to the Staple Act of 1663, which noted that the various regulations were enacted to maintain "a greater Correspondence and Kindness" between the colonies and mother country; to keep the colonists "in a firmer Dependence" upon England; and to render them "yet more beneficial and advantagious" to the mother country by furthering the "Imployment and Increase of English Shipping and Seamen," by increasing the sale of "English Woollen and other Manufactures," by rendering navigation to and from the colonies "more safe and cheap," and by making England "a Staple, not only of the Commodities of those Plantations, but also of the Commodities of other Countries and Places, for the Supplying of them."[1]

The policy embodied in the Navigation System was an old one. As early as 1621 the Privy Council, observing that England would receive the most advantage from the colony of Virginia "if the Commodities brought from thence were appropriated unto his Majesties subjectes" and "not communicated to forraine countries, but by way of Trade and commerce from hence onely," had ordered that "henceforth all Tobacco and other commodities whatsoever" should "not be carried into any forraine partes until the same have beene first landed here and his Majesties Customes paid therefore."[2] In the first Navigation Act, the Ordinance of 1651, Parliament legislated a part of the earlier Stuart program into a basic imperial rule: none of the produce of America, Africa, or Asia was to be imported into England, Ireland, or any English possession except in English ships manned primarily by English subjects. Further, commodities of foreign production could be imported into English territories in foreign ships only if both the goods and the ships belonged to the same place of origin.[3]

The Parliamentary Act of 1651 was merely a preliminary. The Stuart Restoration in 1660 inaugurated a serious attempt to organize the English colonies on the basis of mercantilist doctrines. Charles II returned to England in May, 1660. Since his government refused to recognize the validity of statutes enacted under the Commonwealth, immediate legislative action was required. On the 13th of September Parliament passed "An Act for the Encouraging and Increasing of Shipping and Navigation." Based on the precedent of the Ordinance of 1651, this Act, through additions and corrections, went far beyond its predecessor. The first paragraph made the prohibition against foreign vessels in English colonial trade absolute: "No Goods or Commodities whatsoever shall be imported into or exported out of any Lands . . . to his Majesty belonging . . . but in such Ships . . . as do truly . . . belong only to the People of England or Ireland . . . Wales or Town of Berwick upon Tweed, or are of Build of and belonging to any of the said . . . Territories." [4]

Otherwise the Act required that vessels in the colonial trade should be not only English owned but manned by an English master and a crew three-fourths of whom also were English.[5] Aliens were forbidden to "exercise the Trade or Occupation of Merchant or Factor" in the colonies, while ships of foreign construction could be used in colonial trade only after English ownership had been attested before customs officials in England. An innovation in this Act of 1660 involved certain colonial produce considered especially necessary for English self-sufficiency. Paragraph eighteen required that "no Sugars, Tobacco, Cotton-wool, Indicoes, Ginger, Fustick, or other dying Wood" of colonial production could be shipped anywhere except to England or English territory.

The Act of 1660 provided the legal basis for engrossing the colonial carrying trade to English shipping. It did not, however, necessarily make England the entrepôt for all colonial commerce. As long as English shipping was employed, all commodities except those enumerated in the Act could be carried directly from the colonies to other European countries, while foreign imports into the colonies also were unrestricted if the requirement concerning English shipping was complied with. This oversight was corrected in the Staple Act of 1663, which provided that "No Commodity of the Growth, Production, or Manufacture of Europe, shall be imported into any . . . Colony . . . but what shall be bona fide, and without Fraud, laden and shipped in England. . . ." [6] Under this rule nonenumerated goods could still be taken from the colonies, in English ships, to foreign ports; but any foreign produce taken on board in exchange had to be carried first to England, unloaded, the duties paid, then the cargo reloaded for shipment to the plantations. Such a system had the double advantage of centering all trade on England while permitting the needy Restoration government to increase its revenues by collection of the duties on foreign imports into England.

A decade of operation, however, showed that there remained a fundamental flaw in the system elaborated by the Acts of 1660 and 1663, a flaw arising logically from the misconceptions prevalent in England concerning the nature of colonial commerce. The English legislators had based their regulations on the assumption that most or all of the colonial trade would be handled by shipping sent out from England. In fact, they sadly underestimated the growth of intercolonial commerce. Trade originating in the colonies could not be as effectively controlled as that operating out of English ports. By 1672 it had become obvious to the English authorities that, under cover of intercolonial commerce, some enumerated products were finding their way to foreign markets. In the Act of 1673, passed to stop these violations of the mercantile code, the Parliamentary legislators complained that earlier laws permitted the free exchange of enumerated products between the colonies "without paying of Customs for the same, either at the Lading or Unlading" which greatly increased the "Trade and Navigation in those Commodities, from one Plantation to another," while the colonists "not contenting themselves with being supplied with those Commodities . . . free from all Customs (while the Subjects of . . . England have paid great Customs . . .)" continued to bring into "Europe great Quantities thereof . . . to the great Hurt and Diminution of your Majesty's Customs, and the Trade and Navigation of this your Kingdom." [7] Consequently in the new Act Parliament stipulated that if any vessel came to the colonies to take on board enumerated goods, and "Bond shall not be first given with sufficient Surety to bring the same to England," in that case certain duties were to be paid before the enumerated products could be loaded.[8]

The Navigation Act of 1673 is the only one whose significance needs clarification, since its provisions have caused some confusion. It is generally argued, and accepted, that the Navigation Laws were enacted, not to raise a revenue, but to direct trade to the advantage of the mother country and the home industries. Such arguments were popular in the decade before the outbreak of the Revolution when the colonists objected to the reforms of 1764 on the grounds that they replaced regulations with taxation; the Americans claimed the earlier duties had been intended to guide the flow of trade, not to raise a revenue. Over the years most historians have accepted this basic differentiation between the first Acts and those of the Revolutionary era. The small returns collected in the colonies from the duties on enumerated goods seem to support this interpretation.[9] The Lord Treasurer himself two years after the passage of the Act noted that it had been enacted "to turn the course of a trade rather than to raise any considerable revenue to his Majesty." [10]

The question remains of why, if regulation was the motive, duties were imposed in the colonies. Enforcement of the provisions concerning enumerated commodities in the earlier Acts depended principally on the use of bonds: a ship before going to the colonies was required to give bond guaranteeing that if enumerated commodities were taken on board in the course of the voyage they would be brought to England or English territory and not elsewhere. If evidence appeared showing that this requirement had been violated, the bonds could be put in suit in a court of law. It seems odd that the English government did not think it enough merely to extend enforcement of the bonding provisions to the colonies. A great deal of confusion might have been avoided had they done so. In January, 1676, merely three years after the passage of the Act, the Privy Council's Committee on Plantation Affairs (the "Lords of Trade") were themselves bewildered about the purpose of the duties collected in the colonies. They wondered whether by the Act of 1673 "a Ship that lades the Commodities there enumerated, and payes the Duty there imposed, by declaring themselves bound to another of his Majesty's Plantations be not exempted from any other Bonds, and at free Liberty to carry such Commodities to what part of the World they please." [11] If this interpretation by the Lords of Trade had been accepted, the Act of 1673 would have given the colonists, after they had paid the duties on enumerated goods, the privilege of free trade with the rest of the world.

The attorney general, in answer to a question from the Lords of Trade, predictably rejected that concept. In his opinion, the Act of 1673 did not repeal the Act of 1663, which required ships going from one colony to another to give bond to carry enumerated commodities only to England or other English territory. The Act of 1673, he said, placed a duty on enumerated goods if bond had not been first given, which meant that a vessel going from England to the plantations gave bond to bring the enumerated items "into England only, and in that case no Duty is to be paid at the Plantation." But if a ship came from any other place of origin than England "then the Duty must be paid and also a bond given to the Governours as before to carry the goods to some English Plantation or to England." [12] That is, in the view of the attorney general, both the bonding provisions and the collection of duties were to be enforced in the colonies, which in fact became the rule of procedure throughout the rest of the colonial period.

It is obvious that the motives involved in the enactment of the Act of 1673 were complex, that the new law was something more than a "simple but ingenious remedy" to prevent the introduction of enumerated goods directly into Europe.[13] From the wording of the passage from the Act quoted earlier a certain irritation can be noted in England concerning the colonists' tax-free use of goods for which the English had to pay ample duties: the colonists were not content "with being supplied with those Commodities . . . free from all Customs" while the English "have paid great Customs." Who were these colonists who enjoyed this tax advantage over their English competitors? Clearly they were not those who raised the enumerated commodities themselves; there was no suggestion of taxing them for the use of their own produce. It was the settlers in other areas, where the enumerated goods were not produced, who benefited from the free importation. In fact, it was the northern colonies, particularly New England, that the English legislators had in mind in 1673.

According to mercantilist dogma the northern continental colonies were the least valuable of the British possessions. An area such as New

England actually seemed to have more potential as a competitor to the homeland than as an asset; it produced few or none of the required raw materials and prospered only by adopting trade patterns which appeared detrimental to English interests. A year before the Act levying duties had been introduced into Parliament the Privy Council received a report which noted the possibility that colonies of the New England type would "dayly grow more destructive to the trade of this Kingdome." At the same time the president of the Lords of Trade commented that in twenty years New England was likely to "be mighty and powerfull and not at all careful of theire dependance upon Old England" and suggested that it would be well to "hinder theire growth as much as can be." [14] Lord Culpepper, a member of the Lords of Trade, noted after passage of the Act that it "seems to be wholly made in reference to New England." [15]

Viewed against this background the reasoning behind the imposition of the duties is clear: they were a tax on the intercolonial coasting trade designed to restrict participation by the northern colonies in the exportation and consumption of materials deemed necessary to English prosperity. The specific intentions of the Act of 1673 may be summarized in this way: 1) to ensure that colonial competitors did not enjoy tax-free benefits not available to Englishmen at home; 2) to restrict the intercolonial coasting commerce, particularly in commodities required in England; 3) to limit the colonial coastal trade generally, with a consequent reduction in the shipment of enumerated goods directly to foreigners; 4) to increase the home revenues by increasing the supplies of such taxable imports as tobacco and sugar; and 5) to tighten English control over colonial markets.

The Act of 1673 was not, then, directly connected to the raising of a revenue. But indirectly that Act, and in fact all the Navigation Acts, were related to the procurement of revenue, and that relationship deserves some emphasis. In the wording of the Act of 1673 Parliament noted that colonial evasion of the trade regulations was a "great Hurt and Diminution of your Majesty's Customs." [16] Earlier a letter from the Treasury to the colonial governors, in 1667, had stressed the importance "to his Majesty's revenue in particular that those laws [the Navigation Acts] should be duly and strictly observed." [17] While it is probably true that the English government did not expect the duties collected in the colonies under the Act of 1673 to amount to very much, revenue considerations were still involved: a decrease in colonial handling and consumption of enumerated goods presumably would mean an increase in the shipment of those products to Great Britain, with a consequent increase in the government's collection of import duties. And there is no question about the interest of Charles II in increased revenues. It was, in fact, his government's financial embarrassments that led directly to the creation of the colonial customs service.

Charles II's financial needs upon his return to England were so urgent that he voluntarily assumed an old debt of £250,000, which his father had owed to the former farmers of the customs, on the condition that those creditors would loan him immediately an additional £150,000, "to be paid in within a month." [18] For the same reason Charles II reverted to the arrangements concerning the collection of customs duties in England that had prevailed in his father's day; he put an end to the Parliamentary committee that had supervised the customs since 1643 and once again entrusted the collection to a group of private speculators known as the "farmers." It was a convenient arrangement since, in return for the long-term profits of their "farm," the speculators could be persuaded to make occasional loans to the king. [19]

On the other hand, these new creditors had to be assured of a fair return on their investment. In the same year that the customs were again farmed out, Parliament passed an "Act for preventing Frauds, and regulating Abuses in His Majesty's Customs." [20] In various ways this Act tightened the customs collection and protected the "Officers employed in the Affairs of the Customs" from "Violence used against" them. By this Act Parliament and the king did much to ensure that the customs returns would be high and the farmers' profits adequate.

However, this new law left one problem unsolved; as noted, duties on produce imported into England from the colonies were affected adversely by colonial evasion of the Acts of Trade. Tobacco sent directly to foreign ports, for example, not only benefited England's commercial rivals but also lessened the revenue at home, a loss of which the English government was well aware. As early as 1664 a plan was approved authorizing the farmers to establish agents in the colonies to see to enforcement of the Acts. [21] The Dutch War postponed action for several years, but in 1669 the Lords of Trade recommended once more that the farmers should send agents to America to put a stop to illegal practices.[22] The farmers, however, never were to dispatch representatives to America. Within two years Charles II, feeling his financial position to be more secure, no longer needed to mortgage the customs revenues for the sake of quick loans. In 1671 he put an end to the career of the farmers, so that the first customs agents to go to the colonies were to be royal officers, not representatives of the king's creditors.[23]

The matter of enforcement of the trade regulations had been a problem since the passage of the first Navigation Act in 1651, which had elaborated no special measures for enforcement. Since its major purpose was to cut off Dutch intrusions on the English carrying trade, primary reliance was placed on the navy and its ability to capture foreign intruders in English waters. Otherwise the Act depended on a loose system of voluntary cooperation by private citizens, who received a half share in the proceeds from a seizure for acting as informers.[24] In England itself, of course, the regular customs machinery was available to aid in enforcement.

The Act of 1660 continued the methods employed by the earlier Act. The royal navy was "authorized and strictly required to seize" any foreign vessels found trading in forbidden waters, while informers assisting in seizures were offered one-third of the proceeds. The two innovations in this Act involved the registering of ships and the use of bonds. According to the new regulations, any Englishman purchasing a ship of foreign construction had to register it with the customs officers in the port from which he operated. At the same time, vessels sailing from England for the colonies were required to post bond to guarantee compliance with the provisions concerning enumerated commodities, while ships coming to the colonies from any place other than Great Britain were to post similar bonds with the various governors.[25] This three-fold program of using bonds, registering shipping, and involving the governors in enforcement, was continued and expanded throughout the colonial period.

The Act of 1663 made the governors' duties more explicit. Any person importing "any Goods or Commodities whatsoever" into any colony was required to give a true inventory of his cargo to the governor "or to such . . . Officer as shall be by him thereunto authorized" within twenty-four hours of arrival. No ship was to unload or load any goods until the proper information concerning its cargo, as well as certificates showing that it was English owned and manned, had been offered to the governor. All governors were to take oath for the faithful performance of this trust, on pain of loss of office and forfeiture of £1,000.[26]

Unfortunately, information reaching the English government indicated that these measures were inadequate. In a circular letter to all governors in 1663, the year of the Staple Act, the Privy Council explained that they had made the duties of the governors so explicit and the penalties for nonperformance so high because they had heard of "neglects or rather Contempts" of the king's orders. Ships, it was said, were still trading directly between the colonies and Holland, Spain, Venice, and other foreign ports, primarily because of the failure to take bond and to check for English ownership. In this letter the Privy Council added to the governor's responsibilities by requiring that complete listings of all shipping entering and clearing each colony should be returned yearly to London.[27] Four years later the government, noting the lack of improvement, again felt it necessary to write to the colonial governors, this time charging directly that nonenforcement of the Navigation Acts was caused by "the neglect of duty in his Governours." Repetition of the responsibilities and the penalties did little to correct the situation.[28]

Confronted with the failure of enforcement in the colonies, which not only violated mercantilist ideals but lessened the revenues, the English government turned to the customs service. On the 26th of October, 1671, the first royal customs officer was appointed for the colonies. Rather naturally, since tobacco was a top revenue producer, this first agent was assigned to Virginia. In a letter to the governor King Charles explained the reasons for the appointment: noting that he had put an end to the farm of the customs and entrusted the revenues to the care of a royal commission, he pointed out that a large part of the customs receipts was derived from the importation of tobacco into England. Since numerous frauds were continually being reported, particularly of ships bypassing England to avoid payment of the duties, he was appointing a customs surveyor for Virginia, who would check the bonds and securities offered and see that the proper reports were returned regularly to London.[29] In effect this new customs officer was intended to act as a check on the colonial governor. The first appointment went to Dudley Digges, a native of Virginia, who was provided with an annual salary of £250.[30]

Before Digges had been long in office, Parliament passed the Act of 1673. It has been mistakenly assumed that this Act extended the English customs service to the colonies.[31] Actually the king had already done just that on his own authority in the appointment of Digges. The Act of 1673 gave Parliamentary approval and authority to a prior royal action. After detailing the new duties to be imposed on enumerated goods, Parliament included this paragraph in the new Act:

And for the better Collection of the several Rates and Duties aforesaid . . . Be it enacted . . . That this whole Business shall be ordered and managed, and the several Duties hereby imposed shall be caused to be levied by the Commissioners of the Customs in England . . . under the Authority and Directions of the Lord Treasurer . . . or Commissioners of the Treasury for the Time being.[32]

The wording of this passage, so succinct in contrast to the usual involved and cautious style of such laws, confirms the impression that Parliament here was approving, rather than initiating, a program. In fact, Parliament assumed so little responsibility for the new arrangement that its vague statement that "this whole Business" should be managed by the Customs Commissioners left many questions unanswered, to the future sorrow of the officers sent to the colonies. The colonists were, in time, to claim that only the collection of the enumerated duties was entrusted to the customs officers and not the enforcement of the Acts of Trade and Navigation generally. Obviously, however, from the content of the royal letter appointing Digges, the intention was to use the new officials to ensure obedience to all the commercial regulations. In fact, it is well to remember that the motive behind this extension of the customs service to the colonies, with its hope for a consequent improvement in the effectiveness of the Navigation Acts, stemmed from a desire to increase the revenue. One hundred years later a new effort, in which the customs service was again involved, was undertaken to tighten the workings of the Navigation System for exactly the same purpose. The difference then — and it was an important difference to the colonists — was that the later attempt involved the raising of a revenue in the colonies themselves. On that point England was to lose an empire.

With passage of the Act of 1673 formal organization of the colonial customs service could take place. On November 27, 1673, the first list of officers for the colonies was drawn up. As in the case of the earlier appointment of Digges, the first concern of the English authorities was for those colonial areas which produced most of the enumerated goods. Two customs officials, a collector and a surveyor, were assigned to Maryland, the Carolinas, Virginia, Bermuda, and certain of the West Indies islands. The salary arrangements made for these new colonial bureaucrats are of special interest. To make the amount of the enumerated duties collected as large as possible, the customs officers were paid a percentage of total receipts in their area, the proportion varying from colony to colony depending on the estimated potential yield. In Virginia the collector received one-eighth of the receipts, from which amount he was to pass one-third on to the surveyor. In the Carolinas the collector was allowed one-half of the collection, of which one-third went to the surveyor. In Maryland the division was one-sixth to the collector, with one-third of that to the surveyor.[33]

The establishment of a new imperial agency called for the preparation of an elaborate series of instructions and directions. The collectors assigned to each colony received a detailed list of special orders. Before entering on their office they were required to give bond and take an oath before the governor in their colony for the faithful performance of their trust. They were to determine the best location for a customs house and to appoint deputies to cover the outlying areas. They were to see to it that the masters of all ships not having given bond to return to England reported to their office with detailed information on their cargoes. Before any enumerated goods were loaded on any vessel, the duties were to be collected, while careful accounts were to be preserved of all transactions, with close attention being paid to the detection of possible frauds. They were warned against one possible fraud in particular: since ships having previously given bond to return to England had to pay no duties, the collectors were to see that no goods supposedly intended to be put on board such vessels were instead actually loaded on a nonbonded ship. More generally, they were to check all imports coming into the colony to make sure no commodities were arriving directly from Europe without a stopover in England; they were to insist that every incoming ship report to the governor immediately on arrival to prove it was English owned and manned; they were to be certain that the governor sent home to London the required lists of entries and clearances, while they themselves sent home duplicate lists as well. Finally, they were ordered generally to see to enforcement of all the Acts of Trade and Navigation, particularly the bonding provisions, seizing all transgressors.[34]

The surveyors received their own instructions, which for the most part merely obliged them to see that the collectors did their work properly. They were to keep duplicates of all the collector's accounts, to check and sign all accounts sent home to London, and to watch with particular care to see that the bonding provisions were complied with. All deputies appointed by the collector were required to send copies of their accounts to the surveyor as well as to the collector.[35]

None of the northern continental colonies were included in the original list of officers drawn up in late 1673. Actually, in view of the vagueness of the wording of the Act drawn up by Parliament, there was some doubt in London that it applied to such areas as New England. The duties were levied on enumerated goods only, none of which were produced in New England. Consequently, perhaps it had been intended to place customs officers only where the goods were produced. After some delay, in 1675 this question was referred to the Commissioners of the Customs. They replied that the Act of 1673, as well as all the Acts of Trade, applied to New England as much as to any other colony, which, if the intention was to achieve general enforcement of the Navigation System in all the colonies, was only common sense.[36]

Assignment of customs officers to New England was further delayed by King Philip's War, which ravaged those colonies between June, 1675, and September, 1676. Even so, New England continued to be a topic of consideration in London. In March, 1676, the Lord Treasurer, disturbed by reports indicating that ships from New England were still purchasing European goods directly from Holland and France and distributing them throughout all the colonies with no stopover in England, asked the Commissioners of the Customs to select someone to administer the required oaths to the various New England governors and also "to advise me what you think fit to be further done for the prevention of those practices."[37]

A year later the Treasury, in another letter to the Customs Commissioners, reminded them that there were by now customs officers in all the colonies except those of New England, where "for some weighty reasons" action had been "deferred untill now." The letter continued, "The commotions in those parts being now quieted his Majesty doth now thinke fitt that officers should be forthwith settled there." [38] In response to this royal order the Commissioners undertook to locate a suitable officer for the New England area.

However, some difficulty developed in selecting a candidate for this crucial assignment. Edward Randolph, who knew the region and had useful connections in the English government, seemed a logical choice. He had just returned from New England, where he had served as a member of a royal commission investigating the colonial situation. Unfortunately there was some fear that his participation on that commission had made him so unpopular in New England that he would have difficulty executing the duties of a customs officer. The question was debated at length, and by November, 1677, the Lord Treasurer ordered the Customs Commissioners to nominate someone else "that I might present a fit officer to his Majesty in case of objections against Mr. Randolph as obnoxious . . . to the people." [39]

By May, 1678, the Lord Treasurer had decided against Randolph and ordered the Customs Commissioners to appoint Daniel Whitfield to the New England post. The warrant for Whitfield, noting that an officer was badly needed in New England to prevent the direct importation of European goods and to see that vessels taking on enumerated commodities, which were brought to New England in great quantities, gave bond to go to England, authorized a salary of £100 a year for Whitfield, paid in London until such time as the receipts in New England became adequate for the support of his salary. Whitfield was entitled to appoint deputies in outlying areas, while he himself cared for the major port of Boston.[40]

In the case of Whitfield the Lord Treasurer, for once, had acted too hastily. Edward Randolph had friends in the Privy Council and generally had made a favorable impression through his detailed reports as a member of the royal commission. For the first time, but not the last, political considerations played a part in the operation of the colonial customs service. On May 31, 1678, the king overruled the appointment of Whitfield and ordered Randolph installed in his place, and on June 12 a new warrant was issued naming Edward Randolph collector, surveyor, and searcher of the customs in New England, with the same salary and powers as formerly provided for Whitfield.[41] With the appointment of Randolph, all the English colonies in America were included within the organization of the customs service.

Appointment of customs officers in each of the colonies was not the only measure taken to complete the enforcement system. The effective operation of the Acts of Trade conceivably could be supplemented by extending the preventive precautions into foreign countries, where many of the evasions originated. Obviously English customs officers could not be stationed in foreign ports, but use could be made of the diplomatic and consular officials abroad to report on English shipping trading illegally in their areas, and appropriate instructions were consequently sent to such personnel from time to time.[42] Special agents were even employed occasionally to travel abroad to search out violators; Edward Randolph himself at a later date was sent out on such a mission to Holland "discreetly to inform" himself of transgressors and, if possible, to bring the culprits back "to the next Port of England" for trial.[43]

More important to the future operation of the enforcement system was the use made of the royal navy. By the Act of 1660 the navy was authorized to seize foreign vessels trading in English waters. Unfortunately the later Acts gave the navy no new powers, so that the colonists could claim, with some justice, that ships of war were not entitled to make seizures for violations of any Act but that of 1660. Eventually, in 1687, this loophole was closed. In that year the Treasury, noting that naval vessels off the colonies were finding it difficult to make seizures for general violations of the Acts of Trade, authorized the Commissioners of the Customs to make the naval commanders in colonial waters their deputies, with full power to seize and prosecute ships discovered violating any and all of the provisions of the Acts.[44] In this way the royal navy, in theory at least, was closely tied to the administration of the customs service in the colonies.

One final precaution was taken to ensure the success of the colonial operation. Since the customs officers in the colonies were far removed from the authorities in London, some sort of regular over-all inspection system seemed desirable. That further check was provided in 1681 with the appointment of William Dyer as surveyor general of the customs operations in the plantations. Dyer, formerly collector of New York, had been driven from that colony by the local authorities who had prosecuted him as "a false traitor" for collecting unauthorized duties. On the grounds that the New York courts were incompetent to try his case, Dyer managed to have himself sent to England for trial, where he was speedily exonerated. At first he was reassigned as collector for Pennsylvania and the Jerseys, but then the London authorities decided to make use of his experience in a different way and pushed through his appointment as surveyor general. In fulfillment of his new assignment, Dyer made a general inspection of the customs service in each colony, traveling from Bermuda to New England between 1683 and 1685.[45] In 1685 he was recalled and Patrick Mein went out in his place.[46] These surveyors general had the authority to examine into the workings of all the Acts of Trade, to investigate the conduct of the various customs officers, to suspend or appoint officers as required, to search out illegal goods, and to seize violators of the trade laws. Although the office of surveyor general was not made permanent until later, from the appointment of Dyer in 1683 to the end of the colonial period there was always one or more such official overseeing the customs operations in the colonies.

The creation of the office of surveyor general completed the arrangements made in these early years for the colonial customs service. In every colony at least one collector had been placed, along with a surveyor to check his activities. In Virginia and Maryland, which, because of their tobacco output, were the most important of the continental colonies to the English, the original plan (which prevailed in the other colonies) of appointing one collector who created his own deputies had been soon abandoned. In 1676 Virginia was supplied with seven independent collectors, while in 1685 Maryland was divided into two customs districts, each with its own collector. In both of these colonies, however, there still remained only one surveyor, who had the task of checking the accounts of all the collectors.[47]

The West Indies generally were not included within the normal customs service routine, since the officers there were involved in the collection of the special four and one-half percent duty, which over the years was to become the most valuable revenue of all to the English. Only Jamaica, the Bahamas, and Bermuda were not included in the four and one-half percent area; and of those islands only the Bahamas and Bermuda were coupled with the continental customs service, Jamaica being a special case in itself. In the four and one-half percent area the salaries of the customs officers were paid entirely out of that revenue, which made them an entity apart from the officers in the continental colonies, and they were so regarded by the English authorities.[48] Events in the West Indies rarely influenced the operation of the customs service in the continental colonies.

Except for the regular salary established for the collector in New England, the colonial officers continued to receive a percentage allowance of their total receipts; but, since the collections were discovered to be considerably lower than originally expected, the proportions allowed to some were increased.[49] The English accounts for some of these years are missing, making a statement of the average receipts and expenses impossible. From the three consecutive years for which the accounts have survived, however, the records show that between 1681 and 1684 the continental colonies returned a total of £944 to the English Exchequer, for an average of £315 a year. Roughly two-thirds of that sum was allowed to the officers as salary. But these figures are hardly authoritative, since the only two colonies reporting during that period were Virginia and Maryland.[50] From time to time in the accounts for other years the Carolinas and Jerseys appear. The returns were never very large, but on the other hand the colonial customs service itself during these years, because of the salary arrangements, was never a direct charge on the English Exchequer.

From the English point of view the system evolved out of these measures and arrangements seemed logical and practicable. All the regulations necessary to control and direct the colonial trade to the advantage of England in general, and the royal revenues in particular, had been detailed in formal Acts of Parliament. The English customs department, which operated with increasing efficiency at home, had been extended to the colonies. The royal navy had been deployed to aid in enforcement. Even the diplomatic service abroad had been utilized. It remained to be seen, however, how this system, so impressive in theory, would perform in actual operation.

II

Early Years in the Colonies

THE development of the customs service was merely one particular aspect of the general colonial policy pursued by the Restoration government of Charles II. The long years of civil war, followed by the Cromwellian Protectorate, had left the American plantations relatively independent of outside control. With the return of Charles in 1660 that era of freedom was ended and a new period of increased English administrative activity inaugurated. Behind the renewed English interest in the reassertion of royal authority in the colonies lay a concern for the prosperity of England. As the principal adviser to Charles II once remarked, "Upon the king's first arrival in England, he manifested a very great desire to improve the general traffick and trade of the kingdom, and upon all occasions conferred with the most active merchants upon it, and offered all he could contribute to the advancement thereof." [1] One result of this concern for the promotion of trade was enactment of the Navigation Acts, which were intended to guide the colonies into a proper commercial relationship with England. However, more than the direction of trade was involved here: "The fact of the case was that the principle of mercantilism, as applied to the colonies, . . . presupposed the existence of a high degree of both political and social unity as the condition of its success." [2] In an effort to achieve that "political and social unity" the Restoration government re-examined every aspect of colonial administration, the establishment of the Dominion of New England being merely the most dramatic result of the new policies.

Everywhere the reintroduction of English authority touched upon areas of colonial sensitivity, and, obviously, the new customs officers sent to the colonies, innocently or otherwise, hardly could avoid involvement in the tensions created by this explosive situation. In the first decades of the operation of the colonial customs service, three collectors were killed, two imprisoned, and one tried for treason, while another became the chief magistrate in a successful revolutionary government. The record was not encouraging, but from the experiences of these first officers certain lessons were learned which did much to clarify the nature of the problems facing the English colonial program in America.

Edward Digges, first customs officer in Virginia, apparently had been unwilling to continue in office after the £250 salary he had received prior to the Act of 1673 was changed to a percentage allowance of receipts. In his place Giles Bland, an unwise selection, was appointed collector. Bland's father, a London merchant with connections in Virginia, had earlier written an essay condemning the Acts of Trade and favoring Dutch participation in English colonial commerce.[3] Giles, who first went to the colony to look after his father's large holdings there, was young and, in his father's opinion, somewhat of a "hothead." Generally Giles Bland was not a man to respect established authority, and nowhere in the plantations was there a more authoritarian regime than that of Governor William Berkeley in Virginia.

Even before his appointment as collector of the customs, Bland was involved in a controversy of major proportions. In attempting to settle his family's affairs, he had stirred up a heated dispute with Thomas Ludwell, secretary to the province and one of Berkeley's closest councilors. Ludwell charged Bland with having brought to Virginia forged documents which were to be used to claim property not rightfully belonging to his family. Inflamed by too much liquor, Bland challenged Ludwell to a duel and, when the secretary did not appear, Bland fastened Ludwell's glove to the door of the statehouse as a mark of his cowardice. As a result of this impertinence Bland was fined £500 by the House of Burgesses.[4] It was not an auspicious debut.

Appointed collector, presumably through the influence of his father, Bland continued his feud with the authorities, but this time enforcement of the Acts of Trade, not personal honor, was at stake. Governor Berkeley's position was quite simple: the Acts of 1660 and 1663 entrusted enforcement to the governors and to such officers as they saw fit to appoint. The Act of 1673 imposed certain duties and authorized their collection by deputies of the Commissioners of the Customs. Berkeley would see to enforcement of the Acts and the customs officers could collect their duties as best they might.

In September, 1675, Bland sent a long letter to the governor in which he declared that the collector was not responsible to the colonial authorities but was an employee of the Customs Commissioners, to whom he judged himself "liable to render an Account of my Actings in the said office, and to none others." However, he added, the governor's support was essential, since "without your Honors assistance" the commercial regulations "cannot be putt in effectual execution." So far, Bland reported, instead of cooperating the local authorities had done everything possible to impede his work. One captain who had cleared properly with the collector had been forced by the secretary of the colonial government, Ludwell, to surrender his original clearance and to take out another. At the same time Ludwell had cleared a ship on his own authority without the knowledge of Bland and had refused to give the collector any details of its cargo or destination. Similarly, for want of accurate information Bland had seized one vessel which had properly entered with the governor, opening himself to prosecution for faulty seizure.

On the basis of these complaints, the collector asked the governor to assist in four ways: 1) by appointing a public customs house for all shipping coming into the York and James rivers; 2) by lending his official approval to the customs deputies stationed at outlying areas in the colonies; 3) by backing up the customs officers with certificates of authority from the governor himself; and 4) by seeing that the collector was provided with copies of all bonds taken by the governor's agents. In a general closing observation Bland reported that the Acts of Trade were violated daily, European goods being introduced illegally and enumerated commodities being exported without payment of the duties.[5]

The governor's answer was immediate. The Council of Virginia judged Bland's letter to be an affront to the dignity of the colonial government and suspended him from office, while Berkeley personally told the collector that if he attempted to clear any ships he would, according to Bland, "lay me by the Heeles, withall calling me Rogue Villain Puppy and such like." The collector of the casual (or local) revenues was empowered to act in Bland's place.[6]

Early Years in the Colonies

Giles Bland may himself have been responsible for many of his troubles, but he was not the only one to resent and oppose the authoritarian regime of Berkeley and his coteries of favored planters. Part of Bland's difficulty arose from his position as an outsider intruding on the prerogatives of the established clique that ruled Virginia. Another outsider, Nathaniel Bacon, was the author of the first great colonial rebellion, which, among other results, effectively put an end to the contest between Berkeley and Bland. As a consequence of Bacon's uprising Governor Berkeley fled the colony on August 3, 1676. Bacon himself died unexpectedly on October 18th of the same year. Between those dates Virginia was in the hands of the revolutionary government, one of whose most ardent partisans was Giles Bland, collector of his Majesty's customs. The ultimate collapse of the Rebellion after Bacon's death cost Giles Bland his life. In the bloody vengeance exacted by Berkeley upon his return Bland, and many other participants in the uprising, were hanged as traitors and rebels.[7] Even before the end of the Rebellion, however, Bland had lost his collectorship. On August 21, 1676, the king ordered the Customs Commissioners to find a replacement for the wayward official.[8]

In all probability Bland would have been removed from his collectorship even had he not participated in Bacon's Rebellion. The customs officers alone could not effectively enforce the Acts of Trade. If they were at odds with the local authorities, there were two possibilities — to replace the customs officer or to remodel the colonial government. Of the two, the former was by far the easier, if not necessarily the wiser, course. For the moment in Virginia cooperation between the local government and the royal agents could best be achieved by the appointment of more diplomatic customs officials. It was at this moment that the English government adopted a system of multiple collectors for Virginia in place of the single officer formerly relied upon.[9] Aside from providing better coverage of the numerous creeks and rivers of the colony, this arrangement prevented any one officer, such as Giles Bland, from exercising too much personal authority to the irritation of the local magistrates. Most indicative of the effort made to achieve harmony at this time was the appointment of Philip Ludwell, Bland's old adversary, as one of the new collectors. Ludwell's selection, in fact, was an example of what came to be the predominant characteristic of the organization of the customs staff in Virginia. Throughout the rest of the colonial period the customs officers in that colony were chosen largely from the ranks of the local aristocracy.[10] In this way the English government sought to gain cooperation in the Old Dominion from the local government. One result of this policy was that the history of the customs service in Virginia thereafter was generally peaceful, with no repetition of the unsettling Bland incident.

The Virginia story was replayed in the Carolinas, with one major variation. In Virginia the royal collector, Giles Bland, participated in a rebellion against the established authority; in the Carolinas the collector represented the legal governmental authority and was the victim of a revolt against his administration. On November 16, 1676, Thomas Miller was commissioned collector at Albemarle in the Carolinas.[11] He sailed for the colony in company with the newly appointed governor, Thomas Eastchurch. Stopping at Nevis in the West Indies, Eastchurch met a wealthy widow and "took hold of the oppertunity marryed her and dispatched Mr. Miller for Carolina." Eastchurch made Miller "President of the Counsil untill his arrival and gave him very full and ample powers." [12] In this way the royal collector arrived at Albemarle as the legitimate acting head of government.

A peculiar situation had developed in the Carolina settlement. As the Lord Proprietors later pointed out, the "illness of the harbours" forced the settlers either to send their tobacco overland to Virginia or to depend on merchants from New England who "were the onely imediate Traders with them." [13] In the circumstances the New England sea captains exercised a good deal of influence in that part of Carolina. When the news first reached the colony of the appointment of new customs officers, there was a general uproar. The local authorities were warned by some New England merchants and others that "it would be a great inconvenience for to submit to this paymt and that the New England men did intend to raise their commodities double if such paymt . . . were exacted from them." In obedience to instructions, the Council appointed Valentine Bird as acting collector to receive the duties levied by the Act of 1673 until the new collector arrived. But so dependent was the community on supplies provided by the New Englanders that a compromise was soon arranged whereby the visiting merchants were given a refund out of every collection.[14]

Early Years in the Colonies

Miller, who arrived in Albemarle in July, 1677, made his first official action an order to the acting collector to account for all the receipts he had collected. The rebate to the New Englanders was ended and, between July and November, 1677, Miller gathered in £1,243 sterling value in old and new receipts and seized goods. Even though this amount was collected in commodities, and not in specie, it represented a tremendous imposition on the struggling community. Along with his work as collector, Miller assumed full authority as governor and dealt with the people in a firm manner. He settled a conflict with the Indians and in his own words "brought the people, who . . . were in a miserable confusion by reason of Sundry factions amongst them to a reasonable good conformity to his Majestyes and the Lords Proprietors Laws and authority." [15]

Actually what Miller had accomplished was to unite the feuding factions in opposition to his government. Previously not everyone had been allied with the interests of the New England traders, who, although they might furnish needed supplies, also through their monopoly of the market could obtain tobacco "att very lowe rates." [16] Miller managed to alienate both factions and his fall consequently became merely a matter of time.

In November Captain Zachariah Gilliam arrived from London with a cargo of arms and ammunition. According to Gilliam's testimony, he made entry with Miller as required, but the collector, not content merely to consider his present cargo, asked Gilliam how much tobacco he had carried away on his last voyage. When the captain said nearly one hundred and eighty hogsheads, the collector insisted on payment of the enumerated duties for that previous load, to which Gilliam replied that he "had paid the King his Custom in England & did not judge his Majesty desired his Custom twice." Still, Miller insisted on payment and threatened the captain with arrest should he not comply.[17]

Gilliam's arrival was the spark that was needed. The weapons he gave the inhabitants "for their defence against the Heathen" were turned against the collector.[18] Miller was imprisoned, for a time on Gilliam's ship, and then tried on charges of having expressed treasonable words against the Duke of York and the king. The collection of the customs reverted to normal with the appointment of one of the rebels, John Culpeper, in Miller's place. It was probably no coincidence that the goods Miller had gathered in as payment for the duties he collected had not yet been sent out of the colony. The rebellion was nicely timed to prevent that shipment, and Culpeper took the goods into his care, confiscating all the customs records at the same time. Fittingly enough, the foreman at Miller's trial was one of the traders from New England.[19]

The absent governor, who finally arrived in Virginia in the middle of these events, was forcibly prevented from entering the settlement at Albemarle by the rebels and died in Virginia shortly thereafter. Miller himself, along with his surveyor, escaped eventually to England. There he had Culpeper, who had gone to London to present the rebels' story to the proprietors, arrested, charging him and Gilliam with overthrow of the lawful authority in Carolina.

In this case much depended on the attitude of the Lord Proprietors. At first they seemed inclined to support Miller in a lukewarm fashion. Miller did have "full and ample powers" from Eastchurch but he did "many extravagant things," alienating the people. On the other hand, the proprietors said, Gilliam was involved in the rebellion, and the other leader, Culpeper, "was a very ill man having some tyme before fled from South Carolina where he was in danger of hanging for laying the designs & indeavouring to sett the poore people to plunder the rich." [20]

The Commissioners of the Customs were quite explicit as to their position. They recommended that Miller and the other officers "be restored to their Employment and Estates . . . and be fully repaird . . . for any damage done them." In their opinion it should be made "highly penall for the future to oppose such Collections & Collectors" and the governor and "all in Authority" should be "Enjoyn'd to give all Countenance and assistance thereunto." [21]

Two factors worked to Miller's disadvantage in the hearings on his complaint. First the crown officials were tempted by the thought of recovering all the lost revenue that had been taken from Miller by Culpeper. And secondly the proprietors were more concerned with restoring order to their territory and with making it profitable than with upholding the royal authority. During the hearings on the case the Earl of Shaftesbury, as spokesman for the Proprietors, had presented their argument as outlined above: Miller may have acted unwisely but he had "ample powers" to act for the absent governor. When the case came to trial, however, Shaftesbury completely reversed his position. He interceded for Culpeper, and the Lord Proprietors now stated that Miller *"without any legall authority* gott possession of the government of the County of Albemarle." Since his was not a legal government, there could be no rebellion in the eyes of the law. Consequently there was no case against Culpeper and Gilliam.[22]

In the final settlement of this affair the only casualty was the royal authority in Carolina. Approving certain measures which seemed "the best method for recovery of the arrears of Customs due to His Majesty," the Privy Council dropped the case against Culpeper and declined to reinstate Miller and the other officers to their posts in the colony. At the same time, however, they ordered that Miller and the others should have satisfaction for their personal losses and be freed from any "vexatious suits" in the future. A replacement was sent to Carolina for Miller, who was given a customs post in England.[23]

The long-range effect of this failure to uphold the authority of the royal agents in Carolina was made apparent to one of Miller's successors, George Muschamp, who became collector at Albemarle in 1687. Muschamp attempted to get a conviction in the local court against a ship which he had seized. Admitting that his evidence was not of the best, Muschamp sourly noted that it really made no difference, since the court announced that no matter what the evidence it would throw out the case, claiming "the Benefit of their Charter against me." Since the charter had been granted after passage of the first Navigation Act, the colonial court asserted that their colonists were not bound by its provisions. In such a situation, Muschamp correctly observed, "it will be difficult to maintaine the Acts of Navigation in due force here." In due course Muschamp found his position in Carolina hopeless and obtained a transfer to Maryland.[24]

The Carolinas were not the only proprietary colony to make the operations of the customs staff difficult. In Maryland the son of the proprietor, Lord Baltimore, was the first collector. On the death of his father the new Lord Baltimore recommended Christopher Rousby as his successor in the customs post.[25] Although the proprietor himself selected the new officer, the two did not work in harmony for long. By 1681 Rousby was in England to present his complaints, while Lord Baltimore was urging his removal for misconduct and treasonable words against the Duke of York. Once again, as in Virginia, the trouble lay in the competing jurisdictions of the royal collectors and the local authorities, particularly the collectors of the casual revenues, in the colony.

While Rousby was in England responsibility for the customs operations devolved on the surveyor, Nicholas Babcock. Lord Baltimore and the acting collector differed on the question of whether ships sailing to Ireland should pay the tobacco duty imposed by the Act of 1673. Babcock insisted that they should. Baltimore overruled him and ordered him to clear certain vessels without collecting the duties. The dispute was carried to England, where it was settled in Babcock's favor. Lord Baltimore received a severe reprimand and was ordered to pay the sum lost to the revenue through his interference.[26]

For the moment Baltimore's concern for the possible threat to his charter led to a period of calm relations. But in 1684 the proprietor left the colony and placed a member of his council, George Talbot, in charge of the government. In October, after drinking heavily, Talbot picked a quarrel with Rousby, who had recently returned to his post, and killed him. The fight was preceded by sharp words concerning the conflicting authorities of Talbot and Rousby.[27] Talbot was taken to Virginia, but eventually was released under a sentence commuted to five years' banishment.

Neither the death of Rousby nor the departure of Talbot ended the struggle in Maryland. The words of the captain of the naval ship stationed in the Chesapeake Bay, reporting that "noe officer of the Customes in Maryland can live without a good guard," were perhaps extreme.[28] But Rousby's successor found that little had changed. In April, 1685, the new collector, Nathaniel Blakiston, wrote home that the officials appointed by the colony were interfering with his work. For example, he noted, a local agent of the colonial Council would seize any ship he thought Blakiston might have his eye on. Then that agent, Nicholas Sewall, Lord Baltimore's stepson, would make an arrangement with the captain, and at a mock trial the ship would be condemned and sold at a token price, the purchaser being the same captain.[29]

Against this background it is understandable that both royal customs collectors in Maryland participated in the rebellion against the proprietor in 1689. Blakiston himself was a staunch adherent of the revolutionary leader, John Coode. The other collector, John Payne, was killed in an affair involving the same Sewall who had caused Blakiston such difficulty. At the outbreak of Coode's rebellion in 1689 Sewall fled to Virginia. In January, 1690, he returned to Maryland in a boat which anchored in the Patuxent River. Payne, hearing of his return, attempted to board the vessel during the night and was killed in the brief battle.[30] Payne of course acted as an adherent of Coode's movement, although it is worth noting that he had a legal right to visit any ship entering his waters.

Payne's death, coupled with the accession of the Protestants William III and Mary, enabled the revolutionary movement to climax its efforts with success. An assembly was called, the royal collector, Blakiston, being elected president, and an appeal was made to the new monarchs to make Maryland a royal province. In 1691 the government of the colony was taken into royal control, although the property rights still were left to the proprietor, so that in this colony, for the moment at least, the royal collector emerged victorious.

In Massachusetts the situation of the customs officers in these early years combined the worst features of the problems facing their colleagues in Virginia, Carolina, and Maryland. The charter government of the Bay Colony claimed a privileged status much like that of the proprietary regimes in Maryland and Carolina, while the long established Puritan hierarchy, in its monopoly of power, bore resemblances to the entrenched administration of Governor Berkeley in Virginia. As a result, the settlement of the customs service in Massachusetts was a long and bitter struggle.

After the Stuart Restoration steps were taken to recall Massachusetts, which had assumed the powers and position of an independent commonwealth, to its proper dependence on England. In 1664 a commission was appointed to visit the various colonies. It is suggestive that this commission was provided with two sets of instructions, one relating to Massachusetts and the other to all the remaining plantations.[31] From the beginning the Bay Colony was considered, quite correctly, as a special problem.

After some successes in the other colonies, particularly in settling the boundary dispute between the new province of New York and Connecticut, the English commissioners met with total failure in Massachusetts, where they were forbidden to hold hearings. Consequently the commissioners soon gave up their work in disgust, but not without a slashing verbal attack on the local authorities: "Since you will needs misconstrue all these letters and endeavors, and that you will make use of that authority he [the king] hath given you to oppose that sovereignty which he hath over you, we shall not lose more of our labors upon you, but refer it to his Majesty's wisdom, who is of power enough to make himself to be obeyed in all his dominions." [32]

The English were slow to follow up the threat implied in the commissioners' letter. The Act of 1673 may have been aimed primarily at the New Englanders, but not until 1676 was another official embassy from the king sent to Massachusetts. This time the pressure for action came partly from John Mason and Sir Ferdinando Gorges, who had claims to New Hampshire and Maine and who opposed the intrusions of Massachusetts on those areas. Edward Randolph, related to the Masons by marriage, was chosen to carry a royal letter to the Bay Colony, thus commencing his long career in the plantations.[33] The letter Randolph carried to Massachusetts ordered that colony to send agents to England to answer to the king for the conduct of their province and to explain their position concerning the claims of Mason and Gorges. After presenting his communication, and receiving what he considered to be insulting treatment, Randolph returned to London, full of information on New England and its perversity.

The decision to extend the customs service to New England, and the selection of Randolph as the chief officer, followed.[34] The wisdom of sending Randolph to Massachusetts, despite the fact that he might be personally "obnoxious" to the people, was questionable. The new officer, who during the next twenty-six years was to play such an important role in the development of English colonial policy, was a peculiar man. He combined an intense devotion to duty with a terrifying persistence in pursuit of his objectives. Imprisoned many times, continually insulted and abused, Randolph took it all in stride and returned for more. But many of his difficulties seemed to be of his own making. Armed with his own righteousness, Randolph irritated when he should have soothed and alienated what little support he might have possessed. His view of the colonists as congenital rebels and rascals may not have been far off the mark, from the English point of view, but a wiser man would have displayed more flexibility and practicality. Randolph met every problem head on, and when he met defeat and humiliation so did the authority of England and her colonies. Rigidity was both Randolph's greatest strength and his greatest weakness.

In an unusual outburst of sprightly verse, some Bostonians welcomed Randolph back in December, 1679, when he returned as royal collector, with these words, among others:

> He that keeps a Plantacon Custom-house,
> One year, may bee a man, the next a Mouse.
> Your Brother Dyer hath the Divell played,
> Made the New-Yorkers at the first affraide,
> Hee vapoured, swagger'd, hector'd (whoe but hee?)
> But soon destroyed himself by Villanie.[35]

The reference to Dyer in New York was particularly fitting. The New York collector had been harassed by the colonial courts, until he eventually had returned to England for redress.[36] Randolph, too, soon found the provincial courts the source of many problems. Within six months of his arrival he had missed being imprisoned only by the interference of the governor, who ordered that his bond be accepted for bail. The legal action against Randolph arose from a seizure he made of a ship coming from Ireland, whose captain instituted a £800 personal suit against the collector.[37] And the collector had to depend on these same provincial courts, which had so willingly ordered his imprisonment, for the prosecution of whatever seizures he might make. Between 1680 and the end of 1682 Randolph made thirty-six seizures which he took to trial. All but two were acquitted.[38] At times his investigations were forcibly resisted, as in the instance when the man he left to guard some illicit goods was "sett upon by 4 or 5 persons" and badly beaten, while the goods were carried off to safety.[39]

In the struggle with the royal collector, the local authorities in Massachusetts made full use of every resource. One loophole was provided by the Acts of Trade themselves. The Acts of 1660 and 1663 entrusted enforcement to the governors and whatever officers they chose to appoint to act for them. As early as 1661 the Bay Colony had instructed its governor to "take effectuall course that the bonds be taken of all shipmasters coming hither . . . and returnes made . . . so this country may not be under the least neglect of their duty to his Majestys just commands."[40]

In 1663 officers were appointed at Boston, Salem, Marblehead, Gloucester, and Piscataqua to handle the bonding provisions, while the secretary of the colony was charged with making the proper returns to England.[41] Both of these enactments were adopted merely for the benefit of the English authorities. Massachusetts had no intention of enforcing the Acts of Trade on her own, as shown by the fact that not one report was ever sent to London by the colony's secretary and that fourteen years later the General Court had forgotten that it ever passed such laws.

After the visitation from Randolph in 1676, and while their agents were in England defending the actions of the colony, the Assembly again felt the need to enact at least a token compliance with the commercial laws. In 1677 the General Court, noting that they had been "informed, by letters received this day from our messengers, of his majestys expectation that the acts of trade and navigation be exactly and punctually observed . . . , his pleasure therein not having binn before now signified unto us, either by expresse from his majesty, or any of his ministers of state," ordered the Acts to be observed.[42] Seemingly the visit of the commissioners of 1664, as well as the earlier laws passed by the colonial Assembly, had passed from memory without a trace.

Some seven months before the arrival of the collector in 1679, a committee of the General Court recommended that officers be appointed in the various ports so that "no fraud nor lapse be committed whereby the countrys credit & peace be endaingered."[43] However, not until Randolph had been in the colony for a year did the Assembly finally take steps to implement their previous enactments. In March, 1682, Massachusetts passed a formal Naval Office Act, establishing officials at several ports to enforce the provisions of the Acts of 1660 and 1663.[44]

Randolph correctly interpreted this Act as aimed at him personally. The intention was simply to exclude Randolph from participation in the entering or clearing of ships. The claim again, as in Virginia, was that enforcement of the Acts of 1660 and 1663 was entrusted to the governors, while the royal customs officers were concerned only with the collection of the duties of 1673. Ignorant of the arrival or departure of ships, Randolph could hardly see to the collection of the duties, much less to over-all enforcement of the Acts of Trade. The collector reported that only four captains had entered with him and that he had seen only three bonding certificates since the Massachusetts Act had been passed.[45]

Early Years in the Colonies

In passing this Naval Office Act the Massachusetts General Court clearly encroached on the powers of the governor, since the acts of 1660 and 1663 had assigned enforcement to the governors of the various colonies, not to the legislative assemblies. In 1682, however, the popular majority in the colony which openly opposed Randolph in every possible manner could not depend on the cooperation of the governor. The Puritan Commonwealth of that date was divided into "popular" and "moderate" factions; although the former was the more numerous, the latter group gave Randolph an important nucleus of support.

The origin of the moderate party had an important bearing on the future course of England's colonial policies. "In Massachusetts itself the commercial spirit was steadily growing, and with it went a decline in religious fervor."[46] Trade, it seems, was breaking down the exclusiveness of the Puritan "Promised Land" and carrying the Bay Colony back into intimate economic and social contacts with the European world. In the pursuit of profits, idealism receded in importance. Simon Bradstreet, the governor in 1682, was one of these moderates. He refused to approve the Naval Office Act, which consequently became law only without the participation of the governor, who by the Acts of Parliament was the sole authority for the creation of these naval offices. This fact supplied Randolph with an effective argument against the validity of the Act.

In fact, Randolph made the very most of this division in the ranks of the Puritan leaders. In his letters home Randolph always referred to the opposition as a "faction" of extremists.[47] To him it seemed that the moderates were daily increasing their strength and that, with the proper encouragement, they in time might be able to lead the colony into closer cooperation with the homeland. Joseph Dudley was one of the men Randolph thought might be useful; his comments on Dudley showed exactly what he thought should be done: "Major Dudley is a great opposer of the faction heere . . . who, if he finds things resolutely manniged, will cringe and bow to anything; he hath his fortune to make in the world, and if his Majesty, upon alteration of the government, [would] make him captain of the castle of Boston and the forts . . . his Majesty will gaine a popular man and obleidge the better party."[48]

There was a close connection between Randolph's idea and the creation of the Dominion of New England. In 1677, after Randolph's return from his first visit to the colonies, he had listed at great length

33

the faults of the colonial government of Massachusetts. Among other items, he charged that they violated "all the Acts of Trade" and cost the English revenue over £100,000 yearly.[49] The only solution, he felt then, lay in making New England a royal province. To achieve this, he recommended employing the military forces then in Virginia under Sir John Berry to reduce New England, but at the same time he asserted that the introduction of a royal government would not lack support in the colonies themselves, because of the "Earnest desire of most and best of the inhabitants (wearied out with the Arbitrary proceedings of those in the present Government) to be under his Majesties Government and Laws." Men like Dudley should be involved in the new administration and a pension "allowed them out of the publicque Revenue . . . with Some Title of Honour to be conferred upon the most deserving." [50]

On the basis of that report from Randolph, and from other information available to them, the English government in 1677 had initiated an investigation leading to the end of charter government in Massachusetts and the other New England colonies. Various legal obstacles had to be overcome, but by the end of 1682 the decision had been made, and Randolph was called home to participate in the preparation of *quo warranto* proceedings against the recalcitrant colonies.[51] After a year more of inconclusive maneuvering, the charter of Massachusetts was declared forfeited on the 13th of October, 1684. Randolph himself had the pleasure of carrying the official decree to Boston. It was his moment of triumph.

The creation of the Dominion of New England, which followed the revocation of the charters, was the climactic moment in the implementation of the colonial policy of the Restoration. New England had been the problem-child of the empire. Now it was reduced to passive submissiveness. A giant step had been made towards the achievement of the "social and political unity" required for the fulfillment of the mercantilist ideal.[52] If the experiment in New England were a success, similar reforms could be undertaken in the remaining colonies with every expectation of an equally favorable result. It was consequently a critical moment in the development of the American colonies. Not until the reforms initiated after 1764 were their liberties again to be in such danger. It is impossible not to wonder what the outcome would have been had the English in this early period been able to sustain the vigorous prosecution of this successfully inaugurated program. Economically and militarily the colonies were much weaker then. Could they have successfully defied the power of England? Or would their forced submission have allowed the English time to direct their development, politically and commercially, in such a way as to tie them firmly to the imperial system? Fortunately for the Americans the restrictive policies of the Stuarts were not limited to the colonies alone. The English themselves rose against their king, and the successful revolution in England ended, or at least postponed, the threat to the colonists.

In the history of the customs service in New England the Dominion years represented a period of unspectacular quiet, although Randolph, remaining there as collector, still had his problems. The man he recommended earlier to the attention of the English authorities, Joseph Dudley, at first headed the new administration. Randolph did not easily accept Dudley's new importance and soon was describing him as a man of "a base servile and antimonarchicall principle." [53] Even after a royal governor, Edmund Andros, arrived, Randolph unhappily found himself pushed to the background and generally ignored. In fact he discovered that he even suffered financially under the new order. One of Andros' favorites persuaded the governor "to make him navall officer, and thereby to settle the fees granted the Collector of his Majesties Customs upon the Navall Officer." [54]

In the area of his work as a customs officer, Randolph found his task easier, but he reported that his seizures had inflamed "the people's malice against me." [55] One of his major problems involved a "warm dispute" that he engaged in with Captain John George of the *Rose,* a royal frigate stationed at Boston. The captain insisted on his right to seize vessels even in the harbor of Boston and in doing so interfered with what Randolph thought to be his sole prerogative. At stake were the profits from the division of the proceeds of the seizure. Randolph piously asserted that he cared little who made the seizures as long as "Interlopers" were apprehended but that "in as much as hither to I find by the Acts of trade & practice of other places that it is my Duty to seize and prosecute for his Majestie I do not see how I can [make] omission of that part of my Duty." [56] This dispute was settled to the disadvantage of Randolph, as the Treasury decided in that very year to deputize all such commanders formally as agents of the Customs Commissioners.[57]

There were limitations to Randolph's success in enforcing the Navigation Acts. In the first year of the new government he reported that he had made several seizures, one of which he managed only with the help of the captain of the *Rose*. Generally, Randolph said, "I have provided boates and my men are Diligent, but I dare not Expose my selfe or them as farr as Nantasket which lyes a League below & out of Command of the Castle." [58] But with two frigates, the *Rose* and the *Saint Lo,* cruising off the coasts, and with the major ports and settlements firmly under control of the royal government, in all likelihood the Acts of Trade and Navigation were never so carefully observed in New England before or after.

These halcyon days were of short duration. In 1688 William of Orange and his wife landed in England, and news of the event touched off rebellions throughout the colonies. Governor Andros and his partisans, including Randolph, were imprisoned in Boston and the great experiment was terminated. Randolph explained the revolt of the colonists in terms of their resentment against the Navigation Acts: the "bottom & ground for all their complaints" was that the Dominion government had "endeavoured to have the Acts of Parliament, relating to trade and navigation duly observed & prevented their going out to rob in the Spanish W. Indies & harbour pyrates as formerly." [59] Again he said, "it's not the person of Sr Edmund Andros, but the government itself, they designe to have removed, that they may freely trade." [60]

Perhaps it was to be expected that Randolph, who as collector was responsible for enforcement of the Acts of Trade, should insist that it was their strict observance which infuriated the colonists. Such an argument was merely one way of saying that he had been faithful to his trust and had performed his duties fully. Herbert Osgood had that thought in mind when he wrote that this "interpretation of an issue which was far broader than his language indicated was characteristic of Randolph and of his tiresome insistence on his own deserts." [61] Certainly there was more to the collapse of the Dominion than a desire to "freely trade." But in fairness to Randolph it should be noted that in his statements it was to the governor, and not to himself, that he gave credit for the firm enforcement of the Navigation Acts. And his remark that it was not Andros but "the government itself" which the colonists "designe to have removed" suggests that Randolph had a broader understanding of the problem than has been recognized.

When Randolph referred to the Acts of Trade he meant more than the various regulations laid down by Parliament; he had in mind the mercantilist principles embodied in those Acts and in every aspect of Stuart colonial policy. Along with the remarks quoted above, Randolph also said that the New Englanders had unmasked themselves as "an hypocriticall wicked & By-gothed people" and "that force is the Onely Argument to convince and oblige them to a dutyfull & intire Submission to the Crown & the lawes of England." [62] England sought the "intire Submission" of the colonies not as a desirable abstraction but with an explicit purpose: to guide the development of the colonies to the best advantage of the mother country. The Dominion of New England itself was created "in the interest of trade, defense, and a closer dependence of the colonies on England." [63] If Restoration colonial policy was based on mercantilism, then the heart — the keystone — of that policy was found in the Acts of Trade and Navigation. In that sense Randolph was quite correct to lay the blame for the rebellion on the trade laws. They were the visible sign of a general attempt during the period of the last Stuarts to execute in fact the vision of empire held in theory by so many Englishmen. There was a coherency, a completeness, to Stuart colonial policy that was not to be evident again for seventy or more years.

What could be said of the colonial customs service at the end of the first sixteen years of experimentation? The first impression would be that it was a failure. As one aspect of the general English administrative intrusion on the colonies, the customs officers' experiences more than anything else illustrated the difficulty of the undertaking and the depth of colonial opposition. Some valuable lessons had been learned, however. One problem involved the relationship of the customs staff to other authorities in the colonies. The feud between Bland and Governor Berkeley in Virginia, for example, had seriously impaired the operation of the system in that colony. It was clear that the conflicting responsibilities of the various officials needed definition. The naval office, whether used by the governor, the proprietor, or as in Massachusetts by the colony, had interfered with the customs operations. It too required attention.

Trade and Empire

More generally it had become evident that the "independent" colonies — both the proprietaries and the charter variety — were the source of much difficulty. The customs officers were royal officials, and in those colonies royal authority was weaker than elsewhere. To ensure uniform enforcement of the Navigation Acts some action would be necessary in that area. The colonial courts, too, had proved unreliable. As Randolph in New England and Muschamp in Carolina had discovered, successful prosecutions in those courts were rare. Either the courts would have to be reformed or a new arrangement worked out.

The record of these years clearly indicated that the customs personnel themselves needed greater protection. Not only were they exposed to physical danger but too often they were themselves victims of legal harassment and prosecution for actions performed in the line of duty. Officers in England had been provided with various safeguards by an Act passed in 1662. Unfortunately that Act had not been applied to the colonies. If the colonial service were to function as efficiently as the English system did, the provisions of that Act would have to be extended to the plantations.

During the ten years following the flight of James II from England some, but by no means all, of these lessons were incorporated into a program designed to place the customs service on a workable basis. In that way, at least, the Restoration policies were continued by the new administration. Important differences, however, developed in the execution of colonial policies under William and his successors. Whereas the Stuart effort had involved "meddling on a grand scale with self-governing and self-willed communities," [64] altered circumstances now dictated an attempt to control the colonies externally with a minimum of internal interference. In effect, the new government of William and Mary, repudiating much of the earlier Stuart program, endeavored to find another, easier way to create the proper commercial relationship between England and her colonies.

III

A New Policy Defined

O F THE twenty-five years that William and Mary and their successor, Anne, ruled England, nineteen were occupied with war with France. In the circumstances colonial administrative problems became of secondary importance. Not only were English energies directed elsewhere, but extension of the European conflict to the New World made colonial cooperation a matter of concern. It was not a time for forceful coercion of recalcitrant subjects.

Characteristic of the cautious approach of the new king and queen was the remarkable continuity in governmental personnel maintained, not just in the customs service but in all branches of administration, between the old order and the new. In London important civil servants such as William Blathwayt adjusted to the altered situation with a minimum of discomfort, while in the colonies the continued importance of Edward Randolph emphasized the fact that the new regime intended no immediate, radical break with past policies. King William's employment of Randolph, in fact, must have dismayed many of the colonists who had joined in the uprisings of 1689. Responsible for much of the form and direction taken by the Stuart colonial administration, Randolph had been so attuned to the realities of his position that merely a year before the Glorious Revolution he had heard, with perfect equanimity, of the intention of James II to send Catholic priests to the colonies; Randolph even suggested that the priests might be very useful in wooing the Indians away from their allegiance to the French.[1] Yet under "Protestant William" this most faithful of Stuart employees was not only continued in governmental service but promoted to a higher post; Randolph became surveyor general of all his Majesty's customs in America. Brought to the throne by a successful revolutionary movement, William and Mary wisely made use of the experience and knowledge of all those in the government who were willing to serve the new regime.

Perhaps much of the continuity maintained by King William with the personnel and policies of his predecessor stemmed from the fact that the central problems of colonial administration remained basically the same. The Glorious Revolution of 1688 and the colonial uprisings of 1689 did not remove the fundamental point of friction between England and her colonies. England still insisted on her paramount position, politically and economically, within the empire, while the colonists endeavored to exercise as much home rule as possible. Consequently, continued conflict between English authority and colonial opposition was to be expected. If there were any doubts on that point in London, events relating to the colonial customs service soon made the truth apparent.

One matter on which there was complete accord between the former Stuart administration and the new government of William and Mary was New England; to both governments it was a problem area which required special handling. As soon as word of Randolph's imprisonment in 1689 reached London, the Commissioners of the Customs notified the Treasury that they considered it essential to locate an officer there as quickly as possible.[2] However, on one point their attitude had changed. Now the Commissioners felt that the service in New England might operate more smoothly if the chief officer were a native of the region. Such a man would have a more extensive knowledge of the area and might be more acceptable to the inhabitants. Consequently the post of collector in New England went to Jahleel Brenton, a native of Rhode Island, who had been in London as agent for that colony. In line with the same policy of employing native sons, Sir William Phips became governor of Massachusetts under the new charter.[3]

Brenton's experiences quickly demonstrated that, although England might have a new king and Massachusetts a new charter, the problems of administration did indeed remain the same. Brenton's first undertaking was a mistake, as he tried to punish a ship owner who, according to reports, openly paraded both his past violations of the trade laws and his intention to continue to evade them in the future. Brenton took the owner, Nicholas Page, to court on a charge of having shipped tobacco directly to Scotland in his ship, the *Salisbury,* in the year 1689. At the trial Page argued that William and Mary's Act of Indemnity covered such former misdeeds, and the court agreed with him, dismissing Brenton's case without further hearing.[4]

Eager for revenge, Brenton seized the *Salisbury* again, this time for importing European goods without going through England. Actually Page's ship had taken its cargo on at Liverpool, but Brenton thought its papers were faulty and that some goods had been taken on elsewhere. He prosecuted the *Salisbury* successfully in the Massachusetts courts, but unfortunately the Commissioners of the Customs did not support his case when it went to London on appeal; they felt the ship's papers were in order and that Brenton's charges were unreasonable, so the verdict was reversed.[5] Once again the collector had been defeated by Nicholas Page.

In the contest with Page, Brenton was motivated partly by personal pique and partly by a desire to make an example of a known violator of the commercial regulations. His failure did little to enhance the prestige of his office. In this instance discretion would have been wiser than official zeal. But Brenton's disputes were not restricted to merchants and the local courts. By 1693 he and Governor Phips were open enemies, the break becoming irreparable after Phips led a crowd of "about fifty people" to a storehouse where goods seized for illegal entry had been placed and, "Laying violent hands" upon Brenton, "pulling and dragging him about the wharfe of the said Storehouse," forced the collector to return the goods to their owner.[6] This bizarre episode, with the royal governor and the collector of his Majesty's customs cavorting in such a childish manner, also did little to increase English authority in New England.

Sir William Phips was an irascible, pompous man, and undoubtedly his personality had much to do with the fight between him and Brenton. But basically their contest was merely a continuation of an old and familiar problem, at the heart of which was the conflicting authority of the governor and the collector in enforcement of the Acts of Trade. In June, 1692, the Massachusetts legislature had enacted a new Naval Office Act which, similar to the one in force before the establishment of the Dominion of New England, set up officers at seven different ports in the colony. All masters were required to clear and enter with these officers, but it was stipulated, for the benefit of the English authorities, that these places were not to be "accounted ports for the unlivery or lading of any of the enumerated commodities." [7] The real motive behind the Act was revealed by an order published by the governor and his Council, declaring "that no further office than the Naval Office established by Act of the Province is necessary for clearing and entering ships." [8]

Brenton correctly interpreted this proclamation as "an order forbidding me to enter and clear vessels," adding that Sir William and his naval officer "kept all cocquets and certificates" from him and frequently permitted ships to unload without producing any papers at all. Supported by the governor, opposition to the collector had become general. In one trial, when the jury somewhat surprisingly found for Brenton, the judge "refused to accept any verdict except for the defendant." When Brenton attempted to convince the judge of the strength of his case, the defendant broke into the storehouse and reclaimed his goods by force. [9]

A peculiar tug-of-war followed passage of the Naval Office Act. In the middle were various captains and merchants. A typical example involved Thomas Cobbit of Portsmouth, New Hampshire, who came to Boston with his ship and was told by the governor to enter with the naval officer. Cobbit replied that several people had advised him to enter with the royal collector. Although the governor assured him he did not need to bother with the collector, Cobbit still thought it wise to see Brenton. While he was with Brenton, the captain heard that the naval officer was about to seize his ship. Hurrying to the naval officer, he saved his ship but was forced to surrender all the papers he had obtained from the collector. Later the naval officer refused to return the papers either to Cobbit or to Brenton. [10] Cobbit's story was reversed in the case of another captain who was forced to enter at the customs house after Brenton and his deputies took away the permit to unload that he had obtained from the naval officer. [11]

This ludicrous situation could not last long. By 1694 Brenton had registered formal articles of complaint against Phips in London. Among other charges the collector reported that the governor had forcibly taken seized vessels from the customs officers, that he encouraged captains to rescue forfeited goods, that he terrified the king's officers from performing their duties, that he assisted in passing laws to nullify the Navigation Acts, and that he had confiscated certain prizes and prize money for his own use. [12] Both Brenton and Phips went to England to contest these charges, but the governor died before he was called to account for his actions. While in England Brenton did manage to have the Naval Office Act disallowed, the Privy Council repealing the Act "inasmuch as the powers and directions therein given to the said Officer are, by divers Acts of Parliament, reserved to such Officer or Officers as shall be appointed by the Commissioners of His Majestys Customes." [13] Brenton also requested that if the post of naval officer was to be continued in Massachusetts he might be appointed to the office.[14] This suggestion was not approved, and the naval office and the collectorship in Massachusetts remained separate institutions. But with the death of Phips and the repeal of the objectionable Act of 1692, Brenton's assignment was made easier and the rest of his time in office passed in relative calm.

Brenton's experiences indicated how little the problems had changed since 1689. The courts, the governor, the naval officers, and the inhabitants — all participated in obstructing the work of the collector. In the rest of the colonies Edward Randolph, in his new capacity as surveyor general, found much the same story. Particularly interesting was the situation he discovered in Virginia, where the special effort made after the removal and death of Giles Bland to bolster the efficiency of the customs service by associating it with locally influential men had produced peculiar results.

Randolph arrived in Virginia, the first stop on his tour of inspection, on the 5th of April, 1692. His hopes for immediately undertaking an examination of the operation of the customs service there had to be postponed: "I found the General assembly sitting & could not then enter upon my survey with the Collectors being all members of the Councill . . . ." To pass the time Randolph participated in the trial of a ship the lieutenant governor had ordered seized for presenting forged cocquets (itemized cargo lists) and certificates. Comparison in court of the false papers with real certificates convinced the jury of the truth of the charge, but unsure how to proceed the jury referred the case to the High Court of the province. In Randolph's words, "Coll. Cole the President with the 2 Wormleys & Coll. Jennings, all Collectors of the Customs & the major part upon the bench, did not see cause to give Judgment for their Majesties." Instead they permitted the captain of the ship ("Thomas Meech A Scotchman & an old Transgressor") to give security to produce proper papers on his next voyage to take the place of the forged documents he had presented. Meech was allowed to take on a load of tobacco and leave the colony.[15]

The ruling aristocracy of Virginia was firmly entrenched in power. Not only did Council members monopolize the collectorships but as Randolph reported, "It has been the practice . . . to appoint a Member of the Councill to be Naval Officer where Needfull." Since the same men were appointed "to be Collector . . . of the Customs it gives an Opportunity for connivance att frauds in the remoter parts of the Province." Certain reforms were possible even in the present situation. The collector who had accepted the forged documents from Captain Meech was suspended by the lieutenant governor, and this firm action caused other officers to realize that their posts were no longer to be merely sinecures. The collector at the Lower James thereupon requested "to be dismissed from that and all other publick places which was granted." [16]

Such actions were useful but hardly enough, Randolph thought. In general the collectors were too indifferent to their duties: "not one of them has deputed under officers . . . with power to goe aboard & strictly examine whither their loding [i.e., loading] agree with their Coquet & discover what Tobacco they take aboard." Since the collectors themselves were usually absent on Council business, this was a serious omission. One collector who had appointed a deputy went "once or twice a year to reacon & receive his Share of the fees," but of formal records and accounts there was "not one word." [17]

To correct these weaknesses Randolph suggested that the comptrollers of both Virginia and Maryland be replaced. Philip Lightfoot, the present comptroller of Virginia, was "a very good man" but he only "states such Accounts as the Collectors . . . bring him & sees them sweare to them before the Governour once a year." A man who would keep more active watch over the collectors was needed. Also Randolph suggested appointing certain trustworthy collectors at key stations who could check the work of the others. For all these assignments he had definite candidates in mind whose names he submitted in his letter. To further restrain the evils of plural officeholding Randolph recommended that the naval office posts and the collectorships be "managed by different persons." [18]

Maryland presented a vastly different but equally disastrous picture. Unlike Vrginia, where the "First Families" monopolized the offices, in

Maryland the customs posts were filled by men out to make their fortunes. Most were the creatures of the governor, Sir Lionel Copley. One "before he gott to be Collector of Customs was a poor Atturney not worth a Hogshead of tobacco, nor now if he be forcd to pay the great arreares due from him to their Majesties." The governor's "second Jacall" was George Plater, the collector at Patuxent: "his business has been to plye for wine [and] Brandes for the Governor amongst the ships; he has presented the Governor with a horse & has a young wife at his Excell' service." The governor did his best to protect these men from Randolph's investigations: "the Governor slaves & toiles for Blackstone & Plater." [19] The surveyor general summed up the contrasts between the two colonies in this way: "The Collectors of the Customs in Virginia . . . sitt at home, Masters of vessells outward or Inward bound sweare anything to the best of their knowledge pay their fees & are cleerd, without an Officer seeing them (or their vessell) . . . In Maryland the officers plye like Watermen . . . for he that uses the Masters best has most business." [20]

Aside from the appointment of a trustworthy comptroller for the colony, Randolph thought something could be accomplished through the naval offices. He realized that the Act of 1663 placed such offices under the authority and responsibility of the governors, but in this case he felt it would be wise to take that power from the governor and to appoint someone "by a letter from the Lords of the Committee for trade." Then "the Naval Officer will be a check upon the other Customs house officers." [21]

While in Maryland Randolph attempted to prosecute two ships for violating the Navigation Acts. His evidence seemingly was not of the best, but as was usually true that made little difference. In the first case Randolph's suit was postponed indefinitely on the excuse that the master who would have to defend the charge could not appear in court because he had "killd one of his Saylors att sea." In the other case the court refused to require the master to swear under oath where he had loaded his cargo, and the following disappointments caused the surveyor general to write, "I then forbore to have any further business with the court." [22]

These experiences in Maryland, coupled with the trial of Captain Meech in Virginia, led Randolph to propose "the Necessity of having a Court of Exchequer erected . . . with an able Judge to try all Causes relating to the Crown." Otherwise "itt will be to no purpose to be att trouble & Charge to seize & try Irregular Traders nor to put any of the forfeited bonds in suit." [23] This suggestion by Randolph had intriguing implications. Previously, in the days of the Stuarts, Randolph would have urged the reform of the administration in these colonies from top to bottom. Now a new caution was evident in Randolph's thought. For example, of the situation in Virginia he observed that it would be "hazardous for Capt. Nicholson [Francis Nicholson, the lieutenant governor] to break with the whole Councill . . . till he have an express order to make an alteration fundamentally amongst them." [24]

Realizing that internal reforms in the colonies depended on initiative and support from home, and that at the moment such comprehensive efforts were not envisioned in England, Randolph now suggested by-passing the colonial opposition. In effect, he would no longer depend on authority within the colonies but on the authority of England employed from without. If the colonial courts and governments could not be remodeled, they would be circumvented. If the governors could not be trusted to perform their duties, the naval offices would be removed from their control and appointments made in England. If, in the seductive atmosphere of life in the colonies, individual officers were led from the faithful performance of their assignments, a system would be devised whereby each official would be checked by another. The collectors would be restrained by the naval officers. Both of those officers would be supervised by attentive comptrollers. And over all the surveyor general would periodically keep the staff up to the desired standards.

Implicit in this program was the concentration of immediate authority in London. Appointments would be made, orders issued, and all the important decisions resolved there. Under the Stuarts a major reliance had been placed on officials within the colonies. For example, the collectors in the individual colonies originally had the responsibility for determining the location and number of under-officers to be employed, while the governors through their chosen agents were to see to enforcement of the trade laws. Now these powers, if Randolph's program were adopted, would be removed to England. External, in place of internal, control would become the key to imperial administration.

For the moment Randolph had to content himself with forwarding these thoughts to England in writing, since this survey of the colonies had to be completed before he could return home to urge his proposals in person. In West Jersey he found the collector "become sottish with drinking, he makes use of whom he can get to do the business of the Office." This man he suspended and replaced with "an understanding person of A good Estate." [25] At Philadelphia Randolph found "they harbour Privateers who have brought in a great booty . . . It's an Asylum for Debtors from New Yorke, prohibited Goods are landed there and no law to prevent it." [26]

In New York he found the collector "regular in his Office" but felt there was a great need to place a comptroller there to check the activities of the collector, there having been no comptroller in that colony since the end of the Dominion of New England.[27] Randolph heard of "a Great Fraud" committed by Brenton's deputy at New London; and at Newport, Rhode Island, he found "neither law nor Government"; although he did not approve of Brenton's deputy there, he felt there was no other "person fitt to be employed in that service." [28]

In Boston he found "Mr. Brenton full of Complaints that he [and] his Officers were obstructed in their Duty." One of Brenton's deputies, Randolph was told, "lay 8 dayes in Goal for saying he had a power [to] show for what he did." The surveyor general had a most unsatisfactory interview with Governor Phips, who told Randolph that "the Commissioners of the Customs had nothing to do in this province, their being none of the Enumerated Commodities grown amonst them." Randolph reported that "the appointing a Navall Officer in those Out ports opens a doore to all illegal trade for since the Revolution all the Harbors in New England are become free ports & the Enumerated Commodities are carried to Holland Scotland & Newfoundland without any stop." On the other hand, Randolph wrote that the collector, Brenton, "has been irregular & arbitrary in his proceedings . . . Some vessells he has seized & not prosecuted. Other vessells & Goods he has seized & . . . taken Bond . . . but not yet putt those Bonds in suite." Randolph also accused the collector of accepting half the cargo of one ship for his personal profit instead of taking the case to court.[29]

During the next two years Randolph traveled back and forth through the colonies, spending much of his time in the important tobacco plantations of Virginia and Maryland. His fights with the colonial courts continued; on one occasion he was arrested in Virginia by a sheriff from

Maryland, who acted outside his jurisdiction with the consent of a Virginian justice of the peace.[30] By 1695 Randolph felt his work in the colonies had been carried as far as possible for the moment and requested permission to return to England to report in person on the operation of the Acts of Trade in the colonies.[31] By the end of that year both he and Jahleel Brenton, pursuing his charges against Massachusetts, were in London. If the new government in England had any thought of continuing the policies contained in the Stuart Navigation Acts, with the surveyor general and the collector for the critical area of New England on hand, now was an appropriate moment for decision.

For some time the groundwork had been prepared for reform of the customs system. As early as 1692 the Treasury had asked the Customs Commissioners for suggestions on what should be altered or improved. Primarily they were concerned, at that moment, with the customs service in England itself. But the reply of the Commissioners indicated that some thought had also been given to problems in the colonies. In their report, which was based on items included in a draft of a bill "part whereof had been long since Prepared," the Commissioners proposed that all ships belonging to English subjects, either in England or in the plantations, "bee Registered upon oath in the port to which they at that time respectively belong." No ship would be permitted to have its name altered, but on changing hands the new ownership and port of location might be added to the old registration. Every ship would have to have a certificate of such registration with it at all times.[32]

The Treasury and the Commissioners were still discussing this and other reforms in 1694.[33] Alterations in the customs system were a sensitive issue. Since many men and many interests were involved, agreement was not easily achieved. The Commissioners in their letter of January, 1694, implied that a bill was then before Parliament on that subject, but nothing further developed. A year later another effort was made and a bill particularly aimed at securing the plantation trade was introduced into Parliament. It got no further than a second reading. Two members of the House of Commons wrote that the bill "was so unfortunate as to be cast out the last parliament, but we shall consult with the most judicious in those affairs . . . and endeavor it may have better success now, and if it should be put in with the act that will be brought in to secure our trade against the Scotch East India Company it will go on the better." [34]

Associating the program for customs reforms with the Scottish threat, as suggested by those two members of the House, was an astute move. For many years Scotland and England had been at odds on the subject of trade. The northern kingdom wanted a share in England's commercial empire, while the English were irritated by Scottish encroachments on trade with the colonies. In 1695 the Scots took the initiative, creating their own East Indies company. This Darien Company was to have a monopoly of commerce with Africa, America, and Asia, and all goods imported into Scotland by the company, except tobacco and sugar, were to be duty free.[35] Passage of this Act marked a major national effort by Scotland to bolster its participation in the exploitation of the world's resources.

The English response, predictably, was immediate and angry. From their point of view the Scottish Act was a brazen attempt to intrude on their monopolies. So great was the resentment that King William saw fit to remove his representative in Scotland from office for having approved the Act, and Parliament was mobilized to counter the Scottish threat. A majority for any measure introduced to block the Scottish plans could be easily obtained. Consequently associating a general customs reform with such a measure would help to ensure passage.

No man was more suited to the task of relating the operation of the colonial service to Scottish encroachments than Edward Randolph. The letters he had written since his return to the colonies in 1692 had been filled with references to illegal traders from Scotland. The "Captain Meech" whose ships he tried to have condemned in Virginia was "A Scotchman & an old transgressor." One of the vessels he prosecuted in Maryland had been captained by a Scotsman and the jury which frustrated Randolph's plans had been summoned by a sheriff who was "a Scotch Irishman" and who returned a jury composed of "known Scotch & others their friends." [36] Thoroughly informed on affairs in the colonies, enthusiastic in his opposition to Scottish encroachments, Randolph was an ideal lobbyist for a new Parliamentary bill.

In 1695, Randolph presented two reports to the Commissioners of the Customs, the first of which related directly to the customs service in the colonies. Under eleven headings the surveyor general discussed the weaknesses and suggested remedies. First, the naval officers accepted "persons of small or no estate" to act as security for captains and also too readily cancelled bonds on receipt of forged certificates. This loophole could be corrected if the governors were required to accept only substantial citizens as securities, on penalty of forfeiting £1,000 if they approved insufficient security.

Secondly, since the courts displayed a "general partiality . . . biassed by private interest," a court of Exchequer should be erected in the colonies with judges and attorneys general appointed by the king. Also, because there was no penalty for presenting forged documents, it should be enacted that masters using such papers should suffer twelve months' imprisonment. Randolph was particularly distressed at the freedom with which captains unloaded their cargoes before entering. To prevent this evasion any ship discharging its cargo before entry should forfeit £200, while anyone assisting such enterprises should pay £10 for the first offense, £20 for the second, and forfeit whatever small boats they used in their work.

If bond were given in England before a ship sailed to the plantations, a printed certificate of that fact should be in possession of the captain; otherwise no ship should be permitted to trade in the colonies. Since many Scotsmen entered the colonies to act as agents for merchants in Scotland, all such factors should be considered aliens and prohibited from engaging in trade. Referring again to bonds, Randolph complained that forfeited bonds were never prosecuted unless the offending party was present in the colony. It would be better to order that such bonds were to be prosecuted whether or not the offenders were available, and certificates of such forfeitures sent to England to be acted upon there.

A closer check should be made of Scottish or Irish ships, which frequently employed an English captain to cover the true ownership. Such ships were to be seized immediately; and, if the Englishmen hired to perpetrate such frauds should themselves give evidence, they were to receive one-half the value of the seizure. Collectors were to board any suspicious vessel and take written testimony from the captains as to the ownership and the composition of the crew. Should the captain make a false report, he should be liable to a £500 penalty and loss of his ship. Since a great amount of tobacco found its way from Virginia and Maryland to New England or other colonies, and from thence to Europe, every colony not producing tobacco on its own should set up two ports where tobacco could be imported, and collectors and other officers were always to be on hand at those designated ports to check all entries and clearances. And, finally, Randolph, feeling that foreign privateers were given too many liberties in the colonial ports, suggested that they should not be allowed to "have liberty to reside" until they posted bond to observe the laws with the governor or some other authority.[37]

In his second report Randolph used the Scottish threat to elaborate once again one of his favorite schemes, reminiscent of his suggestions leading to the establishment of the Dominion of New England. Arguing that the Scots planned not only "to let themselves into the trade of all his Majesty's Plantations" but also to purchase "a settlement . . . on the southern shore of Delaware Bay," Randolph prophesied that such a colony would soon rival the Dutch islands as a center of free trade and frustrate all English attempts to control the commerce of the colonies. Actually such a threat was not only farfetched but absurd. The Scots could not "purchase" a colony on Delaware Bay without royal permission, and the area was generally included in the proprietary of Pennsylvania. Even if the Scots instead acquired "one or more islands near the Continent," as Randolph suggested they might, they hardly had the navy or merchant fleet to rival the English as effectively as the Dutch had done. Yet on the basis of this remote possibility Randolph recommended a complete reorganization of the American colonies. It was a transparent attempt to employ "scare tactics" to pressure Parliament into underwriting a general reform program.

Randolph urged that the Carolinas be taken out of the hands of their proprietors, that South Carolina and the Bahamas be put under one government, that North Carolina be merged with Virginia, that the Lower Delaware counties be annexed to Maryland, that West Jersey be added to Pennsylvania and an "active Governor" appointed there, that East Jersey and Connecticut be added to New York, and that Rhode Island should be included in Massachusetts. Because some of the proprietors or members of the charter colonies might "not apprehend the danger that is threatened by the new law in Scotland," those who should "refuse in this time of danger to accept his Majesty's government . . . should be obliged both to accept and maintain such officers as may be needful to preserve the trade to England and the duties to his Majesty." [38]

At the request of the Lords of Trade, the Commissioners of the Customs analyzed Randolph's two reports at length. As to the reorganization of the colonies they pointed out that the whole plan was carefully worked out but rather extreme. All the colonies were "subject to the Acts of Trade, and his Majesty's dominion is over all." Since the various proprietors "are so much tied up to the dominion of the Crown of England as they ought to defend the same at the peril of their lives, and may not alienate a foot to Scotch . . . it were most reasonable, in case more may not be had, that at least all Governors employed by the Proprietors should be sworn . . . to the observation of the said Acts, under penalty of £1,000."

In effect the Commissioners realized that the Scottish threat could not be stretched to cover complete reform of the plantations. As they said, "in case more may not be had" it would be best to settle for what might be obtained. Nothing better illustrated the change in policy from the days of the Stuarts to those of William than the Commissioners' remarks on Randolph's closing proposals to force such colonies as declined to accept a royal government to support enforcement officers: "we are humbly of opinion that his Majesty's officers will best do their duty when wholly independent from any proprietors for their salaries and subsistence." The Commissioners were practical men. If the colonies could not be controlled from within — and in spite of Randolph's dreams that remained a remote possibility — they must be controlled from without. For that purpose "wholly independent" officers were the wisest tool. Within a year's time this realization led to a major alteration in the colonial customs service.

Although they saw little immediate value to Randolph's governmental reorganization scheme, the Commissioners agreed completely with the surveyor general's report on specific alterations in the trade laws. In fact they had already prepared a draft of a bill to be presented to Parliament which was being studied by the attorney general. All but two of Randolph's suggestions required Parliamentary action, the Commissioners reported, and they were included in the bill. But the question of privateers and of the courts could be settled by the royal authority alone. As to the first, the governors should be ordered to take £1,000 security from any privateers — who were really "freebooters, who break all the rules both of Admiralty and trade" — for their "good behaviour to the laws of trade" before they were granted permission to reside. On the subject of courts, the Commissioners pointed out that the king "hath power to erect Courts of Exchequer in the Plantations for trial of causes that have reference to his Revenue, and to appoint the Officers thereof, and with such powers for this end as his Majesty's learned Counsel shall advise." [39]

The bill prepared by the Commissioners was given its first reading in the House of Commons on the 27th day of January, 1696. During the hearings Randolph was called upon to testify several times. By April 13, 1696, both Houses agreed on a final form for the new Act.[40] This "Act for Preventing Frauds, and Regulating Abuses in the Plantation Trade" was the last of the great fundamental Navigation Acts.[41] Whereas the earlier Acts had been predicated on the existence or achievement of a "high degree of both political and social unity" in the colonies,[42] the new Act was realistically based on the status quo. It presupposed a lack of cooperation from the colonists and elaborated in detail, and at length, a comprehensive program to perfect the machinery of enforcement. The two members of the House of Commons who had written that passage of the Act might "go on the better" if associated with the Scottish threat had been correct.[43] The Act of 1696 was a landmark in the development and execution of English colonial policy.

The preface to the Act noted that in spite of the existence of the former laws "great abuses are daily committed, to the Prejudice of the English Navigation, and the Loss of a great Part of the Plantation Trade to this Kingdom, by the Artifice and Cunning of ill-disposed Persons." First consideration in the Act was given to tightening the restrictions on participation by foreign shipping in the colonial trade. No goods were to be carried to or from the colonies in any but English built and owned vessels. The only exception to this new exclusion of foreign-constructed but English-owned ships was in the case of prizes captured and condemned in a court of law. Otherwise only ships of English construction, manned by a crew three-fourths of whom were English subjects, and captained by an Englishman, could trade in the colonies. This provision both decreased the opportunities for fraudulent participation by foreign shipping and encouraged the growth of England's own shipbuilding industry.

Along with the question of shipping, the responsibility of the governors to support enforcement of the Acts was strengthened. Now the oaths they were obliged to take included each and every provision of all the Acts, and failure to take such oath, or to uphold the laws, would result in dismissal and forfeiture of £1,000. The next provision, relating to the naval office, was particularly important. As Randolph and Brenton had suggested, the naval officer played too important a role in enforcement of the Navigation Acts to be left completely under the sole supervision of the governors. The Act of 1696 provided that the naval officers should still be appointed by the governors but that such appointments had to be approved by the Commissioners of the Customs. Further, all naval officers were to give bond to the Commissioners or their agents for the faithful performance of their duties. In this way what had originally been entirely a local office was tied to the official service. Usually the agents representing the Commissioners in each colony would be the regular customs officials, so they would now have a measure of control over their former rivals. Thereafter any naval officer faced removal and forfeiture of his security if he opposed the customs officers or was negligent in his duty.[44]

Perhaps the most important feature in the new Act was the extension of the Act of Frauds to the colonies. This Act, passed in 1662, had protected the customs officers in England against personal harm and had given them extensive powers of enforcement.[45] Under that Act the officers were entitled to general search warrants, known as writs of assistance, and permitted the right of forceful entry in cases of suspected concealment of illegally imported goods. Now these privileges were granted to the colonial officers. In their powers, rights, and obligations, they were made the complete equals of the officers in England.

The next article provided that proceeds from seizures should be distributed as formerly, one-third to the king, one-third to the governor, and one-third to the person who should put the suit in prosecution. To facilitate successful prosecutions, the burden of proof was placed on the defendants in all cases arising from illegal importation or exportation of goods from the colonies. To clear up any doubts as to the meaning of the Act of 1673, it was explicitly stated that payment of the enumerated duties did not excuse a captain from posting bond to carry the enumerated goods only to England or another English territory.

A New Policy Defined

The ninth paragraph of the new law contained implicit recognition of the failure of the Stuart policy of internal control of the colonies. Realistically providing for the existence of an organized opposition to the imperial system in the plantations, it was stated that "all Laws, Bylaws, Usages or Customs, at this time, or which hereafter shall be in Practice, or endeavoured or pretended to be in Force or Practice, in any of the said Plantations, which are in any wise repugnant to the before mentioned Laws . . . or . . . to this present Act . . . are illegal, null and void, to all intents and Purposes whatsoever." The Stuarts had hoped to control the local laws at the source — in the colonial legislatures. King William's Parliament accepted the abandonment — or at least the post-ponement — of that ideal solution. Where they could not control the creation of law they could invalidate objectionable enactments after passage. For the next sixty years review of colonial legislation was a major administrative assignment in England.

Randolph had complained that there were no penalties attached to use of forged papers. Now it was provided that in case such frauds were suspected, the customs officers might require the captains to post an additional bond which would be forfeited if the papers proved to be false. Anyone counterfeiting documents, or knowingly using them, was subject to a fine of £500. The wording of the Act suggested that "Scotch Men" were mainly responsible for such frauds and deserved special attention. Following this article, the authority of the Commissioners of the Customs and the Treasury to appoint as many officers as they thought necessary, and at "any City, Town, River, Port, Harbour or Creek" in the colonies, was specifically recognized, and they were instructed to concern themselves with "better executing the several Acts of Parliament relating to the Plantation Trade." In this way the argument of the colonists that the members of the customs staff were charged only with collecting the duties of the Act of 1673, and not with general enforcement of the laws of trade, was disposed of. Thereafter the collectors and the other officials were the undoubted principal agents of enforcement in the plantations.

The clause relating to the Treasury and the Customs Commissioners also stated that in any "Actions, Suits and Informations that shall be brought . . . in the said Plantations, upon any Law or Statute concerning his Majesty's Duties, or Ships or Goods to be forfeited by reason of any unlawful Importations or Exportations" the jury must be composed entirely of English subjects. Earlier, however, in the section on the distribution of the proceeds of seizures, where it had been decreed that the burden of proof rested on the defendant, the Act had specified that "all the Penalties and Forfeitures" could be recovered in "any of his Majesty's Courts at Westminster, or in the Kingdom of Ireland, or in the Court of Admiralty held in . . . [the] Plantations respectively, where such Offence shall be committed, at the Pleasure of the Officer or Informer, or in any other Plantation belonging to any Subject of England."

These vague references to the procedure to be followed in legal cases arising under the Acts of Trade have been described as showing "how carelessly the act was prepared."[46] In one section trial by jury is clearly recognized, and yet in the other reference is made to the Admiralty courts, which operated without juries. The clause relating to the Admiralty jurisdiction was, in fact, an afterthought. While the bill was in hearing before the House of Lords, a mere two weeks before final passage, Edward Randolph had been requested to present a provision regarding Admiralty jurisdiction in the colonies. Randolph replied that the Act of 1660 provided for Admiralty jurisdiction in the plantations but he prepared a few words to be inserted in the new Act as a precaution.[47] The result was disastrous. The extent of Admiralty jurisdiction remained uncertain and the effectiveness of those courts was sadly impaired for many years.

It would seem to have been the intention of the framers to extend Admiralty jurisdiction to the colonies but to place a major reliance on other courts as well. Possibly they thought to make use of colonial courts of Exchequer. Randolph had suggested that such courts be erected in the plantations, and the Commissioners of the Customs had indicated that they could be established on the royal authority alone, without the intervention of Parliament.[48] In England itself the Court of the Exchequer, not the Admiralty, had cognizance of violations of the Acts of Trade. Logically it would be expected that such an arrangement should be extended to the colonies. In fact, there is evidence that this was done. Certain colonies, including Bermuda and New York, did provide for courts of Exchequer, and by the end of the seventeenth century most governors had been instructed to assemble such courts as needed.[49]

However, in practice, Exchequer courts in the colonies proved unworkable. The colonists had little knowledge of the complex procedure of the English court, and since the personnel of such courts as were established consisted of local inhabitants the new tribunals showed as little desire to support imperial regulations as the other colonial courts.[50] For these reasons the courts of the Exchequer never became a permanent feature of colonial administration. In sixty years' time this failure was to have important consequences; claiming that there were no Exchequer courts in the colonies, the colonists launched a determined attack on the use of writs of assistance by customs officers. Since under the laws these writs could be issued only by the Court of the Exchequer, there was a certain validity to the legalistic quibbling of the colonists on this issue in the days of James Otis. But for the moment, in 1696, the important fact was that establishment of Admiralty courts in the colonies had been given Parliamentary sanction. The details had yet to be worked out, but a major step forward had been made in the effort to achieve enforcement of the Navigation Acts.

The final clauses of the Act of 1696 included definition of a previously confused point of law. The original Acts of Trade had included Ireland in the list of places to and from which trade to the colonies was authorized. A later Act had eliminated Ireland, but in practice many bonds accepted by the customs officers still authorized its inclusion. Now it was definitively stated that Ireland was not to appear on such bonds. Further, in answer to one of Randolph's complaints, it was now required that only "Persons of known Residence and Ability" were to be accepted as security for bonds given in the colonies. Bonds not canceled within eighteen months by presentation of certificates proving that the regulations had been obeyed were to be put in suit.

After providing for a tighter check on ships attempting to trade illegally under cover of "Stress of Weather . . . or by Reason of Leakiness," the Act dealt directly with the Scottish trade threat and the problem of privileged proprietary colonies. No person having any "Right or Property" in the English colonies could "sell or dispose" of any part of his lands to any but an English subject unless permission were obtained from the king. And the proprietary governments were required to see that their governors were "allowed and approved by his Majesty" and that they took the proper oaths to uphold the Acts of Trade and Navigation. If enforced, this provision would greatly enlarge royal authority in the "independent" colonies.

The final article of the Act fulfilled the earlier recommendation of the Commissioners of the Customs in regard to the registering of shipping.[51] No vessel should be "deemed or pass as a Ship of the Built of England . . . until the Person or Persons claiming Property in such Ship . . . shall register the same." The procedure elaborated involved attesting ownership before customs officials in the port to which the vessels belonged, with certificates of such registration being carried by the ships. Restrictions were placed on changing the names of ships, and a central "general Register" was to be kept by the Commissioners of the Customs. Any vessel not having proof of such registration, except small boats "whose Navigation is confined to the Rivers and Coasts of the . . . Place where they trade," should be liable to seizure "as any Foreign Ship."

The length and complexity of this Act speak for themselves. It was an exhaustive effort to achieve enforcement of the Navigation Acts. Where the earlier Acts had outlined the general rules, this statute defined the explicit details. If its provisions could be enforced, no matter what the internal state of the individual colonies might be, England would be assured of the full commercial benefits of empire. The great advance made in this Act was that in no instance did the machinery of enforcement evolved depend on colonial participation. Whether in the final determination reliance was to be placed on the courts of the Exchequer or on Admiralty courts, still the local judicial system had been bypassed by the establishment of special imperial tribunals. In specific terms the agents of the Commissioners of the Customs and the Treasury were designated as the principal officers of enforcement, while such officials as the governors and the naval officers were placed within the reach of the royal authority. The manner and place of trial of offenses against the Acts were left to the discretion of the prosecution; cases could be taken to "any of his Majesty's Courts at Westminster, or in the Court of Admiralty . . . where such Offence shall be committed, at the pleasure of the Officer or Informer, or in any other Plantation." In this way cases were not only removed from the local courts but could be taken out of a given colony to another plantation, or to England itself, if need be.

The same policy prevailed in regard to bonding provisions. Copies of all bonds issued in the colonies had to be forwarded to London. Hearings involving forfeiture of such bonds could be held in London as well as in the colonies. Nor was the registration of shipping left to local control. Even though the royal customs staff took part in the registering of vessels, provision was made for the keeping of a "general Register" in England to prevent frauds. In all its varied aspects the Act of 1696 centered authority on London. Every action was to be checked there, every official concerned with the trade laws appointed or approved there. Nor did the passage of the great Act end elaboration of this system. In the months immediately following three important steps were taken: a network of Admiralty courts was created in the colonies; royal advocate generals were sent out to protect the king's legal interests; and the colonial customs officers were made "wholly independent" by being transformed into established members of the English service. With those actions the colonial customs service came of age.

IV

The System Takes Shape

THE years between 1696 and 1710 were occupied with the settlement of the colonial system along the lines laid down in the Act of 1696. In 1697 the Privy Council issued an order for plans to be drawn up to establish Admiralty courts in all the colonies. The plantations were divided into eleven districts, and the High Court of the Admiralty prepared special commissions authorizing the various governors to erect such courts and to appoint judges, advocates, and other officers as was done in England.[1] The first appointments were only temporary, the real test of the new legal system coming with the dispatch of William Atwood from England in 1701 to preside as judge of the Admiralty for the colonies from New Hampshire through the Jerseys.

Atwood went first to New York, where he was disappointed to learn of the death of Lord Bellomont, who had a reputation as a strict enforcer of the Acts of Trade. But the judge expressed himself satisfied with the support of the lieutenant governor, although he was disturbed by a case decided before his arrival, in which the naval officer had let the guilty party go on receipt of a small payment. Generally Atwood was content with his initial reception, an estimate he was soon to revise.[2]

As well as being judge of the Admiralty, Atwood was also chief justice of the royal colony of New York. In a like manner, Sampson Broughton, the advocate general of the Admiralty court, was also attorney general of the province. As chief justice, Atwood at first experienced some problems, but the support of the lieutenant governor enabled him to write as of October, 1701, "Several here cannot well bear with the execution of the Laws of England; yet I hope I have hitherto maintained their credit in these parts, and the Assembley, as evidence of their approving my endeavours, have added 70£ a year to my salary." He added that although "a great clamour was raised against a sentence of mine in the Admiralty Court . . . that sentence is at peace and the vessel is upon sale." The press of business in New York kept Atwood there longer than he intended, since he was anxious to proceed to Boston, where he felt "the neglect and frauds of the officers of the Customs" would probably keep him from having much to do in the Admiralty court but where he felt his presence was particularly needed.[3] It was at Boston that the judge was to encounter his first open opposition.

In a long report of December, 1701, Atwood detailed his experience in New England. In Connecticut he found the governor and Council of the opinion that his activities as Admiralty judge interfered with their charter rights, but Atwood thought "I left [them] in a disposition to submit to that jurisdiction." However, since the only customs officer in the colony, the deputy Brenton had appointed at New London, was a member of the Council, Atwood expected to hear of few seizures in that colony. In Boston Atwood discovered that Brenton's deputy actively opposed his work. William Payne, the deputy collector, had seized some brandy and wine illegally imported into Boston; but the goods were never prosecuted in court and Payne refused to account for either the goods or their value which he had "suffered to be embezzled and disposed of into hands unknown." Atwood proceeded to hold a hearing on the goods anyway. Both Payne and Ralph Harrison, the comptroller, were called but refused to testify, Payne telling the judge that he was only responsible to the Commissioners of the Customs and further presenting a petition claiming that the creation of the Admiralty court was "an unjust invasion and illegal obstruction of the subject's liberty." Atwood's efforts to force Payne to account for the goods was defeated by the common law courts, which took the case under indefinite advisement and meanwhile ordered that no one was to seize or restrain the "person" of the deputy collector. In this way Payne was removed from the reach of the Admiralty judge's power.[4]

This experience caused Atwood to write that " 'Tis certain unless some farther authority from England check their proceedings, 'twill be impossible for H. M. Admiralty jurisdiction to have any effect there." As to New York, Atwood said that in that miserably divided city his efforts to enforce the trade laws had created less resentment than his attempts to use his authority as chief justice to settle the internal confusion. By this interference in local politics, he reported, he had made "many enemies, perhaps even more than Mr. Weaver [Thomas Weaver, the collector], whose warmth in H. M. service, and great care to prevent irregular trade make many earnest for his removal, of which they think themselves sure upon the coming of a new Governor." [5] Atwood wrote those words in December, 1701. Within a year the new governor, Lord Cornbury, had arrived, and not only was Weaver suspended but Atwood himself as well. Since the new governor sided immediately with their political opponents, Weaver and Atwood were driven into political exile.[6] So after two years of frustration and wasted effort the first royal judge of the Admiralty in the colonies retired in defeat to England.

Atwood's experiences in the north were echoed by those of his counterparts in the south. Joseph Morton, judge of the Admiralty in the Carolinas, wrote in August, 1701, that he had met "with much discountenance and many discouragements." He added that the people there in general were very "adverse from a complyance with the Laws of Trade and Navigation." Morton closed this report by warning that "unless Your Lordships speedily interpose some effectual remedies, unlawful trade will take a deeper root, and spread its branches further in these Plantations." [7] Robert Quary, Admiralty judge in Pennsylvania, when he was replaced in that post, wrote that "I am very glad that I am superseded, and do heartily wish that I never had been concerned." In another report Quary summed up the difficulties that the judges and other royal officials labored under when he observed that as long as the colonists "have the choice of the Council, the Judges, the Sheriffs, and consequently the Juries, and all the other officers, they have nothing to hope for or fear from the Queen's Government." [8]

The selection of a successor to Atwood indicated the attitude of the English government toward the colonial Admiralty courts at the end of the first period of experimentation. Roger Mompesson, who became judge of the Admiralty from New Hampshire to Pennsylvania, was an outspoken critic of the extension of Admiralty jurisdiction. Merely four years before his appointment he had composed a strong defense of the common law courts over those of the Admiralty. Perhaps Mompesson's selection, as Robert Quary charged, was engineered by William Penn to protect his property rights.[9] In any case the appointment of such a man indicated the acceptance, at least for the moment, by the English authorities of the failure of this aspect of the enforcement program. From the arrival of Mompesson to the time of the reforms in 1764 the Admiralty courts, originally intended to bulwark the machinery of enforcement, receded in importance. Atwood's experiences, and those of the other early judges, which showed what effective use the colonists could make of their common law courts, suggested just how great an effort would have to be made to make extension of Admiralty jurisdiction over violations of the trade laws truly effective. It was an effort the English for some time were not willing to make, and so this aspect of the program inaugurated in 1696 was discarded. The local colonial courts, with their juries, retained their dominant position.

The failure of the attempt to extend Admiralty jurisdiction in the colonies was compounded by similar difficulties encountered in the effort to incorporate the colonial office of attorney general into the royal system. Edward Randolph originally had urged that these officials be taken under the royal appointive power, but this suggestion unfortunately was considered unacceptable constitutionally. At first Randolph's plan had the support of both the Customs Commissioners and the newly created Board of Trade, which in one of its reports endorsed the idea of making the attorneys general royal officers. Quoting Randolph, the Board said that the attorney general in Virginia was wholly unfamiliar with the law and the practice of English courts, that the same official in Maryland was a "favorer of illegal trade," and that the attorney general of Pennsylvania had declared that "he served the Province only and thereupon refused to put severall forfeited Bonds in Suit." [10]

Support from the Board and the Commissioners was not enough. The Attorney General of England, Sir Thomas Trevor, was asked for his opinion and declared that, while the king could appoint advocates general to serve in the Admiralty courts, attorneys general, as officers of the local provincial courts, were not properly included within the reach of royal appointive powers. [11] As a result of this ruling the attorney general's office in the colonies remained for a time beyond the direct control of the English government. Since the attempt to strengthen the Admiralty courts had broken down, the local provincial courts continued to be intimately involved in questions relating to the Acts of Trade, and the chief prosecuting official on whom the customs collectors had to depend for the conduct of their cases in those courts was the attorney general, a provincial officer. This double failure concerning the Admiralty courts and the office of the attorney general did not make the task facing the reformed customs staff any easier.

The customs service itself was reorganized at the same time that the first of the new Admiralty courts were being established. On January 17, 1696, the Commissioners of the Customs had observed that "as things now stand, we see a necessity to have many new officers employed, and such as by fit rewards may not be liable to the temptation or connivances which others have heretofore been guilty of." [12] There was, in fact, only one solution to their desire to make the colonial officers "wholly independent": the salaries of the colonial staff would have to be placed beyond the reach of local colonial authorities. Consequently it was decided to add them to the regular English establishment.

On November 20, 1696, the Treasury approved the plans of the Customs Commissioners to pay their officers from the English Exchequer. On the original list drawn up by the Commissioners a total of twenty-nine officers were mentioned, the charge to the Exchequer for their combined salaries amounting to £1,605. Only the officers on the continent and in the Bahamas were included, those in the West Indies continuing to be paid from the revenue of the four and one-half percent duties. The average salary on the new establishment was approximately £45 a year, while most of the officers mentioned were collectors. Apparently in many places the office of comptroller — or surveyor, as it had originally been called — had fallen into disuse. At best it was a post of little profit, with a minimum of authority but onerous responsibilities. On the establishment list only two comptrollers appeared, one in the Carolinas and the other in New England. Only gradually during the following years were these offices revived, and many remained unfilled until after 1764. The collectorship was the important office and generally reliance was placed entirely on the men in those posts. Also on the list was the surveyor general, who was provided with an allowance of £80 a year. [13]

Most of the officers were not new appointees. Time was needed to implement the new arrangements, and for the moment the former officials continued in their posts. However, there was at least one indication of things to come: William Massey, who had "Served as a Deputy Kings Waiter . . . [in] London about 9 years," was sent out as collector at Lewis in Pennsylvania. [14] His appointment testified to the desire of the Commissioners to place experienced and responsible officers in the colonies. Massey was free of local ties and could be expected to be a truly "independent" agent.

Edward Randolph remained as surveyor general. The allowance made to him on the new establishment was in addition to his regular salary and was meant to provide for a boat and four men to help him in his work. As surveyor general Randolph now received a total income of £495, from which he had to pay for a boat and men and for a clerical assistant as well. The Commissioners of the Customs wished Randolph to return to the colonies as quickly as possible to put the new arrangements into effect. Exaggerating the number of new officers to be sent immediately to the plantations, the Commissioners reported that, "in regard it has been thought necessary to form a new establishment of officers . . . for the better putting in execution the several laws . . . which officers (in regard there could not be that reasonable confidence in persons of interest and residence upon the place as in persons disinterested in and unrelated to the place) have been for the most part chosen from hence, and will be therefore new and inexperienced in the Plantations, it may be necessary forthwith to dispatch Mr. Randolph with them to the Plantations . . . to dispose and settle them in their respective places." [15]

Randolph returned to the colonies in November, 1697. With him went the new establishment list and a greatly expanded series of instructions to the colonial customs officers. The original instructions drawn up in 1673 remained in force.[16] To them were now added sixteen new articles. The first of the new instructions related to the Scottish East Indies Act of 1695. The collectors were furnished with a copy of the Scottish Act and warned to keep a careful watch for any encroachments. For the rest, the additional articles merely summarized the various provisions of the Act of 1696.[17] At the same time the Commissioners sent a form letter to all the governors reminding them of their duties and responsibilities to the king and his government.[18]

Once again, fortunately, Edward Randolph in his voluminous correspondence covered his experience during these years in implementing the new system. Between December, 1697, and July, 1700, the surveyor general traveled from one end of the colonies to the other, much of his time being occupied in locating the various officers and selecting replacements where necessary. In Maryland, his first stop, he appointed William

Bladen collector at Annapolis in place of the former officer who had "Remov'd from that Town 20 miles Distant to another Employment." In the same colony, at Pocomoke, he appointed Edward Price as surveyor and searcher to replace John Dashell "who liv'd at too great a Distance to prevent the Illegal Trade Carry'd on where the Boundaries of Maryland & Virginia meet." Such work, in fact, was one of the most important of the duties of the surveyor general. Collectors might die, leave their posts, or resign, and unless periodic checks were made the customs service would suffer accordingly. For this reason Randolph later, when he was in Bermuda, was anxious to find transportation to North Carolina "where Mr. Marchant the Collector at Curretuck dyed in November, 1696, and another man is wanted there." The local authorities in many areas could not be depended upon to provide temporary replacements, or even to notify the surveyor general of vacancies; it was often to their advantage to have the customs house unoccupied.[19]

Another of Randolph's concerns was to see that forfeited bonds were put in suit. He sent letters "to All the Collectors in Virginia to put all forfeited bonds in suite," while in Pennsylvania he "Demanded All forfeited bonds" from the lieutenant governor and would himself have put them in suit "but David Lloyd a Quaker the Attorney General Refused to doe itt Neither would Mr. Markham [William Markham, the lieutenant governor] Appoint Another Person to prosecute them." Randolph also seized various vessels on his own authority as he traveled through the colonies, but his experiences in that line showed little improvement over his earlier disappointments prior to 1696. In May, 1698, he "went to Amboy in East Jersey from New York & seiz'd the Ship Roster . . . for Unlivering Goods not being first Register'd, She was sometime After discharg'd by the Court of Admiralty at New York where I was at charges to prosecute her."

New York itself presented a special problem. The collectorship there had a long history of mismanagement and unfortunate associations with the internal political turmoils. Most of the trouble arose from the fact that the royal collector of the enumerated duties also acted as receiver of the casual or provincial revenues. In his latter capacity he was a local official responsible to the colonial government; consequently his work often became involved in local politics. This unique situation apparently originated in the fact that New York was first the private preserve of the Duke of York. William Dyer, the first collector there, was selected by the Duke and authorized to collect both the royal and local revenues.[20] This combination of functions continued throughout most of the colonial period in New York.

The officer who had followed Dyer in New York, Lucas Santen, had been removed in 1687 by Governor Thomas Dongan for gross mismanagement of the provincial revenues.[21] His successor, Mathew Plowman, had a short and stormy career. He was appointed rather hastily in November, 1687, to replace Santen, but within less than a year William Blathwayt wrote to the governor of New York that he had received "a further Character of Mr. Plowman which is not much to his advantage." He was quickly removed, and Childley Brooke was appointed to the posts, which he still held in 1698 when Randolph made his official visit to New York.[22]

New York in 1698, and for many years thereafter, suffered from the effects of the uprising of 1689. The revolutionary government of Jacob Leisler, which controlled the colony after the fall of the Dominion of New England, had ended with the execution of Leisler in 1691, but the political divisions caused by this event kept the colony in a state of unrest for many years. Childley Brooke had been a member of the Council in the government which had put Leisler to death.[23] Until 1698 this political connection with the anti-Leislerian faction was to his advantage, as the royal governors supported that same group. But in 1698 Richard Coote, Earl of Bellomont, became governor of New York, and, disgusted with the mismanagement of the colony under the former administrations, sided with the faction loyal to the memory of Leisler.

One of the new governor's first actions was to examine the conduct of Brooke in his two offices. Bellomont arrived in New York in April, 1698; by the end of June he had suspended Brooke from all his duties. The governor reported that he found negligence everywhere; trade moved freely where it would, the customs officers were lax in their duty, and the collector was the worst of all. To support his charges Bellomont pointed out that one small seizure made within a month of his arrival put the whole town in "an Uproar . . . [they] look'd on it as a Violent Seizing [of] their property." This reaction, he suggested, was an indication of the previous laxity of enforcement, which led the inhabitants to think it was their right to trade as they wished.[24] Brooke was also charged, along with the former governor, Benjamin Fletcher, with having been in league with the merchants and having profited from association with pirates.

Whether or not these charges were true is open to question. The fact is that until Governor Robert Hunter, during his administration starting in 1710, managed to quiet the factional strife in New York, the chaotic internal political situation was responsible for many personnel changes in all the local offices. Brooke was succeeded by a commission of five men who supervised the collection of the revenues. This commission ended with the appointment of Thomas Weaver as collector and receiver in 1701. Unfortunately for Weaver, in that year Bellomont died and the anti-Leislerian faction, centered around Nicholas Bayard, again took power. The "Articles" exhibited against Weaver by the "principall Merchants," which led to his removal in 1702, were based primarily on his mismanagement of the local revenues and his participation in the political contest against Bayard and his followers.[25] Weaver's successor, Thomas Byerly, in turn was twice suspended from office for political reasons between 1703 and 1723, but he, at least, lived long enough to see the end of the factional strife and the return to "normal" government.[26] In all these cases, although the royal collectors were involved, their difficulties arose from the political contests centering around their duties as receivers of the local revenues. The unfortunate fact in New York was that the effectiveness of the customs service for many years depended on the state of the local political scene. The disruption of the customs service there had little to do with attempts to enforce the Acts of Trade.

New England, of course, was the territory of Jahleel Brenton, who as collector had the authority to appoint deputies throughout the area. Randolph inspected the officers in Rhode Island, in Salem and Boston, and in New Hampshire, at the same time complaining that there were no settled officers in Connecticut, which permitted that colony to evade the Acts freely. Relations with the local courts were still a problem in Massachusetts. Randolph reported that in one trial of some goods seized by Brenton one of the owners, who was a member of the Council, "sat Judge upon the Bench whilst his own cause was Tryed." The naval officer was "a great Promoter of the Illegal Trade," and in general all matters were "Contriv'd for Carrying on the Illegal Trade there with

68

security, Several of the Members of the Councill being cheifly Concern'd therein." [27]

During the next few years Randolph continued his tour of the colonies, bringing order and system to the customs operations, until unexpectedly in April, 1703, he died at the home of a friend in Virginia. With his death an end came to an era in the history of the customs service. Since his first visit to New England in 1676 this man had traveled more extensively in the colonies, accumulated more information, and done more to influence the course of English policy than any other single individual. In a sense Randolph had been the customs service in the colonies. The majority of the officers had been appointed by him in person or by the authorities at home on his recommendation. Every colony had felt the force of his presence, and to a large degree the resentment aroused by the activities of the customs service had centered on Randolph personally. He had endured much and accomplished much. No man again was to exercise such general authority over the customs operations in the plantations. With his passing there came a close to the period of "one man rule." Thereafter the individual collectors increased in importance, while the authority of the surveyors general declined in equal measure. Since 1689 the tendency had been towards centralization of authority in London, and as the system evolved there was no room for one man to carry across the seas in his person all the power that had been Randolph's. Randolph himself had been useful in ordering the arrangements outlined in the Act of 1696; but by 1703 he had outlived his value. With decisions increasingly emanating from London, Randolph was gradually forced to the side lines. He died a lonely, ignored, and antiquated symbol of a bygone era.[28]

Randolph was succeeded as surveyor general by Robert Quary, the displaced Admiralty judge of Pennsylvania, and the final ordering of the colonial customs service took place under his supervision. In his tour of Maryland, in late 1703, Quary found some of the officers "guilty of severall mistakes, neglects, and omissions" but the officers promised to behave for the future. One collector, David Kennedy at Pocomoke, had left his post and gone to England without leave; Quary suggested his replacement. In Virginia the surveyor general found that "the Collectors and Naval Officers are gentlemen of very good characters both for honesty and ability" except for George Luke, the collector at the Lower James. Luke had gone to England, like Kennedy, but left a "scandalous caracter behind him." He married an "infamous" woman who had previously been on trial for her life and narrowly escaped hanging, and together they had led such a life that Luke had made himself "the scorn and contempt of the meanest in this country." [29]

Currituck in North Carolina, Quary reported, was a "small hole where much mischief is yearly done," while the naval officers in Pennsylvania still continued to oppose the customs operations. Generally the surveyor general reported that to secure the trade of the colonies from Pennsylvania to the Carolinas "a small briganteen with an active Master and about 20 brisk men" was needed. Such a vessel would save the Queen the expense of sending "a small man of war . . . which hitherto hath been done" with ill results. The captain of the man-of-war disliked the assignment and "do find one pretence or other always to be at anchor." Quary wanted the brigantine placed under the immediate authority of the governors of Virginia and Maryland.[30]

In his northern tour Quary found New England somewhat improved, although Connecticut was still impossible. That charter colony generally openly opposed the trade laws. Quary wrote that he had "turn'd out all the Collectors in this Government & putt others in their places, which I hope will make some alteration, tho' I must own that I have no hopes of preventing illegal trade." Rhode Island, too, was not a happy picture. Newport had risen to a major port in recent years and there was much illegal trade, which could not be stopped as long as the colony retained its charter privileges. But the old villain, Boston, showed signs of improvement. Formerly there had been a great deal of illegal trade, but the war had reduced Boston's commerce generally, and now the "impoverished" city was more amenable. Still, the extensive coastline, and numerous opportunities to unload goods beyond the sight of customs officers, made trade violations easy. Quary suggested a sloop to cruise continually off the New England coast.[31]

While Quary was engaged on his surveys, the last major alterations in the colonial customs service were being made in England. In 1707 the Treasury learned that Jahleel Brenton was willing to resign his offices. In his place John Jekyll went to Boston as collector, but with an important difference in powers. Brenton had been collector and surveyor for all New England, with the authority to appoint deputies throughout the whole area. Jekyll's commission was restricted to the port of Boston.[32]

The deputy system in New England had been under attack for some years. As early as 1699 the Board of Trade had complained of the situation, with the Earl of Bellomont, governor of New York and Massachusetts, concurring in their opinion. Bellomont had written the Board that Brenton's deputies were generally unreliable. The man in New Hampshire was "a broken Marchant of Boston who has no good Character," while the deputy in Rhode Island consorted with pirates. Bellomont did not hold these faults against Brenton personally; rather it was the system: "I believe a man that's honest and of substance too, would hardly accept of a Deputy Collector's place." The governor recommended separate collectors for Rhode Island and New Hampshire, adding, "I should alsoe humbly advise that all Officers of the Revenue may be Englishmen, and not of these plantations by no means: for they have little Interests and friendships to gratifie, and to speak plainly, they seem here to hate those that are English-born, as if they were foreigners."[33]

Bellomont's suggestions had been seconded by Randolph and Atwood, both of whom had reason to know the character of the deputies at first hand. The retirement of Brenton provided the opportunity to implement their recommendations. As usual it took time to make the arrangements. Jekyll arrived in Boston in November, 1707. Not until June of 1709 were the Commissioners of the Customs ready to fill the other posts. Meanwhile the former deputies apparently continued to act on an unofficial basis.

On the 25th of June, 1709, the Commissioners reported to the Treasury that on the recommendation of Quary, various merchants, and Robert Armstrong (the former naval officer in New Hampshire),[34] they had decided to place collectors at Piscataqua in New Hampshire, at Salem and Marblehead in Massachusetts, and in Rhode Island. They suggested the former naval officer in Boston for the post in New Hampshire, but for Rhode Island and Salem the Commissioners chose two experienced members of the English customs service.[35] This division of New England completed the appointment of customs districts in America that had begun in 1673.

At the same time that the final arrangements were made for New England, the Commissioners acted to increase the over-all efficiency of the colonial service. Experience had shown that visitations by the surveyor general were a continuing necessity. Now the Commissioners reported that twelve hundred miles of coast line were too much for one surveyor general to cover effectively. Consequently they recommended establishing two departments on the continent: the northern to include the colonies from the Jerseys through Newfoundland, while the southern territory would extend from Pennsylvania through the Carolinas, including the Bahamas and Jamaica.[36] The Treasury approved this plan, and Robert Quary became the first surveyor general southern, Maurice Birchfield taking over the northern district.[37] With the adoption of this arrangement the formative years in the history of the colonial customs service came to a close.

The administrative system evolved by 1710 was to remain intact, with some additions but no major alterations, until 1763. From Newfoundland down through the Carolinas, and out to the islands of the Bahamas and Bermuda, there were thirty-four customs districts or areas in 1710, staffed by forty-two permanent officials.[38] The constancy of this arrangement throughout the whole period is illustrated by the fact that by 1760 the number of districts had risen only to forty-five, manned by fifty-eight officials, much of the increase being due to the organization of the new colonies of Georgia and Nova Scotia. Schemes, proposals, and projects to alter and extend the system appeared in generous profusion during those fifty years, but despite the obvious inadequacies and weaknesses actual reform had to await the political changes that attended the accession of a new monarch, George III, in 1760. So for fifty crucial years the major responsibility for the enforcement of the Acts of Trade and Navigation rested on the organization of the customs service as it existed in 1710.

The district farthest to the north, that of Newfoundland, was staffed only by a preventive officer. In the past there had been numerous complaints that a large amount of illicit trade centered on Newfoundland, and it was the duty of the preventive officer to check such activities. His was a purely negative function, as the area was not in itself an official customs port of entry. By 1715 it was felt that such an official was useless, since without a formally organized civil government there, with no courts in which to prosecute seizures and officials to back up his activities, he could accomplish little. Consequently, until Newfoundland was so organized, the preventive officer was removed in 1715 to Boston, where he became the surveyor and searcher.[39]

Nova Scotia was not administered by the customs service until after 1713, so the next post to the south in 1710 was that of Piscataqua in New Hampshire. One man, with the combined title of collector and surveyor, operated there. Massachusetts by this time was divided into two ports or districts — Salem and Marblehead, manned by a collector only, and Boston, which had both a collector and a comptroller. For the rest of New England, there was one collector in Rhode Island and another for Connecticut and its dependencies.

New York was the most completely staffed port as far as established officers went, having a collector, a comptroller, a surveyor and searcher, and a landwaiter. As noted later, various ports were provided with land- or tidewaiters and searchers on an informal basis — that is, on a basis of day-to-day hire as required. However, in New York, where the collector of the enumerated duties was also the receiver of the casual or provincial duties levied by the colony, the matter of salaries was always a problem; consequently the minor officials had been placed on the established salary list of the customs service.

New Jersey had two collectors and two districts, one at Perth Amboy and another at Bridlington, while Pennsylvania possessed three ports: Philadelphia was staffed by a collector and comptroller, and the Lower Counties (now Delaware) had collectors at Newcastle and Lewis. There was also a surveyor provided to supervise activities in Delaware Bay itself.

The largest concentration of officials was centered in Maryland and Virginia. Maryland had collectors at Patuxent, North Potomack, and Pocomoke, surveyors at Annapolis, Wicomocco and Munni, Williamstad, Bahama and Sassafras, and a riding surveyor along the Potomac River. Virginia had six collectors and two surveyors, the former covering the districts of South Potomac, Accomack and Northampton counties, York River, Upper James River, Lower James River, and the Rappahannock River, while the latter guarded the shores of Cape Charles and the Elizabeth River.

North Carolina was divided into two districts, that of Currituck, provided with a collector and comptroller, and that of Roanoke with a collector only. South Carolina was one district centered on Charleston, where a collector was located. Finally, collectors were stationed, one to each, in Bermuda and the Bahamas. The total, once again, was thirty-four districts or areas and forty-two officials. Shortly after 1710 a comptroller was added for South Carolina and the Bahamas, and as mentioned Nova Scotia was provided with a collector in 1713.

Supervising the activities of these various officials were two surveyors general, who divided the continent between them into northern and southern districts, the northern district extending from Newfoundland through New Jersey, while the southern covered the colonies from Pennsylvania through the Carolinas and the Bahamas.[40] Each surveyor general was paid a total of £495 a year, which included a personal salary of 20 shillings a day, plus £50 per year for a clerk and £80 for a boat and four boatmen.

Salaries for the other officials ranged from a high of £160 for the collector at Philadelphia to £35 for the surveyor at Williamstad, Maryland. There were a few oddities, such as the £55 a year paid to the collector at New York, but in most cases the salary was set in relation to the importance and size of a given port. In some cases the annual payments to the various officials included more than personal salaries; the collectors at Newcastle and Lewis, for example, each received £40 per year in addition to their regular salaries for a boat and two men. And at different times various incidental expenses were allowed, such as rent on a customs house or allowances for stationery.

The cost to the English Exchequer of these established officers for the year 1710 was £3,700.[41] The cost in 1760, for comparison, was £4,460, an increase of only £760, emphasizing once again the stability of the system. Against this expense could be set the receipts from the collection of the enumerated duties. Such receipts were irregular and varied greatly from year to year, but the four-year total from the period 1707 through 1711 was £7,305, an average of £1,826 a year. Thus, from the point of view of the English administrator, the colonial customs service in the continental colonies cost the Exchequer slightly under £2,000 a year.

Of the total of over £7,000 received in duties during the four-year period, roughly two-thirds was collected in the West Indies; only one-third, or an average of £640 a year, came from the continent. However, as noted previously, the West Indies were a special case within the imperial system, and the revenue from the four and one-half percent was available for use there.[42] With the officers in the islands being paid from that fund, in effect at no expense to the English, the combined West Indies and continental receipts from the enumerated duties could be used to offset the cost of the establishment on the mainland.

To glance ahead for a moment, over the four years from 1756 to 1760 the customs collectors in the colonies forwarded a total of £20,897 to England, an average of £5,224 a year. The largest part of this sum came, however, from receipts under the Molasses Act of 1733. Discounting that revenue, and considering only the collection of the enumerated duties, which were levied in 1760 just as they had been in 1710, the total receipts were £7,426, for an average of £1,856 a year, remarkably close to the average of £1,826 for the period 1707–1711. Breaking that receipt down further, it appears that by 1760, on an average, only £16 out of £1,856 was collected in the continental colonies. In effect, while the total receipts remained much the same, the share of the contribution made by the mainland had fallen from one-third of the whole to less than one-hundredth, an indication of the course events had taken on the continent during these fifty years.

Along with the established customs officials were others, lesser employees to handle the necessary daily chores. Boston, for example, had only two established officers, a collector and a comptroller, but two waiters were customarily employed there also.[43] In general most customs houses needed, and certainly possessed, one or more clerks to handle the required paper work. The number of these officials is difficult to ascertain, as only the individual port records could have provided complete information on them, and those records are lost. Each collector was allowed to charge certain operational expenses against his account, and in this manner provision was made for these minor officials. It is likely that the opinion of the surveyor general as to the need for such employees would weigh heavily, and that on that basis when each collector's accounts were approved in England such items would be allowed or disallowed as the case might be. In some instances, a collector might prefer to have his work done by deputy, in which case he of course would have to provide on his own for this assistance. To use Boston as an example again, William Sheafe acted as deputy collector there for some thirty years, serving several different collectors. Such deputies, it should be emphasized, did not officially replace the collector, but were rather assistants. Only one collector on the continent was officially authorized to act entirely by deputy, and the rest were duty bound at least to appear to be handling their official assignments in person.[44]

By 1710 the problem of the colonial naval office had been largely settled; in each of the above customs districts the collector's work was intimately involved with that of the naval officer, so much so that the latter may be considered a regular part of the customs service. The Act of 1696 had required that the naval officer give bond for performance of duty to the Customs Commissioners in England, and gradually even the appointment of these officials was removed from colonial control. The effort to combine this office with that of the collector had failed, mainly because of the English enthusiasm for a system of checks and cross-checks, in which every official would have another peering over his shoulder, limiting the opportunity for dishonest transactions. Still, the naval officer had been made to play his part in the customs operation and, in effect at no expense to the Exchequer, the English were provided with another agent of enforcement.

Confused as their relationships might often appear, each of these officials, in theory at least, had distinct and important functions. The central figure of necessity was the collector. On him depended full responsibility for the enforcement of the Acts of Trade and Navigation, and the other officials took their lead from him. Essentially the collector's task was to see that all goods were entered properly in his presence, that no cargoes were loaded or unloaded without his warrant, that the required duties were paid on enumerated items, and that proper bonds were given when necessary. He also was required to have the various acts and regulations on hand for the information of the captains and owners, and when necessary to seize in the king's name the goods, and possibly the ships, of transgressors. In the latter instance, the collector acted as the "informer" in the legal prosecutions following seizure. He had to check bonds and cocquets, keeping an eye out for forgeries, and see that the sureties offered were acceptable. His own accounts were to be transmitted regularly to England, attested to by the comptroller (where one was present) and the surveyor general, and sworn to before the governor. He also, of course, had to transmit the receipts from the enumerated duties to England, when possible in specie or bills, but in commodities if necessary. The matter of quarantine inspection and enforcement was another of his concerns. And the collector was not himself to engage in trade.[45]

The comptroller had the completely negative function of acting as a check on the activities of the collector. Such had been the design for this office in England since the time of Edward the First.[46] He was to keep his own records of transactions in the customs office, examine and sign all accounts and dispatches jointly with the collector, and generally share responsibility for the proceedings at his port. In fact, the comptroller entered more actively into affairs than his position required, frequently carrying out the instructions of the collector or acting for him in his absence.

The surveyor and searcher, of which only one example, that of New York, appears on the 1710 listing, was responsible for the actual inspection and control activities in the harbor. Under his supervision the outdoor officers did their work, tidewaiters boarding incoming vessels, landwaiters watching ships at moor, and searchers examining the loading and unloading process. Only the larger ports warranted such officials, and in most cases all these activities would be combined in one or two men. The officer sent to Nova Scotia in 1713, for example, had the general title of collector, surveyor, and searcher. In the ports where they were found, the ordinary searcher, as the title indicates, would inspect incoming and outgoing vessels and persons of whom "sinister suspicions might be had." [47] Tidewaiters or tidesmen were put on board incoming vessels to ensure that no goods were clandestinely landed before the mooring was reached, and landwaiters took charge at the quay to see that no unauthorized loading or unloading took place. Again, in most cases, all these functions were combined in one or two officers in any given port, at least until the system became more complex and efficient at the close of this fifty-year period.

Most of the surveyors listed on the colonial establishment were in actuality riding surveyors, a rather different matter. These officials had been found useful in England, particularly along the Scottish border, where they patrolled their districts on horseback, guarding against smugglers and illicit traders.[48] The surveyors in Maryland and Virginia were of this type, their special assignment being to watch over the numerous bays and inlets of the extensive coast line there. Very similar was the preventive officer, such as was stationed at Newfoundland to curtail the use of that distant area as a center for illicit trade with the French. Other preventive officers appear to have been used from time to time on an informal basis at certain places, as at Plymouth and Nantucket in Massachusetts.[49] But again the loss of the port records makes it difficult to obtain complete information on these men. In all likelihood a local official, such as a justice of the peace or a sheriff, would be used for this work, with his payment for services being based on a percentage reward from any successful seizures.

The duties of the naval officer, as summarized by an English official in 1713, were "to take an Accot of the Arrival of all Ships trading thither with their Ladings and how Navigated and the like of all ships going from the Plantations or from one plantation to another and to take Security (if not given before in Great Britain) that all Enumerated Goods be carried to Great Britain or from one plantation to another, and no ship can Load or Unload without the permission of this Officer as well as the Collector."[50] Although in theory this official represented the governor, who was required to see to the enforcement of the Acts of Trade in his area, in fact by 1710 the naval officer had become a subsidiary of the customs officials and was indeed little more than a keeper of the official port records. Bonds, for example, were taken out and recorded in his office but were not valid without the approval of the collector. Perhaps his most important contribution was the preparation of the official "naval lists" which contained itemized accounts of all vessels trading to and from the area and which, when forwarded to London, were used by the authorities as the principal source of information on the nature and extent of trading activities. Reduced to a paper-work official, the naval officer had little authority of his own.

The men chosen to execute these various offices came from a variety of backgrounds, but by 1710 certain patterns of selection were already evident. The more important and more remunerative the assignment, the greater the likelihood that it would go to an Englishman with prominent connections at home. Along with the established salary, each official was allowed certain fees for almost every transaction, and so the more active the port, the greater the income. Boston and Philadelphia, of course, were two of the most active of all colonial ports and consequently the most desirable. In 1710 the collector at Boston was John Jekyll, while

The System Takes Shape

John Moore occupied the same post at Philadelphia. Jekyll's uncle, Sir Joseph Jekyll, was not only wealthy and well known but was an influential member of Parliament as well. John Jekyll himself had been associated with Lord Paget when the latter was ambassador to the Imperial Court, and such was his influence that his appointment as collector was forced on the Commissioners of Customs in 1707 by the Lord Treasurer, a rather rare and unusual occurrence.[51] Jekyll served as collector until his death in 1733, when his son (also named John) succeeded him. Altogether the Jekylls, father and son, were collectors at Boston for thirty-four years.

During his lifetime Jekyll took an active part in the affairs of the Church of England parish that had been settled in the midst of Puritan Boston, and it is possible that his selection owed something to the same considerations that obtained the Philadelphia post for John Moore, whose patron was none other than the Bishop of London, the clergyman most closely associated with colonial affairs. The prime concern in Moore's appointment seems to have been a desire to strengthen the English Church in Pennsylvania in the face of opposition from the Quaker proprietor and settlers. Moore himself wrote to the Bishop in 1704 that "Mr Penn & his creatures . . . will appear strenuously my opponents, but I trust in yor Ldps favour to Surmount them all." [52] Nor were his hopes disappointed, as the good Bishop appeared in person before the Board of Trade and obtained their recommendation for Moore.[53] Moore remained as collector at Philadelphia until his death in 1729.

If an individual's connections were good enough, it was in fact even possible to have part of the customs organization rearranged to satisfy his personal needs. In 1710 James Bowles petitioned the Treasurer for the vacant post of collector at Patuxent in Maryland, his qualifications being listed as having been "long abroad in the Country and experienced in Trade." However, the Customs Commissioners had other plans for the post. John Dansey, formerly collector at North Potomack, had suffered greatly as a result of a prosecution brought against him by the owner of a ship and cargo he had seized in the line of duty, and on the recommendation of the surveyor general the Commissioners determined that Dansey had prior claims on the opening. Bowles, too, had his champions, as his father and Sir Henry Furness called in person at the customs board to argue his case. An accommodation, presumably agreeable to all, was reached, by which Dansey obtained the collectorship at Patuxent, the collector at North Potomack was moved to another district, and his place given to James Bowles.[54] Interesting as an example of the use of influence, this instance is also worth noting for the solicitude shown by the Customs Commissioners towards a faithful employee. It is good administrative practice to stand by "one's own," and in that area at least the customs service consistently displayed a commendable degree of wisdom throughout these years.

Along with these candidates of "influence," Englishmen of another type found their way into the colonial service, those who received their appointments as rewards or compensation for past services. George Muschamp, until 1710 collector at Patuxent, Maryland, is a case in point here. His father for twenty-eight years had been associated with the customs in Ireland, as farmer and commissioner, and George had also been employed there. Unfortunately the father died before his accounts had been approved, and in the confusion the family never received any benefit from the arrears due on the farm. Instead the son requested, and obtained, various positions in the colonies, first in Carolina and then finally in Maryland.[55] In a similar manner Maurice Birchfield, surveyor general northern in 1710, had served as a secretary in Ireland for some years with little compensation.[56] Nathaniel Kay, collector in Rhode Island, had previously performed faithfully as a riding surveyor on the Scottish border, while Charles Blechyden, collector and surveyor at Salem and Marblehead, had been employed in the English customs service for some twenty years prior to his appointment in the colonies.[57] In the latter case, however, there was another motive present beside that of rewarding a deserving official, as the English authorities planned to save on Blechyden's salary as "keyman" in London by sending him to the colonies and not engaging a replacement. In this instance the colonial service provided a convenient means to retire a useless official and ease the burden on the overcrowded English operation. One noticeable asset these men all brought to their work was their experience, a valuable advantage in officers entrusted with the execution of policy on distant and isolated shores.

Colonials too, of course, acquired positions in the customs service, on occasion by calling themselves to the attention of the English authorities in a favorable light, although this was not always an easy task. A success-ful applicant of this sort did well to imitate the example of Thomas Newton, who wisely took his case to England in person and benefited from good timing. At just the moment the Commissioners were begin-ning to discuss the extension of the service in New England by replacing the single collector, Brenton, with a flock of new officers, Newton arrived with a claim to their attention based on his long service as attorney gen-eral in Massachusetts. As the attorney general necessarily was frequently associated with the customs house in legal affairs, he could point to his knowledge of the business, at the same time playing up the meagerness of the compensation he had received for his pains over the years. He was rewarded with the place of comptroller at Boston.[58] In general, though, most colonials in these early years entered the service in a different man-ner, by on-the-spot appointments, usually of course to minor positions. Thus John Stackmaple, collector of Connecticut for twenty-three years, was a native of New London. In 1708 the surveyor general toured the district, discovering to his horror that the man acting as collector, al-though a "Pillar of their Church" was "a great Rogue" who dealt in false certificates and encouraged an illegal tobacco trade.[59] That man the sur-veyor general removed, and Stackmaple got the post, in which he was eventually confirmed by the English Commissioners. Or again, in Vir-ginia, perhaps because of the close connections that existed between the tobacco planters and various gentlemen in London, many of the stations in that colony found their way into colonial hands, as in the case of Edward Hill at the Upper James, who was himself the son of a collector. Few rose very high, and they were generally found in the minor offices for which there was not much competition, yet it is still true that a goodly number of the customs positions remained in the possession of native sons throughout this period.

Several of the officeholders can be accounted for in one final type-casting. These were the "schematists" or idea men, either English or colonial, who by dint of continually submitted reports and suggestions on the operation of the system created a reputation for knowledge and diligence, thus earning themselves a place in the service. Such a man was Robert Armstrong, listed in 1710 as collector at Piscataqua. Armstrong had come to New England as secretary to the governor, Bellomont, and through his favor had been made naval officer in New Hampshire. With the unexpected death of his patron, Armstrong wisely returned to England, presented himself as an expert on colonial affairs, while suggesting many of the changes that were made in 1707 and 1710. He so impressed the Commissioners that they set aside the post of surveyor general northern for him as a reward, only to be overruled by the Treasurer, who once again had a candidate of his own. Armstrong had to settle for the collectorship at Piscataqua, but eventually he managed to combine this with the position of deputy surveyor of the king's woods, again by presenting himself as an authority on the needs of that office.[60] Another of this sort was Caleb Heathcote of New York, who became surveyor general northern in 1715. Between 1708 and 1715 this ambitious gentleman corresponded with the English Board, presenting schemes of various kinds.[61] Heathcote owed his success as much to these reports as he did to the prominence of a relative in London. The careers of these men illustrate the difficulties imposed on the English administrators, attempting to govern a continent many miles and days distant from their shores. Firsthand information was at a premium, and it was always a temptation to rely on self-proclaimed experts.

As to the naval officers, for the most part at this period they still owed their appointments to the governors. Some like Armstrong came to the colonies as part of the governor's entourage. Often they were local men, recipients for various reasons of the governor's patronage favors and in that manner tied to the royal administration. As the period advanced, more and more of these offices came to be filled from England and by Englishmen, as the home authorities removed this patronage plum from the gift of the governor.

By 1710, at the opening of the long central period in the development of the colonial customs service, out of confused beginnings a general uniformity had been imposed on the system. Although a modern observer might have serious reservations as to the personnel employed, in terms of average eighteenth century administrative standards the colonial organization possessed a remarkable number of experienced officers. While the failure to establish the Admiralty jurisdiction on an effective basis and to turn the attorney general into a royal officer undermined part of the program before it was completely implemented, still the system generally had been tightened and the customs organization existing in the mother country duplicated as nearly as possible in the colonies. And, after all, it worked well enough at home. Thinking in these terms an English administrator in 1710 might have entertained a certain degree of optimism; yet, as any royal official in the colonies could observe, the problems to be solved remained numerous and the long, crucial decades lay ahead.

V

Reports from the Field

WHILE the home authorities in their distant wisdom might rest content with the arrangements made for the colonial service, their agents in the field were driven quickly to more realistic appraisals of the situation. Their task was made difficult by a combination of many factors. Colonial opposition to enforcement of the Acts of Trade appeared in a variety of forms, ranging from legalistic quibbling to open violence. Separated from the motherland by many miles, the royal officers in the colonies frequently were left to their own devices, forced to make decisions and act without previous advice from home. And too often they found themselves facing the most determined resistance alone and unaided, without the means to summon or command effective support. Communication with England was a painfully slow process, one which taxed the resources and patience of all concerned, while as a capstone to their difficulties there was the geography of the New World itself, a continent of immense size, of innumerable rivers, harbors, and inlets, with infinite local variations. Such conditions imposed an almost intolerable burden on the pitifully small group of officers serving in the plantations and made the truly effective performance of their duties an unattainable goal.

In its different way each of the experiences of the various customs officials during the years following the completion of the system in 1710 served to bring these problems into focus; from the first-hand knowledge thus accumulated, a body of proposals and suggestions for further reform grew up which clearly depicted the realities of the situation while indicating the requirements for future improvements. With the harsh facts thus called to their attention, responsibility for further action then lay once more in the hands of the administrators at home.

Reports from the Field

In 1715 Maurice Birchfield, who for many years had been surveyor general for the northern district, was reassigned to the southern department.[1] Very quickly he discovered that in one of his provinces, Maryland, carelessness and neglect in the customs houses had permitted a good deal of unfinished business to accumulate. Under the Acts of Trade great reliance was placed on the various bonding provisions, the thought being that any captain or owner would hesitate to engage in illicit activities if he knew that detection would mean the forfeiture of his bond and the loss of a goodly sum of money. However, in Maryland the system had obviously been far from effective. Bonds put in suit twenty years before Birchfield's arrival were still outstanding, including several adjudged forfeited in 1695 for tobacco shipped to foreign parts. Birchfield found that these bonds, after having been declared forfeited to the crown, had been recalled on a writ of error and the previous judgment eventually reversed. Seeking to establish the grounds for such actions, Birchfield investigated the story only to find that the bonds had been "Burnt & Destroyed" while the writ of error was in process, making any further effort to stay the reversal of the original judgment of no use.[2]

Undiscouraged by this initial reverse, Birchfield continued his investigations. In 1688 one Philip Lynes had given bond for £1,000 to ship certain enumerated goods directly to England. Evidence was produced that the items had been shipped elsewhere, and, in 1696, a judgment for the crown was given, the bond being declared forfeited. Again the decision was contested and eventually in 1714 a reversal obtained. Once more, as in the previous case, the bond itself had been destroyed in an opportune fire in Annapolis during the judicial hearings. Questioning the manner in which the case had been handled, Birchfield uncovered serious irregularities. In prosecutions of this sort the crown's case depended on the attorney general of the province. Lynes, it appeared, "in order to stop his Mouth" had devised part of his estate to William Bladen, the attorney general; further, on the death of Lynes, Bladen proceeded to purchase the rest of his estate from the other devisees for one-third of its real value. With the prosecuting attorney, at first partially and then completely, interested in the finances of the defendant, the outcome was a foregone conclusion. Bladen, by the way, was also an officer in the customs service, surveyor at Annapolis, a position that he understandably lost in 1718 when these disclosures were made public.[3]

Birchfield's greatest difficulties arose from yet another case involving certain bonds. On this occasion the bonds had been taken to ensure payment of duties and forfeited to the crown. Several gentlemen were responsible for payment on the bond, but instead of offering a cash settlement they signed over to the king certain debts owed to them by others. The receiver general of the province held these obligations in trust for the crown. When Birchfield determined to collect these debts and put "bills in action" against the names he was given, he encountered a major problem: he discovered that he had no way of knowing how much each individual was responsible for, nor could he find any proof whatsoever that the indicated parties actually owed the original offenders anything at all!

In line with the usual colonial practice of obstruction, during Birchfield's investigations the Assembly of Maryland passed an act declaring that no legal actions pending in county courts should continue longer than twelve months, in a provincial or high court of appeals for more than nineteen, or in court of chancery more than twenty-five. As if this act were not pointed openly enough at Birchfield, in the same session the Assembly passed another piece of legislation disabling Thomas Macnamara, who was acting as counsel for the king, from performing his duties. Macnamara "in order to procure some relief against the said Act Came into England, the Act was repealed and he soon after dyed." In general, Birchfield met with so many difficulties and obstacles in his prosecution of these suits "both from the partys and the Gentlemen of the Country, that many of them could not be brought to a Conclusion or a hearing." He failed to finish all the cases within the time permitted by the act, "and by Colour thereof some of the Suits have been dismissed with Costs, the Judges there Imagining, that the King and his Interest (tho' not mentioned) is bound by these Acts." As a final harassment the deputy secretary of the province later brought suit against the surveyor general himself for fees he claimed were due to him for filing bills, returning writs, and so forth, during the above prosecutions. So on one Sunday Birchfield found himself arrested as "his Majesty's Debtor" and ordered to pay the fees. It was of little comfort to him that eventually one legal authority in London, on hearing that the Lord Proprietor was exempted from such fees, tentatively expressed the thought that "the

86

Crown ought to have equall Privilege and Exemption with the Lord Proprietary." [4]

In attempting to straighten out past administrative irregularities and ensure future compliance with the Acts of Trade, Birchfield encountered one of the basic truths of the customs officers' situation: obstruction, not cooperation, was usually to be expected from the local colonial authorities, while in particular the provincial courts and legal apparatus would be employed to the full to delay and frustrate the enforcement of undesirable regulations. There were, of course, the Admiralty courts, and the question naturally arose as to whether those courts could be used for such prosecutions against forfeited bonds, thus avoiding the interference of the local judges, juries, and officials. However, Attorney General Sir Edward Northey in England put an end to such hopes when he declared that suits involving plantation bonds could not be heard in an Admiralty court until and unless it should be expressly so authorized by Act of Parliament. [5]

Another official having his difficulties with the local courts was Nathaniel Kay, collector in Rhode Island. Kay, happening upon five hogsheads of claret which had been smuggled ashore and concealed in a "Backhouse," left the wine in the custody of the sheriff and a guard while he searched for a cart to move the barrels. Before he returned the owner came along with a number of people "in a Riotous manner" and destroyed the hogsheads, as "being armed with axes [they] threatened to kill the Officers in case they resisted." The collector knew better than to attempt to obtain redress in the provincial courts, which he had good reason to know were used by the "Trading people of the Island" in arresting the customs staff "for taking their just fees and put them under very great difficultys and take them in Execution [of their duties] by the Laws made there which never had the King's sanction." But, the collector wondered, what about the possibility of removing such cases to England to be tried in Westminster Hall? The answer this time was yes, the trials could be heard in Westminster, as permitted in section seven of the Act of 1696. [6] Unfortunately at the same time that this possibility was pronounced legally acceptable it was recognized as unworkable in practice, because of the difficulty of transmitting not only evidence but the defendants themselves over the ocean. [7]

Like Birchfield, Nathaniel Kay learned to mistrust the colonial courts, but his hope of solving the problem by wholesale transference of such cases to England was mere wishful thinking. Although in cases involving fines and forfeitures it was entirely possible to use an Admiralty court for the hearing, it is noteworthy that Kay saw no particular advantage there. By this time it had become clear to him and his fellow officers that as an effective instrument of imperial control the Admiralty courts had been skillfully nullified by their colonial adversaries. The means was a prohibition issued by a common law court, which had the effect of stopping the process of any given case being heard by an Admiralty court.

The Lord Commissioners of the Admiralty, in whose province such matters lay, were not unaware of the situation. In February, 1718/19, they wrote to the Privy Council to request a change in the instructions to the governors, mentioning that James Smith, advocate for the court of Admiralty in New England, "represented to us, that the provinciall Judges make frequent and intollerable encroachmts not only on H.M. authority, but on the jurisdiction of the Admiralty in those parts, insomuch as to sett at liberty persons imprisoned by decree of the Admiralty Court for debts and penaltys due to H.M., and to sett aside by pretended prohibitions, all appeals to the High Court of Admiralty, and to issue out writts, for large sums of money against masters of ships and others who sue in the Vice-Admiralty Courts." The Commissioners added that they had "received complaints of the like nature from . . . Courts of Admlty. of other H.M. Plantations insomuch that it appears there is little or no regard had to the authority and jurisdiction of the Admiralty abroad." [8] Earlier the advocate general Smith referred to had himself suffered arrest and a heavy fine of £400 as a result of a prosecution brought against him by two merchants who were unhappy about the actions of the Admiralty court.[9] The judge of the Admiralty court in New England seconded the statements of Smith, adding that the colony had passed "an Act, which not only forbids under a severe penalty, the officers of the Court of Admiralty to take or demand any fees, but such as they [the colonial Assembly] thought fit to establish, and wherein are omitted, not only more than the third part of the articles which occurr in that Court, for which dues have ever been paid . . . but likewise differs from an Act of Parliament." [10] Smith summed up the situation generally by referring to the "intollerable oppressions we lie under occasioned by an utter aversion the great part of the people in these parts entertain against all powers not derived from themselves." The example of Massachusetts, he said, had spread to other provinces, "some of which have no Charters but hold precariously of the Crown," and they too have thrown off "their submission to Admiralty jurisdiction, so that at present it is almost quite suppressed." [11]

The Admiralty Lords felt that it was necessary for the king to "command the severall Govrs. . . . that they do not only forbear giving interruptions to the proceedings of the Courts of Admlty . . . and restrain the provinciall judges from doing the same, but that they give all possible countenance, and assistance to ye judges and other officers." [12] It is a commentary on the situation in England that all these complaints and reports were of no effect. The Privy Council referred the request from the Admiralty to a legal expert, who advised that a new Act of Parliament be passed to clarify the status of Admiralty jurisdiction, but the whole matter thereafter was put aside and forgotten for forty more years.[13]

Kay and Birchfield had discovered, to their sorrow, that the legal machinery in the colonies could be employed most successfully to deter them from their assigned tasks, but that hazard was not the only one they faced. There was also the use of open force. The destruction of the wine casks seized by the Rhode Island collector was a minor outbreak compared to slightly later events in Boston. In December, 1723, the brigantine *William and Mary,* W. Whipple, master, sailed into Boston from Lisbon with a cargo of salt. Not only did it appear that Whipple had stopped above Boston at Piscataqua and clandestinely landed some wine and oil, but the comptroller at Boston, obtaining a search warrant from the lieutenant governor, also found that Whipple had run eighteen skins of Spanish leather and twelve jars of Spanish oil ashore in Massachusetts itself. William Lambert, the comptroller, exhibited a libel in the court of Admiralty against the vessel and goods, and summoned the entire crew to testify, only two of whom appeared, but both gave evidence for the crown. During their testimony, in full court session, the abuse against the two witnesses became so violent that Lambert had to appeal to the court for their protection. The court was adjourned to another day, but when the new session opened once again the witnesses were outrageously treated. When the hearing ended and the judge departed, "some merchants and masters of ships with a great number of other persons in a violent and mobbish manner assaulted the said evidences, kicked and pushed them downstairs and beat one of them so unmercifully dragging him thro' the streets that it is not yet known what may be the consequence." The intervention of the sheriff saved that unfortunate informer, but the threats turned on the customs officers, who were greatly abused and threatened with the same treatment. In forwarding this account of events to the Treasury, the Commissioners of the Customs added that "the Officers of the Customs in New England having at other times been insulted and abused in the execution of their duty, we humbly pray . . . that our Officers and their assistants may be protected in the execution of their duty." [14]

The Treasury Board decided that in this case the governor should "advise the proper method" of action, and the matter was referred to Governor Samuel Shute.[15] Shute's answer was to request "three independent Companys" of troops for his provinces, two for Massachusetts and one for New Hampshire. Shute would have stationed the troops at Fort William in the harbor and in the town of Boston itself. All this he said would appear necessary "from the many Riots and Disorders that have been Committed in the Town" and also from the complaints forwarded from the officers of the Admiralty court as well as the customs personnel.[16] Once again, as in the Admiralty reports, Shute's advice was farmed out for expert opinion and no action taken by the Treasury.[17] Shute's successor felt much the same five years later, as he wrote that "I have seen so much of the Temper of the people of this province, that I humbly conceive that some of His Majestys forces upon the British Establishment, will be necessary to keep them within the bounds of their duty," and he requested that two hundred troops be sent to Massachusetts, similar to the independent companies posted at New York.[18]

In his report on events in Rhode Island, Nathaniel Kay had stated that "the Governour gave his utmost Assistance," [19] but the customs officials were not always so fortunate. In New York Governor Hunter complained that the surveyor general had removed Thomas Farmer, the collector at Perth Amboy in the Jerseys, for nonresidence, although he had a deputy in the port and lived right across from it himself. Hunter claimed that the replacement was as much an absentee himself, and a mere tavern keeper at that.[20] This and the other charges levied against

Birchfield by the governor stemmed from the rivalry between New York and New Jersey, but the governor was successful in driving Birchfield from the scene.[21] Caleb Heathcote, who succeeded to Birchfield's former post by 1715, encountered much the same opposition from Governor Hunter, who asserted that the surveyor general refused to install Francis Harrison as surveyor and searcher in New York, although Harrison had been commissioned by the Customs Commissioners themselves. Once again the governor won his point and his candidate was awarded the post.[22]

In general the customs officials in the colonies were in a peculiar situation, being somewhat of a state-within-a-state — connected with, but basically independent of, the various other royal officials. Consequently it is not surprising that contests of strength between them and the governors should consist of something more than just a struggle over patronage control, important as that issue might be. In Philadelphia the collector and the governor came to a parting of the ways over the seizure of a vessel.

In October, 1724, there arrived at Philadelphia the ship *Fame,* William Lea, master, bringing in various Palatine families who planned to settle in the colony. Investigation showed, however, that under cover of this legitimate enterprise the *Fame* had brought from Holland a large quantity of East Indies goods and various European manufactured items, of a total estimated value of £20,000.[23] A partial listing of the cargo included one thousand gallons of arrack, two hundred weight of tea, French and German brandies, wines (burgundy, claret, and "campaigne"), seventy barrels of gunpowder, cheese, sail cloth, cordage, and iron.[24] It was even discovered later that the owner of the vessel was a merchant in Rotterdam. John Moore, the collector, seized the ship in the king's name and placed four waiters aboard to guard the prize. During the night, however, some sixty or seventy people in disguise "in a tumultuous & violent Manner" cut the *Fame* loose from its moorings and carried it down river.[25] According to customs house reports, all but two of the waiters "being terrified by the menaces of these rioters . . . leapt over board," the remaining guards being forced along with the ship. Once below the city, the greater part of the prohibited goods were put ashore, while the two waiters were kept "so closely confined, that they could give no account to what places these goods were carried." [26]

Moore notified Lieutenant Governor William Keith of the rescue of the *Fame* on the 31st of October. Not until the first of November did Keith take any action, going then from Newcastle, where he was, over to the *Fame*. There, he reported, he was politely received by the merchant on board, who informed him that the collector had made a mistake and that all the goods were covered by cocquets. Keith went back to Philadelphia, and on the 3rd of November called the collector to his house, berating him for not following the ship down river, while adding that, if the proof of illicit activities that Moore had to offer satisfied his doubts, then he himself would go down to the ship and bring it back to the harbor. On the fifth the governor did just that, not neglecting to seize the *Fame* in his own name on a doubt, as he put it, that the collector could prove his prior seizure. To Moore he made the offer that, if the collector would drop his "pretended" seizure and depend on his, he would see to it that Moore would receive as much from it as if it had been his own. Moore, he reported, declined this gracious offer; and so Keith proceeded on his own, taking the case to the regular provincial courts rather than to an Admiralty court, because as he asserted, the governors of Pennsylvania had no right to set up Admiralty judges such as other governors possessed.[27]

Keith wrote home that the collector had "not only been remiss and negligent in his duty . . . but he has from the very beginning of the affair, acted a most deceitful and collusive part." Moore, he claimed, intended to have the *Fame* escape legal condemnation in order to cast the blame on him and "maliciously to asperse my character."[28] The lieutenant governor won the first round in this struggle, as the vessel "and some small part of the goods" were prosecuted on his seizure in the county court of Philadelphia, where on the master's confession of guilt they were condemned and sold at auction for the paltry amount of £600 sterling.[29] Moore, of course, appealed to the home authorities, and was thoroughly supported by the Commissioners of Customs in a report forwarded to the Treasury; but the latter felt that as both "partys are beyond Sea" time was needed to gather all sides of the story, which should then be presented to the Privy Council.[30] Eventually it was decided that the collector could take his case to the proper court in Pennsylvania with the aid of the attorney and solicitor general there, a recommendation that did little to help the collector. Moore meanwhile had commenced a legal action against one of the principal offenders in the case. When it seemed that the Supreme Court was inclined in Moore's favor, the Assembly stepped in and passed an act removing original jurisdiction in any suits for breach of a penal statute from that court, effectively putting a stop to Moore's action.[31] The collector at least had the satisfaction of seeing his rival, the lieutenant governor, removed from office shortly after these events and his replacement by a gentleman who found Keith (who stayed on in the colony for a time) a most distasteful person.[32] Not the least remarkable aspect to this whole story of the seizure of the ship *Fame* was the activity displayed by the collector: John Moore in 1724 was roughly eighty-five years of age.[33]

William Keith, taking advantage of the collector's dependence on the governor's support, employed tactics of delay and procrastination to frustrate the work of the customs house and to earn himself an undoubtedly large personal gain from the irregular proceedings. Opposition from the governor could take a more active form. The customs officials in South Carolina in 1715 reported a variety of complaints. Whenever they would seize a vessel for breach of the Acts of Trade, Governor Charles Craven, on a pretext that it was required for the public service, would commandeer the ship and send it out of the province on a trumped-up mission. Or, if they seized goods for illegal entry, Craven would step in and claim the items as his own, threatening to shoot if they dared to touch his property. Worse yet, the governor ordered all masters of vessels to refuse to let themselves be boarded by the customs house yacht that cruised in the harbor, claiming it had no power to visit incoming ships. He went so far as to have the fort in Charleston fire on the yacht, and on an English man-of-war as well. In one trial of twenty tons of clandestinely imported logwood, the governor appeared for the defendants and passed the time in court jesting about the Acts of Trade. He overruled an appointment made by the surveyor general; and, finally, he was himself concerned in trade, both as an owner of vessels and as an interested party in their cargoes, for which reason he freely encouraged violations of the regulations.[34]

Not only certain governors but the colonial assemblies, as well, served as centers of resistance to the work of the customs service. Birchfield's investigations into the matter of the bonds in Maryland had been complicated by the act passed setting a time limit on legal cases.[35] John Moore had seen his prosecution against a principal violator of the Acts of Trade stopped by an ex post facto alteration in the jurisdiction of the Supreme Court in Pennsylvania.[36] Another example occurred in Virginia when the surveyor general attempted to make changes in the personnel there. Following his instructions to investigate the activities of the various collectors, removing such as did not produce an adequate defense against any charges presented to them in writing, the surveyor general had dismissed George Luke, collector at the Lower James River, in 1714. In his place he appointed Francis Kennedy, whereupon the new collector immediately was taken to court and disabled from filling the position under a Virginia act which said that no one could hold office, civil or military, in that colony unless they had resided there three years or more. It was true that this act included the provision that "such persons as have Commissions from her Majesty her heirs & Successors be excepted"; but as Kennedy, until confirmation of his appointment was received from England, served only on the surveyor general's warrant, the act was interpreted to apply to him. The affair was only settled by an appeal to London and the eventual determination there that the law was repugnant to various Acts of Parliament and so void.[37]

Perhaps the most effective and universally employed restraint imposed by the colonial assemblies on the efficiency of the customs staff was in the matter of fees. Nathaniel Kay in his report on events in Rhode Island touched on this question, when he wrote that the "Trading people . . . do frequently arrest the Officers for taking their just fees." [38] And Judge John Menzies of the Admiralty court in New England had also observed how the fees in the court had been cut by more than a third by the colonial authorities.[39] Such interference by the colonial legislatures was made possible by the vague nature of the policy on fees, as illustrated by the situation in New York. In 1709 the Assembly of that province passed an act settling fees allowed to the various officers, including those in the royal customs service. After study in England, it was ruled that the fees so established were too low and the act was disallowed. Instructions were forwarded to the governor of New York to work out a list with the advice of his Council. The result pleased neither the governor nor the customs officials, as the Council set the fees so low that the governor only granted his consent because the officers otherwise would have been left with no legal fees at all.[40] Similarly one year earlier the Assembly of Rhode Island had passed an act establishing a table of fees at a uniformly low level, with the proviso that collectors and naval officers found guilty of taking higher fees were to be fined; a warrant issued by any of the local justices of the peace would suffice to bring the offender into court.[41] Such an arrangement provided a convenient method for harassment of overzealous officers, and Kay's complaints made seven years later show the act was used exactly for such purposes.

The problem was hardly a new one, even in 1710. As far back as 1679 the Lord Treasurer had wondered about fees in the colonies, "they being uncertaine and different in severall Plantations," and he determined to ascertain "what power the King may have to impose Such fees, considering they will fall most on English Shipping."[42] Nothing came of that enquiry, and the problem remained to plague Lord Bellomont in 1699. Although the naval office was a great trust and required a good man, Bellomont observed, the Massachusetts Assembly had reduced the fees so low he could not find any one to take the post. Bellomont added that the "Assembly retrenched the fees on purpose, for they hate in this Countrey to have their Trade inspected, and will always put wt discouragement they can upon officers who are intrusted with that inspection."[43] In spite of these difficulties, the Commissioners of the Customs in 1716 still optimistically thought they could depend on the legislatures, writing that "if fees were settled for the Officers of the Customs in his Mats several plantations by the respective Assemblys it would be of Public advantage."[44]

Enforcement of the Acts of Trade in a country where "they hate . . . to have their Trade inspected" was hardly an easy assignment. And along with open opposition from the inhabitants the vast area they were expected to patrol complicated the work of the customs officers. Five miles down the river from Philadelphia had proved a safe haven for the ship *Fame* and her illicit activities, as the helpless officers in the city and across in the Lower Counties sought the means to reach her.[45] Without interference the captain of the *William and Mary* had stopped in New Hampshire on the way to Boston, and outside of the sight of the customs officials unloaded part of his cargo.[46] The surveyor and searcher in Charleston, South Carolina, in 1718 complained that the sloop *Charles* had cleared the port without a full cargo and then had proceeded down to "Rebellion Road" to take on a load of undeclared items. In this instance the customs staff was able to give pursuit in their yacht, but far from the harbor and on their own, they proved no match for the armed illicit trader, which forced them to retire from the scene.[47] In Rhode Island the officers found their work made hazardous by the practice employed there by the captains of vessels they attempted to seize; once the customs officials were on board the master would hoist anchor and put out to sea, or threaten to do so, until he obtained a promise that his ship would be left alone.[48] All these difficulties were summed up by Charles Blechyden, collector and surveyor at Salem and Marblehead, who spoke with a frankness permitted by his twenty years of service in the English customs. In reporting on the use made of fishing vessels in his district to smuggle in foreign products, Blechyden wrote that "wee have above 400 vessels belonging to the Fishery and if we had 500 officers it would not prevent this trade; by reason of the largement of the country and the many harbours and creeks belonging to the same." [49]

Amid all these tribulations and reports of colonial violence the customs officials themselves, of course, were not always the injured parties. The surveyor general northern in 1710 was accused of using his official position for personal profit when a foreign ship, loaded with cocoa, was brought into New York as a prize of war. The collector agreed to permit the cargo to be unloaded and stored, after condemnation, while awaiting the payment of the prize duties. Thinking they had to pay the entire duty at once, the captors of the ship agreed to sell six thousand pounds of the cocoa to Mr. Stephen De Lancey. When the surveyor general heard of this, he reportedly tried to include himself in the transaction, promising De Lancey that, if a share of the cocoa was turned over to him, he would see to it that the whole cargo was acquired for a much lower price. De Lancey refused the offer, but the surveyor general still forced the owners of the rest of the cocoa to let him buy some himself. Not content with this, he supposedly later had the owners arrested on damages of £3,000 for refusal to deliver the cocoa where and in the manner he had specified.[50]

John Jekyll, collector in Boston, for all his fine English connections, seemingly was not himself above taking a bribe to allow an unauthorized party to trade in his port. In 1718 a French vessel from Cape François arrived in Boston and was permitted by the collector to unload its cargo of molasses and store it in a warehouse. Later he allowed the captain to sell the molasses for £900. The captain then purchased a new sloop and sailed away to Cape Breton; shortly thereafter his sloop was seized at Canso, and the ship's papers exposed to examination. It appeared from the French captain's records "that the great civilities which had been done him, flow'd from another principle than that of humanity," as beside gifts of wine there were listed presents of £20 to Jekyll and £15 to each of his two waiters.[51]

The venerable John Moore in Philadelphia also was rumored to be involved in illicit activities; it was reported that vessels trading to Barbados from his port entered part of their tobacco cargo as biscuits, thus avoiding the duty otherwise collectable and costing the crown the revenue on seven hundred hogsheads a year. An anonymous letter said that "Some are of the opinion the Collector is concerned with them, seeing they are his nearest friends that practise itt, others ascribe his inactivity and connivance to his great age and riches."[52] Daniel McCarty, collector of South Potomac, Virginia, was accused not only of breaking his instructions by engaging in trade for himself and acting as factor for others but also of using his official position to harass his competitors;[53] while the familiar charge of acting in association with pirates was made against two officials in North Carolina in 1720 by the captain of an English man-of-war.[54]

In all these instances, however, it is well to keep in mind Lord Bellomont's insight when he investigated the conduct of a customs officer who, he found, was "much hated by the Marchants here, but 'tis (for ought I can find) for being carefull and Exact in the Execution of his office." Bellomont added that "a Collectors is the most ungratefull Office in these plantations that can be, if he is Just to his trust in looking into their Trade they hate him mortally."[55] Rumors as to their misconduct were not necessarily to be trusted and, if Lord Bellomont was right, then possibly the louder the complaints the greater the proof of the officer's value. At the same time, given the low state of eighteenth century official morality, malfeasance was probably as widespread in the customs service as elsewhere. In any event, as the various incidents just recounted suggest, had the officials been one and all the most upright of men, still their assignment was so difficult as to border on the impossible. Few men could, or would, struggle alone and unaided against the odds a customs officer faced in colonial America.

From the colonies to the home authorities there flowed an ever increasing number of reports on these events, in all of which the basic weaknesses of the system were illuminated, and in many of which interpretive reviews of the situation were coupled with suggestions for improvement or reform. The story they told was one of confused and contradictory policies, inadequate preparations, and dangerous precedents.

One of the most persistent of correspondents on the need for reform was Caleb Heathcote of New York, a man who was variously a colonel of the militia, mayor of the city, and, after 1715, surveyor general of the customs for the northern district. Heathcote had good connections in London in his brother, Sir Gilbert Heathcote, who had remained behind in England where he "came to rule a host of men in many places as a prince of commerce, forced the reordering of the great East India Company, became an organizer and the governor of the Bank of England . . . Lord Mayor of London, and at last as a baronet died the richest commoner in England, worth close to three-quarters of a million pounds." [56] This contact was particularly helpful after the death of Queen Anne with the attendant restoration of the Whigs to control in England. But by that period Caleb Heathcote had already made a name for himself in official circles as an informed and zealous partisan of the English programs for the colonies. His first projects centered on the unfulfilled potentialities of the plantations as a source of naval supplies, as between 1705 and 1715 he constantly wrote home on the subject.[57] Nothing concrete developed from these efforts, except perhaps that the Board of Trade was impressed and became "willing to reward the author of a programme with honors and with responsibilities," supporting Heathcote's appointment to the customs service.[58]

With his appointment as surveyor general, Heathcote's thoughts turned elsewhere, alighting first on the difficulties presented by the various proprietary and charter governments.[59] A large share of the troubles recounted above occurred in these areas: John Moore in Pennsylvania, Nathaniel Kay in Rhode Island, and the entire customs staff in South

Carolina. In particular the governors of those plantations displayed an annoying degree of independence and greatly complicated the work of the other royal administrators. Recognition of the problem was not new; as far back as the year 1701 Robert Livingston had recommended that "one form of government be establish'd in all the neighboring Colonies on this main Continent," suggesting that the Carolinas, Virginia, and Maryland form one government, New York, the Jerseys, Pennsylvania, and part of Connecticut another, with the rest of Connecticut, plus Rhode Island and New Hampshire being added to Massachusetts.[60] And earlier yet, the Dominion of New England had attempted a similar arrangement for the northern colonies, only to fall apart on the rocks of the Glorious Revolution.

In January, 1716, the new surveyor general wrote to the Treasury that he had heard some time ago that Parliament intended shortly to pass an act "to break" the proprietary or charter governments; this he thought was an excellent idea, as until such was done it would be nearly impossible to regulate the colonial trade. With these offending governments removed, and a better division worked out, it would then be possible to settle a revenue "by a customs and excise on the whole continent, upon an English footing," which could be used to defray all the expenses of the several governments and pay for ships of war to guard the ports as well. Nothing, he added, "can be more reasonable than that all the plantations and dominions abroad should . . . be made to bear the expense they occasion and not remain a dead weight on the nation that severely groans under the debts of which they have been, in a great measure, the cause." If the assemblies refused to provide such a reasonable revenue, he supposed Parliament might with justice "do it for them," as there was no reason the subjects on this side of the ocean should have more privileges than those at home, where a revenue on trade was "a burthen the people of Great Britain have always with great chearfullnesse layd on themselves, and is what they never expect to be exempt from." [61]

From these suggestions it is clear just what the surveyor general thought was wrong with the system. Certain privileged governments were recalcitrant and obstructive; the authorities in the colonies were too dependent on the local inhabitants financially; and the geographical problem was such as to necessitate large scale employment of ships of the royal navy. It was not a pretty picture; in fact, as Heathcote wrote on another occasion, he had difficulty expressing his thoughts in a reasonably brief space, "there being abundance of mistakes, in the management of affairs, Relating to the Revenue, & other ways, which want much to be Regulated, whereby his Majestys Intrest is Greatly Hurt, the Treasury needlessly drained & Exhausted, & many of the services for which vast summes are given, neglected & unperformed, & Things are wrong on so many Accounts." [62] He found collection of the revenue difficult, if not impossible, and on the basis of a questionnaire to all the officers under his supervision he concluded the situation was the same everywhere.[63]

Nor did the activities of the colonial legislatures escape his notice; remarking on their habit of passing acts intended to frustrate the work of the royal officials, Heathcote reported that the English policy of employing threats but no action was dangerous. The charter governments, for example, had frequently been threatened with the loss of their privileges but nothing further being done, they were inspired to greater abuses and confirmed "in that absurd notion of their laws being sufficient in themselves." While "they have a power (as they imagine) of making laws separate from the crown, they'll never be wanting to lessen the authority of the King's officers, who by hindering them from a full freedom of illegal trade, are accounted ennemies to the growth and prosperity of their little commonwealths." [64]

Nathaniel Kay had written home that customs officers were constantly harassed by charges of excessive fee-taking; as his superior, Heathcote knew about his troubles. Kay, he reported, not only had been arrested on such a complaint but, after he had been cleared in a hearing before the governor, his opponents had perversely used the very same disproven fact to re-arrest him and take him "into custody in the custom house, while in his duty, and thence hurried him away, amidst a crowd of spectators, refusing to admit him to bail." [65] Previously the surveyor general had himself experienced difficulties in his efforts to get suitable fees settled on the surveyor and searcher in Boston, when the Assembly not only would not act but "were not so mannerly as to give him any Answer." [66] For this reason he suggested to the home authorities that all fees "be settled on an equal foot" throughout the continent.[67] His recommendations on this point were seconded by Archibald Cummings, the surveyor and searcher at Boston, who wrote that the fees in the plantations should "be Stipulated under one Regulation to prevent Exorbitant fees . . . and that the fees stipulated in the book of Rates by Act of parliament for the port of London and other ports of England might be a Standing rule for them excepting the difference of Exchange and money in each Plantation." [68] Cummings' proposal would have provided the customs officers with a legal regulation to which they could appeal; and, as Cummings was probably aware, although he mentioned the prevention of "Exorbitant" fees, those in use in England were generally higher than those in the colonies, so the customs staff had nothing to lose by such a change.

Archibald Cummings, like Heathcote, was in continual correspondence with the English authorities. Originally he had gone to Newfoundland as an agent of the Admiralty, and being on the spot had been employed by the Customs Commissioners to act for them there, until in 1715 such activities were felt to be useless and he was transferred to Boston.[69] Between 1716 and 1725 he addressed many reports to the Board of Trade and other departments, climaxing his endeavors with one of the most remarkable of all these early proposals.

Cummings' first efforts in 1716 and 1717 were primarily accounts of the size and nature of the trade in Boston; he estimated that for the year ending April, 1717, one hundred and sixty ships, totaling eight thousand tons, had been constructed in that port, while he also kept a watchful eye on the imports of sugar and molasses from the foreign islands.[70] The size of the latter trade led him to his first recommendation, that this foreign produce, on which there was at the moment "no duty more paid here than if our product" should be taxed more heavily so as to bring it up to equality with the output of the British islands which paid an impost on exportation from its place of origin.[71] His difficulties in preparing these reports, coupled with his awareness that other ports did not necessarily provide similar accounts, prompted him to suggest that if "an Inspector General of all the accounts of the import and export of the Continent was appointed it would be a means annualy to give your Lordships a true state of the trade." [72] By 1720 Cummings was ready with more detailed recommendations, which still, however, related mostly to his special interest in the form and extent of trade; it would help, he thought, if the weight of sugar, rice, tobacco, and other products were ascertained according to the English standards, if other measurements, such as the gauge of casks, were standardized, and certain minor duties taken off to encourage trade. He suggested that fees be regulated everywhere, and finally that, as provided in the Act of 1696, all merchants loading or unloading any goods be obliged to take out permits at the customs house to prevent frauds and permit the regular calculation of the value of imports and exports. This latter remark he coupled with the pleas that "all the rules prescribed in that act be Strictly Executed," which request, coming from an official in one of the major ports in America, was commentary enough on the practice there.[73]

His researches on these matters completed, Archibald Cummings was ready for a more ambitious undertaking. In 1722 he wrote home that with the proper urging he could propose a scheme "to raise a fund in the plantations, which would not be burthensome." [74] The response was favorable, and in November, 1722, Cummings forwarded to England an eleven point program of startlingly comprehensive proportions. The title he provided indicated the general purpose of his proposals: a "Scheme for maintaining five or Six thousand regular troops upon the Continent of America" and the "raising of a fund, for ye better support of Governours, and Officers of ye Crown, in the Plantations." [75]

Cummings' plan consisted of eleven separate points, all but two of which related to the raising of a revenue in the colonies. He suggested "That the stamp duties be expended [i.e., extended] to the plantations," that new duties be imposed on foreign molasses, sugar, cotton, cocoa, and indigo, that an excise be placed on all rum distilled in the continental colonies, that all rum being imported into the colonies pay a substantial duty, that new imposts be levied on imports of wine, and that a tax should be imposed on unimproved lands privately owned in the various colonies. His other recommendations included the encouragement of the production of hemp in the colonies, the removal of certain drawbacks on foreign goods shipped to the colonies, and the use to be made of the six thousand regular troops to be maintained in America.[76]

Caleb Heathcote had previously indicated that the problems confronting the English administrators were not simply separate items, to be solved singly as they arose; rather he had viewed the situation in terms of three basic factors, so interrelated as to require a unified solution. Proper regulation in his eyes was not possible while privileged proprietary governments remained in existence, nor as long as the royal officials in the colonies were dependent on the inhabitants financially, while the vast areas to be patrolled could not be handled without further employment of the English navy. Cummings' scheme fulfilled in explicit detail the requirement of Heathcote's general proposals, by providing the funds to implement such a program. Most of the provisions were intended to raise a new revenue to be employed in administering and securing the plantations, and for no other purpose. Heathcote had suggested that if the colonies themselves were unwilling to levy the needed imposts, Parliament could "do it for them"; Cummings pointed out just how it should be done. Employing such a fund to free the hands of the royal officials, to provide for the defense of the colonies, to create administrative unity and conformity, and to ensure proper respect for the Acts of Parliament was a move these men, on the basis of their experience, felt to be not only wise but necessary; in no other way could they envisage a solution to the troublesome and dangerous problems existing in the plantations.

Archibald Cummings was not the only man to recommend the extension of the English stamp act to the colonies. In 1726 Sir William Keith, former deputy governor of Pennsylvania and himself once surveyor general of the customs, proposed various reforms, all of which, he concluded, would be of little purpose "unless a Sufficient Revenue can be raised to Support the Needfull Expense. In order to which, it is humbly submitted whether the Duties of Stamps upon parchments & paper in England, may not with good reason be extended by Act of Parliament to all the American Plantations." [77]

One of Keith's other suggestions would have received ardent support from any customs officer or legal adviser charged with interpreting the vague and often contradictory provisions of the various laws then in existence. He advocated that "the Acts of Parliament relating to the Trade and Government of the Colonies, be revised and collected into one distinct body of Laws, for the Use of the Plantations and such as trade with Them." Presumably such matters as the clarification of the jurisdiction of the Admiralty courts, as proposed by the Admiralty lords, would find a place in this revision, which would have the effect both of clarifying the law and facilitating the work of the royal officials.

Keith also endorsed in full an earlier stand taken by the Board of Trade, which in 1721 had proposed that all plantation business be "confined to one office."[78] The former deputy governor wrote that too often someone coming from the colonies with a complaint was at a loss to know to whom he should apply. To his mind the Board of Trade seemed the logical agency to handle plantation affairs, but such an arrangement would require that the first lord of that Board have daily access to the king. If this were done, Sir William felt, all "Rents, Customs and Revenues and other profits in any manner arising from the plantations would then center in one place," facilitating the flow of business and avoiding repetition and confusion. Not only did the delays entailed by the divided and conflicting jurisdictions of the various departments of the English government make it painfully difficult for a royal official in the plantations to obtain advice or approval of his actions, but at the same time the situation played directly into the hands of the colonial opposition, which had found quickly enough that time was its greatest ally. Could they, by procrastination and quibbling over minor points, in any given case hold off a decision long enough, in all likelihood the matter would be forgotten, or at least decided so long after the fact as to be meaningless.

In a sense that was exactly the message the customs officers in their various reports sent home: time was on the side of the colonists. Habit is a powerful factor to reckon with, as any Englishman should have known, not only the Parliamentary system under which the government of England operated but the fundamental common law of the land itself being so much the result of long continued custom. The various reports and accounts made it perfectly clear that all was not well with the royal administration in the plantations, and that the Acts of Parliament themselves were in many cases given only token lip service. To allow such a situation to continue would be to create dangerous precedents for the future, while the longer corrections were in coming the more difficult their enforcement would be. Not all the advice sent home by the agents in the colonies was wise, or even practicable; but still this general warning deserved attention. As Caleb Heathcote reported, the colonists were only too fractious and independent in their actions, freely nullifying the Acts of Parliament, "which, if they are not kept to a strict observance of, and made sensible of their dependence on Great Britain, as they are daily growing very numerous and powerful, so a neglect therein, may with time, be attended with very ill consequences." [79] In making this situation known, the royal agents had fulfilled their obligations; further action, for the moment, was beyond their control. It was up to the English authorities to take steps to avoid these prophesied "ill consequences," and they had received fair warning that failure to act might well decide the issue by default. There were important decisions to be made; and, after years of ineffectual administration, the need plainly was urgent.

VI

The English Scene

IN April, 1725, a major report on the colonial service was forwarded to the Treasury by the Commissioners of the Customs. Their concern in this case was primarily financial. Since the officers in the colonies received their salaries in England and constituted a charge on the annual budget, the Commissioners "thought it our Duty to examine into the Several Allowances paid to the Officers either by the Establishment or by Incidents." First they considered the various preventive officers and riding surveyors who have "greatly increas'd the Charge on the Revenue." Most of these officials had been created at the suggestion of the surveyors general, but the Customs Board reported they had "by Experience been found useless"; consequently they recommended that those posts "be sunk."

At the same time, in direct opposition to reports from the plantations, the Commissioners decided that the various assemblies had provided generous fees for their officers so that they received an adequate income from that source. In Virginia and Maryland, they further noted, the tobacco duties assessed by the Act of 1673 had been granted to William and Mary College, and the collectors were paid an allowance by the College for handling the receipt of these funds, an arrangement which gave those officers an extra income. More generally the Customs Board pointed out to the Treasury that their officials were not the only agents involved in enforcing the Acts of Trade, since the governors and naval officers also were required to see to their observance.

All these items meant one thing to the Commissioners: a major cutback in the colonial establishment was in order. With their letter to the Treasury the Board enclosed a reduction plan that would save the English government one-third of the current expense.[1] According to these proposals a total of twelve officers would be retired, while one new post would be created. The surveyors at Elizabeth River and Cape Charles in Virginia, at Williamstad, Bahama and Sassafras, Wicomocco and Munni, Delaware Bay, the Potomac River, and Annapolis in Maryland were to be dispensed with altogether, but the surveyor at Annapolis was to be replaced by a collector, accounting for the one new post. Newfoundland was to lose its preventive officer, while the comptrollers at Philadelphia and New York, and the landwaiter at the latter port, were to be discontinued. Many of the remaining officers were to have their salaries reduced — the collector in South Carolina, for example, going from £60 to £40 a year and the collector at Boston from £100 to £40. Under the old arrangement the Commissioners reported the salary bill yearly to be £3,930, while the new plan would amount to only £2,660, creating a saving of £1,270.[2]

The implications of this scheme are obvious. At a time when the reports from the colonies were filled with stories of colonial opposition, of inadequate provision for the enforcement of the Acts of Trade, the Commissioners of the Customs undertook to reduce their staff to a bare minimum. Their proposals were not designed to create greater efficiency in the service, as in their own words the prime considerations were financial. Either the Commissioners were unaware of the situation in the plantations, or they chose to ignore it. Both explanations contain an element of truth.

Nothing could better illustrate the confusion existing in London over events in the colonies than the appearance of Newfoundland on the Commissioners' reduction chart, since the preventive officer at Newfoundland much earlier had been removed to Boston, where he was employed as surveyor and searcher.[3] In fact, in 1721 the Customs Board itself had reported to the Board of Trade that there was no use stationing officers at Newfoundland until that area was equipped with a regular civil government.[4] Yet in 1725 the Commissioners listed Newfoundland as one of the places to be "struck off ye Establishment" and the £150 a year salary "not to be paid." At the same time they included the surveyor and searcher at Boston on their list. All this confusion arose simply because the officer removed to Boston in 1715 had continued to receive his salary on the English accounts under his former title as preventive officer at Newfoundland. The Board of Trade in 1725 knew these facts, but the Commissioners of the Customs did not.

Four years earlier the Board of Trade had prepared an exhaustive study of the colonies for presentation to the king. It closed with these words: "We the rather mention this, because ye present method of despatching business relating to the Plantations is lyable to much delay and confusion; in as much as there are at present no less than three different ways of proceeding herein, that is to say, by immediate application to your Majesty, by one of your Secretaries of State; by petition to your Majesty in Council, and by representation to your Majesty from this Board; whence it happens that no one office is thro'ly informed of all matters relating to the Plantations." [5]

Obviously there was a good deal of justice to this complaint by the Board of Trade. In fact, two, and possibly three, other government departments could have been added to their list; along with the Privy Council, the Secretary of State, and the Board of Trade, the Treasury and the Admiralty played a part in colonial administration, while the Customs Board itself also might well be considered a separate department. The result was, as the Board of Trade reported, and the Newfoundland incident illustrated, that "no one office is thro'ly informed of all matters."

The Board of Customs Commissioners was technically a sub-department of the Treasury. Established in 1671 by royal patent, it had been combined in 1723 with the Scottish Customs Board; in 1725 the Commissioners were fourteen in number, seven residing in London, five in Scotland, and two in the English outports.[6] Colonial affairs were the province of the London Commissioners. A study of the correspondence between these Commissioners and the Treasury suggests that within its field of special interest the Customs Board was treated with respect by the Treasury; the latter might initiate action by requesting the Commissioners' advice on a given matter, but the Board's expert knowledge was thoroughly recognized and usually accepted.[7] The Treasury remained the final authority for all actions taken by the Commissioners, in effect operating as a board of review for appeals from their decisions, while it also functioned as the intermediary between the Customs and the other departments. In brief, the position "of the Customs Commissioners in the machinery of state was that of a body of ministers through whom a higher controlling power operated to secure enforcement of trade laws, yet who were themselves responsible for the due execution of such laws." [8]

The composition of the Board of Customs Commissioners was so stable as to make it the eighteenth century counterpart of an organization staffed by permanent civil servants. A complete turnover of personnel never occurred. Death or retirement of a patent-holder was generally the only way openings on the Board arose, and on only four occasions were as many as four of the fourteen Commissioners replaced in one year.[9] Many of the members served for long terms: Sir John Stanley, 1708–1744; Sir John Evelyn, 1721–1763; Edward Hooper, 1748–1793; and Brian Fairfax, 1723–1750.[10] Continuity was considered so important for this office that an unusual arrangement was made to ensure no lapse in the Commissioners' powers and right to office on the death of a sovereign.[11] Long tenure and special consideration in effect showed that in regard to the customs service a "certain subordination of political influence to effective administration" was practiced.[12]

Relative freedom from political pressures was an asset, but it did not necessarily ensure complete efficiency. For implementation of its decisions, the Board was dependent on the Treasury. In the eighteenth century the Treasury was the largest of the departments of the English government, so large in fact that a catalogue of its activities is necessarily incomplete. As distinct from the Exchequer, the Treasury proper exercised general financial control over the operations of the entire government. The Treasury Board, which consisted of the First Lord, the Chancellor of the Exchequer, and three junior lords, carried on a voluminous and continuous correspondence. A partial list of departments and individuals included in their routine business gives some indication of the breadth of the Treasury Board's concerns: the Privy Council, the Secretaries of State, the Customs Board, the Admiralty, the paymaster of the forces, the Excise Office, the Exchequer, the auditor of plantation affairs, the commander in chief in America, the colonial agents, the surveyor of the woods in the colonies.

In spite of its size the Treasury always had more problems to consider than there was time available. The result was that this most central of departments could never devote its entire attention to any one matter. For this reason, perhaps, the Customs Board was permitted greater freedom of action than might otherwise have been the case. But for the identical reason the Customs Commissioners could never rely entirely on the Treasury for guidance. Frequently they were left to their own devices and had to depend on the other departments of the government for what help they could get, particularly in regard to colonial business, which was a minor matter for the harassed Treasury Lords.

The procedure in the case of the seizure of the ship *Fame* at Philadelphia will be recalled.[13] John Moore, the collector, forwarded an account of his tribulations to the Customs Commissioners. They in turn, approving his actions, urged the Treasury to support him fully. The Treasury, however, was too busy to spend much time on the case itself and merely replied that because both "partys are beyond Sea" the decision should be left to the Privy Council. The result was that Moore never did obtain real satisfaction.

Over the years the Privy Council itself had lost much of its importance in colonial affairs. The creation of the Board of Trade in 1696 had restricted the Council's concern with the plantations, but one particular category of colonial business had been expressly reserved to the Council. By royal order all appeals from any of the colonies were to be heard by a committee of the Privy Council. It was the activity of this committee that "principally maintained the position of the privy council as the highest court for colonial appeals." [14] The determinations of the Privy Council were embodied in an Order of the King in Council, which was the highest authority in the Empire, save only an Act of Parliament itself.

Despite its participation in the Philadelphia customs dispute, the Privy Council was in fact remote from active involvement in the normal routine of plantation affairs. Primarily the appeals brought to its attention were of a judicial nature. Rarely, and only at second hand, was it concerned in the creation or execution of general policies. In an age when Parliament and the beginnings of the cabinet system were working major alterations in the English form of government, the Privy Council was a relic of the past and so closely associated with the power of the crown as not to be trusted with complete control of the colonies. So it, like the overworked Treasury, was unable to provide the centralized leadership that was needed.

For a time it had been hoped that the Board of Trade would serve as a coordinating body in colonial administration. Provided with eight permanent members, each with a salary of £1,000 a year, the Board between 1696 and 1715 was quite active in plantation business.[15] One limitation on its effectiveness is frequently overlooked: the Board was not concerned solely with the colonies. Trade in general was their province, and a great deal of their time and labor was devoted to such matters as commercial treaties with Sweden or the drawing up of instructions for envoys and agents abroad. In short, the Board functioned as a catchall for problems relating to trade and was expected to provide expert opinion on many and sundry questions. As a consequence the Board of Trade regularly fell behind in its work and left many requests for aid from the colonies unanswered for long periods.

The need for one central body to handle colonial affairs was widely recognized. Sir William Keith in his "Short Discourse" had suggested that the Board of Trade should fill this function. To this proposal, Keith added that, if such were done, the head of the Board would have to have "daily access to the King." [16] Here Sir William touched upon the major weakness of the Board: legally it was only an advisory body. It had no executive authority of its own and indeed could not even force other departments to heed its advice. After 1715, as the First Lord of the Treasury and the Secretaries of State assumed increased importance under the Hanoverian kings, the Board declined in influence. The consequences were serious. The existence of the Board provided the other departments with a convenient excuse to evade responsibility for the conduct of colonial administration. Increasingly urgent questions involving the plantations were lost in the dead files of the Board, which all too often found itself vainly importuning the other offices to consider its reports. A brief effort was made in 1751 to bring the Board to equality with the other departments, but that proposal collapsed over the very problem of "daily access to the King." [17] So throughout the colonial period the most informed section of the English government on colonial business was the least effective and important.

The main executive responsibility in colonial affairs resided with the Secretary of State for the Southern Department. As early as 1704 this officer had been granted a title indicating that he had "charge of plantation affairs." [18] The great advantage the Secretary possessed over the Board of Trade was the right of approach to the king. Because of this asset the Secretary did indeed become the "intermediary between the king and the other parts of the British government." [19] If any one official had the power to bring unity to the determination of colonial business, the Secretary did. Unfortunately, like the Treasury, the Secretary had much more to consider than the plantations. Anything from diplomatic relations with France to trade agreements with small Mediterranean states were his province. In the eighteenth century officials clung with might and main to all the prerogatives of their offices. Authority, even if not regularly exercised, was not lightly surrendered, a truth Lord Halifax was to discover in 1751 when he attempted to enlarge the powers of the Board of Trade. After 1715 what power the Board of Trade had possessed was taken from it by this increasingly important Secretary, "who often ignored it." [20] Too busy to oversee everything, the Secretary only erratically concerned himself with colonial administration. The Board of Trade could not act without the support of the Secretary, and so a further wedge was driven between the creation and execution of an informed colonial policy.

The last of the agencies mentioned earlier, the Admiralty, was the most unfortunate of all. The section of the Admiralty generally concerned with colonial administration was the High Court. The great Act of 1696 had authorized the establishment of Vice-Admiralty courts in the colonies and had entrusted a share in the enforcement of the Acts of Trade to them. As the high court of appeals for cases originating in these courts, the English Admiralty Court theoretically had an important role to play. In fact, Vice-Admiralty jurisdiction was hotly contested by the colonials, and until the reforms of 1764 the courts in the plantations were forced to concentrate primarily on routine maritime questions, such as seamen's wages or contracts. The Admiralty Board had reported the truth when in 1719 it said that "there is little or no regard had to the authority and jurisdiction of the Admiralty abroad." [21]

Discussion of the Admiralty suggests a fundamental weakness in the organization of the English government. There were a number of special agencies to handle special problems, but no one body to centralize and coordinate activities. Legal questions were divided among the Privy Council, the High Court of Admiralty, and the Exchequer. Matters of trade were shared by the Board of Trade, the Secretary of State, the Treasury, the Privy Council, and the Customs Board. Governmental problems were equally the concern of the Secretary of State, the Board of Trade, and the Privy Council. The result was fragmentation both as to the creation and execution of policy.

In such a situation it was only too possible that information available to one department would not necessarily be known to another. The ignorance of the Customs Board concerning Newfoundland in 1725 was merely one more example of this general confusion. It was a weakness which was to be corrected only partially in the critical decade leading to the outbreak of the American Revolution.

Organizational failings in themselves of course need not be decisive. With the proper leadership nearly any form of government can produce results, and reform is always possible. But for nearly forty years more after 1725 little was done to assert English authority in the colonies or to correct the obvious administrative defects in England itself. England in those years belonged to the Whig party of Sir Robert Walpole and his successors. Their aims did not necessarily involve a tightening of imperial control in the plantations, and so they too must share in the responsibility for these years of inaction.

Prosperity, not glory, was the keynote of Whig thought. The first speech from the throne drawn up under Walpole's direction openly avowed this policy: "In this situation of affairs, we should be extremely wanting to ourselves, if we neglected to improve the favorable opportunity which this general tranquility gives us, of extending our Commerce upon which the riches and grandeur of this nation chiefly depend. It is very obvious that nothing would more conduce to the obtaining so publick a good, than to make the exportation of our own manufactures, and the importation of the commodities used in the manufacturing of them as practicable and easy as may be; by this means, the balance of trade may be preserved in our favor, our navigation increased, and greater numbers of our poor employed." [22]

This policy of the Whig leaders was not due solely to their association with the commercial interests of the nation, although that connection undoubtedly existed and played its part. As much as the Whigs were the party of commercial growth so too they were the party of the Hanoverian succession. The threat of a Stuart restoration was real to these eighteenth century politicians, and their policies were shaped accordingly. Time was needed to establish the German kings securely on the English throne, and stability and prosperity were the best means to achieve that end. They became the basic aims of the Walpole "system."

In the most penetrating analysis yet made of the politics in these middle years, John B. Owen quietly corrects many earlier misapprehensions.[23] Parties may not have existed then, in our modern sense, but there was a validity to the division between Tories and Whigs. The Tories were, in fact, as Owen points out, "by and large the most stable element in the whole House of Commons." [24] Their stability came from their devotion to tradition and their character of "independent country gentlemen." As Sir Lewis Namier has shown, by the end of this period "Tory" had become synonymous with the idea of "independent country gentlemen," and certain distinct attitudes were characteristic of this group: concern for the Church, "persistent opposition to the Court, disregard for pensions or places in the central administration, and a longing for greater influence in the sphere of local government." [25]

One ingredient in "Toryism" has not received the attention it deserves. It is commonly accepted, for example, that William Pitt's success as the great war minister owed much to Tory support. In fact Pitt was very solicitous about these allies throughout his career.[26] If indeed it is true that the "war policy of the elder Pitt, incorporating essential elements of the Tory creed, gave them further cause for satisfaction," then perhaps there is more to be said about "Toryism" than has yet been offered.[27] In the absence of clearly defined distinctions between parties and policies, concrete observations are difficult. It becomes a matter of recreating a "climate of opinion" or an amorphous set of attitudes and generally held conceptions. Yet clearly there was such a thing as a "Tory attitude" present in the eighteenth century, and it obviously had some relation to basic assumptions about the empire and imperial policies. There would undoubtedly be numerous objections raised to any effort to label the Tories as the party of imperialism, but it seems fair to suggest at least that the expectations of the advantages to be gained through the possession of an empire held by the small landholding gentry, the "independent country gentlemen," differed from those held by great magnates and the commercial groups.

The English Scene

Understanding the meaning of "Tory" is perhaps a backward approach to a definition of Whiggism, but the truth is that while it may be difficult to define "Tory," "it is impossible to define 'Whig.'" [28] As the dominant political force of the period the Whigs reflected many of the varied aspects of life in that day. England was ruled by an oligarchy, an aristocracy of titled wealth. Land, speculation, and "place," these were the sources of the nobility's power; "the variety of their economic enterprise aroused a keen interest in many aristocrats in the commercial destiny of their country and lifted their eyes beyond the confines of their own broad acres." [29] These were the men who controlled England's fate and directed the course of empire. J. H. Plumb has recreated the political scene in this manner:

> The ambivalence of attitude between the aristocracy and the smaller gentry gives an edge to local politics . . . which otherwise they might lack. It kept alive the old struggle of whig and tory . . . And this too must be remembered — they [the gentry] were far more numerous than the whig oligarchs who ruled their lives. After Walpole had brought peace to the land, the growing prosperity of the country in which they shared, tended as year followed year, to soften their asperity and bring them to a grumbling indifference. But they could never be ignored. Their representatives in Parliament, the independent country gentlemen, could act decisively in the conflict between factions . . .This conflict within the landowning classes sharpened the struggle for power at Westminster. [30]

Prosperity, then, was the key to Whig thought. The wisdom of this policy at home was evinced by the reduction of the opposition to "a grumbling indifference." In England it brought political stability and ensured the establishment of the Hanoverian monarchy. In the colonies it was a different matter. If the gentry were inclined to regard the empire much as they did their own relationship to the land — territorial expansion representing so many new acres added to their holdings — the Whig oligarchs combined their landed interests with a deep involvement in the commercial welfare of the country. Looking "beyond the confines of their own broad acres," they saw the growth of trade and the spread of English manufactures as the ultimate aim. Their colonial policies were shaped accordingly.

Walpole himself had no hesitation in initiating drastic reforms if he felt them warranted. In his first three budgets after taking power in 1722 he revised and tightened the customs system in England and increased the number of officers there.[31] This action was necessary to provide financing of the government's operation and to avoid economic chaos. It concerned only Great Britain. Walpole's exterior policies were to maintain peace, particularly with France, and to facilitate the flow of English commerce. To these aims the colonies could best contribute by creating no new problems and by cooperating voluntarily in the advancement of the motherland. To keep the colonists content required a policy of appeasement, not of coercion. Consequently for Walpole and his successors the guiding principle became to let well enough alone. "Quieta non movere" thus became Walpole's political maxim in colonial administration.

In the words of Basil Williams, inaction in the administration of the colonies "was largely due to Walpole's set policy, perfectly congenial to Newcastle's own inclination, of interfering as little as possible with the colonies." [32] England was the first of the prime minister's concerns, as illustrated by a remark he made in 1739. Urged to force the plantations to contribute financial aid by imposing direct taxes there, Walpole replied, "I have old England set against me, do you think I will have new England likewise?" [33]

If the ignorance of the Customs Commissioners on matters under their immediate supervision illustrates the confusion existing in governmental organization, a fitting memorial to the Walpole leadership is found in the fate of the Customs Board's proposed reduction. They received little or no attention and were never implemented.[34] Neither was the Board of Trade's plea that plantation affairs be centered in one office. The Whig leaders were quite impartial in their adherence to the creed that well enough should be left alone. Colonial administrative details were only erratically of concern to them, so little was accomplished in that area. "Salutary neglect" was not an accident but a precise policy.

If administrative reform in the colonies was of minor interest to the oligarchs, in another way the plantations were prominent in their thoughts. Pursuit of patronage was not only a habit for Englishmen in these years; for many it was a way of life in itself. Thus colonial offices could not long escape the notice of the politicians at home. By 1760 this aspect of the colonial scene had been woven deep into the political fabric of England; neither the customs service nor any of the other branches of the colonial governments was untouched by this pernicious practice.

The position connected with the customs service which was the most readily available as a political prize was the naval office. Although incumbents in this post were obliged to give bond to the Customs Board for the performance of their duties, and in spite of the fact that their work was intricately involved with that of the customs officers, right of appointment to this office never belonged to the Customs Commissioners. Originally the place was entirely within the gift of the various governors, but by 1715 many of the naval officers in the West Indies had obtained their post through the intervention of the home government. Gradually the practice spread to the continental colonies. The excuse first offered was that the naval office needed close supervision from London to prevent the taking of excessive fees, which hindered trade.[35] Afterwards no excuse was offered.

A typical and well-documented case was that involving Benjamin Pemberton and the naval office in Massachusetts. Until 1733 the governor of Massachusetts filled the office as he wished; Jonathan Belcher, then governor, had looked to his own interests by dividing the prize between his son and son-in-law.[36] Much to Belcher's chagrin, Pemberton sailed into Boston harbor in 1733 with a royal order for his installation as naval officer. Pemberton's claim to consideration by the home authorities was based primarily on a reported loss of a ship he owned in 1729, which, according to Pemberton, had been seized by the French on a pretense that it was sailing too close to Martinique.[37] In his straitened circumstances Pemberton left nothing to chance and took his case both to London and to the French court itself, where he was said to have been "so impetuous" that he obtained the order he brought to Belcher.[38] Considering Walpole's policy of peace with France, the story is plausible.

Many years later Pemberton recalled the situation in 1733 in this manner. When first the Massachusetts naval office was called to the attention of the English administrators, he reported, there was some fear that "the King's taking the Grant of this Office into his Royal Gift would be an abridgement of the Governour's perquisite in that particular . . . [but it was decided] that the Crown had long ago done, and continued to do the same in several of the Plantations, that nothing in the Charter or constitution of this Province any way interfered, [and] that although Mr. Belcher, the then Governour, might perhaps think hard of it's being taken from him personally, no future Governour here could think so." [39]

Pemberton was correct on at least one point; Belcher did indeed "think hard of it's being taken from him personally." He knew enough to obey the royal order, but he did so only momentarily and only partially. The warrant he gave Pemberton for the office was good at the governor's own pleasure, not at the king's. In this way Belcher ensured that, when and if he could do so with impunity, he could remove Pemberton on his own authority. Meanwhile he began what became a battle of "interests" in London.

In this struggle Belcher was somewhat handicapped by the fact that his original patron, Lord Townshend, was no longer available.[40] Instead he wrote to the Duke of Newcastle and Walpole, but he committed a tactical error by going behind their backs and writing to the president of the Privy Council and the speaker of the House of Commons as well. As Pemberton correctly observed, such action was sure to displease the patronage-conscious Newcastle.[41] Pemberton in turn relied on his friends, Delafaye and Horace Walpole, and was also defended by the Duke of Newcastle.[42]

Pemberton was successful in retaining his office, partially as the result of the activities of William Shirley, whose later fame as the most resourceful of Massachusetts' colonial governors has clouded the fact that previously he had been one of the most persistent and ruthless of place-seekers. For a time he was Belcher's friend and ally, until it became obvious that the governor could be of no further use. Then Shirley callously turned on Belcher and, in spite of a direct request not to interfere in the affair, applied to Newcastle for the post of naval officer for himself.[43] The confusion his entry into the contest created helped to defeat Belcher's plans, although Shirley himself did not win the post. Later when Shirley became governor his first act was to remove Pemberton (who still served only on Belcher's warrant) and to place his own son in the post of naval officer. Eventually Shirley too had to bow to Pemberton's connections at home, and the latter was finally secured in his post by a warrant at the king's pleasure.[44]

The Pemberton story, with variations, was repeated in other colonies. In Virginia, Henry McCulloh discovered that one of the naval offices had escaped the notice of the authorities at home. As McCulloh worded it, the post of naval officer at the Lower James being part of "a divided River had slipt ye Knowledge of ye Offices untill given in by me." Being interested in obtaining the post for himself, McCulloh pointed out that there was a precedent for overriding the wishes of the governor, as in "ye year 1742/3 Mr. Couraud was appointed by patent for York River in sd province, in ye room of the Governour's Son, who then enjoy'd it by his Father's appointment." [45]

The situation in South Carolina was more complex. Alexander Murray, the person sent out to exercise the authority of the naval office there, was a deputy for Apsley Brett, his "principal," who remained in England. In the circumstances, Murray reported, the governor became "very inquisitive about the Naval Office and I'm told hinted to some of his Friends that he intended to appoint an officer, for by Act of Parliament he has that power." The governor, Murray added, "may likewise perhaps insist that you should reside here agreeable to your Mandamus." Quite correctly, Murray felt that a short letter to the governor from "Mr. Pelham would go a great way to clear all his doubts." Such was the case, and Murray held the post until his death. A deputy like Murray in effect hired the office from his principal on the basis of an agreed annual payment from his income, as indicated by Murray's request that "a reasonable abatement in the Rent" be made in view of his troubles. [46]

Benjamin Wheatley, who was granted the naval office in North Carolina, echoed the sentiments of many of these men when he objected to having his warrant "pass the seals" in the colony instead of in England. Nor did he wish to have a residency clause included: "So uncertain a tenure as that during pleasure, being obliged to reside there, the expense of the voyage & other necessary Charges, leaving my friends at home, the risque of being taken, all considered, & if I should by any unforseen accident unhappily be removed, may instead of being of service to me, end in my ruin. My Lord, with these inconveniences, should the Governor retard my being put into the immediate possession of the office, which the Situation of my affairs cannot admit of, I must be in a miserable condition." [47]

Although the restrictions were a bit more onerous in the regular customs service, the encroachments of the place-seekers did not stop with the naval office. The actual officers appointed by the Commissioners of the Customs were not permitted to indulge in absentee officeholding generally, but still the positions were eagerly pursued. Charles Henry Frankland, who with one brother on the Admiralty Board and another in Parliament succeeded without difficulty in 1740 to the collectorship in Boston formerly held by the Jekylls, had his choice of either being governor in Massachusetts or collector in Boston and chose the latter post. Also provided for with a brother in the Admiralty, Andrew Elliot later had no difficulty in occupying the collectorship in New York.[48]

The Admiralty Lords in general were in a good position to obtain favors for their candidates; in their own right they controlled many patronage prizes and so other officials gladly cooperated with them. Thomas Gadsden, collector in South Carolina from 1722 to 1741, earned his place through the favor of Sir Charles Wager, First Lord of the Admiralty, who used his influence with Walpole.[49] Wager was also successful in moving Joseph Hull from a position in New Jersey to the collectorship in New London, which Hull preferred.[50] Another of Wager's candidates had a multiple claim to consideration. Charles Paxton, who was to play a vital part in the dramatic events of the sixties, was recommended to Walpole by Wager because "he is the Son of an old Captain in the Navy, who retir'd to New England many Years ago: and is, I believe, very well qualifyd for what is desired." [51] Paxton was hardly dependent on Wager in this application, however, as his brother was a trusted employee of the Treasury; earlier the Treasury minutes record that the Board would "know of Mr. Paxtons Bror, who my lords intend to provide with some Employ, whether he will accept of the office of a Deputy Kings waiter in the port of London." [52]

Such cases represented a more or less justifiable exchange of favors between administrative departments. But political considerations also contributed their share of appointments. An intriguing game of shifting interests was enacted over the collectorship at Piscataqua in New Hampshire. In 1736 Samuel Solly had gone to Roanoke, North Carolina, as collector through the patronage of Sir George Oxenden. Oxenden at the time was an intimate of Walpole, had been Lord of the Admiralty, and was then on the Treasury Board. In 1740 Solly moved to the collectorship at Piscataqua. In 1756 James Nevin, who wanted the post at Piscataqua, saw to it that the First Lord of the Treasury, the Duke of Devonshire, was notified that Solly "had been long a Lunatick, & consequently incapable of performing the Duty of his Employment." [53] Supported by the king's close friend, the Earl of Bath, Nevin offered to pay the "Lunatick" £50 a year from his own profits if he were given the post. This arrangement seemed reasonable to Devonshire, and Nevin became collector in New Hampshire. However, his troubles had only just begun.

By October, 1757, Devonshire had been replaced at the Treasury by the Duke of Newcastle, and other political interests were at work. On the 24th of October the Earl of Bath wrote to Newcastle that some friends and relatives of Solly, "on a pretence that it may be more convenient, & easier to the Captains, by reason of the distance of some of the Ports," had requested that a second collector be appointed to divide the salary and advantages of the post in New Hampshire.[54] As far as Bath was concerned the motive was mere revenge against Nevin for displacing Solly, but actually it was the handiwork of yet a third party in the contest.

Samuel Waldo was a wealthy New England merchant with extensive landholdings in Maine. Having been second in command to William Shirley at the siege of Louisburg in 1745, Waldo felt entitled to special consideration. In 1756 he was in England petitioning for the payment of £1,340 as salary for his service at Louisburg, plus £1,000 for personal losses.[55] With difficulty he received the £1,340, but nothing more. But there were other ways to take advantage of his position. With him in England was his son, Francis. In March, 1757, Francis Waldo, reporting to the Treasury that there was no customs house within one hundred and fifty miles of his home at Falmouth in New England, requested that the port be made a customs district and that he be named collector.[56] Samuel Waldo, with his commercial connections, had no difficulty in persuading the "most considerable Merchants of the City" to testify to the need for a customs house at Falmouth, and Francis got his appointment.[57]

Not only were Nevin and the Earl of Bath annoyed at this intrusion on their territory but they were incensed by the partition that was decided upon; according to Nevin, the territory assigned to Waldo was even greater than had been first requested, leaving him with little of his own for a district. Consequently Nevin requested that his Piscataqua port be extended seven miles to the northeast and twenty miles to the south-west in order to retain his hold over York in Maine, which Waldo's warrant assigned to the Falmouth district, and to expand to the southward to the Newbury River to offset the territory lost to Waldo. In this at least he was successful.[58] The Earl of Bath felt that this whole affair had all the appearances "of a concerted Job"; and the possibility cannot be ignored that Samuel Waldo and his fellow merchants, faced with the arrival of a new official in place of the ineffectual Solly, undertook to make Falmouth a port of entry for their own convenience.[59] Certainly Falmouth was hardly the busy district Francis Waldo depicted to the Treasury, and the American Commissioners after their coming in 1767 found the customs business there poorly managed in the extreme.[60] It was an ideal location for ships on the way to Boston to stop off and unload any goods that might cause difficulty in the more strictly guarded port.

Boston itself was the center of another patronage contest, when Sir Charles Henry Frankland finally surrendered his place as collector there in 1757. Samuel Waldo asked for the post for himself, depending once again on his services at Louisburg and calling attention to the expenses he had been put to by his "Seven Years Solicitation" in London.[61] But Boston was not a backwater port like Falmouth, and it was the object of careful scrutiny by greater men than Waldo. By the time Waldo made his application, the Duke of Newcastle and the Marquis of Rockingham had made tentative plans for the vacancy.

On August 17, 1757, the Marquis wrote Newcastle that his friend Quarme had not quite decided yet whether to accept the place or not; Quarme's problem was that he was "Unwilling to think of a Temporal Transportation tho' the Terms are both Honourable & Profitable." Still Rockingham was not ready to surrender his friend's claim so soon. Perhaps, he suggested to Newcastle, he could find someone else to go who would be willing to provide some allowance for Quarme; the only danger to that arrangement was that possibly, if Newcastle approved it and Quarme accepted, then the Duke might think further favors unwarranted. What Quarme really desired was "the first Vacancy in the Commission of Stamp-Tax or Salt." Rockingham told Newcastle that if these plans were agreed to, and Quarme were not eliminated from future consideration for other offices, he "could make, More than one, Good friend of Mine Happy, on whose account I must some day become troublesome to your Grace." [62]

Newcastle answered that his "Good little Friend, the Chancellor of the Exchequer, would not make Two Additional Commissioners of the Stamps" so that he was "inclined to your other Scheme." [63] After consulting with his protégé Rockingham wrote that Quarme preferred to wait for an opening in the Stamp Office, but until such time as that was available he "must request . . . that you would suffer him to be Quarter'd on the Person, who will reap the Benefit of Quarmes Non Acceptance of the Collectorship at Boston." The Marquis had heard of a gentleman who he thought would accept the place and agree to pay Quarme some £300 a year. If this plan were acceptable, then when Quarme received his appointment to the Stamp Office Newcastle could have that £300 to dispose of as he wished. Rockingham asked the Duke not to let the man he had in mind know about all these things, as "he will come more readily into it if he hears it first from me, and thinks he has no chance of the whole." [64] If certain other conditions were met, Newcastle was perfectly agreeable to this arrangement and wrote that Rockingham's man could "have the place, & give what He, & you please out of it to Quarme." [65]

Either the man the Marquis had selected discovered the truth or he too was unwilling to undergo a "Temporal Transportation," for the man who went to Boston was Benjamin Barons, who had not figured in the correspondence between Rockingham and Newcastle. Barons had been in the colonies previously, serving as secretary to the governor of New York; he was a protégé of Sir Charles Hardy, a former governor of that colony who was influential in English political circles through his connections with the Admiralty. Barons himself was not without "interests" of his own, as shown by an incident in 1750 when a ship belonging to him came from Lisbon to Boston with a cargo of salt. Having no register to prove English ownership, it was seized and condemned. The Customs Commissioners upheld the condemnation, but the Treasury received such a flood of testimony on behalf of Barons from London merchants and "distinguished people" that the king's one-third share of the seizure was remitted to Barons as a form of settlement.[66] Whether or not, with these strong connections, Barons had to share his profits with Quarme unfortunately is not recorded. In any event Quarme would not have received much benefit, as Barons' career in Boston was brief and stormy.[67]

Negotiations between Rockingham and Newcastle had been carried on in a gracious and subtle manner. Jonathan Acklorn was quite blunt. In August, 1757, he wrote to Newcastle that he had learned that the merchants of Connecticut had petitioned for the creation of New Haven as a legal port of entry. The Board of Trade had approved and was now waiting for a report from the surveyor general. Acklorn wanted the new post for his brother-in-law, Joseph Harrison of Newport, Rhode Island. In a cocksure manner, Acklorn reminded the Duke of his services in procuring votes in the last election and requested the appointment of Harrison.[68] Newcastle was most cooperative, and Harrison got the post. Later Joseph Harrison moved to Boston as collector, serving in that capacity during the critical period from 1766 to 1773. His son inherited the collectorship and was the last of the royal collectors of the customs in Boston.

In spite of these examples there was another side to appointments in the customs service. The collection of the revenue was an important matter, one which Walpole and his heirs did not take lightly, with the result that there was a "certain subordination of political influence to effective administration." [69] One applicant for a post was informed that the Duke of Newcastle could only appoint "the properest person to an office of so great consequence to the Revenue." [70] Another place-seeker ruefully reported that "the Commrs of the Customs are very alert on Appointments," although he still hoped in his case that the Treasury might be persuaded to overrule the Commissioners.[71] One gentleman was refused the collectorship at Boston because "the Commissioners of the Customs have objected to him on account of his Commercial connections." In this instance the applicant was a merchant involved in the sugar trade and the Customs Board feared that "he might be tempted to encourage the illicit Trade carried on between those Islands & the Continent of America." The applicant offered to show that he did not now have "£100 engaged in any branch of trade whatsoever" and promised that if the Commissioners would point out how the illegal trade in sugar could be stopped he would gladly put their plans into execution, but he got neither the Boston post nor any other in the customs service.[72]

The fact is that the role of patronage in English politics has frequently been misrepresented. Although Acklorn might refer to the votes he had procured for Newcastle, and Pelham might consider giving Thomas Pitt the governorship of South Carolina on a "condition of Mr. Pitt's giving the Government his interest in the several Boroughs where he is concerned,"[73] patronage was not the decisive political instrument often pictured. The best description of the use of patronage has been given by J. B. Owen: "Patronage was necessary; it was not, and never could be, sufficient. Its primary purpose was to provide seats and salaries for the 'men of business,' on whose work and abilities the security of the Government depended; for the rest, it had the character of private charity rather than public corruption, and as a constitutional lubricant between executive and legislature it was always of subordinate significance."[74]

As a feudal lord had been expected to look to the welfare of his retainers, so in the era before the formation of modern political parties the heads of government were counted upon to share the advantages of their positions with their followers. Men such as John Carteret or William Pitt who overlooked this aspect of their duties were often less effective than they might have been; as leaders unconcerned with political realities, their tenure of office was usually brief. Such a man as the Duke of Newcastle, in spite of the scornful treatment he is accorded by modern commentators, in his way played a vital and indispensable role in the transformation of English politics from an age of feudalism to modern times. Without such men eighteenth century England might have been a different, and far less happy, land, a country of ineffectual government and general political turmoil.[75]

In 1758 an American colonist wrote that the English politicians, "having been so careless for many years past of the character and abilities of the civil officers appointed for America, that most of the places in the gift of the Crown have been filled with broken members of Par-t, of bad, if any principles, pimps, valet de chambres, electioneering scoundrels, and even livery servants. In one word, America has been for many years made the hospital of Great Britain for her decayed courtiers and abandoned wornout dependents."[76]

Although there may have been grounds for this sarcastic complaint in other sections of the colonial administration, including the naval offices, the use made of the customs service as a hospital for the dispensation of "private charity" was a somewhat different matter. Many applicants did object, like Quarme, to a "Temporal Transportation"; others, like Wheat-ley, feared the "risque of being taken." Yet the attention paid to appoint-ments by the Commissioners, and the residency requirements insisted upon in the customs service, made the employment of deputies most difficult. Annuities provided a happy solution to this problem.

The importance of Charles Henry Frankland's connections has already been indicated, but when this man, so influential in his own right, took office as collector in Boston it was on the condition of paying a £200 a year "annuity" from the profits of his place to the Duke of Newcastle.[77] Newcastle did not of course keep these funds for himself; out of it he provided for "a poor long expecting Disappointed Friend."[78] By this arrangement Frankland held office in his own name, avoiding the problem of a deputy, while one of Newcastle's dependents was taken care of without being obliged to quit the country.

If a man as important as Frankland could be quartered upon for £200, lesser men could expect harder bargains. The scheme plotted between Rockingham and Newcastle, outlined previously, supplies an extreme example. Rockingham's man, Quarme, wanted the Boston post but did not wish to leave England. A deputy was not possible; so Rockingham proposed an annuity for Quarme of £300. But there was an additional ingredient in this transaction: Newcastle too expected to share in the profits. He wanted the payment he had received from Frankland, the previous collector at Boston, continued. The terms Rockingham finally agreed to were that whoever obtained the post "was to Continue the Payment of yr £200 & also to pay Quarme a further Annuity out of the profits of the Place."[79] Newcastle wondered "Who is your Friend, that would allow that, and also give Quarme something for the present?"[80] But the Duke added that in any case "I must have Two Hundred Pounds pr An. for two Friends, to whom I have been engaged, I believe, before you return'd from abroad."[81] Thus these two English politicians expected whoever went to Boston to furnish them with a double annuity.

Another letter to Newcastle shows that annuities could be derived in a different manner. In 1742 William Gage wrote that Mr. Arburthnot, the collector at Antigua, had just died. This officer, Gage reported, had obtained his post through the recommendation of a Mr. Board and in return had paid Board a yearly annuity from his profits. Gage now wanted Newcastle to let Board recommend someone else for the place so he could continue to receive his annuity. Even better, Gage thought, would be an arrangement by which the Duke found something else for Board; then Newcastle could have the annuity to use for his own purposes.[82]

Fourteen years later another collector at Antigua died of an indisposition "brought upon him, by looseing £5,000 Sterling in one Night at Play." This collector had paid an annuity of £200 a year to "an Old Gentleman in Sussex," a situation which was called to Newcastle's attention by George Munro, who wrote the Duke's secretary that he could "find Sufficient Security to pay £400 a year out of it, on the exchange of London, which . . . would enable His Grace to oblige more of his Friends." In this case, again, the applicant, Munro, did not wish to leave England himself and offered such a high price as an inducement for the Duke to procure permission for him to operate by deputy.[83]

The workings of this annuity system rather naturally brings up the question of the value of the posts in the customs service. Some of the smaller positions obviously were not involved in such arrangements; they were worth little enough as it was. As late as 1763 the governor of Virginia reported that of the six collectors acting in Virginia only one had any income worth mentioning.[84] Yet the larger places seemingly were quite remunerative and well able to bear the burden of such extra charges. Often these offices were more valuable than the English authorities realized. During the struggle over the naval office in Massachusetts Governor Belcher wrote to a correspondent in England that the post was worth £550, Massachusetts currency. Yet to his son Belcher estimated the true value of the office at £1,200.[85] Benjamin Pemberton, inexperienced at the business, did not know how to get the most out of his place at first, and thought it worth only £120 sterling in 1733.[86]

The loss of £5,000 in one night might break the spirit of any man, but the collector at Antigua who died of an indisposition caused by such an event earned a good income; his place was estimated to be worth £1,000 per year.[87] Newcastle and Rockingham expected to receive annuities to the value of £500 from the man going to Boston as collector, who would have been left with an income of £300, as Newcastle reported the value of the place to be £800 a year.[88]

Actually the value of all these places was probably higher; during the long years of neglect many illicit practices grew up which make the determination of real worth impossible. Compositions are one example. If a ship was detected in illegal activities, it was liable to prosecution, which might entail loss of both the ship and cargo. From the captain's, or owner's, point of view any settlement that could be reached with the detecting official was desirable. On the other hand, because of the impotency of the Admiralty courts and the prejudices of the local courts, successful condemnations were long and difficult matters; often the case would have to be carried to London. And, too, there was always the danger that the customs officials, if they persisted in prosecuting, might themselves be taken to court on a variety of charges in revenge. Few royal officials relished the thought of facing a local jury. Consequently an accommodation was the logical answer. The officials would "compose" the affair out of court for a fair sum and the only loser would be the king's revenue.[89]

The most accurate figures on value come from a later period. After the collapse of the customs service in the colonies in 1775 many of the refugees received compensation for their losses. Strict inquiry was made into the legitimacy of such claims, and the resultant statements may be regarded as the most dependable available. Allowance must be made for the changes in enforcement after 1763, but there was not necessarily such a difference as might at first be supposed. A large part of the profit of the individual posts prior to 1763 came from the "extras" an officer earned by such activities as agreeing to a "composition" or accepting a bribe. After 1763 it became the policy of the English government to put a stop to these practices by increasing the "extras" an officer could earn by the faithful performance of his duty; officially authorized rewards took the place of the unofficial and illegal "extras." In this way presumably what income the officers lost through the disappearance of the former illegitimate profits was equaled by their gains through sharing in the distribution of seizures and through particular rewards for particular services. In short, the value of the places after 1763 was probably much the same as earlier, only the manner in which it was derived was different.[90]

Francis Waldo, collector at Falmouth, reported in 1776 that he had received no income for over a year. To illustrate the extent of his losses, Waldo listed his earnings from "legal and accustomed fees" for the period 5 April, 1774, to 5 April, 1775, at £400.5.8; with the salary he was allowed of £100 per year Waldo's income for the minor port of Falmouth was over £500.[91] Since Falmouth was one of the most wide-open ports in North America, Waldo probably made as much earlier from "neglect" of duty.

If Waldo's district was small and unimportant, Boston was one of the most active of all ports. The last collector, Richard Acklorn Harrison, has left us a detailed account of his profits. Harrison's income schedule for the year 1775 was as follows:[92]

Salary:	£100
Fees at Boston:	£1,138.11.6
Fees at Nantucket:	£200
Share of Seizures:	£100
Gross receipts:	£1,538.11.6
Deductions for payments to four clerks and deputy at Nantucket:	£298
Net income:	£1,240.11.6

These figures for Boston compare favorably with the Duke of Newcastle's earlier estimate of £800. Allowing for the fact that the information available to Newcastle was probably under the true value, and for the possibility that increased trade and stricter enforcement may have raised the income slightly after 1763, it is reasonable to presume that Boston was worth roughly £1,000 a year to its collector. An interesting comparison to English customs posts is possible here; after his flight to England, Harrison for a time was placed on a pension list. Eventually he was appointed collector at Kingston on Hull. Although Harrison was probably glad to have the office, he took a sharp drop in income; at Kingston he earned £230 per year in salary and £120 in fees, for a total of £350, or only slightly more than one-third of his Boston receipts.[93]

One of the most important of the customs posts in London was that of chief searcher. The income of that office suggests that the best of the American positions were equal to or slightly more valuable than their English equivalents. In 1763 the chief searcher reportedly received a salary of £120 per year, which was subject to deduction for the land tax, payment of six pence in the pound to the Civil List, and one shilling in the pound general tax on salary and perquisites. After these deductions, and payment of £80 per year to a deputy and £45 per year for a waterman, the final net value of the place including profits from fees was £500 a year.[94] A safe presumption would be that American incomes ranged from a low of £100 per year at the smallest posts to £1,000 at the most active. Compared to the English establishment the minor posts were less profitable, and the important places as profitable or more so, than similar offices at home. The major difference was that there were more large ports in England than in the colonies and consequently more good positions to be distributed.

The fact that annuities rather than deputies were the basis of the patronage system in the customs service effectively negates the frequent charge that the operation of the system was impeded by offhand selection of irresponsible deputies by their English principals. Each of the men sent to the colonies was examined by the Customs Board. As long as Newcastle and the others secured their annuities they were perfectly content that the officers chosen were the best available. That responsibility they left to the care of the Commissioners of the Customs, and the evidence is that those men performed their work with at least some objectivity.[95] Standards, either moral or ethical, were not high in the eighteenth century; the failings of the customs service personnel were those of the century in general and not of the manner of appointment in particular.

Of course, faced with the necessity of paying a given sum yearly to some English "retainer" an officer might be led to squeeze as much from his position as possible. Consequently he might be too eager to make a composition or take a bribe. This would be true, however, only as long as such illegal activities presented the best way of supplementing one's income. If it became possible to make as much, or more, from the faithful performance of one's duty, there is no reason to suppose that such officers would not operate quite efficiently. The blame for the long years of corruption and nonenforcement lies more heavily on the policy of "salutary neglect" than it does on the personnel involved. Left to their own fate, unsupported from home in the face of determined opposition, little remained for these men but to adjust to their circumstances and make the best of a difficult situation. After 1763 these same officers bore the brunt of the English efforts to recoup the mistakes of previous years, and they performed in a creditable, sometimes surprisingly heroic, manner.[96]

Even in the few cases where deputies were employed they were not necessarily a misfortune. Grosvenor Bedford, collector for Philadelphia, was entitled by his special warrant to operate through a deputy. Philadelphia from 1733 until 1771 was thus entrusted to a series of men representing Bedford. For the thirteen-year period from 1746 through 1758 Bedford's deputies sent a total of £813 to England as receipts from their port.[97] Not a large sum; it averages only a little over £60 per year. But during this same period, Boston contributed not one shilling. The contrast is even sharper for the years when the Molasses Act first began to be enforced. From 1759 through 1761 Philadelphia returned £2,927 to London as receipts under the Act of 6 George II; Boston contributed £9. And all this was accomplished with much less popular discontent and opposition in Philadelphia than in Boston. If this was a test of the deputy system, England might have done well to put it into effect everywhere.

It was not necessarily the selection of personnel that was the disastrous feature of the involvement of colonial officeholding in the web of English patronage. The real danger lay in centering all political activity in London. To the English authorities such a policy seemed wise; just as they centered all trade on the homeland, so they felt it important to concentrate authority there. It was an unfortunate mistake. Royal officials in the colonies needed all the support possible, and the control of patronage is a necessity for effective political administration. This advantage was denied to the officers abroad.

When Benjamin Pemberton arrived in Boston to take the naval office from the control of Governor Belcher, the latter argued to the English ministers that such action "tends to undervalue him to the people of the Country." [98] William Shirley, although he had attempted himself to wrest the office from Belcher's control, when he succeeded to the governorship let the Duke of Newcastle know that loss of that office would lower him "very much in the eyes of the People." [99] In the customs service itself the plea was for "an actual Superior upon the Spot." What was required, the author of that remark reported, was that a "Man of Weight, Character and Influence" might occupy the office of surveyor general to keep the officers who were "removed at a great distance" attentive to their duties.[100] In actual fact the surveyors general had little authority to discipline or control the officers they were intended to supervise. When they did remove a man for misconduct frequently they found their judgment reversed in England.[101] They had no power of appointment, except on an interim basis, and even that authority was severely circumscribed.[102] In such circumstances it was difficult to produce a man of "Weight" and "Influence."

The failure to use the power of patronage properly was two-edged: it destroyed the ability of officials on the spot to build up centers of support for the imperial policies, and it permitted the colonists to bypass local authority more or less at will. In 1767 Governor Francis Bernard of Massachusetts, commenting on the opposition he faced, pointed to the past history of that colony: the "faction" had driven Governor Shute from the country; William Burnet's heart had been broken; Belcher had been removed on charges which appeared false "almost before the Ink of his dismission was dry"; Shirley had departed for different reasons; Thomas Pownall had stayed only a brief moment. The faction's success in forcing the repeal of the Stamp Act, Bernard observed, had merely continued this tradition, and every triumph from Shute's day to his own had contributed to the arrogance of the opposition.[103] The tradition Bernard referred to was a logical product of the operation of the English system.

Many years before the time of Bernard, Lieutenant Governor Gooch of Virginia had asked the English authorities to consider "how absolutely necessary Rewards as well as Punishments are to maintain Authority in any Government." To remove the "Power of rewarding Merit" leaves an official "a Province rather like that of an Executioner to inflict Punishments." [104] Gooch might have added that the royal officials, like executioners, rarely were able to achieve popularity. The concentration of the power and authority associated with patronage in London was perhaps the gravest of the mistakes made in this period. Untrustworthy officers should have been removed; good officials should have been trusted. Responsibility is nothing without authority, and that the colonial officials never really possessed. As Gooch commented, the system as it operated permitted "the most unworthy, if they happen to have friends at Home, to look upon their Superiours with Disdain and bid them Defiance," a remark that is as applicable to the operation of the customs service as to all the branches of the English administration in the colonies.

The English Scene

Inefficiency in departmental organization, indifference to reform, and the misuse of the power of patronage — such were the predominant characteristics of the English colonial administrative system in these middle years. It should have been no surprise to anyone that eventually it would be not just the local royal representatives but the home authorities themselves whom the colonists would "look upon . . . with Disdain and bid . . . Defiance." When that day arrived, a total breakdown of authority could be expected. The history of the operation of the customs service during these middle years suggests that the groundwork was laid for just such a disaster.

VII

The Fallow Years

FOR a brief moment in 1735 it seemed that the policy of "salutary neglect" was to be abandoned. Two years earlier the West Indies planters had achieved their long-desired aim. The Molasses Act of that year imposed a prohibitive duty on the produce of the foreign sugar islands when imported into the American colonies. Contrary to traditional interpretations, this Act was not solely the result of planter agitation. Over the years many officials other than those immediately concerned with the islands had called attention to the dangers of the situation. In 1716 Archibald Cummings had noted that foreign sugars entered the colonies in a favored manner, since they paid "no duty more . . . than if our product" while escaping assessment under the four and one-half percent.[1] In 1720 William Gordon observed that New England obtained over one-half of its molasses from the foreign islands; if such trade were restricted, the consumption of the produce of the English islands, which was subject to the four and one-half percent as well as the enumerated duties, would be increased.[2] In 1725 the combined New England customs staff, from the surveyor general to the surveyor and searcher at Boston, sent a memorial to the Board of Trade, requesting that the provision trade, particularly in horses, from their area to the foreign islands be stopped. The major exchange item in this trade was sugar or molasses, which hurt the English islands; but also prohibited goods such as Dutch "linens, french lulstring and alamodes, wines and brandies" were supplied by the foreign merchants and often run ashore in New England. Since such activities, "for want of more officers cannot be so well prevented," a general prohibition of the trade was needed.[3]

Any question touching the four and one-half percent received careful consideration in England. Not only was the revenue from that tax considerable, but the English authorities were free to use it as they wished. In 1726, for example, Governor Shute, who had been driven from his province of Massachusetts because of the bitterness engendered by the salary question, was provided for from this fund.[4] The figures on the receipts from the four and one-half percent at the time of the passage of the Molasses Act are revealing. In 1727 over £20,000 was paid into the Exchequer from this source; from 1730 to 1733 receipts reached a low of less than £8,000 a year. Immediately after Parliament enacted the Molasses Act, returns rose to a peak of over £40,000. Thereafter they fell precipitously.[5]

Concern for the revenue of the four and one-half percent, encouraged by suggestions from various colonial officials, lent support to the case presented by the West Indies planters. Even so, the Molasses Act was not easily obtained. At first the planters attempted to gain satisfaction through the Privy Council, but exasperating delays entailed by interdepartmental indecision and by the procrastination of the agents for the continental colonies led "the sugar colonies to turn to parliament as the only sure agency for reform in colonial affairs." [6] In 1731 the House of Commons passed a bill to prohibit the importation of foreign sugar, molasses, or rum into Great Britain or any part of the empire while also forbidding the exportation of horses and lumber to any foreign sugar colony. The parliamentary session ended before the House of Lords acted on this measure, and the same fate overtook a second effort made in 1732. In May, 1733, the Molasses Act finally was passed by both Houses. In its final form the Act replaced a total prohibition of the importation of sugars from the foreign islands with a prohibitive duty.[7]

Later laxity in enforcement has tended to obscure the real story of events in the years immediately after passage of this Act. Some commentators suggest that the Act was never taken seriously and that it was enacted as a meaningless concession to the planters, but the evidence indicates that originally, at least, the English government expected its provisions to be observed. In August, 1733, the Treasury wrote to the Commissioners of the Customs on the subject of the new Act, ordering the Commissioners to instruct their surveyors general in the colonies to appoint proper officers "where wanted, to put into Execution an Act of Parliament of the Sixth year of His present Majesty." Further, the

Treasury wanted to know "what additional Number of Officers at each place will be absolutely necessary to perform the Duty and at what Allowances." [8]

One year and a half later the Commissioners replied that they had received an answer from the surveyor general northern and that certain new officials were being employed "upon Tryal." Since the New England colonies were the most active participants in the sugar trade, all the new officers were assigned to that area, Salem and Marblehead in Massachusetts being provided with a surveyor and searcher (who was also to act as a landwaiter) at £40 a year, and Rhode Island with a combination searcher and landwaiter at the same salary. Boston also received a tidesurveyor at £50 per year, plus a boat and two men, each of whom was to be paid £20 a year. The additional expenses thus incurred were to be covered by the receipts under the new Act. [9]

In the first year a total of £330 was collected under the Molasses Act. Receipts through 1737 averaged £249 a year, while from 1738 through 1741 the average return was £76. [10] These figures speak for themselves. After an initial attempt at enforcement the situation quickly reverted to normal, with laxity and evasion again becoming the rule. Receipts rose again after 1741, primarily because of the activities of the British fleet in American waters during the war. But between 1738 and 1750 a total of only £5,603 was collected on the produce of the foreign islands imported in the normal course of business, while £7,616 more was received from duties on captured prizes.

Although nonenforcement may not have been the original intention, it was a foregone conclusion. The painful fact was that the administrative machinery in the colonies was completely inadequate. Even with the new officers New England, for example, possessed only ten regular officials and a handful of lesser functionaries, hardly enough to ensure strict observance of an unpopular measure. By 1739 the facts were so obvious that a bill was introduced into Parliament to make the Molasses Act effectual, but it failed of passage. [11] Ten years later another effort was made but it too was talked to death in numerous hearings. [12] Until Parliament should act to implement its new law the situation remained much as described by the governor of Massachusetts in 1737: "The Sea Coast of the Province is so extensive & has so many Commodious harbours, that the small number of Customs House Officers are often complaining they are not able to do much for preventing illegal Trade. Nor does the Sugar Act take any great Effect; great Quantities of foreign Molasses are still brought into this Province, and much of it by way of Rhode Island." [13]

That the Molasses Act was permitted to become a dead letter was partially due to other steps taken to relieve the distressed West Indies planters, who gradually realized that one of their major handicaps was the prohibition against shipping their produce directly to European ports. Even the operation of the drawback system did not compensate for the increased charges they faced through being forced to ship via England; consequently they were at a disadvantage in competing for the continental markets. The planters petitioned Parliament for the removal of this restriction, receiving satisfaction in the Acts of 1739 and 1742 which, if they did not allow rum and molasses to be shipped directly to Europe, at least did remove the prohibition on sugar itself.[14] This concession meant more to the planters than the unenforceable Molasses Act and probably explains the failure of the bill to tighten the provisions of that Act which Parliament was considering in 1739.

More important, perhaps, than this temporary muffler put on agitators for the Indies was the end of the Walpole era of international peace. In 1739 England went to war with Spain. Walpole's reluctant acceptance of involvement in a contest with Spain marked the beginning of the end for his long career. At the same time the end of peace also fundamentally altered relations between the motherland and her colonies. Cooperation and mutual good will were now more important than ever. It was not a time for coercive measures. In 1740, for example, an expedition was planned against the Spanish islands in the Caribbean, and all the colonies from the Carolinas to New England were asked to contribute levies. So seriously did the English regard this undertaking that Governor Belcher of Massachusetts, who had survived numerous other crises, finally was removed for his failure to collect the required number of troops.[15]

Between 1739 and 1763 England was at peace for only six years. The War of Jenkins' Ear merged into the War of the Austrian Succession, which ended only in 1748. By 1754 England and France were again at war in the preliminaries to the climactic Seven Years' conflict. Both these great contests were fought in the colonies as well as in Europe. Consequently active colonial participation and aid were a necessity. Nor were the English authorities as free to look to colonial affairs as formerly. The correspondence of such an official as the Duke of Newcastle, until 1748 Secretary of State, indicates that the conduct of war was an all-encompassing task. Colonial business, at best, was always on the periphery of administrative consciousness. In wartime it was completely relegated to the background. Reform would have to await the return of peace. Until then officials in the colonies had to do their best without further support from home.

After 1735 no more was heard of plans for a general increase in the customs establishment in the plantations. Typical of the attitude prevalent in this period was the answer given by the Customs Commissioners to a request made by Governor James Glen of South Carolina for more officers to enforce the Acts there: "We cannot propose . . . the putting the Revenue to any further expence, it being impossible to appoint Officers at every Creek & River in the Province." [16] Governor Glen well might have replied that it was equally impossible to expect the six officers then stationed in his province to ensure observance of the laws.

Between 1738 and 1760 certain additions were made to the customs service. Georgia, after becoming a crown colony, was equipped with a collector, a comptroller, and a searcher. Even before Governor Glen's protest two new ports had been added in South Carolina, at Wynyaw and Port Royal, while major changes were made in North Carolina, as Beaufort, Bathtown, and Brunswick became ports of entry. Maryland obtained a new district at Chester and Patapsco, while New Jersey added Nova Casaria to its port list. Along with the additions in New England noted above, and the organization of Falmouth in Maine discussed earlier,[17] Nova Scotia added a surveyor and searcher to the collector that had been stationed there since 1713. For the most part these changes were made gradually. They represented no concerted plan for a major expansion of the service.

The story behind the creation of one of these new posts illustrates the process in general. In 1752 James Stirling sent a memorial to the Treasury reporting that a large area of Maryland was not effectively covered and requesting that a new port of entry be established and that he be appointed collector. His application was supported by "distinguished" gentlemen who knew Maryland, and, after a brief correspondence between the Treasury and the Customs Commissioners, Stirling was given the new position. The original petition had been read at the Treasury on the 29th of April; the decision had been made and the warrant authorized by the 12th of May. In fact, the whole affair was so speedily transacted that the Customs Board never did have time to investigate properly the need for the new district. The Commissioners indeed did not even read Stirling's memorial, merely telling the Treasury that the important men supporting Stirling seemed to know what the situation was and so they had no objections to offer.[18] It was an offhand manner of arriving at an important decision.

Many years later a dispute over the boundaries of the district originally assigned to Stirling led to disclosure of the true story of his original appointment. In 1752, it was reported, "Stirling then a Doctor of Divinity living upon the said River [the Chester in Maryland], . . . by his Interest obtained a Commission as Collector of that River" before the other officers in Maryland knew of his petition. Later, upon representation the Commissioners of the Customs investigated and discovered that the granting of the commission had been wrongly and unfairly obtained. Rather than vacate a warrant which had already been issued, they approved a compromise by which Stirling was to hold his post until his death, after which no new appointment would be made and the former arrangements would be re-established. In itself this policy of procrastination is a commentary on English administrative practices; even more typical was the end result. When Stirling died in 1765 the former promise had long since been forgotten and a new officer was quickly appointed to his post. As late as 1772 a heated contest over the boundaries of the old and new districts absorbed the attention of the customs staff in Maryland to the exclusion of their duty as agents of the English government.[19]

At a time when a large portion of an officer's income was derived from fees, the larger the district the larger the income. Maryland was not the only colony disturbed by such disputes. In Nova Scotia the collector took matters into his own hands. Originally Hilbert Newton, the collector, had been ordered to reside at Annapolis, but in 1724 the Commissioners of the Customs moved him to Canso "upon a representation that it was become a more considerable place of Trade than Annapolis." By 1750 Newton felt another move was in order, Halifax now being the most important and active port. The collector's problem was not so much one of districting as it was of intrusion on his rights. All Nova Scotia was his territory, but in his absence the naval officer at Halifax had made that port his own. Newton asked the surveyor general for approval for his move to Halifax but was refused. He proceeded on his own.

The governor of Nova Scotia wrote to the Treasury that in spite of his objections, and in defiance of the instructions of the surveyor general, Newton had moved to Halifax. Governor Edward Cornwallis added that the "Naval Officer is active and diligent in his duty to see the Acts of Trade . . . put in force" and that in his opinion "a Customhouse here for some time would be very detrimental to the Settlement."[20] The governor intimated that until Halifax was commercially well established the presence of customs officials could only serve to discourage trade.

The Commissioners of the Customs replied that they had not ordered Newton to Halifax but the same reasons that had dictated his former moves indicated that "he should now have the liberty of Keeping his Office at Halifax, where it is necessary for the service there should be a Collector as well as a Naval Officer." For the rest, Newton would just have "to take the best care he can of the business at Annapolis and Cansoe, and of all the Bays and Creeks within the Province . . . as we do not think it proper to propose . . . putting the Revenue to any additional Expence."[21] In this one instance, at least, the customs officer was successful in his contest with the governor. Hilbert Newton, in fact, did very well at Nova Scotia. When a surveyor and searcher was authorized for the province, Newton's son got the appointment, and when Newton finally died another son became collector in his place. From 1713 until the end of the colonial period the customs service in Nova Scotia was completely a family affair.

Nothing could be more illustrative of the general laxity of enforcement in these years than the intrusion of the deputy system, in a bastard form, into the customs service. From the earliest years deputies had actually been employed — but as assistants, not replacements. The rules of the customs service required the presence of the principal officeholder on the scene, but in the absence of strict supervision this regulation was easily evaded. Sir Charles Henry Frankland, collector at Boston, employed William Sheafe as deputy collector. Shortly after his arrival in Massachusetts, Frankland wrote the Duke of Newcastle that "this is the finest Country & Climate I ever saw Yet I begin to grow Sick of the people."[22]

The Fallow Years

Involvement with a young girl kept Frankland in the colony longer than he intended, but eventually he returned to England and even resided in Portugal for a time.[23] During his years of absence Sheafe performed the duties of the Boston customs house. As in the case of Bedford's deputies at Philadelphia, this substitution was not necessarily unfortunate; Sheafe was a conscientious worker who performed well in the crises that arose later.

A less fortunate example was found in Rhode Island, where in 1742 the judge of the Vice-Admiralty court reported that the collector for Rhode Island "for many years last past has not resided there but farms out the same." At a later time the judge added that the port "at present is filled by a Deputy Collr who must be presumed to Rent ye Office from his Principle." The result was that Rhode Island was "Virtually a free port." [24]

Such evasion of responsibility was possible because of the ineffectualness of the administrative system. Theoretically the surveyors general should have corrected these faults; however, their powers were severely limited and generally their opinions carried little weight in England. To make the situation worse, the surveyor general northern in these years was Thomas Lechmere, of whom it was reported that "he is at present thro' Age incapable of inspecting the Proceedings of the several Ports within his District" and who although "Brother to Lord Lechmere was perhaps never equal to the Duties of that Post." [25]

The letter that provided those reflections on Thomas Lechmere effectively summed up the general situation of the customs service. No considerations, the author reported, "will restrain the Trader in pursuit of Gain, but those arising from his own Interest." The customs officers might be remiss in their duty but what can be done "where most Effectual Methods are found out to evade them"? A thorough investigation of the operation of the whole system was needed but it would be most difficult and "how certain and inevitable his Destruction must be who was Known to move it from hence." His next remarks indicate the usefulness of ports such as Falmouth in Maine and Stirling's in Maryland: "There are Ports here that scarce Serve to any other purpose than to Screen a Clandestine Trade, and to Furnish permits for Goods illegally Imported," while as long as that "is the Case Vigour in one Port could only serve to banish Trade from that place without answering a common Good; for a General Evil requires a General Remedy." The experience of many customs officials was distilled in the author's closing statement, which he coupled with a plea for closer supervision of their conduct: "We are here removed at a great distance from Our Superiors, and Continuing long in the same place degenerate into Creoles, and at length forget Mother Country and her Interests."

Just how bad was the "General Evil" which was demoralizing the isolated officers and which required a "General Remedy"? As to the Molasses Act there is no question. All historians of this era agree that the merchants and officials, from the governors to the tidewaiters, combined to undermine any effort to enforce its provisions. The testimony of a merchant from Salem, Massachusetts, in 1758 shows what actually took place. Timothy Orne wrote to one of his captains that, "Since you Sailed from here our Officers have recd Orders not to Enter foreign Molasses as heretofore. The Vessells that have arrived since those orders have been admitted to Enter about One Eighth or Tenth part of their Cargo paying 6d Sterling p. gall. Duty for what is entered — which is more than twice as much as was given before." [26]

According to this evidence, prior to the orders given in 1758 for stricter enforcement of the Molasses Act, only a small part of any given cargo was entered in the customs books, and a lower duty than authorized collected on what was entered. Even after 1758 only a fraction of the molasses was taxed. What was true of Salem was probably true elsewhere. A compromise was reached between the merchants and customs officials at the expense of the English Exchequer. It was the only solution possible when total enforcement was not feasible.

The exact extent of the trade in foreign molasses will never be known, but at a safe guess it was enormous. When the duty on molasses was lowered to one pence per gallon in 1766, and levied on both foreign and British products alike, there was no longer any need to falsify the returns. Between 1768 and 1772 imports listed as coming from the English islands fell from 326,675 gallons to 125,466; during the same period foreign imports rose from 2,824,060 to 4,878,794 gallons, suggesting that false entry and not clandestine smuggling had been the main problem earlier.[27] In 1766 Massachusetts was reported to possess fifty-one distilleries each producing one hogshead of rum a day, while New York had twelve such refineries.[28] In 1762 nine thousand hogsheads of molasses were officially imported into Massachusetts. If only one-fifth of this amount, calculated at the conservative figure of sixty-three gallons to a hogshead, came from the foreign islands £2,835 in duties should have been collected. Official receipts from the duty on molasses from all the continental colonies for that year were only £718. Since it is likely that more than one-fifth of the nine thousand hogsheads was of foreign origin, the defrauding of the revenue was even greater than these figures indicate.[29]

Modern historians are in accord as to the Molasses Act: evasion of its provisions was persistent and general. Observance of the other Acts of Trade in this period is a more controversial question. In the most recent work on the subject, O. M. Dickerson comments as follows: "When all the known evasions are consolidated and compared with the known legitimate trade, the proportion of irregular trade is exceedingly small. Writers seem to assume that the occasional case of smuggling was representative of general conditions. There is no adequate foundation for such assumptions." [30]

In his pioneer work in this field G. L. Beer, perhaps more wisely, noted that the "chief evasions were connected with the Molasses Act; but in addition it became apparent that the trade with the enemy was also to some extent connected with the direct importation of European goods from foreign countries." [31] More cautiously, Lawrence Harper concludes that as far as exportations were concerned "illicit trade constituted only a small fraction of the legitimate commerce." On the question of the importation of European goods Harper tends to support "the hypothesis that the inward trade was reasonably law-abiding." [32]

A quantitative answer to this problem is of course impossible. Illegal trade does not leave official records. Yet from the evidence available it is possible to suggest the nature, if not the exact extent, of illicit activities. At least the type of information available to the English government can be ascertained. For the rest only general, and undoubtedly controversial, conclusions may be offered.

Many of the objections raised by such writers as Dickerson to the high estimates sometimes given of the amount of smuggling can be answered easily. Dickerson points to the fact that during the later period of nonimportation agreements there was a real scarcity of goods in common use. But this of course was after the British had tightened their methods of enforcement of the Acts and hardly applies to the previous years. Again he stresses the "nature of the offerings of merchants advertised in the newspapers." Such evidence is not conclusive, because prohibited goods were liable to seizure even after importation if indications of illegal entry were discovered, and it is not to be expected that the merchants would indict themselves in public print.[33]

More generally Dickerson bases his arguments on the more than six hundred percent increase in British exports to the colonies between 1700 and 1770, which may be coupled with the fact that after the Revolution American trade still continued to concentrate on England. However, such evidence merely indicates that most of the colonial trade may have centered naturally on Great Britain, which was unquestionably in advance of the other European countries commercially and industrially. It bears no relation to the matter of the effectiveness of enforcement of the Acts of Trade. Evasion, if it occurred, would involve those items which England herself could not supply as readily or as cheaply as other nations. Information on the trade in these goods is a logical method for arriving at a decision as to the extent to which the Acts, and the customs service, determined the course of trade.

Generally speaking, the opportunities for illegal trade were considerable. The customs officials were few in number and weak in authority. The American coast line was extensive and exposed; as the Commissioners reported, it was "impossible to appoint Officers at every Creek & River."[34] For long periods the English were indifferent to, or diverted from, problems of colonial administration. In such a situation many peculiar practices developed.

Composition of seizures has been mentioned earlier.[35] Not only were successful condemnations hard to achieve because of the weakness of the Admiralty courts and the prejudices of the local juries, but the customs officers were members of the communities in which they resided and had to think of their personal relationships as well. As one Providence merchant pointed out to an eager young officer, he should remember that "he an't out of the reach of wantg the favr of this town."[36] Such pressure could be remarkably effective.

The testimony of Timothy Orne of Salem earlier indicated how the duties on molasses were compounded for a fraction of the real amount. This same merchant provided a glimpse of another aspect of the illicit trade. After cautioning his captain about the changes in enforcement of the Molasses Act, Orne advised him to buy cotton, cocoa, cables, anchors, cordage, and canvas instead of molasses. These items Orne suggested should be sent "Home a little in a Vessel as Stores for the Vessel that bring them." [37] This use of ship's stores was one of the flagrant abuses of this period, since every vessel was entitled to carry a certain amount of goods as part of its regular supplies. Orne meant that the items he ordered should be divided up and brought back in various ships as part of these "stores." There would be no difficulty in passing small quantities through the customs, and, if necessary, the officers could probably be persuaded, at a reasonable price, to overlook such false entries.

A good general summary of relations between customs officials and merchants in this period was offered by Governor Bernard of Massachusetts, when in 1764 he came to the defense of a collector charged with malfeasance in office. It was unfair, Bernard said, to attack an officer on the grounds of his conduct prior to the reforms of 1764. Since the new instructions had been received this particular collector had been thoroughly faithful to his duty. Previously, like "every other Custom house officer in North America" he had overlooked the importation of foreign sugars and molasses without full payment of the duties. In common with all the others he used to ignore Spanish and Portuguese trading vessels which came in, usually with a cargo of salt, but with small quantities of wine and fruit also. Again, as was the general rule, the collector had accepted presents of lemons and wine from these traders, but, unlike other officers, he had never taken payments offered as an inducement for neglect of duty. Bernard stressed that the failings of this collector were those of the system in general and not of that officer in particular.[38]

If such admissions could be offered in defense of the conduct of an official, how much worse the whole truth must have been! The impression derived from such accounts is of a nearly total breakdown of authority prior to 1764. When an officer did perform faithfully it was not necessarily just from the local inhabitants that he could expect trouble. In 1756 Robert Palmer, collector at Bathtown in North Carolina, seized a ship with the approval of the governor and the surveyor general, the vessel being condemned and it, and its cargo of salt, sold at public auction. When the English merchants who had chartered the ship heard this news they threatened to have the collector removed "for doing my duty and Complying with the Acts of Trade." The merchants claimed to have great interest with Sir George Lyttleton, which was probable, since the ship's name was the "Lyttleton"! In October, 1756, Palmer wrote to the secretary of the Treasury, whom he had met, pointing out that he too had some "interest" at home, having obtained his post through the recommendation of the Duke of Queensberry. He pleaded with the secretary to intervene with Sir George for him.[39] However, his efforts were of no avail, as shown by a memo from the Treasury to the Commissioners of the Customs, dated a year later, indicating that a legal action had been commenced against Palmer in England.[40]

Nor were the merchants entirely dependent on the forced or voluntary good will of the officers in their ports. In those days of slow communication authentication of documents was generally impracticable. Consequently forged or false papers were difficult to detect and easy to obtain. In 1748 the Quincy brothers of Boston wrote to one of their captains about goods he was to purchase in Holland. On his way home they advised him to go through the Orkney Islands, where he was to contact Andrew Ross, who was the only "Gentm to be depended upon." Ross specialized in getting vessels "clear'd by the lump for so much wthout unloading." [41] In effect this meant that a Scottish customs official was providing false papers, showing that ships had broken bulk in Great Britain and paid the proper duties as required by law. There was little a colonial officer could do in such a case.

Outright forgeries were evident in another case. In 1759 it was reported from New York that John Cannon and John Pintard of Norwalk, Connecticut, were the "Persons that have Procured most of the fictitious Clearances, from the Customhouse at Newhaven, for the Merchants here." This information was supported by a letter obtained on a pretense from the unsuspecting Cannon and Pintard, who in their own words claimed that they had "got several Vessels Clear'd . . . for Five shillings N. York Currency . . . we have Teen [i.e., ten] Pound for Our Trouble & Expences." [42]

Under the Navigation Acts foreigners were not permitted to trade in the English colonies, but there were ways to avoid that provision also. In 1748 a Dutch ship for a time freely traded in the ports of Jamaica and South Carolina; claiming that the winds prevented her from reaching her destination at Curacao, the vessel obtained permission to dispose of her cargo in Jamaica. The trade was so good that she sailed away and soon returned with more goods which again were sold on the same pretext. Finally the South Carolina officials put an end to her career and had her condemned.[43]

Such flagrant violations were not really necessary. Charter parties were an easier and more subtle method. In 1758 Lieutenant Governor James De Lancey of New York reported on the case of a ship belonging to a merchant of Boston, Joseph Rhodes, who had arranged to have "a Charter Party . . . drawn between him and one John Hodgson of Amsterdam." Supposedly the ship was engaged by Hodgson to carry goods from Holland to St. Johns in the West Indies. In fact the cargo of tea, rope yarn, and other items, was "an improper Cargoe for the West Indies," and care was taken before the ship left Holland to obtain permission for a stopover at Rhode Island on the way to St. Johns to receive instructions from Rhodes on "how to proceed after the End of the Voyage." Rhode Island was out of the way, and there had been plenty of time for such orders to have been given before the ship sailed. That Rhode Island, not Boston, where Rhodes lived, was chosen as the stopping point is evidence enough of the real intentions here. As De Lancey pointed out, the purpose of these "pretended" charter parties was by securing "liberty to touch at one of the English Ports on this Continent" to "privately land their Cargoes in fraud of the laws of Trade." This particular ship was seized and taken into New York; but condemnation was impossible since nothing could be said to be forfeited until actually landed. Since the Navigation Acts came under the category of penal statutes they had to be "construed Strictly & cannot be extended by an equitable Construction."[44]

Peter Faneuil of Boston presents an interesting case. As reported, "he seems to have been a factor rather than (or at least as much as) an independent merchant and the correspondents on whose cargoes he earned his largest commissions were Frenchmen."[45] Some of the goods he handled arrived in New England in French ships, which, to avoid the hazards of this illegal activity, were provided with two sets of papers and even "by putting two alternative masters, English and French, in command of her."[46] Detection of such frauds was difficult, as many of the ships concerned had been built and registered originally in New England, their sale to foreigners not necessarily being recorded. Robert

147

Dinwiddie called attention to this trade in 1736 when he reported that the French and Dutch bought colonial built and registered ships, keeping the registers, and with a few British sailors carried on a commerce with the American colonies.[47]

If intimidation or corruption of customs officers, the purchase of false papers, or secret agreements with foreign merchants was not enough, clandestine landings were always possible. Former Governor Charles Hardy of New York, on taking leave of his province in 1757, summed up his experiences in regard to its trade: it was common practice for vessels "to come from Holland, stop at Sandy Hook, and smuggle their Cargoes to New York, and carry their Vessels up empty." There was no requirement that ships could not pass through customs in ballast, so that the only hope of stopping this trade was to detect the smugglers in the act of landing the goods. Hardy reported that he had attempted to arrest this evil practice, but the merchants merely "took another Course, by sending their Vessels to . . . Connecticut." The goods were easily brought into New York from that neighboring colony.[48]

Once again confirmation of this official complaint may be found in the papers of various merchants. In 1736 James Browne wrote one of his captains "to bring too [i.e., stop] down the river and send your cargo some to Road Island and some up here in boats, so as not to bring but a few hhds up to my wharf." [49] Browne was concerned with molasses, but his use of coasting vessels or "lighters" was typical. Thomas Hancock, uncle to the famous John, was deeply involved in the Dutch trade, with the Hopes of Amsterdam acting as his agents there. Hancock exercised great care that no intimation of his activities should leak out. To one of his captains who was in Holland he wrote, "neither bring so much as a Letter for anybody here, but what shall come under Cover to me & be Carefull that your people bring no Letters neither for any one." Hancock added, "when you have finished your Business proceed for Cape C[od] New England, speak with nobody upon your passage if you c[an] possibly help it." The reason the captain was to stop at Cape Cod was to unload his cargo, which would be brought up later to Boston by Joshua Atkins or some other good man who "will doe the Business faithfully." [50]

Such were some, but by no means all, of the possibilities and methods for evasion. The question of the content and the volume of such trade remains, the first being the easier point to answer. In fact a generalization on the content of illegal trade in this period is even possible: the goods involved were those which at a given moment England could not, or would not through its tax policies, supply as plentifully or as cheaply as other areas. Other than molasses, most of these items were procured through Holland or the Dutch islands in the West Indies.

This conclusion is easily illustrated, the Hancocks of Boston again providing a case study. Until 1737 Thomas Hancock seemingly had little to do with illicit trade. One of the major items in his business, paper, came from Holland; but the operation of the drawback system in England made it possible to obtain the Dutch paper through his agents in England for a reasonable price. At the time English paper was neither so good nor so plentiful as that from Holland. Unfortunately in 1737 the drawback on Dutch paper was stopped. Hancock soon engaged in a direct trade with Holland, while his orders for paper from London fell off correspondingly.[51]

Gunpowder was another important item in this trade. As Governor George Clinton of New York reported in 1752, the consumption of gunpowder was very great in the colonies, "where every Man is in the daily use of fire arms, and yet it will be found, that the exportation of Gunpowder from Great Britain, cannot to any degree answer such an Expence." [52] The demand for this commodity in the plantations was greater than England could supply, with much of the gunpowder coming from Holland.

In 1739 Archibald Kennedy, collector of New York, seized some casks of gunpowder which were discovered aboard a pilot boat off his port. It was proved in court that the powder had been brought from St. Eustatia in the ship *Mary and Margaret* and "unladen from her between Sandy-Hook and the Narrows, and put on board the said Pilot Boat." The *Mary and Margaret* and the casks were tried in the Admiralty court, but a common law prohibition nullified the whole legal action.[53] Eighteen years later gunpowder was one of the major items imported from Holland which disturbed Governor Hardy so much,[54] while, in the tense months before the outbreak of the Revolution, this trade was to take on a desperate quality, as the colonists prepared for the possibility of hostilities.[55]

Along with ammunition, tea was a standard commodity in the illicit trade. Even O. M. Dickerson agrees that this item was worth the risk of smuggling, reporting that at no time "prior to 1767 was the probable saving of British customs duties by smuggling less than a shilling per pound, and on several occasions it was at least three shillings per pound." [56] The reason for this situation was that tea was used as a source of revenue by the English government. Certain drawbacks were allowed on exportation to the colonies, but the basic customs duties collected in England were not. Consequently tea from England was generally more expensive than from elsewhere. It was included in the cargo of almost every ship seized or examined on suspicion of involvement in illegal trade. That tea should later play such an immediate role in the breakup of the empire seems only proper.

Other items appear from time to time in this trade. Canvas, important to the shipbuilding industry, was listed regularly in the ships' cargoes and in the merchants' orders placed abroad. Coffee and cocoa brought about Thomas Hancock's first serious brush with the customs officers. [57] Both cocoa and canvas figured in the orders Timothy Orne gave to his captain in the West Indies. [58] The other commodities Orne suggested as possible purchases — cotton, cordage, anchors, and cables — appear occasionally. Much of the commerce must have centered on the luxury trade, including wines and French brandies. In 1742 William Bollan of New England wrote that from Holland his area was supplied with "Reels of Yarn or spun Hemp, paper, Gunpowder, Iron and Goods of various sorts used for Men and Women's Clothing." To make his point more effectively, Bollan closed by saying, "I need only to acquaint you that I write this clad in a Superfine French Cloth, which I bought on purpose that I might wear about the Evidence of these Illegal Traders." [59]

All this information concerns the inward trade. What did the colonists export? For the commodities obtained through the West Indies the answer is obvious. The colonists supplied the foreign islands with provisions. One such cargo reportedly contained fifty-one boxes of spermaceti candles, six thousand bricks, eleven thousand shingles, one thousand staves, eleven hundred hoops, onions, cutlery wares, cheese, bread, beef and pork. [60] The ships carrying these goods might themselves be part of the trade; Timothy Orne's captain was instructed to sell his vessel, along with her contents, if a satisfactory price could be arranged. [61]

In return, as well as molasses, sugar, and rum, or European goods, bills of credit might be accepted. These in turn could be used to pay for goods purchased directly from Holland. A letter from Thomas Hancock to his agents, the Hopes of Amsterdam, illustrates yet another aspect of this direct trade. In 1742 Hancock wrote that he was sending a "Cargo of Choise Good New River Chipt wood" which he expected to bring a better "price than Commonly wood is sold at." Also he shipped twelve bags of cotton which he had obtained at St. Eustatia, and "Eight hundred Horns." One of his ships was to be sold in Holland as well. In exchange he wanted various items, including "a Sett of Riging for a Brigantine or Snow." Further he asked the Hopes "what Sorts of flowered Silks & Damasks may be had with you." [62] William Bollan's "Superfine French Cloth" may well have come over in one of Hancock's ships during this period.

Presumably a certain number of staple items found their way to Europe in this commerce. It was reported that rice from South Carolina was being carried to Holland by ships from Rhode Island.[63] Certainly there was no reason for these ships to go empty to Europe. On the other hand it was perfectly possible for them to carry their enumerated cargoes to England, unload them there, and then proceed to Holland. Consequently the loss to England from this aspect of the trade may have been less than it would appear. Drawbacks and bounties helped to center most of the tobacco, rice, and indigo trade on England.[64] It was the introduction of European goods directly into the colonies which seemed to disturb the authorities for the most part.

Discussion of the form and the content of the illicit trade suggests certain conclusions as to its volume. The commerce in itself was in the nature of a supplement to regular trade, the merchants adjusting their activities to the needs and the profits of the moment. At no point, except possibly in the frantic months preceding the outbreak of the Revolution, did illicit trade even approach the legitimate English trade in volume or value. Even such an inveterate participant as Thomas Hancock handled most of his affairs through his London agents, and his ventures in Holland were carried on with their knowledge and aid — which would hardly have been the case had Hancock's Dutch involvements been other than a fringe activity — with the major share of his commercial transactions being centered on Great Britain.[65]

The major importance of illicit trade lay not in its volume but in its effect. The evidence suggests that the colonial merchants were restrained from such activities by the economic advantages of trade with England rather than by enforcement of the laws. When evasion was profitable, it was usually possible; the colonists could indulge in it with relative freedom. The consequences were serious, since a general disrespect for law was a logical result. The customs service, as well as the other branches of the English administration, was affected accordingly.

In 1752 Governor Clinton of New York wrote that his province was controlled by "Merchants, who find their private advantage in the breach of these Laws, they must of consequence do all they can to weaken the Administration by which these laws are to be put in execution." Officials were made "Sensible that the only way for them to prosper, or to be rewarded, is by a Neglect of their Duty, and that they must Suffer by a performance of it." Such intimidation extended "from a Judge to a Constable, and from a Governor to a Tidewaiter." Clinton added, "It is not easy to imagine, to what an enormous hight this transgression of the Laws of Trade goes in North America." [66]

Rhode Island was a prime example of the cumulative effects of these factors. A proprietary colony, it had long been a source of trouble to the English but its charter rights were still intact. The governor therefore was "the Creature of the People & his Naval Officer . . . the same . . . both lyable to be removed at the next Annual Election in Case by any Unpopular Act they incur the Displeasure of the Freemen." [67] An attempt was made to correct one of these faults by appointing a naval officer from England, Leonard Lockman, who although originally a "Native of Hanover" had lived for many years in Barbados. Later, he had moved to the continent but had been "Cast away twice" in hurricanes on trips to the Indies. In consideration of his "hard Case" he was given the naval office in Rhode Island in 1743. The appointment proved of little use. Lockman reported that upon his arrival he "met with the greatest Obstacles & repeated Interruptions from the Governor & General Court . . . who would not even admit the Oaths to be administered." Lockman shortly requested a new assignment.[68]

The other officer on whom enforcement of the Acts of Trade depended, the royal collector, was not even present in the colony; he "rented" his post to an unauthorized deputy, whose activities are illustrated in a letter that came to the attention of the legislature in Jamaica in 1749 when some correspondence between a French merchant of Dominica and merchants in Rhode Island was uncovered in a seizure case. The Frenchman wrote that he had put on board one of his ships some barrels of lemons and oranges for the deputy collector's wife and that he would send her "Plats de fayance" as soon as possible. Relations were so safe and friendly that Cholet, the merchant from Dominica, planned to visit Rhode Island himself "au mois de Mars prochain." [69]

The English authorities were fully informed on these affairs. If they took no action it was not from want of advice. In 1743 Governor Shirley of Massachusetts wrote that the illicit trade was such that "without the speedy Interposition of the Parliament to stop it, it must be highly destructive . . . and finally weakening the Dependance which the British Northern Colonies ought to have upon their Mother Country." To him it seemed that the trade might grow "to so strong an Head as that it will be no easy Matter wholly to subdue it." [70]

In the same year William Bollan reported that "there has lately been carried on here a large Illicit Trade . . . by importing into this Province large Quantities of European Goods of almost all sort from divers parts of Europe." Bollan referred specifically to the men who acted in the colonies as factors for Dutch merchants. [71] Five years later Shirley warned that such advice as he and Bollan had previously offered should not be ignored: "Persons upon the Spot seem to have better Opportunities of discovering by Experience of the Operation of those Acts, & the various Mischiefs arising . . . from Illicit Trade than the best Judges can have at a Distance." [72]

In 1752 the governor of New York advised that examination might show that "Holland and Hamburgh receive more benefitt from the Trade to the Northern Colonies, than Great Brittain does, after the expence that Great Brittain is at, when their support is deducted." [73] Specifically referring to the customs service, the governor of New Jersey in 1754 reported that "as there are many Creeks and Rivers at distances from them, illegal trade may be carried on beyond their power to prevent it." [74]

Along with reports on the situation numerous recommendations for corrective action were continually forwarded to London. Such reports ranged from the specific to the general, much of the later reform program being anticipated in this correspondence. One consistent complaint concerned the Admiralty courts. Governor Shirley of Massachusetts, for many years advocate general in New England, was particularly outspoken on this subject. He was disturbed that not all offenses were within the jurisdiction of these courts, observing that there was little hope for improvement until "all Branches of the Acts of Trade or at least those of 15 Car II cap. 7" were subjects for Admiralty consideration.[75]

William Bollan recognized this difficulty and many others as well. Having cases under 15 Car II heard in common law courts merely meant "trying one Illicit Trader by his Fellows, or at least by his well-wishers." Further, the geography of the country was such that there were numerous places to land goods clandestinely, while corruption was so ingrained in the character of the colonial merchants that their oaths were worth nothing. To correct these failings Bollan recommended that the Admiralty courts be given jurisdiction over all offenses under the Navigation Acts, which would require an Act of Parliament, since the colonial courts had questioned Admiralty jurisdiction and stopped all actions by common law prohibitions. Of interest because of later events, Bollan urged that actions of detinue be brought against importers of prohibited goods. Such a change would mean that personal actions could be initiated against offenders themselves instead of merely against the goods and vessels involved.[76]

Robert Auchmuty too recommended extension of Admiralty jurisdiction. But equally important to him was evasion of the Molasses Act and the inability of the small customs staff to cover more territory. Correctly he interpreted the high duties of the Molasses Act to mean a total prohibition of trade to the foreign islands, "to avoid wch the Unfair Traders Strain their Inventions." If such duties "were Lowered in proportion as not greatly to Exceed ye Contingent charges of Running" smuggling would be much reduced. A second result would be a fund created by increased revenues "sufficient to pay Sallaries for severall Preventive Officers, who now are wanting." [77]

In recognizing the necessity of coupling any movement for reform with the creation of a general fund Auchmuty was not alone. Many years earlier Archibald Cummings had written at length on the subject, pointing out exactly how such a fund could be raised.[78] Some of these ideas had since penetrated to London itself. In 1744 the governor of New York reported that two documents published and circulated in England had been called to his attention, one of which concerned the means for advancing and protecting settlement in the colonies, while the other urged establishing, by Act of Parliament, stamp duties in all the colonies. With great insight Clinton warned that the "people in North America are quite Strangers to any Duty but such as they raise themselves and was such a scheme to take place without their Knowledge it might prove a dangerous consequence to his Majestys Interest." [79]

Nor was the pamphlet that so concerned Clinton the only writing on this subject. Many of Archibald Cummings' proposals were echoed in a document which suggested various ways to raise a fund for defense in the colonies. In fact, Henry McCulloh, the probable author of this scheme, might well have been familiar with Cummings' plan. His fourteen point program recommended a six pence tax on rum and other liquors distilled in the plantations, a three pence duty on molasses, a tax on slaves imported, an excise on liquor sold in America, a poll tax, and a stamp tax. With other duties the author expected his plan to raise the improbable sum of £327,000. [80]

Another report, also probably from the pen of McCulloh, urged that anyone assisting an illicit trader be severely punished, that anyone resisting a customs officer pay a £500 fine, and that all land be surveyed so that it might be properly taxed. [81] The most remarkable proposal associated with the above schemes was that the various governors should appoint, or have elected, delegates to go to England to sit in Parliament. At least the author was aware that colonial approval was a necessity for such plans. More practically it was recommended that the Board of Trade be given increased powers so as to centralize the administration of the colonies. [82]

Beside the question of Admiralty jurisdiction previously mentioned, and the shortage of officers, attention frequently was called to the problem of fees. In spite of the earlier pleas for action this matter had remained unchanged, the local authorities acting as they wished. The legal adviser to the Board of Trade in 1737 reported that the "practice of lessening the Fees of the Officers appointed by the Crown prevailes so much in the Colonys abroad that . . . His Majesty's Gracious intentions . . . must be soon entirely defeated." [83] So little weight was given to this report that sixteen years later the Treasury did not even know what the policy on fees really was; they had to ask the Customs Board for advice.

The Commissioners replied that it was usual for the fees of officials in the colonies to be regulated by the local assemblies and approved by the Privy Council. The Treasury finally sent their particular problem to the Board of Trade for further study.[84]

From the earliest years the various governors had asked for more active support from the royal navy. Certain ships were stationed off the colonial coast; from time to time they played a part in seizure cases. Unfortunately they were few in number, and relations between the Navy and the customs officers were never of the best.[85] Part of the problem lay in the right of the customs officers to act as informers in all trials involving evasion of the Acts of Trade. A suggestion was offered to correct this fault also; in 1749 William Bollan added to his previous recommendations by urging that all royal ships of war be authorized to make seizures on their own and that the proceeds from successful prosecutions so initiated might be distributed one-half to the captain and crew of such ships.[86] Later this idea was to figure prominently in the reforms of 1764. For the moment it was ignored.

More generally this same William Bollan expressed explicitly the feelings of many of the colonial officials when he complained that the Acts of Trade themselves were a source of great trouble: they were vague and contradictory. Provision by provision Bollan analyzed the Acts and pointed to their deficiencies. While there were enough specific problems to warrant action, there was one fundamental reason for Parliament to gather all the various regulations into one great uniform Act. The Navigation Acts legally were penal statutes; as such, their provisions had "to be taken strictly and not by Intendment." Simply put, this fact meant that there could be no flexibility in interpretation of the Acts. Their words had to be considered literally and the intent of the authors could play no part in legal decisions. As Bollan said, "the Freedom of Navigation & Commerce given by the Common Law shall not be understood to be taken away, and new Rules to be enforced by heavy Penalties . . . without clear & express Laws for the purpose." [87] Too often in the past English legal opinion had decided that administrative efforts to implement the Acts in one way or another violated some provision of the law.[88] To prevent legal complications from nullifying the operation of the Navigation Acts in the future the intervention of Parliament once again was required, to consolidate and clarify beyond a shadow of a doubt the basic provisions of the laws.

These and other problems continually were called to the attention of the home authorities. It would be incorrect to say that these reports had no effect. Sporadically the English government took notice of the situation and went through the motions of taking action, as indicated in the circular sent in 1750 by the surveyor general southern to the collectors under his supervision which noted that "Upon an information that great Quantities of European and East Indian Commodities, particularly Linnen and Tea, are run into his Majesty's Plantations in America by the French, and Dutch, and others, the Commissioners of the Customs have directed me to use my utmost Endeavours to prevent these Frauds for the Future." [89]

More important, in 1748 George Dunk, Earl of Halifax, became president of the Board of Trade. Halifax, who was associated with the Bedford faction in British politics and had long been an opponent of Robert Walpole, was an ambitious, energetic, and able official. Under his guidance an attempt was made to correct some of the numerous defects in the system by restoring the power and authority of the Board. By 1752 Halifax had obtained a royal Order in Council entrusting control of correspondence with the governors and patronage rights (excepting those belonging to the Customs and Admiralty departments) to his Board.[90] Some of the words of this Order might have been taken bodily from earlier reports from the colonies. The governors were told that for "the greater regularity and dispatch of business" it had been decided that "correspondence be confined to, and pass through, but one channel."

In 1750 the West Indies planters took advantage of the revived status of the Board of Trade in an attempt to secure enforcement of the Molasses Act. They asked that the northern colonies be prohibited from importing molasses and sugar from any foreign settlement, that ships of war be empowered to search any merchant vessel, that the royal captains and crews be allowed liberal rewards for seizures, that sloops of war be stationed off New England, that customs officers be stimulated to action by greater rewards and penalties, and that the governors might be exhorted to do their best to stop such trade.[91] As usual, however, the hearings at the Board revolved into a protracted contest between the sugar planters and the agents for the northern colonies, with the result that all the arguments were referred to the various colonies for consideration, and no further action was taken.[92] An appeal to Parliament was equally ineffectual.

Halifax's elaborate plans for the Board, in fact, were short-lived. By accepting collaboration with the Pelhams he had alienated the Duke of Bedford, who had great influence with the king. A necessity for Halifax's hopes was a seat in the cabinet and access to the king; only with those rights could Halifax maintain equal status with the Secretary of State. Bedford saw to it that his request was refused. On leaving office as Secretary of State the Duke reportedly told the king that as soon as he was gone "one considerable part of it, America, was to be lopp'd off, & thrown into the hands of the first Commissr of trade, Lord Halifax," which was being done "to promote the Scheme of engrossing all power to *Them* & their Creatures." [93] In effect Bedford warned the king that it would be a diminution of his royal authority to suffer powers to be transferred from the Secretary of State, who was under immediate royal control, to a more independent agency such as the Board of Trade. All the Duke of Newcastle could thereafter report to Halifax was that he had tried but that the king absolutely refused to receive the president of the Board into the cabinet council.[94] A few more years of fruitless activity by the Board followed. Then in 1754 the struggle for control of the Ohio Valley began, and colonial administrative problems gave way to more pressing concerns.[95]

The temporary revival and speedy eclipse of the Board of Trade was a fitting commentary on these long years of inaction. Recognition of the importance of alterations in colonial affairs had supported Halifax's attempt to increase the prestige of his department; political considerations, and a French war, caused his plans to fail. Halifax's experience suggests that three essential changes were to be required before the English government could be stimulated to take effective action in the colonial field: the continual warfare had to end, the need for a strengthening of the colonial system had to gain general acceptance, and a realignment of English political groups had to be achieved. All these factors were to be realized between 1758 and 1763. Thereafter reform was possible — and probable.

However, the men who in 1763 undertook to consolidate England's great empire might have done well to ponder the heritage of years of neglect. In 1743 a report on the non-enforcement of the Acts of Trade had concluded with the prophecy that if the situation were allowed to continue, "the Illicit Traders will by their Numbers, Wealth and Wiles have got such power in these parts that Laws and Orders may come too late from Great Britain to have their proper Effect against it." [96] Twenty years later this forecast was a reality. If there was any moral to the history of these years it was that reform, when it came, was not to be easily accomplished.

VIII

Reform

THE freedom with which the American colonists evaded the Acts of Trade and Navigation from time to time may have been of momentary concern to the English authorities, but one particular aspect of the illegal commerce persistently and increasingly irritated the British. With only six years of peace between 1739 and 1763 much of this trade was in the form of direct communication with England's declared enemies in time of war. Such activities appeared to the English as not only illegal but traitorous. Eventually anger led to action, and a start was made on the road to reform.

The first reports on this trade were made as early as the War of Jenkins' Ear. In 1743 it was noted that Spanish goods were being introduced into the colonies, a commerce that was handled by naturalized French refugees living in the English plantations. Under cover of forged documents they visited the Spanish possessions as subjects of the French king; once the transactions were completed, they put aside that disguise and resumed their role as English colonists, importing the goods into the continental plantations. It was even suggested that this commerce extended to direct trade with Spain itself.[1]

With the entry of France into the war the problem was compounded, since the northern colonists were accustomed to securing great quantities of molasses and sugar in the French islands. Provisions were the medium of exchange. Yet to supply the French with such items enabled the enemy to withstand the efforts of the British navy to starve them into submission. Such trade may have been an economic necessity for the northern colonies, but in another sense it was a flagrant violation of their duty as English subjects. A variety of maneuvers were employed to disguise this commerce.

The most common excuse involved prisoners of war. In the leisurely atmosphere of eighteenth century warfare, exchanges of prisoners were frequently arranged. Transport was of course required. Under a flag of truce ships would carry the prisoners to an agreed place of exchange. The possibilities of the situation were obvious. The French needed supplies; the colonists needed the trade. An accommodation was easily reached. In 1748 Governor Shirley reported that over a period of eighteen months sixty vessels had sailed from New England, primarily from Rhode Island, to the French islands. One solitary French prisoner on board was thought to be enough excuse. Were this trade stopped, Shirley said, the enemy islands would soon have to capitulate, as had almost happened in the case of Martinique towards the end of Queen Anne's War.[2]

What was an irritant in the War of the Austrian Succession became a major concern in the next conflict. In June, 1757, Lieutenant Governor De Lancey of New York forwarded evidence of "a pernicious Trade," which he reported was handled in this manner: "The Method they take is to go to Monti Christo [i.e., Monte Christi], a Spanish Port in Hispaniola, where the Master and Mariners stay, and they get a Master and a Crew of Spaniards to go with a Pass to Port Dauphin, or some other French Port . . . By this indirect Way his Majesty's Enemies are supplyed. What Remedy to apply to this Evil may be difficult to say."[3]

The depositions De Lancey enclosed in his letter showed that during seven and one-half months fourteen ships from Boston and Rhode Island visited Santo Domingo. One captain was a Dutchman living in Rhode Island; another was a Frenchman who had married and settled in that colony, while yet another Frenchman, who had a wife and family in New York, had moved to Monte Christi to handle the business of the New England merchants there. Along with the New England ships, a large Spanish vessel came in with flour and provisions obtained "at and from Philadelphia"; another ship came from Jamaica with beef from Ireland.[4]

Two weeks after De Lancey sent his letter, Governor Hardy of New York forwarded his own report, including evidence that a ship from New Jersey had gone to the Dutch island of St. Eustatia with provisions for the French. Testimony taken from two crew members from another vessel, the *Speedwell* of Rhode Island, showed how they had gone to Christi and sold provisions there and at Havana as well.[5] What had happened was quite simple. A system of "free ports" had sprung up to supplement the flag of truce trade.

St. Eustatia, a neutral island belonging to the Dutch, at the beginning of the war served as a center for trade between the colonists and the French. Under English law, provisions were considered contraband goods in wartime. To avoid the charge of dealing in contraband items, the Americans shipped their provisions to the Dutch island, where in turn the French gathered their molasses. Unfortunately for the Dutch the English made an early effort to break this trade. Arguing that in peacetime the French did not allow foreigners to trade with their islands, the British declared such trade between the Dutch and the French could not be permitted in time of war. Under the "Rule of 1756" the English government authorized seizure of Dutch ships engaged in this commerce, and the navy was employed to make the order effective.[6] As a result the trade at St. Eustatia was considerably reduced.

As soon as that victory was achieved, the British were confronted with another problem. The Spanish also were at that point neutrals, and Monte Christi on the island of Hispaniola was declared a "free port" by Spain. Between 1757 and 1760 the trade at Monte Christi assumed fantastic proportions. It was estimated in 1760 that between four and five hundred ships had taken on cargoes of French molasses there in one year.[7] According to one British admiral, "the newly established free Port of Monto Christi . . . exists no where, but in the airy Regions of Imagination," since there "is here No City, No Town, No Port" but only a few huts.[8] Eventually, after numerous legal difficulties, the "Rule of 1756" was extended to cover the Monte Christi trade. By 1761, for a moment at least, that commerce too was greatly restricted by the activities of the British navy.

Meanwhile during those same years the old flag of truce trade also flourished. In September, 1758, Governor Francis Fauquier of Virginia reported that Rhode Island still carried on a regular trade in prisoners: "The Rhode Island Men knowing there were 60 french prisoners at Boston, sent four Ships from Providence to Boston at their own Expence, and put fifteen on board each ship by which they skreen'd four Cargoes of provisions . . . to Port au Prince." A captured letter from a Frenchman on one of the islands added force to the governor's claim that the English war effort was seriously damaged by this trade: "Every day we are on the verge of great want; without the help of our enemies we would be obliged to live, as you told us, on what the colony produces. Our condition is hard . . . we know very well that it is not within the power of French commerce to aid us." [9]

As late as October, 1760, acting governor Cadwallader Colden of New York wrote that he was convinced that "the Merchants in this place have been too generally concerned in this illegal trade, & that the merchants of Philadelphia have been more so." In this instance Colden referred not to the flag of truce trade but to another, more immediately concerned with the customs service. According to Colden the officers in Connecticut, Rhode Island, and New Jersey aided and abetted the New York merchants by providing them with certificates of cancellation for their bonds given in New York. The provisions would be shipped from New York to the other colonies, where a certificate of landing would be given. There seems to have been no problem in shipping the goods onward from those three colonies to the French islands. "Besides this," Colden added, "I make no doubt, provisions are privately sent off, from some of the many ports on this coast where there are no officers. The officers of the customs assure me, that clandestine illegal trade cannot otherwise be prevented, than by Cruisers properly Stationed." [10] In the same year that Colden made this report Pitt sent a circular letter to all the governors on the subject of "illegal and most pernicious Trade" carried on with the French and ordered them to put a stop to it immediately. [11]

Actually, reports on the contraband trade had already had important effect in England. Events started in 1757 were to lead in a direct line to the Sugar Act and the reforms of 1764. A notation in the *Journal* of the Board of Trade, under the date of November 3, 1757, records that, after reading letters from Governor Hardy and Lieutenant Governor De Lancey of New York, the Board decided to undertake a general investigation of illegal trade in the colonies. Their secretary was ordered to search the files and present to the Board all papers received at any time from the colonies on that subject. [12]

The results of the secretary's labors were embodied in copies or extracts from twenty-six letters, ranging in date from 1739 to 1758. The first was from Lieutenant Governor George Clarke of New York in which he said that "if some Method be not fallen upon whereby Illicit Trade may be better prevented, I doubt it will be to little purpose to bring any cause . . . to tryall by a Jury, and the Officers of the Customs will from thence be discouraged from exerting themselves in . . . their duty." [13] The last was the letter from Governor Fauquier cited above. In between were reports from the judge of the Admiralty in New England, the governors of New York, Massachusetts, New Hampshire, and various of the islands, and private parties. Prominently placed were the communications from William Bollan discussed earlier.[14] The total import of these letters was that much was wrong in the colonies and that corrective action was badly needed. These twenty-six letters represented a choice selection from the files of the most informed of all the English departments on colonial affairs.[15]

It was a critical year of the war, and there were many distractions. But by November, 1758, the Board had considered their secretary's report. Because so many of the questions raised touched upon the revenue, the Board decided to consult the Commissioners of the Customs. A draft of a letter to the Commissioners was ready in that same month, but unfortunately for the Board of Trade at this point they touched upon a sensitive question of interdepartmental relations.

Years earlier, in the reign of Queen Anne, when Sidney Godolphin had been Lord Treasurer, the Board of Trade had been prohibited from carrying on a direct correspondence with the Customs Commissioners, an action which had resulted from Godolphin's determination to put the Board in its proper place and to preserve the powers of his own office.[16] Now this tradition caused a major delay in the Board's investigation. Anticipating some difficulty the Board again searched in its files and found precedents for their request. Correspondence from 1730 through 1737 showed that, although the Commissioners had once informed the Board that they would not give their opinion on colonial acts of assembly "unless they are Commanded by the King in Council or the Lords of the Treasury," they eventually had conceded the point and actually had attended some of the Board's meetings.[17]

The Commissioners of the Customs were not easily convinced. When they finally did receive the Board's letter in February, 1759, they wrote to the Treasury that they had heard directly from the Board and that the practice in the past had been for them to answer the Board only through the indirect channel of the Treasury.[18] This policy was continued and the Commissioners' reply to the query from the Board of Trade was handled by the Treasury.

The letter from the Board explained to the Commissioners that they had the workings of the Acts of Trade under consideration, and that great difficulties were apparent. The Board wanted to know if the Commissioners had received any communications from their officers "of any Doubts and Difficulties attending the Execution of the said Laws." Copies of the twenty-six letters were also forwarded to the Commissioners and they were requested to report on them "so far as concerns His Majesty's Revenue of Customs, and the Conduct of such of their Officers as Superintend the Execution of the Laws . . . whether the Remedies therein proposed are properly adapted to the Evils complained of, or what other measures it may be proper . . . to take." [19]

Meanwhile the Treasury itself had become interested in the question of enforcement of the Navigation Acts in the plantations, the reason for their concern being evinced by their order of October 27, 1957, in which they told the Customs Board to bring their accounts of the gross and net produce of all the duties under their care up to date.[20] The war effort was beginning to take its toll, and the Treasury Lords were uneasy about their ability to meet the financial requirements imposed upon them. Consequently a general tightening of the system was begun.

In line with this policy the secretary to the Duke of Newcastle, then head of the Treasury, in January, 1758, wrote to the Commissioners that the Duke had heard "that the Officers of the Customs in America do receive improper and illegal Fees for conniving at Clandestine Trade, and particularly the Entry of Foreign Rum, and Molasses . . . and that this has been done particularly at Boston for many years last past." [21] The Commissioners replied that they would have the matter investigated by their surveyor general and "inform the officers they will by Law be liable to the Penalty of Loss of Employment and double Costs and Damages for taking illegal Fees." [22]

In February the Treasury issued an order that customs officers were to have no more leaves with pay unless such a provision were expressly included in their warrants. Further, in the interest of efficiency, from that time on all requests for leaves were to be referred to the Customs Commissioners for their opinion.[23] The report of the Commissioners on their investigation showed that there was ample evidence of a connection between illegal fees and illegal trade; consequently the Treasury at the same time ordered the Commissioners to investigate further and to suggest methods to correct the evil.[24] In this way pressures from the Board of Trade and the Treasury were combining to force the Commissioners of the Customs to prepare a general report on the colonial service.

On May 10, 1759, the Commissioners of the Customs sent an important document to the Treasury, containing their answer to the Board of Trade's letter and their own general opinions on the colonial service. Referring to the twenty-six letters, the Commissioners said that the problems outlined there could be covered under three headings: 1) importations of rum and molasses from the French islands; 2) imports and exports to and from Europe, "particularly Holland and Hamburgh"; 3) supplies of provisions furnished to the French colonies. The Commissioners added that they could hardly be expected to cover every question that had been raised in the last twenty years but that they could make certain generalizations from the evidence.

As to the importation of rum and molasses, they wrote, "So long as the high Duty on Foreign Rum, Sugar, and Molasses, imposed by the Act of the 8th of his present Majesty (and then intended, We apprehend, as a Prohibition) continues, the running of those goods . . . will be unavoidable . . . and yet it is extremely difficult to forsee, how far it may be expedient to attempt to remedy this Evil by an alteration of this Law, which was passed, at the request of the British planters."

On European goods the Commissioners felt that "the great Extent of the Coast very much favours the running thereof, before the Masters make their Reports at the Customhouse"; a strict check of clearances was the only means to prevent this form of evasion, and their officers had been ordered to perform that duty with great care. In regard to the exportation of enumerated commodities to Europe, there was little the colonial officers could do. Bonds not canceled within eighteen months might be put in suit, but such cases "must be carried on in the ordinary course of proceedings in the Colonies, where it is apprehended, that Verdicts . . . are not so impartial, as in England." Finally, on the supplies of provisions furnished to the French, the Commissioners pointed out that such trade was carried on even from Ireland, which was much further away and more easily supervised from England. If such were the case, it was unreasonable to think that the officers in the colonies could do much to stop that trade.[25]

Attached to the Commissioners' report was a review by their solicitors of one of William Bollan's letters which had discussed points of confusion in the wording of the Acts of Trade. Their discussion of Bollan's specific complaints did little but accentuate the vagueness of the Acts by illustrating the numerous possible interpretations of their provisions. But on two general questions the solicitors did offer advice. Bollan had said that trials by juries were a waste of time; the only remedy he felt was an extension of the power of the Admiralty courts. Also, prosecutions to recover the value of goods illegally imported but dispersed before they could be seized were a necessity. To the first point the solicitors said that they could not express an opinion; it was a matter for Parliamentary action. On the second they agreed that personal actions concerning dispersed goods "may be tryed, but it is conceived such Prosecution must be Commenced within one Year after the Offence, if Prosecuted by a Quitam Action, and within three years if Prosecuted by the King's Advocate for the use of the Crown only." On the subject of general reform of the Acts of Trade, the lawyers revealed the habitual caution of their profession: "We are apprehensive that any Attempt to Alter them for the sake of Correcting small Inaccuracies may be hazardous and attended with dangerous consequences not to be forseen by Us." [26] The solicitors might not have been so restrained had they themselves been faced with the problem of enforcing the confused and complex provisions of the Acts of Trade in the colonies.

Three months after this customs report had been sent to the Treasury, and forwarded by them to the Board of Trade, the Board made its own presentation to the Privy Council. All the northern colonies had been involved in the trade with the French, the Board said, adding that over one hundred and fifty ships from the continent had been found "at one time in the Road of Monte Christi." French ships did not even bother to maintain a pretense of landing their goods on shore but merely loaded them directly on board the American vessels. Whether this trade was facilitated by powers possessed by charter colonies, like Rhode Island, which were inconsistent with the provisions of the Navigation Acts or from "Defects in the framing of those Laws, or from the Neglect and

Corruption of those, whose duty it is to watch over the Execution of them, We cannot take upon us to say." Wherever the fault lay, corrective action was needed.[27]

It was hardly possible in these most crucial years of the war to undertake major alterations in the administrative system. At the same time certain other factors also combined to postpone action. Seventeen hundred fifty-nine was the "Year of Miracles": Quebec, the heart of French North America, fell to Wolfe; Guadaloupe, the gem of the West Indies, was captured by the English. These great victories revived the confidence and enthusiasm of the British, and money was more readily placed at the government's disposal, temporarily quieting the fears of the chronically anxious Duke of Newcastle. The capture of Guadaloupe also eased the problem of trade in foreign molasses, as the produce of that island could now be legally imported free of duty into the colonies. And the increasingly effective control of the Monte Christi trade seemed to promise eventual success in eradicating that evil.

Discussion of enforcement of the Navigation Acts slowed but did not cease. In February and March of 1760 the Treasury considered new information on the Monte Christi trade, which they referred to the Customs Commissioners and the Board of Trade. They also studied carefully the report the Board of Trade had sent the previous year to the king, noting that the Privy Council had the whole matter under examination, so that for the moment no further action on their part was required.[28] A year later, once more at the instigation of the Board of Trade, the Treasury, the Customs Commissioners, and the Board jointly took up consideration of the French trade.[29] At this point, reform obviously was not far away.

What was the attitude of the colonies on the eve of reform? Certainly it was hardly promising. The extent of the wartime trade with the enemy suggested that colonial cooperation was not easily achieved, while various other incidents indicated that any attempt at forceful alteration of existing habits would encounter strenuous opposition. In 1760 two men who attempted to call attention to evasion of the Acts in New York were jailed to keep them quiet.[30] In 1761 the governor of New Jersey reported that the new emphasis on strict observance of the laws was difficult to implement. In one seizure case the master of the ship "by buying off some Evidence and Removing others" made the issue so doubtful that a special settlement had to be arranged.[31] But the most critical situation, as usual, existed in Massachusetts.

The episode of the writs of assistance is a famous part of the history of the Bay Colony. The speech of James Otis in opposition to the application of the customs officers for the issuance of these unrestricted search warrants was credited by John Adams with opening the move towards independence.[32] Astute handling by Thomas Hutchinson, chief justice of the colony, dampened the excitement by the end of 1761, but not before the constitutional basis of relations between England and her colonies had been thrown open to public debate. The arguments over the writs were mainly theoretical and abstract. More concrete was an issue which predated, and contributed to, the attack against the use of the writs.[33]

For many years it had been accepted practice for the customs officers in Massachusetts to use a share of the proceeds from successful condemnations to pay for information leading to the original seizure. To protect informers from reprisals, the customs officials merely told the Admiralty court the amount arranged, and no names were mentioned, the expense being deducted from the gross receipts of the condemnation. It was a system open to flagrant abuses, but from the point of view of the customs service there was much to recommend it. When the treatment of the informers in the case heard in the Admiralty court in 1722 is recalled, the need for secrecy is apparent.[34]

In August, 1760, Benjamin Barons arrived in Boston as the new collector. Earlier in his career, as a London merchant, one of his own ships had been seized and condemned by the customs officers at Boston, which did not necessarily make for friendly relations between Barons and the older customs officers.[35] More important, Barons was out to make his fortune. Previous collectors had done quite well, more through harmonious relations with the community of merchants than through strict attention to duty. The Jekylls, for example, who had been collectors at Boston from 1707 to 1740, had become respected members of the community. When the elder Jekyll died in 1733 the *Boston Weekly Newsletter* reported that "by his courteous Behaviour to the Merchant, he became the Darling of all fair Traders . . . with much Humanity [he] took pleasure in directing Masters of Vessels how they ought to avoid the Breach of the Acts of Trade." [36] Sir Charles Henry Frankland, successor to the Jekylls, had become a leader of Boston society. As had been said by a customs officer earlier, such men were "removed at a great distance" from their superiors and often, "Continuing long in the same place degenerate into Creoles, and at length forget Mother Country and her Interests." [37]

Benjamin Barons, too, sought to ingratiate himself with the local commercial aristocracy, and made no effort to hide his plans. By the middle of October Governor Bernard could report that the collector's intention of allying himself with the colonial faction which was opposed to effective enforcement of the Acts of Trade was common knowledge. Bernard tried unsuccessfully to reason with Barons. Calling in the surveyor general and the judge of the Admiralty court was equally ineffectual.[38] Barons thought he had discovered a way to assume the leadership of the commercial community and he was not to be dissuaded.

The weapon Barons employed was to expose to public view the practice of making secret payments to informers. There was a legal argument on his side. By the Act of 6 George II, the king's one-third share of proceeds under the provisions of that Act were to go to the colony. Deducting the cost of the trials and the expenses of paying for informers had eaten into that share. Consequently Barons charged Charles Paxton, the officer who had been responsible for most of the seizures, with defrauding the province of its rightful money. At his instigation the treasurer of the colony went to the Admiralty court and demanded an accounting of the funds that should have accrued to the province. Meanwhile Barons obtained some of the bills of cost issued by the court to pay informers and showed them about the town to inflame the citizens.[39] Bernard himself was attacked for his opposition to Barons, the charge in his case being misconduct in the issuance of a register for a ship.[40]

A general meeting of the merchants was called and the bills of cost presented to the gathering. Barons wrote Bernard that if he did not approve the resolves issued by the meeting, and also disavow Paxton and his party, his administration would be ruined. Barons' attitude was made clear in the testimony of Ebenezer Richardson, whom Barons charged with being an informer for Paxton. Barons reportedly told Richardson that if he would work for him he would pay more than Paxton. The collector added that although he had many proofs of illegal activities he would not seize the offenders because he did not wish to distress the town and wanted to be free to call the people his friends.[41]

Barons was suspended from his office by the surveyor general, Thomas Lechmere, who told the collector he had done so 1) because Barons had tried to prevent execution of the Laws of Trade, 2) because he had attempted to ruin the effectiveness of the Admiralty courts, 3) because he had tried to intimidate the customs officers, 4) because he had attacked the authority of the governor, 5) because he had been negligent in entering ships, and 6) because he had attempted to rescue a ship seized by Paxton and publicly berated the sheriff who went to Paxton's aid.[42] These seem solid grounds for removal, but the surveyor general wrote to the Commissioners of the Customs that he had not given the full articles of complaint to Barons. Instead he gave him only general headings as above, because Barons was an expert at making use of every scrap of paper to influence public opinion in his favor.[43]

As the result of Barons' activities five legal actions were commenced against the customs officers in Massachusetts. In Barons *v.* Lechmere the collector charged the surveyor general with suspending him on insufficient evidence. Barons even had the aged Lechmere arrested until bail was arranged. In Barons *v.* Cradock the man who was appointed to take Barons' place during his suspension was charged with taking office on insufficient authority. In Barons *v.* Paxton the collector charged Paxton, who was surveyor and searcher, with improperly appealing over the head of his superior to the surveyor general. In Grey *v.* Paxton the colonial treasurer charged Paxton with defrauding of the revenue. And in Erwing *v.* Cradock a man who earlier had been permitted by the Admiralty court to settle a claim against his ship for half value attempted to get back his loss by suing the collector for false action.[44]

Governor Bernard quite correctly was distressed by these events, writing that his first year in office had been employed in defending the customs officers against "the attacks of a party formed & supported by Mr. Barons Collector of this port." The opposition's idea was to ruin the efficiency of the customs service by constant common law actions against individual officers. Bernard warned that "it will depend upon the Vigorous Measures that shall be taken at home for the defence of the Officers, whether there be any Custom House here at all."[45] However, such a total collapse of authority was not yet at hand. The invaluable Thomas Hutchinson, as chief justice, gave the heat of the moment time to abate and then, on appeal, reversed the unfavorable decisions of the lower courts. Only Erwing *v.* Cradock went to London on a further appeal, and an adjustment was arranged in the colony before a final decision on that case was made.[46]

Barons did not lack supporters. Thomas Lechmere, possibly hurried to his grave by his arrest and imprisonment, died in the middle of these events, and his successor, John Temple, for reasons of his own saw to it that the detailed charges Lechmere had kept from Barons were made known. Temple's action was the beginning of a long contest between him and the governor and several of the other customs officials, a power struggle which nullified much of the efficiency of the customs service in the colony for years and which contributed later to the failure of the American Board of Customs Commissioners. Certain Boston merchants also wrote to the Treasury on behalf of Barons, but their support probably did him as much harm as good. Barons' involvement in the meeting of protest was merely coincidental, they said. He had been interested because the crown had been defrauded and they had been concerned because the colony had lost some revenue. In a manner that was to become increasingly popular, the merchants appealed to their English ancestors: "From them we sprang and like them we hate Tyranny." [47] Predictably, Barons was not reinstated in his office.[48]

For one year and a half in Massachusetts in this instance the colonial opposition, making good use of the local courts and exploiting personal rivalries between the royal officers, had effectively frustrated the operation of the customs service. The cause had been a gradual tightening of the English administration in response to wartime conditions. The reaction of the merchant community in Massachusetts should have served as a warning to the English authorities of what could be expected generally in the colonies if and when sudden and more dramatic reforms were inaugurated.

In London, meanwhile, the movement toward reform received new impetus. The official entry of Spain into the war in 1762 revived the conflict in the West Indies, and the provision trade again became a subject of careful scrutiny. In April of that year General Jeffrey Amherst was aroused to indignant protest, complaining to both surveyors general that little could be accomplished as long as the customs officials continued to neglect their duty. Some of them, evidence showed, even assisted the pernicious commerce "by granting Certificates for Cargoes that never were Delivered." Amherst provided the surveyors general with a list of vessels that had purportedly gone to various English colonies but in reality had traded directly with the enemy.[49] Similarly, the commander in chief personally sent a circular letter to the governors stressing the necessity of putting "a stop to such infamous practices, particularly at a time when there is the greatest demand for provisions to supply the King's troops." [50] All these documents were forwarded to London for the enlightenment of the home authorities. Thus, even on the eve of peace, the inconstancy of the American colonists was made painfully evident to the exhausted British. A reason — one which everyone could understand — was added to the staggering size of England's war debts for forcing the colonies to bear their share of the expense. Within a year a complete overhaul of the colonial system was initiated.

Between 1760 and 1763 a series of developments prepared the way for reform of the colonial administration. The Peace of Paris left England the acknowledged mistress of the seas and possessor of one of the great empires of modern times, while the completeness of her victory seemed to assure at least a brief period of peace. At the same time, disgust with the wartime conduct of the colonists, coupled with the seemingly critical size of the national debt, provided a convincing argument for action, one which could be utilized effectively to gain acceptance for the innovations. And, finally, the accession of George III to the throne wrought fundamental alterations in the political establishment in England.

For over thirty years under the cantankerous but malleable George II the Whig politicians, from Walpole to Newcastle, had remained in control as necessary links between the separate poles of Parliamentary and royal power. The new king, intentionally or otherwise, altered that situation. Within five months of the beginning of his reign George III broke the ranks of the professional Whig politicians and placed his tutor, Lord Bute — a man with no substantial contacts in either House — in the cabinet as Secretary of State for the Northern Department.[51] From that moment Bute clearly possessed the "favor of the closet," while Pitt and Newcastle, through their hold on Parliament, still exercised the "power of the cabinet." [52] It was, obviously, an intolerable situation.

It has been said that the "main theme of British domestic politics from 1760 to 1770 is the search for a stable Administration which would command the confidence of both Crown and Parliament." [53] Such was certainly the case after George Grenville lost the support of the king and fell from power in 1765. But between 1762 and 1765 an equilibrium of sorts was achieved for a moment, just long enough to implement the fateful decision to reform the colonial administration. The dictatorial Pitt was driven from office in October, 1761, over the rejection of his proposals for war with Spain. What he could not direct, Pitt said, he would not be responsible for.[54] Newcastle, the arch-type of the outmoded politician, found himself out of office for the first time in over forty years, as he followed Pitt into exile in May, 1762, defeated in a Council meeting on the question of financing the European campaign for that year.

Lord Bute through the favor of the king and the elimination of his rivals thus inherited sole responsibility for the conduct of the administration. The king in effect had made his own prime minister.[55] But Bute, who was no politician, soon found the difficulties of his relationship to Parliament too heavy a burden; shortly after the signing of the Peace of Paris he asked, and was granted, leave to resign. At the king's request, however, Bute "arranged the Ministry which was to succeed him." [56] What was required was a man who knew Parliament. Bute's first choice, Henry Fox, declined to head a new administration, but Pitt's ambitious brother-in-law, George Grenville, was receptive. He took over the Treasury and became first minister in April, 1763. Not so close to the "favor of the closet" as Bute had been, Grenville still temporarily managed to combine the "power" and "favor" in his person. Thus momentarily the political situation was stabilized, and effective action was possible. The moment for reform in colonial administration had arrived.

George Grenville himself over the years has received much of the credit — or blame — for inaugurating the measures which led to the loss of the colonies. Perhaps more than any other man Grenville was horrified by the size of England's debt. Of him it was said that he considered "a National saving of two Inches of Candle" as important as all Pitt's great victories.[57] Within a month of the time he took office the Treasury ordered the Customs Commissioners to explain why the American revenues amounted "in no degree to the Sum wch might be expected from them." [58] But Grenville's role in these events has been exaggerated at the expense of the truth. The movement towards reform — and even the direction chosen — had a deeper base than the whims or fancies of one man.

The Treasury had noted in 1760 that the Privy Council was considering the subject of colonial trade.[59] A month before Grenville became head of the Treasury, Charles Townshend caused some excitement by proposing in a speech in the House of Commons that an American revenue be raised immediately by lowering the duties on French molasses and enforcing their payment. The furor this speech aroused was not due to the nature of Townshend's suggestions, but rather because Townshend had made this statement on his own without the prior knowledge of the ministry of which he was a part. As George III commented: "this subject was new to none, having been thought of this whole winter; all ought to have declar'd that next session some tax will be laid before the House but that it requires much information before a proper one can be stated, and thus have thrown out this insidious proposal; I think Mr. Townshends conduct deserves dismissing him or the least making him explain his intentions." [60]

Townshend himself had long been an advocate of a uniform plan of reform for the colonies. As early as 1754 he had formulated a program which included extending the stamp tax to the colonies. "A remodelling of the plantation governments was his aim, for which a necessary corollary was the raising of a revenue by Parliament." [61] Lord Halifax, Townshend's superior at the Board of Trade in 1754, also had advocated taxing the colonies in order to strengthen English interests there.[62] And their recommendations had not gone unnoticed even at that time. In 1755 two prominent members of Parliament had informed the agent representing Massachusetts that "it was intended, by some persons of consequence, that the colonies should be governed like Ireland, keeping a body of standing forces, with a military chest . . . [with] the abridgement of their legislative powers, so as to put them on the same foot that Ireland stands." [63] During the war discussion of such reforms was continuous enough so that Governor Bernard, before taking up his duties in Massachusetts, could refer to the idea that "the appointments [i.e., the salaries] of the Governors should be settled by Parliament so as to make them independent of the people" and remark that this "has been much talked of and cannot be done too soon." [64] And by 1763 even Lord Bute, in the midst of his own personal political crisis, could agree that reform of the colonial administrative machinery had top priority.[65]

Perhaps the best description of the situation facing the English government in 1763 was given by a colonial customs official. Writing from Boston, Comptroller Nathaniel Ware suggested that now was the moment to achieve the proper subordination of the American colonies to the interests and authority of the English government, "for which happy purpose never could a more favorable opportunity than the present have offered, and if an effectual reformation be not introduced before those troops are withdrawn which could have been thrown in upon no less occasion without giving a general alarm, one may venture to pronounce it impossible afterwards, and also to add, that the Northern Colonies ripened by a few, a very few more years to maturity, must, agreeably to nature's ordinary laws, drop off from that stock whence they originally sprung; which policy may long retard, though perhaps not finally prevent." [66]

Comptroller Ware was not alone in his concern about the future course of American growth and development. An expert analysis of the colonial problem, which was read and approved by Lord Bute (and passed on to Grenville), was based on the proposition that "His Majesties possessions in North America are so many times more extensive than the Island of Great Britain, that if they were equally well inhabited, Great Britain could no longer maintain her dominion over them. It is therefore evidently her Policy, to set bounds to the Increment of People, and to the extent of the Settlement in that Country." [67] The Proclamation Line of 1763 itself was based at least partially on the same proposition. As the Board of Trade later noted, the principle was adopted "and approved and confirmed by his Majesty" after the Treaty of Paris that the westward expansion of the colonies should be confined "to such a distance from the seacoast, as that those settlements should lie *within the reach of the trade and commerce of this kingdom* . . . and also of the exercise of that authority and jurisdiction, which was conceived to be so necessary for the preservation of the colonies in due subordination to, and dependence upon, the mother country." [68]

The first action in pursuit of the "due subordination" of the colonies was taken even before Bute left office. In March, 1763, Grenville, as First

Lord of the Admiralty, sponsored a bill to increase the participation of the royal navy in enforcement of the Acts of Trade. Enacted in April, the new law was entitled, "An Act for further Improvement of his Majesty's Revenue of Customs . . ." In paragraph nine the "Hovering Act" of 5 George I was extended to the colonies. Thereafter any vessel below fifty tons was included in the provisions authorizing the customs officers to inspect ships hovering off the coast of the colonies, seizing those which did not proceed on their voyage after being warned. Paragraph four authorized the king to divide proceeds from seizures as he saw fit in order to encourage the employment of ships of war in the prevention of smuggling.[69]

The "Hovering Act" was merely a preliminary. On April 22 the Treasury considered the problem of financing the ten thousand troops Bute had authorized for the colonies. It was estimated that the total charge for this force would come to £224,903 a year.[70] The colonies would have to contribute towards this expense. England's war debt stood at £137,000,000 in January, 1763. The interest on borrowed funds was nearly £5,000,000 a year. The national yearly budget was only £8,000,000.[71]

On May 21 the Treasury asked the Customs Commissioners to consider the American Revenue. On July 14 the Treasury requested a list of all officers serving in the colonies. They revealed their urgency by ordering the Commissioners to present their report by the next Friday.[72] On the designated day the Commissioners presented to the Treasury a report of far-reaching significance.

In their report the Commissioners began by pointing out that the Act of 1673 had been passed to lay duties on the colonial coasting trade that was being used to carry on a foreign commerce. In spite of the levying of those duties, they reported, the total revenue under that Act for the last thirty years came to only £35,216. To the Commissioners this indicated an obvious failure. They referred the Treasury to the report they had made on this subject in 1759 at the request of the Board of Trade. As to the Molasses Act, the Commissioners commented that when it had been enacted they had appointed some new officers and given additional instructions, but the total revenue from that Act for thirty years was only £21,652. Recently receipts had risen, but that seemed to be caused more by the number of wartime prizes carried into the colonies than by

regular returns. Again they referred to the 1759 report and their statement that, as long as the high duties remained, smuggling would be
widespread.

On the conduct of their officers, the Commissioners regretted the
"Collusive Practice of the Officers . . . themselves, who at this Distance
from Inspection, are too easily led off from their Duty, to their Interest,
in a Country, where the strict Observance of the former, is rendered
highly difficult and obnoxious." In justice to the officers, the Commissioners added that many of them had reported that a lowering of the
duties was essential. At the same time, so many officers were absent on
leave or otherwise that the efficiency of the service was impaired. They
should be ordered back to duty.[73]

Receipts from colonial duties under both Acts averaged £1,800 a year,
the Commissioners said. Expenses in 1760 were £4,700. Since then new
establishments in the conquered territories had raised the cost to £7,600.
In some areas the customs officers made excessive profits from connivance
at illegal trade. In others they took too large fees: "We apprehend that
the Practice of Fees and Perquisites is a great inducement to many of
these officers to betray their trust." So, the Commissioners suggested that
American officers be allowed no fees at all and instead be given an allowance out of receipts. This recommendation was one way to settle the
problem Archibald Cummings had raised forty years earlier.[74]

The day after this report was received the Treasury met to consider
both it and the earlier one made in 1759 which the Commissioners had
referred to. Of the Commissioners' three proposals to compel officers to
residence, to abolish fees, and to lower the molasses duties, the Treasury
thought that the last two would require the authority of Parliament.
The first, however, could be implemented immediately, so the Commissioners were told to order all their officers to their stations.[75] On the 29th
of July the Treasury again took up the Customs reports. This time they
asked the Commissioners just what action Parliament should be asked
to enact. Also they wanted a further report on distribution of seizures.
And finally they notified the Commissioners that the Secretary of State
had sent a circular letter to the colonial governors ordering them to see
to it that the civil officers did everything possible to help in revenue
matters.[76]

On September 16 the Commissioners submitted the report that served as the basis for the Sugar Act of the next year. In ten explicit articles they outlined a fundamental reorganization of the colonial system. Incorporated in their proposals were the results of years of advice from numerous officials. The first suggestion simply noted that the provisions of the Molasses Act "have been for the most part, either wholly evaded, or Fraudulently compounded." To "diminish the Temptation to Smuggling" and to secure "the just Collection of these Duties" the Commissioners recommended a lower duty.

Secondly, to strengthen the bonding provisions, they proposed that all masters be required to carry with them certificates to show that bond had been given to take enumerated goods only to Great Britain or another English colony. This would facilitate examination at sea. Because ships might give bond and clear customs, only to take on a cargo afterwards, they recommended that masters be required to give bond to cover any foreign molasses they might take on board after leaving port. Again to enable frauds to be discovered at sea, the ships were to carry certificates of such bonds at all times. Any molasses found on board not covered by proper papers would thus prove intent to defraud the revenue.

The fourth provision advocated authorizing the seizure of any vessel found within two leagues of the shore with enumerated goods or foreign sugars not expressly accounted for by cocquets or certificates. No goods were to be loaded on any ship until all the particulars of content and ownership were given to the customs officers. As a sixth point, all fines and duties were to be paid in sterling. Noting that many vessels returned from Holland and stopped in Great Britain, particularly in the Orkneys, clearing only a part of their cargo, the Commissioners asked that no ship be cleared in Great Britain unless the entire cargo were unloaded and properly reloaded.

The eighth proposal was that any vessel stopped two leagues or less offshore, having goods on board not produced at the port of clearing, and not producing cocquets to cover them, should be liable to seizure. To facilitate the settling of controversies about the distribution of proceeds from seizures, a uniform system was urged as the ninth point. The final proposal coupled recommendations that Cape Breton and Newfoundland be provided with regular customs officers with the thought that although "we are sensible of the great Burthen, upon the Revenue from the present Establishment . . . Comptrollers . . . might be useful

Cheques on the Collectors and be agreeable to the general System of the Customs." [77]

The response of the Treasury was quickly made. On September 21 they ordered the Commissioners to prepare a draft of a bill to be presented to Parliament. Only the first eight of the proposals in the letter of the 16th were to be incorporated in the bill. The last two suggestions were already within the power of the Treasury and the king. The Commissioners were sharply reminded that revenue was not the only purpose of these revisions. They were to tell their officers not only to look to the increase of the revenue but also to "the prevention of the Clandestine Trade, which it was the object of those Acts to suppress." [78] The two secretaries to the Treasury were started on an investigation to determine at what rate the new molasses duty should be set. [79] To complete the whole project, on September 22 the Commissioners of the Stamp Duties were ordered to prepare a draft of a bill to extend those taxes to the colonies. [80] Within a period of four months the entire program for reform was outlined.

On October 4 the Treasury took the final step of notifying the Privy Council of its investigation. In its famous letter the Treasury reported to the king that the revenue arising in America was "very small & inconsiderable, having in no degree increased with the Commerce of these Countries & is not yet sufficient to defray a fourth part of the Expense necessary for collecting it." [81] Not only was the revenue, "through Neglect, Connivance & Fraud," impaired, but commerce was "diverted from its natural Course & the Salutary Provisions of many wise Laws to secure it to the Mother Country are in a great measure Defeated." The expense of providing for the defense of all the colonies made a larger revenue essential. In a close echo of the words of William Bollan, the Treasury added that the colonies' "vast increase in Territory and Population makes the proper Regulation of their Trade of immediate Necessity, lest the continuance and extent of the dangerous Evils . . . may render all Attempts to remedy them hereafter infinitely more difficult, if not utterly impracticable."

The Treasury listed the actions it had already taken. New orders had been given to the customs staff, additional officers authorized where needed, and regular accounts requested. These steps had been taken to help in the "Suppression of the contraband Trade which has hitherto been carried on with too much Impunity." The Customs Commissioners had strict orders "immediately to dismiss every officer that shall fail to pay obedience to these Instructions, or be any way deficient in his duty." But only so much could be accomplished within the framework of existing laws. Parliamentary action was needed. Particularly, the Treasury told the Privy Council, for the support of the customs officers and the preservation of the revenue, a uniform plan was required "for establishing the Judicature of the Courts of Admiralty in that Country." This request was made approximately forty-five years after the Lords of the Admiralty had noted that there was "little or no regard had to the authority and jurisdiction of the Admiralty abroad." [82] With the presentation of this letter to the Privy Council the groundwork was completed for the introduction of a major reorganization of the imperial structure.

Actually the passage of the Sugar Act in the next year was in the nature of an anticlimax. The most dangerous, but possibly the most essential feature of the program, had been abandoned before the Bill was presented to Parliament. Every suggestion in the past for raising a revenue in the colonies had been coupled with the idea of using such a fund to improve both the defense and the administration of those areas. Originally this idea had been incorporated into the plan to increase colonial revenues. As early as May, 1763, the ministers had considered using the new income to finance both the military and the civil establishments in the plantations. In January, 1764, estimates of all the colonial civil establishments were read at the Treasury. According to one report, as late as February 11, 1764, Grenville still thought of using the new revenues to relieve colonial officials of dependence on the local assemblies.[83] And, according to the testimony of John Adams, this plan was not unknown to the colonists. Commenting on Oxenbridge Thacher and his activities between 1763 and 1765, Adams later wrote that "his favorite subject was politics, and the impending, threatening system of parliamentary taxation and universal government over the colonies . . . From the time when he argued the question of writs of assistance to his death, he considered the king, ministry, parliament, and nation of Great Britain as determined to new-model the colonies from the foundation, to annul all their charters, to constitute them all royal governments, to raise a revenue in America by parliamentary taxation, to apply that revenue to pay the salaries of governors, judges, and all other crown officers." [84]

Trade and Empire

Unfortunately for the English, the main source of income, the lower molasses duty, was expected to return only £77,775 a year.[85] The military establishment would have to be provided for first. If the new revenue proposals were a success, possibly then the civil officers could be taken care of by later measures. This meant that, for the moment, the governmental authorities in the colonies would be less effective than could be desired. It was a compromise that did not bode well for the success of the new program for strict enforcement of the Acts of Trade.

The new Bill was introduced in the House of Commons on March 9, 1764. Horace Walpole recorded that Grenville answered questions "with more art than sincerity," but there was little debate. "There were a few more speeches . . . but no division." The second and third readings on the 22nd of March and the 5th of April encountered little opposition. Sent to the House of Lords, the Sugar Act became law with no further questions. The House of Lords did not concern itself actively with money bills.[86]

The purpose of this "Act for Granting Certain Revenues in The British Colonies," as set forth in the rest of the lengthy title, was to continue the Molasses Act (which was about to expire), to employ the new revenue to provide for the defense of the colonies, to explain certain provisions of the Act of 1673, to alter various drawbacks on exports from Great Britain, to prevent smuggling, and to secure the trade between the motherland and the colonies. Its provisions were to take effect as of September 29, 1764.[87]

Paragraphs three and four dealt with the molasses duty. Although the Act of 6 George II "hath been found in some degree useful, yet it is highly expedient that the same should be altered, enforced, and made more effectual." The Molasses Act was continued, but after September 29 the duty would be three pence instead of six. Paragraph ten placed the new funds raised by the lower duty and imposts on wines and other items at the disposal of Parliament, to be used for the defense and security of the colonies.

The provisions immediately related to the customs service began with paragraph eighteen, which totally prohibited the importation of foreign produced rum and spirits into the plantations. Section twenty incorporated one of the suggestions of the Commissioners, by requiring all masters carrying foreign sugars or molasses to have with them at all times a certificate that bond had been given to take the goods only to Great Britain or another English colony. Paragraph twenty-one ordered that such certificates should be turned in by the captain at the port of arrival.

In one of the longest sections, paragraph twenty-three noted that the Act of 12 Charles II had required the posting of sureties to the amount of £1,000 (for ships under one hundred tons) or £2,000 (for vessels of one hundred or more tons) to ensure that the enumerated commodities would be carried only to Great Britain or one of her possessions; "notwithstanding which, there is great Reason to apprehend such Goods are frequently carried to Foreign Ports, and landed there." Also great amounts of foreign molasses and syrups were run ashore in the colonies. Consequently, echoing the Commissioners' request, thereafter even ships not carrying enumerated goods at the time of clearance would have to give surety that if those commodities were picked up later they would be taken only to the designated places. No goods were to be loaded on any vessel on pain of forfeiture until such sureties were provided. Again, the masters were to keep a certificate with them at all times to show that they had obeyed these regulations.

The other provisions to ensure enforcement can be briefly summarized. Ships found with enumerated goods within two leagues of the shore, not producing certificates covering the same, were liable to seizure. Coffee, pimentos, coconuts, whale fins, raw silk, and hides and skins were placed on the enumerated list. No wood included in the definition of naval stores, as set out in the Act of 8 George I, should be loaded until bond had been given to carry it to Great Britain. To prevent the use of coasting vessels in smuggling, no goods were to be loaded on any ship to be carried from one colony to another until a permit for loading had been given by the customs officers. Cocquets were required to show the contents of all vessels employed in such intercolonial trade, whether or not the cargoes included enumerated or dutiable commodities.

Ships being cleared in Great Britain to go to the colonies should take on their entire cargo there. Anyone involved in altering or forging papers, or knowingly using them, was subject to a £500 fine. Vessels hovering off the colonial coast had forty-eight hours to leave, after which they were to be seized. Masters making fraudulent entries were liable to damages to treble the value of the goods involved. People aiding illegal activities were to be fined. Duties and fines were to be paid in sterling.

Proceeds from condemnations were to be divided one-third to the collector for the use of the king, one-third to the governor, and one-third to the informer, except that seizures made at sea by the navy were to be divided one-half of the gross to the ships making the seizure and the rest to the king. Another important provision placed the burden of proof in seizures involving the nonpayment of duties on the defendants. And, finally, paragraph forty-one climaxed the whole new system by permitting the informer or prosecutor in any case involving breach of the Acts of Trade to have the hearing in the court of his choosing, including "any court of Admiralty . . . or . . . any court of vice-admiralty which may or shall be appointed over all America."

The Sugar Act, as passed by Parliament, left many problems unsolved, particularly in its failure to relieve the colonial officials of their financial dependence on the colonists. But it was a beginning. Some of the more obvious loopholes in the machinery intended to enforce the commercial regulations had been corrected. Improved enforcement would mean increased revenues. And properly employed, the augmented revenues could in turn be used to strengthen the whole imperial structure. While it had been necessary to abandon, for the time, the idea of independent salaries for the major colonial officials, because of the expense of the military establishment, still even the presence of the troops might have a salutary effect. When the question of troops for America was first discussed, the Board of Trade suggested that one of the prime considerations was "the stationing of Troops in order to awe the British colonies," while another proposal noted that the "provinces being now surrounded by an Army, a Navy, and by hostile Tribes of Indians . . . It may be time . . . to exact a due obedience to the just and equitable Regulations of a British Parliament." [88] Yet another suggestion recommended that forts be erected at the entrance to all the "Principal Harbours" in the colonies and so situated as to "protect, and at the same time Command" the towns, which would "better serve to secure the Dependence of the Colonys." [89] More practically, the Treasury itself noted that the troops could be used in the ports which caused the most difficulty in order to increase the authority of the customs officers.[90]

The truth is, of course, that the Sugar Act was, and was intended to be, merely the first step on the road to imperial reform. As Horace Walpole commented concerning Grenville and his attempts to raise a colonial revenue, "To say that his plan would be confined to present assistance as then chalked out was what neither himself pretended, nor was it by any means adequate to the mischiefs the attempt might produce. He himself termed it but an experiment towards further aid, and as such the Americans immediately understood it." [91] The problem, simply, was whether such a slow, step-by-step approach as that under-taken by Grenville was practicable, given the well-documented record of colonial opposition, because, of course, the issue touched upon went far deeper than a mere increase in taxes for the colonists. As Grenville himself later noted, the "right of taxation" and the question of "sovereignty" ever have been and "must be inseparable." [92] And the point was clearly understood by at least some in the colonies. In the first major reply to the actions of the British government, James Otis, after disposing of the nonsensical (as he saw it) distinction between internal and external taxation, observed that if taxes are imposed on any people *without* consent, they cannot be said to be free. This barrier of liberty being once broken down, all is lost." [93]

Given the seriousness of the issue, and the long heritage of neglect and nonenforcement of British authority within the colonies, perhaps the piecemeal approach adopted by Grenville seemed wise. But there was a danger involved. To alert the colonial opposition without at the same time strengthening the imperial machinery to the point at which it could enforce the government's program in spite of resistance in the colonies might be to court disaster. The Sugar Act, coupled with the simultaneous discussion of extension of the Stamp Act, revealed English intentions. The test would come when the nature, and the extent, of colonial opposition became known.

A Time of Troubles

A T THE same time that Parliament acted to provide the legislative basis for implementation of the mercantilist imperial ideals, major alterations were made in the colonial customs service. Under the original plan adopted in 1673 surveyors — or comptrollers, as they soon came to be called — had been established in every colony to supervise the work of the individual collectors. During the long years of neglect and indifference these offices had all but disappeared. In 1760 there were only five such officers included on the establishment list.[1] In their report of September 16, 1763, the Commissioners of the Customs had written that although "we are sensible of the great Burthen, upon the Revenue from the present Establishment . . . Comptrollers . . . might be useful Cheques on the Collectors and be agreeable to the general System of the Customs."[2] This recommendation of the Commissioners was put into effect. Between 1764 and 1766 twenty-five comptrollers were added to the colonial staff.[3] Such a substantial increase in the establishment was an indication of the seriousness with which the government approached the task of enforcing the Acts of Parliament.

Along with these appointments the Customs Commissioners themselves were provided with a new plantation clerk to handle the increased business.[4] Another step taken to raise the efficiency of the service was the appointment of additional surveyors general. In October, 1764, the Commissioners informed the Treasury that both the southern and northern districts were too large for one man to cover and suggested that the continent be divided into four customs areas. The surveyor general northern would cover the colonies from Newfoundland through Connecticut. The Eastern Middle District would include New York, the Jerseys, Pennsylvania, and Canada. Maryland, Virginia, and the Carolinas would be in the Western Middle District. The Southern

District would now cover only Georgia, the Floridas, the Bahamas, and Jamaica. A fifth surveyor general would patrol the West Indies.[5] The Treasury quickly approved this new arrangement. John Temple, surveyor general northern under the old plan, continued to care for his now somewhat reduced district. Randolph, former surveyor general southern, became surveyor of the new Western Middle District; while the post of surveyor and comptroller for the Carolinas and the Bahamas was abolished and William Randall, who had held that office, became head of the Southern District. The only new appointee was Charles Steuart, commissioned surveyor general of the Eastern Middle District.[6]

Not only were new officers appointed and the regional arrangements altered but steps were also taken to tighten the administrative checks on the personnel of the colonial service. Since 1758 several orders had been issued directing absentees back to their posts. Now it was provided that all officers being sent out to the colonies should be thoroughly instructed in their duties at the Customs House in London before they took office. No officer could go to his post until the Treasury had received from the Customs Commissioners a certificate that he had fulfilled this requirement.[7] Inherent in this regulation was the expectation that most of the new officers would be sent out from London and not selected in the colonies. The advice offered some sixty-five years earlier by Lord Bellomont that "all Officers of the Revenue may be Englishmen, and not of these Plantations by no means" was finally to be adopted.[8]

At the same time these changes were initiated in the customs service a move to improve the effectiveness of the Admiralty jurisdiction in America was made. The individual colonial Admiralty courts were left untouched, but a new court with jurisdiction over all the colonies was established at Halifax in Nova Scotia. Thereafter any offense against the Navigation Acts could be taken to that court instead of to the local tribunal at the discretion of the prosecuting officer. The obvious intention was to provide a court removed from local involvements where the royal officials could expect to find a more impartial settlement of their cases. Selected to preside over the new tribunal was William Spry, related by marriage to William Pitt. He was to receive a salary of £800 a year paid from the profits of his court if possible and, if not, from England. Unfortunately for Judge Spry, and the plans of the English government, few officers felt it worth the trouble to take their cases all the way to Halifax. For most of the period Spry sat in official splendor at Halifax, vainly awaiting the arrival of disputes requiring his services. His salary for the most part was paid from England. An effective solution to the problem of Admiralty jurisdiction had yet to be found.[9]

With so many new officials being dispatched to the colonies the inadequacies of the previous operations were dramatically highlighted. Thoroughly indoctrinated with the relatively orderly and efficient practices of the English service the new officers set out for the colonies with confidence. What they found in America was, in some cases, appalling. In June, 1764, for example, John Earnshaw arrived in Virginia to take up his post as comptroller at the Upper James. In his own words he "could not find at Williamsburg, or in any other part of the upper District . . . any Customs house, Collector, or other Customs house Officer." All he did find was William Dennis, clerk to the naval officer, who "did personate & in a manner transact the business of Thomas Skottowe Esqr. Collector." Earnshaw never did hear from the rightful collector, Skottowe, during his brief stay in Virginia. From an acquaintance he learned that the collector lived at Charleston in South Carolina and had visited his district only once since his appointment. The comptroller reported that the customary procedure was that, when a ship arrived, the captain showed his manifest to the naval officer, who gave him a permit to unload and reload. The ship then went away and discharged its cargo with no supervision whatsoever. When the new cargo had been taken on board, again with no examination, the naval officer cleared the vessel, while his clerk signed the clearance in the name of the absent collector. To complete his discouragement, Earnshaw found that the Virginia legislature would permit him to take no fees. Originally he had been told that his office would bring in up to £300 per year. Without fees, all Earnshaw received was his salary of £30 a year. After a stay of six months the new comptroller returned to England to report on his experiences. In his accounting to the Treasury and the Commissioners Earnshaw spoke for the other comptrollers sent to Virginia.[10]

The situation in Virginia was particularly bad but not unique. The first visit of the new naval cutter to Casco Bay in 1765 found the customs house conducted in the greatest confusion and laxity.[11] Of Falmouth in Maine the Commissioners of the Customs reported in 1765 that they had received "Accounts of the Business of the Customs house being in the greatest confusion, Vessels arriving & sailing daily without paying any regard to the Regulations . . . or without so much as taking the least Notice of the Customs house." [12] The problem of fees was universal. Until 1765 the English government had left the matter of fees to the colonial legislatures. Some assemblies had enacted statutes covering fees allowed to the customs officers. In other colonies informal consultations between the collectors and various merchants had produced an acceptable schedule. Now not only were numerous new officers being dispatched to the colonies who were not included in such arrangements, but the right to determine the size of the customs officers' fees had become a powerful weapon in the hands of the local assemblies. Earnshaw and his fellow comptrollers in Virginia had discovered that the legislature there would not recognize their offices and denied them the right to take any fees. In the situation action by Parliament was again required.

In 1765 Parliament passed an Act to settle the problem of fees. To prevent any colonial tampering with the former arrangements it was stated that all officers were entitled to collect such fees as they had customarily received on or before the 29th of September, 1764. For the new officers, it was provided that they should be allowed to take such fees as were received by similar officials in the nearest port in the colony. If no port in the colony had established fees, the nearest port in any other colony should be used as the model. Further, where comptrollers were authorized no legal fees by the colonial assemblies, or where such fees did not amount to one-third of those allowed to the collectors, the comptrollers were legally entitled to take fees to the one-third the value of those permitted to the collectors.[13]

The wording of this Act of Parliament seems plain enough. But it did little to settle the disputes over fees. Since in many areas the fees allowed as of 1764 were authorized by custom and not by law, it was quite possible for the colonists to question the claims of the customs officers as to what was the established rate. Roger Hale, a former officer in the customs service in London who had been sent to Boston to replace the irresponsible Benjamin Barons, reported that the fees taken in Boston had been in effect for twenty years with no objections. In his eyes they were not only reasonable but less than those taken elsewhere and only one-tenth of those taken in England. As long as the colonists were not harassed by the strict enforcement of the Acts of Trade, the customs officers were allowed to take those fees. In a sense those fees had been a form of bribery. Now, with strong measures adopted to enforce the Acts, the colonists no longer found the bribes useful. Instead they planned to use the fees to force the officers to quit their posts by making them of little profit. In reporting on the efforts of the Massachusetts legislature to lower all the fees, both Governor Bernard and Collector Hale indicated that the attempt was made in revenge for the new regulations.[14]

Typical of the difficulty the English encountered in putting their plans into execution was the peculiar situation that developed in Canada. The British authorities were not unaware of the burdens their plans imposed on the colonists. When customs officers were established in the new province of Canada it was decided that they would be permitted to take no fees at all. This was done partly to relieve the struggling communities from the burdensome impositions and partly "as an Experiment towards preventing Altercation or Collusion, between the Trader and the Officers in this Infant Settlement." In place of fees the new officers were provided with higher salaries than was usual in the colonies. The collector received £300 a year, the comptroller £200, the Surveyor £200, and the waiter and searcher £100. If the collection amounted to over £20,000 a year the officers were to receive a bonus of one shilling in the pound distributed proportionately among them.[15]

Three hundred pounds was a good salary, but the collector in Canada was well aware that without fees his income was less than a third of that of the Boston collector. When Parliament passed its Act on fees the collector and the other officers in Canada realized that they had a legal excuse to start receiving fees. The Act made no mention of the special provisions made for them and merely said that ports where no fees were established should follow the procedure at the nearest port. Since the fees in New York were the highest in the colonies close to Canada the collector chose that port as his model. With the permission of the surveyor general he and the other officers began to take regular fees,

A Time of Troubles

When the Commissioners of the Customs heard of this maneuver they acted quickly. Informing the Treasury that in spite of their large salaries the customs officers in Canada were now taking fees, the Commissioners recommended that the salaries be substantially reduced. Thereafter the collector received £100, the comptroller £70, the waiter and searcher £60, and the surveyor £70. The Canadian officers soon discovered that they had lost more than they had gained. Their income from fees in the "Infant Settlement" was smaller than they had anticipated, and the next six years were spent in an effort to correct their mistake. The result was constant confusion, discord between the customs officers and the governor, and one more complaint furnished to the colonial opposition.[16]

If the English effort to enforce a coherent and orderly colonial system found the customs service ill-prepared and suffering from the years of neglect, the colonial opposition exhibited no such weakness. Part of the new program involved the stationing of naval cutters off the coast of America to guard against clandestine landings in the numerous rivers and bays. Lieutenant Thomas Hill was in charge of the first such ship to cruise off Rhode Island. Acting on his new authority as a commissioned officer of the customs Hill attempted to inspect and seize a vessel in the waters of the colony. He was received in what the Admiralty termed a "riotous" manner by the inhabitants, who forced the gunners of the harbor fort to fire on the royal ship. In spite of Treasury orders that the affair should be thoroughly investigated, and anyone who engaged in "an Act so highly criminal as resisting all legal authority, and actually firing the Guns of his Majesty's Ports against ships of War" should be prosecuted to the fullest extent of the law, no further action was taken.[17] The united front presented by the colonists made investigation difficult, and more important problems soon intervened. Elsewhere the story was much the same. In New York the commander of the royal cutter was jailed after the Admiralty court had ruled against a seizure he had made, although the captain had made the seizure on the advice of the attorney general.[18] The customs officers, too, felt the effect of the increased opposition the new regulations aroused. The collector at Pocomoke in Maryland reported in 1765 that he had been brutally assaulted in the execution of his duty.[19] A forcible rescue was made of a seizure at Newburyport in Massachusetts early in 1766.[20]

A similar occurrence took place at Falmouth in Maine in the same year.[21]

The most publicized outbreak took place in Massachusetts. In May, 1764, John Robinson became collector of the customs in Rhode Island. From the beginning his experiences were unfortunate. The governor had refused to swear him into office, and within a short time of his arrival a vessel seized on the order of the surveyor general was rescued by a mob of disguised citizens.[22] In April of the next year a ship named the *Polly* entered at Newport from Surinam. Her cargo was entered at the customs house and the vessel proceeded elsewhere to unload her molasses. Robinson meanwhile became suspicious of the small size of the entered cargo and determined that the *Polly* should be thoroughly examined. He overtook the ship at Dighton in Massachusetts on the 6th of April, 1765, four days after the original entry had been made. On board he found nearly double the reported amount of molasses.

Robinson of course seized the *Polly* but could not find enough men at Dighton to sail her back to Newport for trial. Leaving two of his men in charge of the ship, the collector returned to Rhode Island to find a crew. In his absence a mob boarded the ship, stripped her of her cargo and all her furnishings, allowing the *Polly* to run ashore. Robinson hurried back to Dighton with a large party of armed marines and sailors, only to find that a warrant had been issued for his arrest on a charge brought against him by the captain of the *Polly*. Eager to give the colonists no cause to complain that he had ignored the law, the collector submitted to arrest and was taken to Taunton where he was jailed.[23]

To this point the story of the *Polly* was a simple, if flagrant, example of colonial opposition to the work of the customs officers. But the aftermath of the rescue of the seized cargo exposed one of the fundamental weaknesses in the customs service. Both the place where the seizure had been made and the town where Robinson was imprisoned were within the jurisdiction of Massachusetts. The governor of that colony and the surveyor general had long been at odds. Both were ambitious men, and the new emphasis on strict enforcement of the Acts of Trade gave the surveyor general an importance which rivaled that of the governor. Both were involved in enforcing the Acts but the limits of their responsibilities had never been defined. Anxious to assert his new authority

Surveyor General Temple claimed the sole right to see to the observance of the trade laws. In his view the governor was merely a local civil official who, when required, should bring the support of the government to the aid of the customs officers. Unless requested to do so, Temple thought the governor had no authority over the customs service in any manner at all. Governor Bernard, in turn, felt that anything affecting his administration was his concern and that the conduct of the customs officers was immediately within his power of review.

When Temple had first arrived in Massachusetts the struggle between Benjamin Barons and the merchants on one side, and the other customs officers and the governor on the other, had been at its height. Resenting the interference of Bernard in the affair, Temple had given certain documents to Barons, indirectly helping him in the contest.[24] In Bernard's words, the surveyor general had "discovered an haughty jealousy of me & my office." For a time after the departure of Barons there was a truce between the two rival officials; but when the Sugar Act was passed and the new regulations sent out to secure the strict observance of all the Acts, the feud flared anew. Partly the contest involved the power of patronage. By binding all the customs officers to himself alone Temple thought to build the surveyor general's patronage into an office of overriding central importance. Bernard sought to combine patronage within the customs service with other openings available to him in order to increase the prestige of and support for the royal government in Massachusetts.[25]

The first casualty in the struggle between the governor and the surveyor general was the collector in Salem. James Cockle was numbered among the "friends" of the governor and so incurred the wrath of Temple. In March, 1764, Cockle discovered that a large amount of molasses had been imported into Salem on forged certificates. He went to the governor and consulted with him on what should be done. Bernard advised that the molasses should be prosecuted and proof of the fraud obtained from the governor of Antigua, where the cargo had been taken on board. With that decision made, Cockle informed Temple of the affair. The surveyor general saw his opportunity, censured the collector for attempting to prosecute the goods instead of collecting the duties he felt should be paid, and suspended Cockle from office. Temple's argument was that Bernard and Cockle wished to prosecute instead of collecting the duties because in that way they would share in the distribution of the proceeds from the condemnation. Temple asserted that the owner of the goods should be allowed to make a post-entry report at the customs house and pay the duties. In that way the entire sum would go to the royal revenue. The surveyor general's argument was peculiar in that he seemed to think that the importer of illegal goods, if discovered, could then pay the duties and escape prosecution. Such a system would have been an open invitation to every merchant to try his hand at smuggling; if detected, he would merely have to pay the duties that would have been collected had he reported his imports as required by law. He would have nothing to lose and everything to gain. But Temple was not concerned with the logic of his argument; he was after Cockle and any complaint would do. To this charge, the surveyor general added testimony to show that Cockle had accepted a bribe and that the customs house books in Salem showed that he had juggled the records of entries of foreign molasses into his port.[26]

In the contest over the collectorship in Salem, Temple emerged the victor. After he had written the Commissioners that Bernard and Cockle had taken the case to court and settled for a composition for one-third the value of the seizure, because they could not produce enough evidence to have it condemned, his suspension of Cockle was confirmed and a new officer appointed for Salem. Of the governor Temple wrote that he was intent on "traducing all Customs house Powers, and taking upon himself to determine all things concerning them."[27] In return Bernard reported that Temple hoped to be "by much the greatest Man in America," which he intended to achieve by "assuming a Power of dispensing with penaltys and forfeitures at discretion; making the Traders dependent upon, & subservient to one only."[28]

The second casualty in the contest between Bernard and Temple was Roger Hale, the collector of Boston. When Barons was removed in 1762 the English authorities were shocked enough by the manner in which this political appointee had conducted himself to determine on a more suitable candidate as his replacement. The man chosen, Hale, was an experienced officer of the London customs service and a trusted employee of the Commissioners. On their recommendation he was given the much sought-after post in Boston.[29] Hale attempted to remain neutral in the feud between the governor and the surveyor general but found it impossible to do so. Temple acted as if every officer not aligned on his side was an enemy. Accusing the collector of being the governor's "friend," he told Hale he would "make him sick of his office" by sending him constantly on unpleasant assignments. Boasting that he had eight governors "under him," Temple also told the comptroller that he would receive the same treatment. Hale replied that he could not perform his duties if harassed on one side by the governor and on the other by the surveyor general. Angered by this response Temple struck the collector, and a duel of honor was scheduled. Governor Bernard used his authority to prevent the meeting, but the damage had been done.[30] Hale was discouraged by the whole failure of his work in Boston and returned to his old post in London. And the struggle between Bernard and Temple was not yet finished.

When the Rhode Island collector seized the *Polly* and was imprisoned in the Taunton jail he notified Temple of his plight. The surveyor general provided bail for him and obtained his release. But Temple was not satisfied to wait for the slow workings of the law to correct the injustice done to a customs officer. He wanted immediate support furnished to Robinson, even if it meant calling up the militia to teach the inhabitants a lesson. Bernard was not eager to aid the surveyor general and did not wish to risk doing irreparable harm to the royal government by hasty and extreme action. As a result little was done to help Robinson, who did however manage to get the *Polly* afloat again and secure her condemnation in the newly established Admiralty court at Halifax. Bernard was annoyed at this insult to the objectivity of the Admiralty court in New England and felt that an unnecessary slight had been cast on the judge in the court there as well as on the other officials who were trying to create support for the government. Temple in turn accused the governor of being concerned only because he lost his share in the proceeds of the condemnation of the *Polly,* although no one profited very much from the disposal of the stripped and damaged ship.[31]

The colonial opposition viewed all these events with open delight. The departure of the displaced Collector Cockle from Salem was hailed "by firing guns, making bonfires, entertainments, &c; and the Surveyor General [was] much applauded by the merchants."[32] Temple, in fact, became a hero to the colonial opposition and had their support and backing as long as he was in office. Unfortunately the division in the ranks of the royal officials was not restricted to the colonies. In London the Customs Commissioners and the Treasury, acting on the information furnished them in Temple's letters, strongly argued his case. The Secretary of State and the Board of Trade, supplied with documents from the governor, supported Bernard. The result was that both men were continued in office and the feud sputtered on for many years longer. When Temple later was appointed to the Board of American Commissioners of the Customs in 1767 much of the effectiveness of that agency was impaired by bitterness and disunity created by the ancient rivalry.

The feud between the governor of Massachusetts and the surveyor general of the northern district was not the only division in the ranks of the royal agents that did damage to the imperial cause. The captains of the ships of war discovered that their new activity in enforcement of the Acts of Trade was not always welcomed by the customs officers. The Act of 1696 had extended the Act of Frauds of 1662 to the colonies. Under the latter statute customs officers were entitled to act as informers in all cases involving violation of the trade laws. Although now the naval captains were commissioned as regular customs officers, the officials on shore who formerly had the sole right to take a seizure to trial only grudgingly surrendered their privilege. As informers they were awarded one-third of the proceeds of the condemnations. When the captains took their seizures to trial themselves the proceeds were distributed one-half to them and one-half to the crown.

When the Admiralty was first called upon to participate more actively in the program for enforcement they had suggested that just such a competition would develop. One of the admirals reported that the navy personnel would probably receive little reward for their pains, as the judges, lawyers, and other officials would recognize no seizure they made as being within their rights unless it took place on the high seas. As the Admiralty pointed out, it was important that such a situation not be allowed to develop, since the major advantage of employing the navy consisted in its ability to cover the bays, rivers, and inlets not within the range of the regular customs officers.[33] However, with no central agency in England responsible for the execution of a uniform and consistent colonial program, it seemed impossible to achieve harmony among the royal officials in the colonies, each group being answerable to a different department at home.

The first royal captain to make a seizure in the waters of Massachusetts found his prize taken from him by the customs officers. He had seized a cargo of molasses, only to have a customs officer board the ship and seize the cargo again. The captain protested this intrusion on his rights but was soothed with the promise that he would be awarded one-third of the proceeds anyway. Then to his chagrin he discovered that the surveyor general took an active interest in the affair and decided not to prosecute at all. Not only did the captain lose his profits but in the process a clear violation of the Acts of Trade was allowed to pass unpunished.[34] In New York another captain received so little cooperation from the customs staff and the legal authorities that not only was a seizure he had made released by the Admiralty court but no steps were taken to protect him from being prosecuted in revenge by the owner, with the result that the captain of the royal cutter passed some time in jail until his release was ordered from England.[35] Such feuds continued up to the eve of the Revolution itself. As late as 1773 Admiral John Montague complained that his naval captains received no support from either the customs officers or the civil authorities. At one point, in disgust at the whole enterprise, the Admiralty suggested that if the navy was to bear the expense and the customs service receive the profits, in all fairness the cost of maintaining the various sloops and cutters should be assigned to the Customs Commissioners.[36]

Disputes over fees, contests over the respective authority of the governors and the surveyors general, feuds between the regular customs staff and the royal captains — such were the unfortunate characteristics of the new program to assert the administrative authority of England over her colonies. In these years Britain reaped the rewards of her years of neglect. The colonial system that had evolved by 1764 was a composite of accidents, compromise, and unfulfilled projects. Time was needed to bring order to the system, but time was just what the British did not have. Their new regulations and enactments aroused an immediate angry response in the colonies which strained the machinery of imperial control to the breaking point before there was time to effect the necessary

197

improvements. Nothing better illustrated the failures of these years than the peculiar response of the various colonial officials to the crisis brought on by the passage of the Stamp Act in 1765.

The Stamp Act was an integral part of the Grenville program. It was designed to provide the revenue needed to support the imperial projects through the assessment of internal taxes in the colonies. Many years earlier the governor of New York on hearing of a project to extend the stamp tax to the colonies warned that the "People in North America are quite Strangers to any Duty but such as they raise themselves." [37] The Grenville ministry ignored such cautions and in one decisive act imposed an internal stamp tax on the colonists.[38] The resultant uproar surprised even experienced colonial officials with its intensity.

News of the passage of the Stamp Act was at first greeted with an outburst of angry oratory. Patrick Henry rose to immediate intercolonial fame on the news of the stand he had taken in the Virginia House of Burgesses in support of resolutions condemning the action of Parliament. At the suggestion of the Massachusetts Assembly an intercolonial meeting was summoned, the famous Stamp Act Congress. From this assembly came resolutions denying the right of Parliament to impose internal taxes in the colonies and requesting immediate repeal. Interestingly, two of the thirteen resolutions concerned the previous Acts of Parliament as well as the Stamp Act. Article nine complained that the duties imposed by "several late Acts of Parliament" were extremely "Burthensome and Grievous" and the collection of them "absolutely impracticable" because of the shortage of specie. The eleventh article stated that the "Restrictions imposed by several late Acts of Parliament, on the Trade of these Colonies, will render them unable to purchase the Manufactures of Great-Britain." There was some thought given at the Congress to demanding the repeal of all the Acts of Trade as well as the Stamp Act, but the majority settled for an express denial of Parliament's right to impose internal taxes, with no direct statement regarding its right to regulate trade through the collection of duties.[39]

By autumn of 1765 it was clear that the colonists intended to make a determined stand against the Stamp Act. When the names of those appointed to collect the new taxes became known they were burned in effigy, some forced to resign their commissions, while the homes and property of others were damaged by rioters. There was no doubt as to what the colonists would do when the stamps first arrived, but there was a question as to what the various royal officers would do. The first cargo of stamps arrived in Boston in September. Governor Bernard clearly indicated the problem created for the colonial authorities by the unwise haste of the English ministry in enacting this measure: "to send hither Ordinances for Execution which the People have publickly protested against as illegal and not binding on them, without first providing a power to enforce Obedience, is tempting them to revolt." [40]

In the difficult situation the royal officials performed as might have been expected. Each refused to take responsibility for what happened and excused his concession to the popular furor on the grounds of lack of support from the other authorities. With the stamp collector forced to resign his office by the mob, Governor Bernard used the excuse that he was not authorized to distribute the stamps to have them stored in safety in the fort in Boston harbor. His denial of responsibility left the other authorities unsure as to how to conduct their affairs. Should they carry on as usual without using stamp paper or should they refuse to permit any transaction at all? Bernard hoped that if all the ports were closed, and the courts as well, the anarchy and economic pressure would force the colonists to accept the Act.[41] The only difficulty was that, lacking the strong support that should have been provided from home, no official was willing to make such an all-out stand at the risk of his life, property, and position. The English ministry had ignited a conflagration at a time when the colonial administrative authorities were ill-equipped to uphold the imperial policies.

For the customs officers the problem centered on the question of entering and clearing vessels without stamped forms. The comptroller and the acting collector (Hale having returned to England) in Boston asked the surveyor general for advice. Temple evaded giving them a direct answer and merely told them to apply to the attorney and advocate generals for an opinion. When the customs officers did so, they received further evasive answers. The attorney general went so far as to have a friend write that he was so ill with "Rheumatism in his right Arm & Shoulder" that he could not hold a pen or "attend to any business." By the 7th of December the customs officers had to give in to the pressure of the merchants and, after obtaining from the former collector of the stamp taxes a statement that no stamped paper was available, they began to enter and clear ships with certificates of their own devising, showing that no stamps were available. Typically, the surveyor general, who had helped them in no way, took credit for holding the merchants off as long as possible. Temple wrote the Commissioners of the Customs that "I found means to put them off from the 1st of November till the 16th Instant, when the Collector and Comptroller assured me that not only their lives & property, but the Kings Money was in the greatest danger." [42]

The comedy enacted at Boston was repeated elsewhere. In Virginia the man who carried the stamps to the colony merely said that he had none available for the customs houses. With that excuse at hand the surveyor general authorized the collectors to clear vessels with a certificate that stamps were not available. In Philadelphia many ships had hastily taken on a fraction of a cargo before the stamps arrived and thus were free to continue loading and clearing with no difficulty, having commenced loading before the Act was effective. By the time this ruse had lost its value the collector was willing to follow the example of other ports and issue clearances as usual. The surveyor general of the Western Middle District noted that "impossibilities will not be expected of us, and that from the Nature of our Case our Conduct will stand justified," while the surveyor general of the Eastern District explained his actions in various ways but emphasized that he really had no choice in approving the issuance of regular clearances. [43]

The unfortunate Stamp Act was repealed early in 1766. English pride was assuaged by the coupling of repeal with the Declaratory Act asserting Parliamentary supremacy over the colonies. In spite of the fine words, the imperial cause had been severely damaged by the ill-timed effort to tax the colonies before either the colonial authorities or the English government was willing, or able, to back the attempt with the forceful measures required to enforce an unpopular measure on a recalcitrant people. A fateful portent for the future was the fact that, while the repeal of the Stamp Act passed only over the objections of a sizeable opposition in Parliament, the Declaratory Act was enacted unanimously in the House of Commons and was opposed by only five votes in the House of Lords. [44] A trial of strength in America was merely postponed, not abandoned. When it came, if the lessons of 1765 had had their proper effect, the English administrative machinery should have been better prepared to uphold the imperial program.

The triumph of the colonial opposition in the matter of the Stamp Act could only serve to increase the problems of the officers attempting to enforce the Acts of Trade in America. In Rhode Island the customs officers were the unfortunate victims of bureaucratic stupidity in London. In 1765 the collector had seized two vessels for violation of the trade laws. To their annoyance Judge John Andrews of the Admiralty court hurried the trials before they had time to prepare their cases adequately, while the advocate general refused to conduct the crown's prosecution. The collector and comptroller complained of these and other events in a detailed letter to the English authorities. In this correspondence they made several general remarks about Andrews and the whole government of Rhode Island. The judge, they claimed, had been hand-picked for his post by the merchants during the last war. They also expressed their opinion of the advocate general in no uncertain terms. Acting as if Rhode Island were a royal colony, with a governor appointed by and responsible to the king, the English authorities forwarded copies of the customs officers' charges to Governor Samuel Ward, presumably thinking he in turn would investigate and correct the wrongs. Instead the governor gave the letter to the legislature and consequently the words of the customs officers became known throughout the whole colony. As the collector and comptroller wrote in October, 1766, "Your Honors may naturally suppose that such an unpopular Topic would at any Time have rendered us extremely obnoxious to the People; but happening at so critical a Conjunction, it could not fail of inflaming their already Kindled Rage to the utmost Height." The closing paragraph of their letter is worth noting at length:

as the interest of the Mother Country & this Colony is deemed by the People almost altogether incompatible, in a commercial View, any officer who out of zeal for the first exposes another officer who favors the latter, will be . . . threatened as an Enemy to this Country . . . and Distruction must be inevitably his Doom, if the helping hand of the Mother Country is not stretched forth to espouse his Cause . . . and every good Man however disposed to do his Duty, must content himself with remaining a passive Spectator of Evils he dares not resist.[45]

The Admiralty judge answered these charges in a letter to the Treasury, in which he said, as to the charge that being a native he favored the colonial cause, "I trust Your Lordships will consider this . . . a meer vapour, which went off in their Heat, that faithful Servants to the Crown are to be found among the Natives of America and that the Geography of an man's Birth hath nothing to do with his Merit or Demerit." [46] In spite of these fine words Andrews proceeded to follow a peculiar course for a loyal British officer. He filed a bill of indictment in the local courts charging the customs officers with defamation of character. Later he sued the collector for £10,000 local currency and won his case. Robinson appealed to the Privy Council but left the colony before his request for reversal of judgment was heard. With his departure Andrews dropped his prosecution. [47]

While in Rhode Island the successful opposition to the Stamp Act emboldened the colonists to harass the customs officers with legal prosecutions, the result in Massachusetts was more dramatic. The Sugar Act had imposed a duty on madeira wines, a favorite drink of the colonists. In September, 1766, the customs officers in Boston received secret information that Daniel Malcom, a strenuous opponent of the trade laws, had several casks of wine on which he had paid no duty hidden in his house. The officers went to investigate and Malcom permitted them to see every room in his house but one, which he claimed was rented by another man and was not his to show. After several hours of argument the customs officers withdrew and secured a writ of assistance. They returned with the sheriff but this time Malcom shut himself in the house and refused to communicate with the officers. A crowd gathered, the sheriff was told that if any attempt was made against the house hundreds more would be summoned by the ringing of the bell in the North Church. Thus intimidated, the customs officers withdrew, deeply conscious of their public humiliation. [48]

It might seem odd that this seemingly minor affair should have achieved such quick fame, but the colonists appreciated Malcom's open defiance of the hated officers, particularly because it had involved the infamous writs of assistance which Otis had attacked so eloquently years before. On the other side the customs officers were determined to make an example of Malcom. In their view he was clearly guilty of contempt of the law. They appealed to England for support, which they found the

Commissioners of the Customs and the Treasury ready to supply. Once again the peculiarities of the legal status of the Acts of Trade brought their hopes to defeat. As penal statutes, the Acts had to be interpreted literally. Although writs of assistance had been granted by the colonial courts for years, and despite the fact that some four years earlier the governor and his supporters had successfully combatted a complaint by the colonial opposition that the writs were illegal, now careful legal examination in London proclaimed that the colonists had been right and the royal officials wrong. The attorney and solicitor generals of England declared that writs of assistance were not valid in America. Their argument was exactly that used earlier by Otis: the Acts of Parliament only provided that such writs could be issued by the Court of the Exchequer. There were no Exchequer courts in the colonies, consequently no legal writs could be issued there. They advised the Treasury that no action could be taken against Malcom "inasmuch as the Writs of Assistance by Virtue of which they entered the House and Cellar was not in this case a legal authority." [49]

The Treasury was properly horrified by this ruling. They required their own solicitor to resubmit the question to the attorney general, pointing out that writs had been issued in the colonies in the past and particularly that an act of the Massachusetts legislature itself, made in 1700, establishing a superior court, stated that such a court should have all the powers lodged in "the Courts of the King's Bench, Common Pleas, and Exchequer within . . . England." This act, the Treasury Lords thought, had been made in connection with the Act of 1696 and clearly created an Exchequer court in the Bay Colony.[50] The legal authorities refused, however, to revise their opinion which was based on the wording of the Acts of Parliament themselves. Consequently any thought of making an example of Malcom had to be abandoned. The publicity given to the incident backfired. Malcom became a hero, and instead of proving the folly of opposing the enforcement of the laws his case became one more well-known defeat for the cause of English supremacy.

The most celebrated event in the aftermath of the Stamp Act disaster occurred in South Carolina. The problem there dated back to the passage of the Sugar Act itself. In that statute an effort had been made to tighten the control of vessels employed in the coasting trade in America. It was apparent from the beginning that the various provisions covering small vessels used in the intercolonial trade would be enforced in South Carolina only with difficulty. In March, 1766, Governor William Bull had reported to the Treasury that he felt it was a hardship on coasting vessels carrying rice in and out of the colony to be stopped continually by the men-of-war. He suggested that such ships be allowed to take out passes good for six months at a time to free them from such problems.[51] An unfortunate incident occurred in late 1766 after the governor had given orders that the fort in Charleston harbor should stop all decked vessels over twenty tons attempting to leave without proper clearances. The gunner at the fort mistakenly fired on an undecked boat sailing past the fort. The result was great "disquietude in the Town" during which the acting collector dared not leave the customs house because of the threats of the "mob of Boatmen and others."[52] Two other factors added to the tension. The presence of the men-of-war off the coast was a constant irritant. Complaints against their continual interference with the coasting trade led the Treasury in October, 1766, to request the naval ships to curtail their activities if it could be done with safety to the revenue.[53] And finally there was the omnipresent problem of fees.

The regular collector of Charleston had retired in 1766. As a temporary replacement the governor appointed Edward Davis. Davis acted as collector from July, 1766, through March, 1767, when he was replaced by Daniel Moore, sent out by the Commissioners in London. While collector, Davis had continued to use the fee table established under his predecessor. The former collector, Hector Berenger de Beaufin, however, had been a respected member of the mercantile community, having become during his twenty-four years in office much like the "Creoles" described earlier. While the merchants were willing to allow such a man substantial fees, they had no intention of bestowing a like favor on any official sent out from England, who would in all probability be less sensitive to their needs than Beaufin had been. When Moore took over the collectorship Davis warned him that the merchants would not tolerate the high fees taken previously. Moore ignored his warnings and the ground was prepared for a contest of strength.[54]

On the 23rd of May, 1767, Captain James Hawker of his Majesty's ship *Sardoine* attempted to inspect a ship entering the Charleston harbor. In his words the previous practice in Carolina was for vessels "never to call at a Customhouse, to give the required Bonds, or to take the necessary papers . . . they unload without entering and so loaded again, without paying the least regard to the Customshouse." [55] Hawker was determined to stop such practices and tightened his inspection of ships in the coastal waters. The vessel he attempted to search on the 23rd of May reached the wharf before the boat Hawker dispatched pulled alongside. When his men attempted to board the ship they were beaten and forced to "leap over Board." A crowd gathered on the shore and Hawker was informed that "if any of the Boats belonging to his Majesty's ship . . . should put off with an Intent to go on Shore or to board the Schooner they wou'd fire at them." Hawker rose to the occasion in dramatic fashion, and stationing himself in the prow of a barge "with the British Flag in my hand," sailed towards the wharf. The crowd showed little respect for his heroism but the owner did produce the ship's papers, which proved to be acceptable. Hawker contented himself with this victory, although he recorded his horror that the drummers of the colonial militia during the affair "beat to arms, not to quell the mob . . . but to collect them together." He added, "This is hardly credible, but it is really fact." [56]

The redoubtable captain was more determined after this episode than before. In the same month he seized a ship, the *Active* of Charleston, for carrying enumerated goods without certificates. Hawker enlisted the support of the new collector, Moore, and proceeded to take the seizure to trial. The judge of the Admiralty court required that the captain give security to pay costs in case the trial should be decided against him. No one in Charleston would act as security for Hawker except the collector himself. In Hawker's words, Moore "was in high esteem with the Inhabitants before he became my Security . . . by which, and his saying He could not overlook such glaring Irregularities, the major part of the Merchants are so irritated . . . that they are resolved upon all means to oppress him." The captain warned the Treasury that if Moore were not supported their "Authority and Deputations will be treated with the greatest Insult and indignity, and it will be out of the Power of the Officers to observe your Directions, or at least to execute them." [57]

Unfortunately for Captain Hawker the vessel he seized had been engaged in trade *within* the colony of South Carolina. Hawker thought that such vessels were required to carry papers covering the enumerated goods aboard but such a requirement had never been enforced in America. To add to his problems every available legal adviser in the colony had entered into an agreement not to be "concerned for the Crown in any case relative to the Schooners employed in the Trade of that province." The attorney general of the province, who was also judge of the Admiralty court, refused to give advice on a case which he would have to hear himself as judge. The case offered by Hawker and Moore was consequently of necessity entrusted to an inexperienced young advocate who did little to help. The case eventually was decided against Hawker; but a reasonable ground for seizure was recognized, freeing him from the threats of suits brought against him in revenge.[58]

Even before the eventual fate of the *Active* was decided another series of incidents had developed that climaxed the struggle in South Carolina and made the names of Daniel Moore, Henry Laurens, and Judge Egerton Leigh familiar throughout the colonies. In the case of the *Active* the crown officers had experienced difficulty in obtaining legal advice. All the established lawyers had agreed not to handle the trial for Moore and Hawker, which was done because the "body of trading men, very few excepted, entered into a combination and made a purse to engage every lawyer in the Province." Henry Laurens was "a man of Fortune and the principal person concerned in the combination." He had declared that any of his ships "Tho' confessedly coming from another province, shall not enter or clear at any Custom house, and has set up two Justices of the peace in Georgia as Customshouse officers to take bonds." These words of Collector Moore explain the events that followed. The customs officer thought that by forcing the leading merchant of the colony to acknowledge the authority of the trade laws, even as they concerned coastal vessels, he might establish his authority once and for all.

In the same month that Captain Hawker seized the *Active* Laurens had dispatched the *Wambaw,* a schooner of about fifty tons, to his plantation in Georgia. There the ship took on a load of shingles and returned to Charleston. The *Wambaw* did carry papers to cover its trip from Georgia to South Carolina, but they had been obtained not from regular customs officers but from the justices of the peace Moore had accused Laurens of setting up for his own convenience. Since the ship involved was decked and well over twenty tons, the collector saw his opportunity to force Laurens to admit publicly the validity of the coastal trade regulations. He offered "the owner that if he would come to the

Customhouse & acknowledge his Error, and promise for the future to pay due regard to the Acts of Parliament" the present violation would be overlooked and the *Wambaw* permitted to make a regular entry. What Moore was after was not one successful seizure, but rather a public retraction of his previous stand by the leader of the opposition. Laurens understood the issue clearly and refused Moore's offer.[59]

While the fate of the *Wambaw* was being discussed, another of Laurens' ships, the *Broughton Island Packet,* came to Charleston also from Georgia but with a cargo of firewood instead of shingles. It too was seized by Moore for being involved in intercolonial trade with no papers or bonds to cover its shipment. In the case of the *Active* the attorney general, who was also judge of the Admiralty court, had refused to give advice to the customs officers in a matter which might come before him in his judicial capacity. Now, however, under pressure from the collector, and on payment of £50, he did consult with Moore and approve the seizures. Seemingly the collector was assured of success in his attempt to make an example of Laurens. Once again he had difficulty in finding a lawyer to handle the case and had to rely on an inexperienced advocate.

Judge Leigh, however, was more than a multiple officeholder. He was also Henry Laurens' uncle. When the two ships came to trial Leigh attempted to achieve a compromise acceptable to all parties. Laurens had admitted that the shingles in the *Wambaw* were intended for public sale. On the other hand he claimed that the wood in the other vessel was for his own use. Leigh seized upon these points and condemned the *Wambaw* but released the *Broughton Island Packet*. The *Wambaw* was sold hastily back to Laurens for £120 local currency. Laurens had to pay the court costs in the case of the condemned *Wambaw,* amounting to £277. In the other case the costs were divided, two-thirds to be paid by Laurens and one-third by the customs officers. If Leigh had hoped to settle the dispute by this clever maneuver, he was sadly mistaken. The issues involved touched upon a more basic problem than a personal contest between two men. The collector and comptroller of Rhode Island had noted that the interests of England and her colonies were "deemed by the People almost altogether incompatible, in a commercial View." [60] That inherent incompatibility was the basis of the contest in South Carolina. Whatever the rights and wrongs of a given case, Moore represented the assertion of English authority, while Laurens characterized the opposition of colonial commercial interests to measures harmful to their well-being. No courtroom decision, no matter how astute, could solve that fundamental division of interests. Laurens himself clearly recognized the seriousness of the issues involved. In a letter to a friend, Laurens described his troubles with the collector, closing by saying, "but I have tired you with the outline of a Mans conduct which in the space of Six Months has given more plague to the Trading people here, than all the Officers of the Customs put together since the memory of the oldest Merchant among us." He added, "yet as this is a dispute of no trifling consideration, I could not forbear saying so much to a friend — if the Tax to be gathered by a British Stamp Act was so odious to the Americans, in what light must that Man appear who dares attempt by his own arbitrary power to levy upon one trading Port a thousand or £1500 Sterling annually, and . . . hold other Money legally collected from them . . . over their heads — 'I can sweat them at Law with their own Money' — Good God! is it possible for freemen to bear this?" [61]

Even while the trials of the *Wambaw* and the *Broughton Island Packet* were being heard, Collector Moore was driven from his post. In the words of the searcher of the customs in Charleston, "Just at this time Mr. Moore was most cruelly prosecuted by a combination of Merchants, with respect to fees upon Indigo Certificates which was determined in his favor, but other prosecutions being prepared against him, He thought it prudent to leave the Province in order to represent those matters at Home." [62] The conduct of the trials was left to this searcher, George Roupell, who in Moore's absence became both the presiding officer in the customs house and the principal target of the opposition's anger. These events received a good deal of attention not only in South Carolina but throughout the colonies and made Henry Laurens a symbol of heroic opposition to British tyranny. This affair, which began with the seizure of the *Active* by the captain of a royal man-of-war, developed into a veritable *cause célèbre* and furnished effective new arguments to colonial propagandists who were daily engaged in their own paper warfare against the encroachments of British authority.

The contest in South Carolina was only the most noteworthy of the failures of English policies in these years. Daniel Moore and Captain Hawker attempted a trial of strength with the colonial opposition before they were assured of their ability to see the affair through to a successful conclusion. Moore, new to the colony, undoubtedly underestimated the determination of the opposition he faced. At the same time he unquestionably overestimated the amount of support available to him. In much the same way the English government, starting in 1764, embarked on a program designed to solidify control of their empire before the machinery of imperial administration was equal to the effort involved. The imperial system in 1764 was a mechanism rusted and corroded by years of neglect and disuse. As one customs officer reported, there were many things wrong in the colonies but they were "so strongly rooted by Habit and profit, that time alone with wise measures properly executed can remove them." [63] Instead of accepting this truth, the British attempted at once to alter the habits and customs established in practice for years. If the period from 1764 to 1767 is regarded as the first round in the contest between the imperial will of Great Britain and the independent aspirations of the colonies, the advantage clearly belonged to the colonists. As George Roupell, the searcher in Charleston, reported, "I have been upwards of twenty years Searcher of this port, but never Knew anything like the disposition of the people at present." [64]

What the English had achieved in these years was not the fulfillment of their imperial dreams. Rather they had given unity and direction to the colonial opposition before England itself was ready or able to enforce its decisions. A man such as Henry Laurens was not a born rebel. He was a conservative merchant, alienated by what he felt to be an arbitrary and unwarranted intrusion on his commercial practices and interests. In effect he refused to be exploited for the benefit of the mother country. Arguments as to the right of Parliament to levy internal taxes as opposed to its right to regulate trade in his case were without meaning. No question of taxation was involved in his dispute with the customs officers. Laurens' annoyance centered on the attempt to control his coastal trade with the neighboring colony of Georgia. For years he had been free to send his ships on such trips as he wished. Now because the English felt, with some justice, that the intercolonial trade was used to defeat some of the provisions of the trade laws, Laurens was to be forced to obey new and onerous regulations that added to his expenditures both in time and money.

Laurens refused to conform to the new regulations. In his view he was the equal of a merchant in England and his welfare should be as much the concern of the English government as was that of their own men of business. When his interests were ignored, he felt it necessary to protest. With no constitutional method available to carry his objections to England, he acted in the logical manner; he used the belligerent atmosphere of his native colony to make good his complaints. In doing so he coupled himself, his influence and prestige, irrevocably with the colonial cause. Fittingly, Laurens was destined to become president of the Continental Congress, and to preside over the dissolution of the ties that bound the colonies to the British Empire.

The case of Henry Laurens was symptomatic of the whole range of problems existing between England and her colonies in those years. The principles of the mercantilist doctrine were avowedly those of exploitation: the colonies existed for the benefit of the motherland. Even the members of the Stamp Act Congress recognized the reality of that doctrine. Robert Livingston of New York wrote that he and many others felt that unless "Britain could regulate our Trade her colonies would be of no more use to her than to France or any other power." [65] Such men wished to recognize England's right to regulate their commerce but not her right to tax them. In one of his finest moments William Pitt argued for repeal of the Stamp Act in this manner:

. . . that the Stamp Act be repealed absolutely, totally, and immediately. That the reason for the repeal be assigned, because it was founded on an erroneous principle. At the same time, let the sovereign authority of this country over the colonies, be asserted in as strong terms as can be devised, and be made to extend to every point of legislation whatsoever. That we may bind their trade, confine their manufactures, and exercise every power whatsoever, except that of taking their money out of their pockets without their consent.[66]

Pitt's eloquent words were effective in forcing repeal of the Stamp Act. But the "Great Commoner" might well have been asked when in history had absolute legislative power ever been divorced from the power of taxation. The experiences of the governors of Massachusetts in their effort to obtain a settled salary, as well as the crisis in New York over supply of the provincial treasury, had illustrated many years earlier that the "power of the purse" was an inseparable component of effective government. The evidence of one hundred years of experimentation had shown that the colonists would not necessarily conform voluntarily to the dictates of the English government. To coerce them, or to mold them into the desired relationship, the English authorities in the colonies had to be relieved of dependence on the colonists for their livelihood. Such an undertaking was expensive, perhaps beyond the capacity of England itself to fulfill. To implement such a program the total resources of the empire would have to be tapped, and that necessarily involved taxing the American colonists in some form. More realistic than the fine words of William Pitt was an answer offered by another Englishman some years later to the same argument that the colonists would accept control of their trade but not taxation: "And then . . . after we have made all these concessions, and removed every thing . . . which can . . . check . . . their smuggling, then, they tell us, that they will cheerfully consent to the operation of such acts . . . of parliament, as they shall find to come within their description of acts of trade . . . after having taken away all authority of parliament to command the observance of these laws . . . they may . . . cheerfully leave them to their operation. Stript of all means of enforcement . . . they well know that they will have no operation at all." [67]

Behind all the rhetoric of these years was one basic fact. The intentions of imperial Britain were incompatible with the aims of the colonists. One or the other would have to give way, or a final test of strength was inescapable. England was determined to exploit its great empire, to fulfill the mercantilist ideal that had lain dormant for a century. Many colonists were equally resolved to defend the atmosphere of relatively unrestricted development in which they had existed for many long years. Both sides had constitutional arguments to justify their positions. The Acts of Trade, embodying the basic principles of the mercantilist doctrine, although never effectively implemented in practice, had come to be accepted by the colonists in theory as legitimate legislative measures. Consequently the English could relate their new enactments to the the failures to achieve the desired coordination of the diverse interests of the empire in the past and argue that the supremacy of Parliament had always been recognized before and was still paramount in 1764. Whatever measures Parliament thought fit to enact were the laws of the empire.

In turn the colonists could base their contentions on the reality of the imperial system as it had operated in the past. For them the constitution

X

Fulfillment

CHARLES TOWNSHEND, the man who "lived too long" and "died too soon," occupies a peculiar place in history. That astute observer of men, Charles James Fox, once remarked that Townshend "must be left to that worst enemy, himself: care only being taken that no agreeableness, no wit, no zealous and clever behaviour . . . ever betray you into trusting him for half an hour." Another contemporary mourned the fact that Townshend's mind and imagination were "so superior to the powers of his heart! The one shewing him many precipices and the other not affording a spark of constancy to support him." Newcastle, experienced politician that he was, simply noted of Townshend that "there is no depending on him." Historians generally have accepted contemporary opinion and Charles Townshend has been immortalized as the brilliant but "unpredictable and erratic" Chancellor of the Exchequer who "dazzled the House" and lost an empire. "Like a schoolboy on a lark" the irresponsible Townshend rose in Commons in January, 1767, declared that he would "assert his own opinions," proposed a taxation scheme for America, and so with this act of "wild impetuosity" reopened the wounds inflicted earlier by Grenville.[1] Unfortunately, this attractive interpretation of the origin of the Townshend Acts ignores the fact that, as Sir Lewis Namier has disclosed, Charles Townshend himself had formulated his program for colonial reform as early as 1754 and in 1767 he "carried into effect the scheme which he had put forward as a very junior minister in 1753–4: a steadiness of purpose with which he has not been credited."[2]

The truth is that there was a consistency not only in Townshend but in British imperial policy in this period that is frequently lost to view. In the confusion of shifting political alliances and realignments, the problem of the colonies has been submerged and distorted. Even the Rockingham ministry, credited with repeal of the Stamp Act and acclaimed as the friend and patron of the American cause, could not escape the logic of England's imperial position. While the Declaratory Act may be discounted as little more than a theoretical gesture, another statute enacted under that ministry indicated that not even those who associated themselves with the American position could abandon completely the program launched by Grenville in 1764. In 1766 the duty on molasses imported into the colonies was lowered from three to one pence. While seemingly a concession to the colonists, in actuality this was a rejection of their fundamental contention that trade regulation was acceptable but that taxation was not. The lower molasses duty imposed by the Rockingham Whigs was to be collected on all molasses entering the colonies, whether of foreign or British origin. Unlike the earlier Acts which involved only foreign molasses, this all-inclusive tax could in no way be termed an attempt solely to regulate trade. On the contrary it was a clear and unmistakable tax levied by Parliament on the colonists. Ironically, not only was this Act destined to bring in more revenue than any other taxation measure imposed on the colonies, but the purpose of the Act as stated in its preface was identical to that expressed in the Sugar and Stamp Acts: to defray "the necessary expenses of defending, protecting, and securing the British colonies and plantations in America." [3]

Nor did this Revenue Act of 1766 stop with a revision of the duties. The bonding requirements of the earlier statutes were extended. Previously ships taking on goods included on the enumerated list were required to post bond to carry those items only to England or English territory. Now it was stated, "in order more effectually to prevent such goods being privately carried from any British colony . . . into foreign parts of Europe in vessels that clear out with non-enumerated goods, as well as to prevent the clandestine importation of foreign European goods into the said British colonies," every ship loading "any goods not particularly enumerated in the said Acts" should give bond not to land its cargo anywhere in Europe north of Cape Finisterre other than in Great Britain. This sweeping prohibition of direct trade between the colonies and Europe was coupled with an even more startling pronouncement that "all sugars which shall be imported into Great Britain, from any part of the British colonies . . . on the continent of America, shall be deemed and taken to be French sugars." The importers of such sugars were required to pay three pence per hundredweight on their entry into England, and no drawbacks or rebates were to be allowed. This provision was an admission of the failure of the attempt to control the importation of foreign sugars into the continental colonies, and by decreeing all sugars exported from those plantations to be of foreign origin the British government hoped to put a stop to that unfortunate loss of revenue.

The fact that such measures could be passed by the "friends" of the colonists indicates the full extent of the divergence of American and English interests. The "Old Whigs" might take advantage of American opposition to the Stamp Act to undermine the Grenville ministry; the Americans, in turn, might make a hero of that stout champion of liberty, John Wilkes. But in each case it was more a matter of expediency, and perhaps of naïveté, rather than principle that brought the two sides together. Even Pitt, who was elevated close to sainthood by the colonists, found it difficult to pursue his policy of moderation once he assumed office. In Pitt's case the specific cause of trouble was the Mutiny Act. Although the Rockingham ministry had amended the original Mutiny Act (passed under the Grenville ministry) so as to prevent the quartering of troops in private homes, the colonists still found its provisions objectionable. The dispute over the Act reached critical proportions in New York, where the Assembly flatly refused to comply with its regulations, claiming that it too represented a form of internal taxation. In this way the "troublesome question of Parliament's right of taxation in the Colonies was . . . resurrected." [4] The attitude of the colonists on this issue helped to strengthen the position of those who wished to follow a "hard line" policy towards the Americans. As one correspondent described the situation, "Ill and groundless reports have been circulated, as though the Colonies were even yet in a state of tumult and confusion (or, as some of them are pleased to term it, rebellion)." [5] Even Pitt himself was angered by the attitude of the colonists: "New York has drunk the deepest of the baneful cup of infatuation, but none seem to be sober and in full possession of reason." [6] It was in this atmosphere of deepening suspicion and distrust that the Townshend program was introduced.

The William Pitt who succeeded Rockingham as prime minister was a far cry from the man who had taken office in 1758 and rallied the nation around him. Pitt in 1766 was old, tired, and subject to strange, incapacitating spells of depression. Titular head of the new ministry, he spent much of his time in retirement in the country, leaving his cabinet colleagues to muddle through as best they might. In such a power vacuum the initiative lay with the man who had the "answers." In this case that man was Charles Townshend. Not only had Townshend conceived a coherent colonial policy as early as 1754 but in 1763 he had specifically developed a colonial taxation scheme which had not been acted upon. In effect, he came to office in 1766 with a colonial program already in mind.[7]

In January, 1767, Townshend, without consulting his colleagues, announced in the House of Commons that he knew how to raise funds in the colonies in a manner acceptable to the colonists. Prodded further by Grenville, Townshend pledged himself to make such an attempt. The result was an Act levying duties on imports of glass, lead, paint, paper, and tea into the colonies. The revenue to be raised was expected to amount only to £40,000 a year, but Townshend pointed out that his Act was merely a beginning and further impositions could be made later after this precedent had been established.[8]

Much has been made of the fact that Townshend acted on his own responsibility in this affair. Lord Rockingham reportedly stated that the Townshend duties "originated from no plan or policy whatever, but were merely the result of picque and passion" on Townshend's part. Another contemporary observer reported that the Act establishing the duties "stole through the House; no man knew how it passed."[9] Such statements are misleading. Any proposal to tax the colonists had wide support in Parliament; in fact, when pressed by his colleagues in the cabinet to explain his original unauthorized promise to raise a substantial colonial revenue, Townshend replied that he had in effect merely been responding to the mood of the House, which was "bent on obtaining a revenue of some sort from the colonies." Even his disgruntled colleagues had to admit that Townshend was correct in his appraisal of the prevalent attitude toward the colonies in the House. And, while Townshend's irresponsibility in reviving the question of a colonial revenue on his own authority has become a celebrated incident, actually at the time his contemporaries took little or no note of his behavior in this instance.[10] An indication of the connection between the dispute over the Mutiny Act and the enactment of the Townshend duties is the fact that in his speech presenting his taxation scheme (May 13th) Townshend devoted most of his time to discussing the appropriate punishment to be meted out to New York and only dealt briefly with his revenue proposals at the very end.[11]

An illuminating insight into the exact nature of Townshend's plan for the colonies is shown in a communication he sent to the Duke of Grafton. Townshend originally had intended to present a bill outlining his proposals on May 5th. He delayed this move until May 13th, and the reason for the delay, as he explained it to Grafton, was simply that "the opportunity has not been taken of soliciting his Majesty's assent to the proposition of independent salaries for the civil officers of North America." When he did introduce the bill, according to Horace Walpole, Townshend asserted that "The salaries of governors and judges in that part of the world must be made independent of their Assemblies." In regard to Townshend's plan the agent for South Carolina reported back to that colony that "out of the fund arising from the American duties . . . His Majesty should be enabled to establish salaries . . . better suited to support the dignity of the respective officers, and for which to be no longer dependent upon the pleasure of any Assembly." [12]

Here lay the heart of the Townshend program. The proposal for a colonial civil list which had been discarded by Grenville for want of sufficient funds was to be Townshend's first concern. The bill introduced belatedly by Townshend on May 13th contained this preamble:

> Whereas it is expedient that a revenue should be raised, in your Majesty's dominions in America, for making certain and adequate provision for defraying the charge of the administration of justice, and the support of civil government in such provinces where it shall be found necessary, and towards further defraying the expenses of defending, protecting, and securing the said dominions; we . . . grant unto your Majesty the several rates and duties hereinafter mentioned.[13]

Paragraph five of this Act expressly authorized the royal government to use as much of the new revenue as was considered necessary to ensure the administration of justice and the support of civil government. The army, which had priority in Grenville's day, now was to be cut back, withdrawn from the interior, and stationed in the coastal areas of the colonies.[14] Not only could the troops be used more effectively in the various ports to overawe the colonists but the consequent savings could be assigned toward the payment of the civil officials. Unlike Grenville, Townshend put the solution of administrative problems ahead of military considerations. The £40,000 to be raised by the Townshend duties would not pay for all the administrative officials in America, but it would provide an emergency fund to be used, as the preamble to the Act indicated, as "necessary." The revenues could then be gradually increased in the future until a complete reform of the colonial system had been effected. Such was the promise — or the threat — inherent in the Townshend program.

The creation of the new duties was only one part of the total project. To clear up one of the weaknesses of the former system paragraph ten of the revenue act settled the dispute over the writs of assistance by authorizing the "superior or supreme" courts in each colony to issue them at will. And at the same time the customs service itself underwent a fundamental reorganization with the establishment of a new American Board of Customs Commissioners. It has been suggested that Charles Paxton, surveyor and searcher at Boston, was responsible for introducing this idea to Townshend.[15] Paxton was in London in 1766–67 and might well have presented such a proposal. He had been a customs officer in Massachusetts since 1733 and was familiar with the problems created by the absence of a central authority in the colonies to supervise and coordinate the operation of the system. However, whatever role Paxton may have played in the creation of the new board, one of the primary reasons for its establishment was the difficulty encountered in utilizing the American revenues raised since 1764 to pay the expenses of the troops stationed in the colonies.

After the passage of the Sugar Act the question of the distribution of the funds raised under its provisions was debated at the Treasury. Payment of the salaries of the troops had been let out on contract to certain individuals. In April, 1765, it was decided to permit the agents of those contractors to receive the required funds directly from the individual collectors in America, giving the collectors in exchange bills of credit which could be forwarded to the Exchequer in England. The Commissioners of the Customs agreed to this proposal and authorized their officers to pay their receipts over to such deputy paymasters for the army as should be established in the colonies. One of the major considerations in this arrangement was to "prevent as much as possible the bringing of Specie out of the Colonies." [16]

However, within a year the Commissioners were not so pleased with the plan. Because the customs collectors were spread throughout the colonies from New Hampshire to Georgia, in some way the receipts had to be gathered together in a central location. The contractors did not wish to bear the expense of sending their deputies to each port, while the Commissioners were equally reluctant to permit their officers to carry the money to the paymasters wherever they might be. They objected to having their officers leave the ports they were to supervise and also felt the removal of the receipts was a risky business which they would rather not manage. Instead the Commissioners suggested that deputy paymasters be established in the more profitable ports to receive the money from the collectors. The less important ports would still send their returns directly to London.[17]

The dispute was still being debated early in 1767. In January the Treasury noted the difficulty of negotiating the bills of exchange and the small sums of money turned over to the paymasters in the colonies. Proposals to abandon the whole plan and to let the supply of money to the troops in America out completely on contract were discussed.[18] The Customs Commissioners were asked for their opinion. In their answer the Commissioners combined the problem of financing the troops with the establishment of a Board of Commissioners to reside in America. Their remarks were in effect a frank appraisal of the history, the failures and results, of one hundred years of experimentation with the colonial customs service. The theme of their report was that because of "the great distance of America, rendering Correspondence with the Officers . . . there, very tedious and liable to great uncertainty & interruption, the Instructions and Orders of this Board can have but little effect." The body of the text they presented to the Treasury is worth quoting at length, containing as it does a commentary on the earlier history of the customs service:

Negligent, Partial, or Corrupt Officers, will from that Circumstance furnish themselves with specious pretences either to defeat or elude the directions sent them; and the diligent and faithfull Officers, willing & desirous to do their duty must be under great discouragement for want of ready assistance, information and support. The truth of this General observation has been long known & felt, but the Oppression the Officers . . . labour under in America (more especially some parts of that Continent) have lately grown to such an enormous height, that it is become impossible for them to do their duty, not only from the outrage of Mobs but for fear also of vexatious Suits, Verdicts & Judgments in the Provincial Courts, and even of Criminal Prosecution therein . . .

We are further to observe that the uncertain Aid of Governors, and the Institution of Surveyors General of the Customs in America are found to be very inadequate means either to prevent or redress the mischiefs derived from the great distance We are at, For tho' the Surveyors General are necessary in the present mode of conducting this Revenue there, yet in many cases of great importance where Actions from various causes are liable to be misrepresented here, it would neither be prudent in them, nor indeed are they legally Authorized to give such decisive orders & countenance to the inferior Officers . . . as the Exigence of the Case may require.

[At present the system must] almost wholly depend upon the Prudence, Resolution & good Conduct of those several Surveyors General . . . and yet as We have already observed their power (great as it is to be trusted to an individual) is not sufficient to attain the Ends for which it is given. The Scene lies so remote, that this Board must generally judge of Matters there by the light in which they are stated to Us by their Representations and Reports, without any probability of a check upon them.

The Commissioners closed by pointing out that effective rewards and punishments were the only way to keep the customs personnel attentive to duty but that as it was there were such delays, particularly in administering punishments, that "the great purpose of Example is but imperfectly obtained." Consequently they recommended the creation of a Board of Commissioners to reside in America as a solution to these problems.[19]

By this time the Treasury had become intrigued with the thought of the establishment of an American Board and asked the Commissioners to offer more explicit proposals separately from the question of payments to the military forces in the colonies.[20] By July, 1767, the Commissioners had prepared a detailed plan for the new Board and attended the Treasury Lords in person to present their suggestions. They proposed a Board consisting of five members, each receiving a salary of £500 per year. They would be provided with four clerks, the chief clerk (who would also act as Registrar of Seizures) receiving £100, the second clerk £60, and the two others £40 each a year. Further the Board would have a solicitor

Fulfillment

(£200), who would have clerical help of his own, amounting to £160 a year. Other officers included a Cashier and Paymaster, a Comptroller (to check the accounts of the Cashier), an Inspector of Imports and Exports, and two roving Inspector Generals to be used as the Board saw fit. The total yearly salary bill for this proposed establishment amounted to £4,500.

That expense would not, however, be a completely new imposition on the strained British revenues. The Commissioners pointed out that savings to the amount of £2,491 could be made by eliminating various officers no longer required. The plantation clerk and his assistant would not be needed in London, saving £600. Reduction of other clerical help would add £236 to that sum. And finally the dismissal of the surveyors general would cut £1,685 from the costs of the establishment. The Commissioners did not include the salary of the surveyor general of the West Indies on this list, since he was paid from the four and one-half percent revenues, but they pointed out that his salary too could be saved by having the new inspectors general tour that area from time to time. Not including that saving, the cost of the new establishment would increase the expenses of the British government by only £2,000 a year.[21]

The Treasury approved this plan except for the suggestion that the new Board have authority over the West Indies as well as the continent. After consulting with various representatives of the West Indies planters and merchants, the Treasury Lords informed the Commissioners that the islands were to be continued under the old arrangements and not combined with the continental areas. The arguments for this distinction are interesting for the light they throw on the English attitude towards the mainland and insular colonies: "the Communication & intercourse is constant and regular between the West India Islands and Great Britain where all the Merchants who carry on that Trade reside." Therefore it would be inconvenient for the West Indies merchants to have to deal with a Customs Board in New York or Philadelphia where they had little business and no agents. In the plan as finally approved, only the Bahamas and Bermuda were placed under the supervision of the American Board. The rest of the islands, including Jamaica, continued under the care of the London Commissioners.[22]

Later criticism of the conduct of the men appointed to the new American Board of Customs Commissioners has tended to obscure the care with which they were chosen. O. M. Dickerson has written that the "selection of the personnel was unfortunate" and that the American Commissioners were typical of the "new race of customs officers" who descended on the colonies like a swarm of parasites in 1767 to fatten themselves on the spoils of empire.[23] In fact, in the case of all but one of the appointees, whose background is not known, each of the new Commissioners had earned the consideration of the Treasury Lords in some manner. Charles Paxton not only was the possible author of the idea for an American Board but had served long and well as a customs officer in Massachusetts, had borne the brunt of the struggle against the merchants and Benjamin Barons in 1761–62, and had won the enthusiastic recommendation of Governor Bernard for his conduct.

John Robinson had gone to Rhode Island in 1764 and had attempted in spite of many obstacles to enforce the Acts in their entirety until driven from the colony by the threats of legal prosecutions by the judge of the Admiralty court. Henry Hulton had served as plantation clerk to the London Commissioners since 1763 and had previously been a customs officer in the West Indies. John Temple had made a name for himself as surveyor general northern since 1761. Although he had been involved in many disputes with Governor Bernard and others, to the Customs Commissioners in 1767 it seemed that he had done so from a legitimate desire to increase the effectiveness of his office. The last and "unknown" appointee was William Burch, new to the colonies but possibly a former customs officer in Scotland. Charles Steuart, former surveyor general for the Eastern Middle District, was assigned to the important post of cashier and paymaster, while a solicitor was chosen after the Board was established in America.[24]

The location of the new Board was considered at length — New York, Philadelphia, and Boston all being discussed. Unfortunately the reason for the choice of Boston is not recorded. There are many possible explanations. Boston was the most active of the centers of opposition to the English administration; stationing the Commissioners there would lend their authority and prestige to the work of the local customs officers. Perhaps Boston was selected because it was the nearest of the major ports to Halifax, where the headquarters of the British navy in America was located; the Treasury Lords may have recognized the importance of co-ordinating the activities of the customs service and the navy. Or possibly the Board was set up at Boston merely because it was the nearest of the three major ports to England. The American Commissioners, like their counterparts in England, were to be under the supervision of the Treasury and communication between the two departments would need to be as swift as possible to ensure complete efficiency.

The creation of the American Board was not allowed to depend on the authority of the crown alone. Parliament was called upon to legislate the Board into existence to obviate any possible questioning of its legality by the colonists. The Act authorizing establishment of the American Board explained that it was done because in the past the customs officers in the colonies had been "obliged to apply to the said commissioners of the customs in England for their special instructions and directions upon every particular doubt and difficulty which arises" and also because "all persons concerned in the commerce and trade of the said colonies and plantations are greatly obstructed and delayed in the carrying on and transacting of their business." The American Commissioners were granted all the powers and authority "for carrying into execution the several laws relating to the revenues and trade of the said British colonies" as had previously belonged to the Commissioners of the Customs in England.[25]

The Treasury later described the reasoning behind the creation of the American Board in this way:

The Design of those who recommended the establishment . . . to Parliament, and the intention of Parliament in adopting it, were to give arrangement, regularity, and improvement to the collection and receipt of the American Duties; to carry remedy and redress nearer to the grievances which had long been observed to prevail and to encrease by reason of the distance of the superintendancy and controul of the Board of Customs in England, and by a more immediate interposition of authority to support the officers of the Revenue on one hand, in detecting and suppressing the Frauds and Enterprizes of illicit Trade; and on the other to protect the Commerce and secure the Property of the fair Merchant from the abuse of power and the insolence of inferior officers.[26]

Many years earlier a customs official in America had written that "a General Evil requires a General Remedy" and that what was needed

223

was "an actual Superior upon the Spot."[27] In effect, the creation of the Board of American Commissioners was Townshend's answer — the answer of the English government — to that long-standing problem.

Concurrently with the establishment of the American Board came reorganization of the Vice-Admiralty court system in the colonies. Since the first establishment of the jurisdiction of the Admiralty courts in 1696, report after report had indicated that those tribunals were of little value. The special court set up at Halifax in 1764 had proved equally useless. The distance involved, and the complications attendant on removing a case from one of the other colonies to Nova Scotia for settlement, had limited Judge Spry's activities to a few unimportant hearings.

As early as 1765 it had been suggested that courts similar to that at Halifax be established at Boston, Philadelphia, and Charleston. In those convenient locations they would be readily available to crown officers who experienced difficulty in obtaining satisfaction in the local common law or Admiralty courts. Charles Townshend died unexpectedly before he was able to complete his program. But before he died, he approved a draft of a bill to create several new superior Admiralty courts in America. By July, 1768, that proposal had been approved by Parliament and four new courts were distributed in America. One replaced the old court at Halifax, while others were located at Boston, Philadelphia, and Charleston. These new tribunals had original jurisdiction equal to that of the provincial Admiralty courts in any case involving breaches of the trade laws and appellate power to review decisions made in the lower courts.[28]

The final step in the reform program was taken after Townshend's death with the creation of a new Secretary of State for the Plantations. Again, the drama associated with the political battles being fought in London in these years has clouded over the actual significance of the establishment of this office. Since Hillsborough, the first occupant of the new post, belonged to the Bedford faction, and since the separation of American affairs from the office of Secretary for the Southern Department marked a diminution of the powers of Pitt's protégé, Shelburne, there is an obvious temptation to ascribe the creation of the new office to political considerations. But it was only in the selection of Hillsborough for the position, not in the establishment of the new secretaryship, that politics played a part; actually, the establishment of such an office had been long under consideration and would have occurred earlier but for the vagaries of English politics.

Since the time forty-five years earlier when Sir William Keith had suggested that if the colonies ever were to be properly administered it was necessary that responsibility for the conduct of affairs be centered "in one place," similar ideas frequently had been urged on the British government.[29] One of the most effective advocates of such centralization of authority was Thomas Pownall, whose *Administration of the Colonies* (published in 1764) pointed out the dangers of divided responsibility.[30] There is evidence that even before the appearance of Pownall's tract the creation of a new secretaryship was considered and that Charles Townshend was in fact offered such a post in 1762 during Bute's administration.[31] It is an indication both of Townshend's political importance and of the high esteem in which his knowledge of colonial affairs was held in these years that, when the Rockingham ministry in 1766 contemplated the establishment of a separate colonial department, Charles Townshend once again was proposed for the office. But for his short tenure of office, Rockingham undoubtedly would have set up such a position, although without Townshend, who refused to serve under him. The Earl of Chesterfield probably best summed up the general feeling in this period when he wrote in 1766 that "if we have no Secretary of State with full and undisputed powers for America, in a few years we may as well have no America." [32]

Most suggestions for setting up a central bureau of American affairs had envisaged transforming the Board of Trade into a Department of State. Halifax in 1751 and later had tried to do just that but had been frustrated by his inability to secure cabinet rank.[33] When the Rockingham ministry took up the problem they at first intended to merge the Board of Trade into the new American Department, but the king disapproved of this plan. As a result when the new office was set up in January, 1768, it was separate and distinct from the Board, although Hillsborough eventually did combine in his person the two offices of American Secretary and President of the Board of Trade.[34] Unfortunately, while the establishment of the new office was an improvement from an administrative point of view, the selection of Hillsborough for the position was unwise. Hillsborough, along with other members of the Bedford faction, was dedicated to ruling America with an iron hand. His appointment, and his behavior once he was in office, were partly responsible for New-castle's comment that the "Doctrine of doing everything by Force prevails now Everywhere." [35] More important, perhaps, than his addiction to the doctrine of force (which, after all, he shared with many others at the time) was the fact that Hillsborough was easily panicked and given to hasty decisions. In the long run he was to contribute markedly to the growth of colonial opposition to English policies.

With Hillsborough's appointment the major components of Townshend's system were assembled. The key to his program lay in the use to be made of the revenues arising in America. In effect, what he proposed to do was to raise funds in America to relieve the royal officials there of any dependence on the inhabitants. "A remodelling of colonial government was Townshend's aim, to which the raising of a revenue by act of the British Parliament became a necessary corollary." [36] One hundred years earlier the Stuarts had thought to achieve the same end merely by asserting their authority in America. The Dominion of New England had represented the execution of that policy in practice. Now, a century later, merely to assert the authority of England was not enough; Grenville had tried to do just that with disastrous results. Townshend's approach was more subtle. Realizing that nothing could be accomplished until and unless English political authority within the colonies was strengthened, Townshend intended to use money taken from the colonists themselves to finance a gradual revival of imperial power. Officials and adherents of royal government would be financed and lavishly rewarded from the American revenues. At the same time the collection and enforcement machinery, as well as the whole administrative apparatus, would be tightened. And, as royal government became more effective, the available revenues in turn would be increased. In effect, taking advantage of increasing resentment among Englishmen at the conduct of the colonists and of the equally widespread desire for a tax reduction, Townshend introduced a program which was intended to correct the one fatal flaw of the previous colonial system. If effective, it would ensure the combination of absolute legislative authority with the "power of the purse." Hopefully, the result would be the realization, at last, of the conception of the empire as a network of interrelated parts, all dedicated and devoted to one primary purpose — the sustenance of the welfare and prosperity of England.

XI

Collapse

A significant but fatal experiment in colonial administration began in 1767 with the establishment of the American board of customs in Boston, Massachusetts.[1]

IRONICALLY, what should have been a beginning was instead an ending. The American Commissioners arrived in Boston on November 5, 1767. Within eight months' time they had been forced by mob action to flee the city and take refuge in a harbor fort, protected by the guns of an English man-of-war. Their humiliation, and the speed with which it was accomplished, were a measure of the temper and effectiveness of the colonial opposition. As the brief, dramatic history of the American Board illustrated, the Townshend plan, for all its subtle logic, was the right program enacted a half century or more too late.

The arrival of the Commissioners actually came off better than expected. When news of their appointment had first reached America, Governor Bernard had reported that the opposition in Massachusetts was divided in its reaction to the Townshend Acts; the merchants in general were indifferent, while the "faction" of extremists was disturbed both by the complacency of the merchants and by the measures taken to relieve the royal officials of financial dependence on the local inhabitants. Bernard warned that the situation was inherently explosive: "the Faction or their underlings give out that they intend to do something when the Commissioners of the Customs come; and particularly threaten Mr. Paxton who is understood to be one of them."[2] But public apathy led the "faction" to call off its plans, and the Commissioners were greeted not by violence but by a satirical procession. Carrying figures representing the Pope, the Pretender, and the Devil (the last bearing the name "Charles" in honor of Paxton), a crowd of citizens followed the Commissioners from the dock through the town. Otherwise their arrival was marked by no disturbance.[3]

Although the colonial opposition at first held its hand, it did not take the members of the Board long to understand the exact nature of their situation. In one of their early letters, they reported to the Treasury that already it was apparent that the customs service in America suffered from a lack of support from the civil authorities. During the last two and one-half years, they noted, there had been only six seizures in all of New England, only one of which was prosecuted to effect. Somewhat forlornly they remarked that earlier the customs officials had been "resisted and defeated in almost every Attempt to do their duty when the Right of Parliament to lay external taxes was acknowledged." Now that the right of Parliament to lay any taxes whatsoever had been questioned "we . . . expect that we shall find it totally impracticable to enforce the Execution of the Revenue Laws until the Hand of Government is properly strengthened."[4] Nor did Governor Bernard have any illusions on that subject. When asked by the Commissioners for assistance, he replied that he had none to give. As royal governor in a "popularly" dominated colony, he was powerless. His authority, Bernard reported, would have to be strengthened before he could do much in support of the Board.[5] Both Bernard and the Commissioners correctly assessed the critical issue of the moment; quite simply, they were involved in a race against time to bolster the support available to royal government in America before a final trial of strength was forced upon them.

In March, 1768, open opposition to the Board first appeared. As reported by Bernard, Daniel Malcom, "a little trader" who had made a reputation for himself earlier by his resistance to the customs officers, expecting the arrival of a vessel from the Madeiras, approached the customs officers and asked what indulgence he might expect in regard to the duties. Told none at all, Malcom replied that he was pleased to know exactly how matters now stood. When the ship arrived, he had it anchor below the town and unloaded a reported total of sixty pipes of wine, which were then smuggled into Boston and hidden in various cellars. The next day Malcom's captain went to the customs house and entered as having come in ballast from Surinam. Since no one could be found to inform on Malcom, he suffered not at all. In fact, three days after his successful coup, Malcom presided over a general meeting of the merchants of Boston, called to discuss opposition to the new British measures. As Bernard pointed out, this meeting was in a sense the first extra-legal assembly to be called in Boston in protest against the Acts of Parliament, previous discussions having been carried on in the regular town meetings.[6]

The irritating Malcom affair was merely a foretaste of things to come. From the moment of the appointment of the American Board the colonial customs service as a whole centered on its operations, a fact that was obvious both to the Commissioners and to the opposition groups in Massachusetts. Consequently, more than local antagonisms were involved in the campaign of harassment undertaken against the Board and its members. It was obvious by March, 1768, that Sam Adams and the other leaders of the "faction" were waiting for the right moment to display their strength. A continuance of the truce that had been in effect since the arrival of the Commissioners could have been maintained only by a deliberate refusal on the part of the members of the Board to exercise their authority. Since the Commissioners could not procrastinate forever, the moment, the incident, the opposition was looking for inevitably would arrive. Fittingly, it was John Hancock, one of the wealthiest and most influential of Boston's merchants — a man who had earlier stated publicly at a meeting of the General Assembly that no customs officers would be permitted on board his ships — who ignited the spark that drove the Commissioners from the city.

On April 7, 1768, one of Hancock's ships, the *Lydia*, arrived in Boston. Two tidesmen were put on board by the collector. While they were there Hancock and a crowd of followers, including Malcom, boarded the ship. According to the laws, customs officers were permitted to board a vessel either to search for illegal goods or to see that no goods were unloaded without the knowledge of the authorities. In the former case they were free to inspect the entire ship, but if their orders were merely to watch for attempts to smuggle goods ashore the law specified only that they might remain on board.

Hancock ordered his captain not to let the tidesmen below deck on pain of dismissal. However, the following night one of the officers, thinking he was unobserved, went below to look the cargo over. Hancock was summoned and confronted the tidesman, surrounded by eight or so followers, including once again the ever-present Malcom. Intimidated by the show of force, the tidesman stated that he had no orders to search the boat. Thereupon Hancock had him forcibly carried on deck, while the companion-way was fastened shut behind them. Malcom the meanwhile shouted, "Damn him, hand him up; if it was my vessel, I would knock him down."

Again, as in the earlier incident involving Malcom's cellar, this minor affair was blown up into a major incident. In the tense expectant atmosphere of Boston in that year very little was required to ignite an explosion. The Commissioners wished to make an example of this affair, fearing that if such flagrant intimidation of the outdoor officers was allowed to pass, no tidesman would be able in the future to perform his duties. However, once again the technicalities of the laws defeated their intentions. The tidesman had said that he had no orders to inspect the cargo. Consequently, he legally had no right below deck, so that there was no case against Hancock. The fact that the officer made such a statement surrounded by a crowd of unfriendly men in the dark hold of the ship made no difference. The matter had to be dropped.[7]

While the case of the *Lydia* was still being discussed, another of Hancock's ships, the *Liberty,* arrived in Boston, coming from the Madeiras with a cargo of wine. The captain entered twenty-five pipes of wine at the customs house. It was reported that much more wine was actually on board, but the two tidesmen stationed on the *Liberty* stated that nothing more than the reported cargo was discharged from the vessel. However, the Commissioners, remembering that Hancock had given out "in public that if we the Commissioners are not recalled, he will get rid of us before Christmas," were not convinced that all was well with the *Liberty.*

The outdoor officers were one of the weak links in the operation of the customs service. The most exposed to danger, they were also the most open to bribery. In fact there were few if any checks on their activities except that they usually worked in pairs. Generally, it was reported that either intimidation or bribery was frequently effective in inducing them to ignore their duty. Only two months before the arrival of the *Liberty* the Commissioners themselves had informed the Treasury that they had discovered that the local outdoor officers were guilty of collusive practices. As a corrective, the Commissioners had appointed more tidesmen, but all that had been accomplished was to further irritate the merchants.[8] Similarly, a few years later the collector at Philadelphia reported with disgust that of the ten tidesmen in his port two were under suspension and three others under suspicion for complicity in various illegal entries.[9] Now in the case of the *Liberty* a strange tale unfolded.

A month after the arrival and unloading of the *Liberty* one of the tidesmen, Thomas Kirk, went to the collector and comptroller and told them the following story. On the night the *Liberty* had docked in Boston he and his fellow tidesman had been put on board. The other officer soon had too much to drink and staggered off home. One of Hancock's captains later came on board and suggested to Kirk that he should permit the wine to be unloaded. According to Kirk, he refused that suggestion and was thereupon forced below deck and locked there for three hours. During that period he heard men at work, moving the cargo about and possibly unloading some. When he was finally released, Hancock's captain threatened that if one word of the affair was reported to the authorities Kirk's property, and indeed his life, would be endangered. Kirk kept his silence for a month, but during that period the captain who had threatened him died. The tidesman then felt free to carry his story to his superiors, or so he reported.

The truth behind this story told by Kirk will never be known. It is possible that he was lying, either at the request of the collector and comptroller who wished to revenge themselves on Hancock or for reasons of his own. Perhaps Kirk had permitted the wine to be unloaded, accepted a bribe for doing so, and then after the captain had died thought he could make more by "informing" to his superiors. Or perhaps Kirk was telling the simple truth. Hancock had previously shown that he knew how to use intimidation effectively and Kirk may have really been frightened into silence. William Baxter, who has made an exhaustive study of Hancock's papers, reported that he could find nothing to either prove or disprove Hancock's statement that there were only twenty-five pipes of wine on board the *Liberty*.[10] Considering Hancock's earlier public defiance of the customs officers, as well as the activities of Malcom, the collector had good reason to suspect that Kirk's story was true. At any rate it seemed a good opportunity to make an example of the "infatuated" merchant.

The collector and comptroller, on the advice of the solicitor to the

American Board, seized the *Liberty*. In the process they unleashed a storm of angry opposition far beyond anything the Commissioners had expected. By their hasty action the collector and comptroller precipitated a crisis which left the Commissioners in a difficult situation. The case against Hancock and the illegal unloading of the wine was not, to say the least, particularly strong; it depended on the testimony of one man, given long after the fact. Although both their own solicitor and the attorney general of England thought there was enough evidence to take the case to trial, the Commissioners wisely decided not to let the trial stand on the matter of the wines and Kirk's testimony. When the *Liberty* had been seized on June 10th, it was discovered that a new cargo already had been put on board. No permit to load had been taken out by Hancock. It had been customary in the past, in spite of the letter of the law, for ships to take on cargo before clearing at the customs house. Still, the legal requirement was that no vessel should take on any goods until a permit had been obtained. On that point the customs officers had a good case against Hancock. The ship itself was tried and condemned on the grounds of loading before permission had been given.[11]

Success in that test was tempered for the Commissioners by the humiliation of a flight from Boston. When the customs officers had seized the *Liberty* on June 10th, a crowd had gathered and they had been abused, hit by stones, and threatened with reprisals. Much of the crowd's anger was caused by the determination of the officers to anchor their prize under the guns of the royal man-of-war then in the harbor. They feared that leaving the *Liberty* at the wharf would be an open invitation for the "faction" to attempt a forcible rescue. With the help of marines from the man-of-war they managed to take the *Liberty* to a safe anchorage. The royal marines were abused equally with the customs officers during the whole operation.[12]

The following uproar was so great that the Commissioners themselves had to flee to the safety of the same man-of-war which guarded the *Liberty*. Disturbed at the violence of the outburst the Commissioners thought "to pacify the Town" by returning the ship to the wharf and to the possession of Hancock. They opened negotiations with Hancock to that effect, asking that in return he would promise to abide by the decision of the Admiralty court when the case came to trial. At first it seemed that this plan would be successful. Hancock was anxious to get his vessel back and may even have initiated the compromise idea himself. But while he was debating whether or not to accept the offer of the Commissioners, all the leaders of the "faction" called upon him and urged him not to give up this opportunity to win a propaganda advantage over the English. Hancock finally refused the overtures of the Commissioners, who consequently failed in their hopes of restoring quiet to the town. They finally sought refuge in the fort in Boston Harbor, which was offered to them by Governor Bernard. The Commissioners at this point had been in Boston less than eight months.[13]

Many years before, William Bollan had suggested that the trade laws would never be enforced adequately until the customs officers were authorized to prosecute the people involved in violations of the Acts as well as the ships or goods in question. This proposal had been revived in the discussion that had taken place in 1759. Now the attorney general of England reported that it might be well to bring suits against the men involved in unloading the goods from the *Liberty* as well as against those obstructing the seizure.[14] Feeling that in spite of their attempts to prevent the affair from playing into the hands of the "faction," the case of the *Liberty* had become an open trial of strength, the Commissioners decided to initiate a personal action against Hancock and some of his associates.

The trial of Hancock and five alleged accomplices was commenced in October, 1768. The crown lawyers asked judgment against each man for £9,000, treble the estimated value of the wine supposedly smuggled ashore. Hancock was defended by a young lawyer, John Adams. Much of Adams' argument was based on constitutional theory. In fact, the crown's case was extremely weak. It depended mainly on Kirk's belated testimony coupled with the public statements and actions of Hancock prior to the arrival of the *Liberty* in Boston. The hearings dragged on through the winter until in March the decision was made to drop the case against Hancock and his associates. With the words, "Our Sovereign Lord the King will prosecute no further" the Commissioners admitted defeat.[15] On this occasion more harm was done than merely exposing once again the weakness of royal authority in America. Hancock became a hero for thousands of colonists. The arguments of Adams were echoed from one colony to the next. Of equal importance was the fact that English troops were sent to Boston.

From their retreat in the harbor fort the Commissioners reported that they could not return to Boston until measures were taken for their support. Governor Bernard hesitated to call for troops in his own name, fearing that if he did so the anger his action would arouse would ruin any further aid he might be able to render to the royal cause in Massachusetts. General Thomas Gage in New York was willing, indeed eager, to send soldiers to Boston to assert English authority but could not act without either a request from Bernard or orders from London. Finally, the English ministry decided the time for firmness had arrived and dispatched four regiments to Boston. The "Sons of Liberty" threatened to oppose the landing of the troops with force, but the colonists were not yet ready for such extreme measures. The troops landed in September, 1768, and remained there until the fateful day of the Boston Massacre a year and a half later.[16] Indirectly Hancock and his ship, the *Liberty,* had commenced a series of events leading to open revolution.

Although the affair of the *Liberty* took on added importance because it involved the Commissioners of the Customs themselves and led to their flight from Boston, an equally famous — and disastrous — seizure was made at the same time in Charleston, South Carolina. The feud there between the customs officers and Henry Laurens had lost none of its bitterness in the months following the trials of the *Wambaw* and the *Broughton Island Packet.* George Roupell, left to handle the cases by the collector who fled the province, was sued by Laurens for £5,000 damages. In releasing the *Broughton Island Packet* Judge Leigh had failed to decree a probable cause of seizure, leaving Roupell open to such a suit. Although the judge himself acted as Roupell's lawyer in the common law trial, Laurens won a verdict of £1,400 local currency against the customs officer. That sum was eventually paid for Roupell by the Customs Commissioners, but the officer was determined on revenge.[17]

Roupell's opportunity came when one of Laurens' ships, the *Ann,* took on a cargo in Charleston. Although the main cargo, rice, had been entered properly at the customs house, the captain had neglected to report various other small items taken on board. According to the Act of 1766 all goods, enumerated or nonenumerated, had to be declared. Roupell took advantage of the captain's omission and seized the *Ann.* At first he hoped to use his prize to force Laurens to admit his guilt in the earlier case of the *Broughton Island Packet,* which would in effect reverse the decision against Roupell in the common law suit. Laurens declined to accept this scheme, and Roupell was forced to take the *Ann* to trial.

Once again Judge Leigh presided over the hearings. His decision in this case was in line with his earlier rulings; he acquitted the *Ann* but declared a probable cause of seizure and assessed the costs of the trial to Laurens.[18] Actually there was little else Judge Leigh could have done. Although it had never been customary previously to enforce the Act of 1766 so strictly, the captain of the *Ann* had broken the letter of the law. On the other hand it seemed unfair to condemn Laurens' ship on a technicality not previously insisted upon by the customs officers. Despite the difficulty of the judge's position, Laurens was infuriated at the verdict and broke off all relations with his uncle.

As a result of this trial Laurens opened a propaganda warfare against the whole customs service and Judge Leigh in particular. In February, 1768, he published extracts from the hearings to illustrate the arbitrary nature of Admiralty court justice. Leigh answered with a pamphlet entitled *The Man Un-Masked*, to which Laurens in turn responded with a further publication of *Observations* on the conduct of the customs officers and the Admiralty courts.[19] The publicity given to this affair served to crystallize public opinion and to furnish such propagandists as Sam Adams with effective arguments for a united front against the incursions of imperial authority.

By the autumn of 1768 it was obvious that the experiment undertaken in the establishment of the American Board was a failure. Centralization of the customs service had served merely to give focus to the colonial opposition. The Commissioners came to symbolize the existence of an arbitrary external authority, and every successful attack on the Board or its members took on the aspect of a major colonial victory. Rather belatedly, the Treasury realized this point and cautioned the Commissioners to remember the delicate nature of their situation. From the point of view of the Commissioners, driven into hiding a mere eight months after their arrival, such advice must have seemed gratuitous. In July, 1768, the Treasury Lords advised the members of the Board to act with firmness and resolution in executing the laws but "at the same time to conduct themselves . . . with such temper and discretion as may give no just grounds of complaint." Naïvely, the Treasury predicted that "such a Conduct . . . will most effectively tend to raise in your officers reverence for your Authority and in the People of America a cheerful submission to the Duties imposed on them by the Parliament of Great Britain." [20] The Commissioners — and the other officers in America — knew only too well how impossible it was to act with firmness and still give the colonists no cause for complaint. In Salem, Massachusetts, for example, a month before the Treasury wrote those words, a boat belonging to the customs house was seized by various of the local people, carried to an area beyond the reach of rescue, and burned.[21] A month after the Commissioners received the reprimand from the Treasury, one of the tidesmen in Salem was tarred and feathered, carried about the town, tied to the Liberty Pole, and warned never to show his face there again. Only five days later the customs officers guarding a seizure at Cape Ann north of Salem were forcibly locked inside a warehouse by a reported crowd of seventy or more men while the goods were carried off.[22] In these circumstances the decision for the customs officers was not how to act with caution but whether to act at all.

Unfortunately, the efficiency of the American Board was further reduced by a feud among its own members. Charles Paxton and John Temple were old enemies, the ill-feeling between them dating back to the episode of Benjamin Barons nearly a decade earlier. Paxton had the majority of the Board on his side, and Temple's official isolation was furthered by the fact that he and Governor Bernard had long been at odds. Partly the dispute centered on personalities; both Temple and Bernard, as well as Paxton, were ambitious men, jealous of their prerogatives and powers.[23] But involved in this feud was also a fundamental disagreement on the nature of the imperial system and the proper role to be played by the royal officials in America. Paxton and Bernard stood for firmness and a determined effort to assert English authority. Temple believed that in practice the officials should do all they could to mitigate the severities of the laws of Parliament. In Temple's opinion the commercial welfare of the colonists was hurt by "the unnecessary Severities occasioned by our instructions" and he reported sympathetically that since 1767 trade in America had been greatly reduced and "what remains has in a great measure deserted its usual Channel." [24] While Bernard or Paxton might argue that the longer English authority was not exercised the greater the degree of contempt for that authority evidenced in America, Temple argued that such views seemed "to flow rather from an anxious desire of lighting up a war between these colonies and their mother country"; he preferred to act upon "principle" and to endeavor "to regulate and settle revenue matters upon an equal, moderate, and practical system." [25]

While Temple's "practical" approach had much to recommend it, still in terms of the immediate situation his attitude made him a highly unsuitable person for membership on the American Board. His policy of catering to the needs and demands of the colonists was in direct opposition to the policies (and instructions) of the other members of the Board, and Temple's activities did inestimable harm to the effectiveness of the Commissioners. Thomas Hutchinson explained the internal troubles of the Board in this way:

The popular clamour against four of the Commissioners and not the fifth is easily accounted for. It was said the Commissioners would cause new changes and new and heavy burdens upon Trade. The people wished therefore that the Surveyor General might not be superseded. The Commissioners exerted themselves to restore the Acts of Trade which for two or three years together no officer dared to carry into execution: Penal Laws which have been disused from opposition made by the People are considered as more grievous when revived than when first enacted: The People, therefore, have always wished to see the Board abolished and [the] Surveyor General restored.[26]

Temple was not bothered by the harassment his colleagues experienced. While they took shelter in the harbor fort, he continued to live in Boston and come and go as he pleased. This was true both in 1768 after the seizure of the *Liberty* and again in 1770 when the Commissioners once more retreated from Boston in the aftermath of the Massacre. Temple continually complained that he was not permitted to see any documents, that the others never consulted him on important matters, and that generally he was ignored. In turn the other Commissioners felt Temple was not to be trusted with any information, as he was quite likely to pass anything he learned on to his colonial friends. The reluctance of the Commissioners on this point was echoed by Thomas Hutchinson; when Hutchinson had some confidential news for the members of the Board, he stipulated that it be kept "from the knowledge of the Fifth." [27]

The first test of strength between Temple and his colleagues centered on the collector at Salem. Four years earlier Temple, as surveyor general, had driven Bernard's protégé, Cockle, from that post.[28] John Fisher, the man who replaced Cockle, knew to whom he owed his post and acted accordingly. In 1768 Fisher was still loyal to Temple. Paxton and the other Commissioners tried generally to replace Temple's adherents with officers of their own choosing. For example, the searcher and preventive officer that Temple had set up at Nantucket in 1764 was pushed aside. In this particular case, however, the Commissioners had good reason to mistrust Temple's man; the officer at Nantucket, Timothy Folger, was not only an active merchant but had been a close associate of John Hancock.[29] Fisher in Salem was a different problem, one not so easily settled.

A report on conditions in Salem given to the Commissioners by their inspector general, John Williams, had noted that there had been no seizures in that port since December, 1764. This unblemished record could not be attributed to the good behavior of the inhabitants, since "every Owner and every Master of every Vessell coming with dutiable goods within the Limits of this Port are concerned in Smuggling." Checking the incoming ships carefully, Williams found that five of them imported a total of sixty-two thousand gallons of molasses. Using those ships as an average, the inspector estimated that the seventy vessels which had brought molasses to Salem the year before probably imported over nine hundred thousand gallons; the official entries for the previous year showed only three hundred and sixty thousand gallons imported. Williams reported that the loss to the revenue on molasses and sugar brought into Salem probably amounted to £4,000 yearly. He cited one particular incident in which one ship, the *General Wolf*, entered one hundred and eleven casks of molasses at the customs house. The inspector claimed that more than that amount had already been shipped out of Salem, supposedly all taken from the *General Wolf*. In his opinion it was an obvious fraud.[30]

The four Commissioners thought that Williams' report gave them a good reason to remove Temple's friend from Salem. Fortunately for Paxton and his associates, the boat carrying part of the cargo from the *General Wolf* out of Salem was seized by a royal cutter. The boat's papers showed that the entire cargo had been legally imported into Salem in the *Wolf* and the duties paid. But a check of the contents showed that the casks on board the coasting vessel contained seven thousand

and seven hundred gallons of molasses. The *Wolf* supposedly had imported only six thousand and eight hundred gallons. On the basis of this discovery the Commissioners charged Fisher with failing to collect the full duties, giving false certificates to a merchant engaged in illicit trade, and doing so without the knowledge of the comptroller.[31]

Fisher replied to these charges in what the Board considered was an impertinent manner. He stated that he had no control over what a merchant did with his cargo after it was legally entered. The importer might shift his molasses around, putting it into larger barrels or casks if he wished. When the molasses was re-exported, all the master was required to do was to apply to the collector for a cocquet to cover the goods; customarily the collector accepted the word of the master as to the fact that the goods had been legally imported in whatever vessel he designated. In this case, Fisher said, the master had obviously deceived him, but there was nothing he could have done to prevent it. As to the charge of not consulting the comptroller, Fisher said it was never done in such matters as cocquets for re-exports.[32]

The four Commissioners answered that Fisher's explanation was not only inadequate but insulting. They suspended him, but Temple refused to sign the order with them. To the Treasury the four Commissioners wrote that they had suspended Fisher for misconduct and for expressing himself in a way no board could countenance and still maintain its authority. They asked the Treasury to uphold their decision and at the same time requested permission for the Board to carry on its affairs even if one of their members would not participate or sign their orders.[33] In their answer the Treasury Lords refused to take sides in the dispute, which they correctly attributed to the feud between the majority of the Board and Temple. Commending both the zeal and attention to duty displayed by the American Commissioners, the Treasury said that while there seemed to have been reasonable grounds for enquiring into Fisher's conduct the evidence offered to prove his misconduct was not sufficient. Reminding the Commissioners of their previous advice to act with firmness but so as not to give offense, the Treasury Lords added that they were "unwilling for many reasons to order the suspension of Mr. Fisher to be taken off by an immediate interposition of their own authority but they desire and direct You to Cause this Act to be done by an order of your own board." Aside from the face-saving permission to reinstate

Fisher on their own order, the four Commissioners' only consolation in this affair was the Treasury's confirmation of their request to carry on their business even if one of their members would not participate. Thereafter any three of the Commissioners could act in the name of the whole Board.[34]

The internal squabblings of the Board members, the turmoil aroused by the seizures of the *Liberty* and the *Ann*, as well as the humiliation of the flight from Boston to the shelter of the harbor fort, led the English ministry to reconsider the wisdom of having sent the Customs Commissioners to reside in America. There was a tone of weary resignation in the letter the Treasury sent to the Commissioners in June, 1769, asking that "all former Dissentions shall be buried in Oblivion." [35] So general was the discouragement with the operation of the Board that in 1770 the ministry seriously considered recalling the Commissioners and refrained from doing so only because such an action might be interpreted as a surrender to the colonial opposition.[36] In one area, it is true, the American Board was not a total failure. Under their handling and supervision the revenues in America produced more than ever before. From September, 1767, to September, 1769, slightly under £30,000 was collected — a sum much less than had been expected, but still a substantial improvement over the previous years. The cost of administering the customs service, however, had also risen; during those same years the salaries and expenses totaled over £16,000.[37] In spite of the size of the expenses not only was the American service for the first time no longer a charge on the English Exchequer but it showed a profit. £14,000 was a good deal more than had been available to the British government in the colonies in the past. And it could be expected that the revenues would increase over the showing of this first year and one-half of operation.

But other than this partial success in the area of the revenue, the American Commissioners — and the customs service generally — gave a poor account of themselves. In 1769-70 a comprehensive survey was made of the American customs operation. No better commentary could exist on the failure of these years — indeed on the failure of the one-hundred-year history of the customs service — than the results shown in this survey.[38] Even the boundaries of some of the legal ports were not known with precision: "It has been taken for granted, that the limits of this Port [Philadelphia] begins where a line divides Pennsylvania from New

Castle Country . . ."; "The Boundaries of this Port [Roanoke, Virginia] never settled"; "How the boundaries of this District [York River, Virginia] were originally settled not able to say, but from long usage . . ." In some places the collectors had little to do with any transactions: "The Collector [South Potomac, Virginia] resides up the River . . . carries on the Business by deputy." Smugglers operated freely in each and every port and colony: "Many vessels which trade to the foreign Islands neither enter or clear at any Custom House [Falmouth, Maine]"; "Smuggling in this district [Rhode Island] is carried on to a very great degree"; "Large quantities of Tea, etc. brought in Small Boats [Perth Amboy, New Jersey]"; "Much Smuggling from Holland, France, and the West Indies, and publicly advertised the goods of the Manufactures of those Countrys to be sold [Charleston, South Carolina]." In some places the problem was geographical: "The Harbours, Rivers, and Creeks along this coast [New Haven, Connecticut] are many and commodious for smuggling." In others, legal loopholes served to mask the smuggling trade: "The officers much destressed for a rule of conduct respecting the coasting trade [South Carolina]." Generally there was a shortage of customs personnel to do an effective job; in spite of the growth of the Boston district there were still no regular customs officers "but at the Port of Entry except at Plymouth and Nantucket; at all the others, Vessels load and unload without the inspection of any officer." Similar complaints had been made a hundred years earlier by the first customs officials sent to America. And the suggestions for improvement offered in this report were familiar too: an increase in the "water guard" in particular and in the size of the customs staff generally. Seemingly, one hundred years of development had left the customs service close to its starting point.

The problems, and the failures, of the American Board were not unique. The whole Townshend program was rapidly revealed as a serious miscalculation. The basic problem was nicely outlined by Governor Bernard. Recounting an episode in which some molasses which had been forcibly rescued from the customs officers was returned to the customs house on the orders of the leaders of the "faction" who wished to prove their basic respect for legal procedures, Bernard commented that it all proved that Massachusetts did indeed have an effective government, only it is not "ours but the peoples." [39] Aimed at increasing the effectiveness of royal government in the colonies, the Townshend program touched upon the most sensitive area of Anglo-American relations. In doing so, it raised a storm of protest in the colonies and united the colonial opposition still further. Townshend had counted on time to make his program effective. But time was not on the side of the English.

Open opposition to the Townshend Acts had been slow in appearing. Many colonists hesitated to repeat the excesses associated with the Stamp Act riots and hoped that in time the English ministry could be convinced of its mistake in a more orderly manner. Aware of the general reluctance to resort to extreme measures, Sam Adams and his associates moved with caution. A carefully worded circular letter was sent by the Massachusetts House of Representatives to the assemblies of the other colonies. With becoming restraint the letter protested the loyalty of the authors to the king, stressed the impracticability of arranging for the Americans to be represented in Parliament, and emphasized that consequently the independence of the various colonial assemblies was their only guarantee of freedom.[40]

The Massachusetts leaders hoped by means of this letter to stimulate a joint response by the colonies to the English measures. But at first the reaction was disappointing. Pennsylvania, for example, under the influence of Joseph Galloway, declined to consider the letter which was fit only for the "selectmen of Boston, and the mob meetings of Rhode Island." [41] At that moment Hillsborough chose to send his own circular letter to the governors of each colony. Ordering the governors to see either that the Massachusetts letter was condemned by their legislatures, or that the legislatures should be dissolved if they declined to do so, Hillsborough in effect gave substance to the fears expressed in the communication the Bay Colony had sent out. It was Hillsborough's letter, not that from Massachusetts, that was condemned in colony after colony as a tyrannical encroachment on their legislative freedom, and the colonial opposition took on new strength and solidarity.[42] Eventually, the colonists united in agreement to use commercial pressure to bring the English government to its senses, and nonimportation agreements generally went into effect in the various ports and commercial centers of America.

Even before the implementation of the nonimportation agreements the English ministry had given evidence of second thoughts on the Townshend program. The small returns under the Acts, coupled with the opposition they aroused, led the ministry in 1768 to debate repeal. The ministry itself was divided in its opinion; Grafton and some others wished to repeal all the Acts and rely on the earlier Acts of Trade, the molasses duties, and the Declaratory Act to uphold English authority. Lord North and others of his thinking felt that the right of Parliament to tax the colonists had become inseparably associated with the imperial supremacy of England; to give way completely on that issue would be, in effect, a resignation of supremacy. The compromise arrived at was to repeal all the Townshend duties except that on tea, which remained a symbol of the rights and powers of Parliament. Lord North, now in power, argued that repeal was not so much a concession or an act of appeasement as it was a well-timed move to divide the colonial opposition and to end the nonimportation agreements.[43] On the latter point he was correct, as nonimportation gradually collapsed after repeal, and there were many colonists to argue that in the long run their interests always prevailed in London.

The key to the policies adopted after 1770 by North lay in the circumstances of his rise to power: "North's quiet accession to power was possible because America and Wilkes had called into being a new conservatism supported not only by the King's Friends but by every other major group. Those means of corruption at the Crown's disposal did not create North's steady majorities. Rather they arose out of a frightened reaction against radicalism at home and abroad."[44] North's was a conservative ministry, dedicated to the maintenance of the status quo. In colonial affairs his desire was to retain both English supremacy and American attachment to the empire. The central question was simply where "to put a term to American pretensions."[45] It was in his failure to solve that problem that the immediate origins of the Revolution lay. Yet the difficulty of North's situation should not be underestimated. Those English politicians who had long and vigorously opposed the colonial programs of the last decade at this critical moment had no creative solutions of their own to offer. Pitt could agree with North — or Townshend, for that matter — that England's paramount position had to be maintained: The Americans "must be subordinate. In all laws relating to trade and navigation especially, this is the mother country, they are children; they must obey and we prescribe."[46] But he presented no practical arrangement to make that doctrine acceptable to the colonists. Another moderate, Dartmouth, revealed the essential barrenness of the middle-of-the-road approach in this period when he argued that if the colonists only would "admit of duties for regulation of trade, and will add to that a revenue for the support of Civil Government, and such military force as they themselves shall desire to have among them, I think we may soon be agreed." [47] In such a situation it is not surprising that North found it advisable to do as little as possible.

In fact, of course, North had no intention of resigning England's authority over her colonies. His thought was merely to avoid contributing further to the development of radicalism in America by the enactment of hasty or unwise measures. In the debate on the continuation of the duty on tea, North made it clear that his eventual aim was to reduce America to its proper dependence on England.[48] Between 1770 and 1773 a waiting game was played, as North hoped to win the day by postponing a direct conflict over the issue of imperial supremacy until the colonial opposition had been reduced and lulled into manageable proportions.

In these years of comparative calm the brunt of the anger of the colonists was borne by the customs service. The customs officers, particularly the Commissioners, were the one remaining visible evidence of the English policies of the preceding years. As such they were the obvious target of attack for those dedicated to ending once and for all England's claim to control the destinies of America. The Commissioners were described as "so many BLOOD SUCKERS upon our TRADE" who by their "disolute Lives and Evil Practices" threaten America "with a curse more deplorable than Egyptian Darkness." [49] In line with Lord North's policy, and in spite of such attacks, it was the job of the Commissioners and the customs officers to procure as much revenue as possible with as little offense as possible. During these years the customs officers walked a tightrope between North's desire to prevent damaging incidents and the radicals' determination to maintain a continuing opposition to British designs.

In one sense the customs service was successful in these years. Without the Townshend duties, the American revenues were less than desired, but still they were considerable. The accounts of Charles Steuart, the cashier and paymaster, show that under all the Acts in force as of 1770 the following receipts were made: 1769–70, £34,389; 1770–71, £31,347;

rescuers, but in revenge he was prosecuted on a charge of having wounded one of the sailors in the boat he seized and required to spend some time in the local jail, while his quarry escaped and carried the boat and its cargo off to Philadelphia. Still determined, Hatton had sent his son to Philadelphia to warn the collector there to watch for the arrival of the rescued boat. Inspecting the harbor, his son found the boat already arrived. Realizing that they were discovered, the crew of the boat organized an attack on young Hatton, who was dragged from place to place, beaten savagely, tarred and feathered, and even had hot tar poured into open wounds he had previously received in helping to make the original seizure. In the words of the Philadelphia collector, young Hatton was tortured "in the manner above related an hour or more." During that time no public official came to his aid, nor any private person for that matter. As a result of this ordeal, young Hatton lay for a time near death and when he did recover had lost the use of his right arm.[52]

From this whole affair Hatton received little satisfaction. The authorities in New Jersey disclaimed any responsibility since the seizure had been made in the bay and not within their jurisdiction. At the same time, however, Hatton was prosecuted by the common law courts for attacking and wounding a sailor during the affray. Seemingly if New Jersey had authority over that charge, they had equal jurisdiction in the matter of the rescued seizure. But, of course, they simply did not wish to act. As to the barbaric treatment accorded to his son in Philadelphia, no one could be found to testify against the guilty parties and the case was dropped after a brief investigation. As commentary on the Hatton incident, the collector of Philadelphia offered these words: "In short, the truth of the matter is, the hands of Government are not strong enough to oppose the numerous body of people who wish well to the cause of smuggling . . . What can a Governor do, without the assistance of the Governed? What can the Magistrates do, unless they are supported by their fellow Citizens? What can the King's Officers do, if they make themselves obnoxious to the people amongst whom they reside?"[53]

Other incidents too were allowed to pass with little notice. In Boston the comptroller general of the American Board was molested on his way home one night, while one of the tidesmen was attacked "by disorderly men and boys and Negroes also" who tarred and feathered him and carried him about the town. His ordeal lasted for over four hours.[54] The relaxed policy which permitted these deeds to go unpunished had its dangerous aspect. When in 1772 the people of Rhode Island attacked and destroyed the royal customs cutter stationed in the waters, Thomas Hutchinson wrote to London that if England "shows no resentment against that Colony for so high an affront . . . they may venture upon any further Measures which are necessary to obtain and secure their Independence . . . ." He added that if the offenders in the *Gaspee* affair were not punished "the friends to Government will despond and give up all hopes of being able to withstand the Faction." [55] Although aroused to appoint a commission to investigate the destruction of the *Gaspee,* the ministry of Lord North only half-heartedly supported the enquiry and dropped the case when the commissioners reported that they were unable to assign the guilt to any particular citizens in the chaotically "democratic" colony of Rhode Island. The only result of the *Gaspee* investigation was the addition of several hundred pounds to the sums paid out by the cashier of the customs service from the American revenues. [56]

During this period, although unable to protect their officers, the American Board Commissioners did at least achieve harmony in their own ranks. John Temple was recalled to England in 1770 and replaced by Benjamin Hallowell, the former comptroller of Boston, who had been in England reporting on the riots created by the seizure of the *Liberty.* [57] With the departure of Temple the Commissioners worked in close cooperation and did their best to perform their duties with the required caution. When urged to start prosecutions against various bonds which had not been canceled as required, the Commissioners advised the Treasury that "finding that it had not been usual to enforce the Laws in this particular" they felt to do so now would only serve to increase "the general opposition to the Revenue Laws." In reply the Treasury said that they would leave the decision up to the Commissioners with the hope that they would put such bonds into suit as soon as it could be done without trouble. [58]

The Commissioners in fact had learned the lessons of the previous years only too well. In 1772–73 the English ministry debated a revision of the Acts of Trade. Their thought was to remove the onerous requirement that coasting vessels should carry cocquets; instead the captains of such craft would give bond yearly to the customs officers. Should any be found contravening the laws, the bonds could be prosecuted. Also, all ships would be required to come directly to the various custom houses and not anchor at a distance, while the captain reported to the collectors. The Commissioners were asked for their advice on these and other points. While in general they agreed that the new provisions were needed, they added that they were "in doubt of the expediency of attempting to enforce any unpopular Regulations whilst the Authority of Government is so feeble." They closed by writing "Upon the whole we submit it to your Lordships Consideration whether it be adviseable to attempt any new Regulations in Trade untill some more effectual Provision be made for supporting the Authority of Parliament and carrying the Acts of Trade and Revenue into execution." [59] Such advice was perfectly congenial to Lord North, who was resolved to continue his program of cautious waiting. The bill to revise the trade laws was allowed to drop from sight. The prime minister, and his royal patron, were playing for time. Every year saw more colonial officials added to the list of those receiving their salaries from the English government. Typical of North's approach was the special allowance given to the commander of the naval forces in America, who after 1770 was provided with a fund of £1,500 to entertain and "court" the colonists in the various ports.[60]

However, Lord North himself once had observed that the dispute with the Americans would continue as long as Parliament claimed the right of taxation and they denied it.[61] In the same way, one of the American radical leaders, Sam Adams, earlier had affirmed that "things will never be properly settled in America untill the Parliament has repealed all the Acts affecting the American Trade from the 15th of Charles 2 to the present time." [62] Nor was Adams blind to the dangers posed by North's delaying tactics: "Perhaps there never was a time when the political Affairs of America were in a more dangerous State; Such is the Indolence of Men in general, or their Inattention to the real Importance of things, that a steady and animated perseverance in the rugged path of Virtue at the hazard of trifles is hardly to be expected." [63] His fear was that, given time, North's delaying tactics, combined with the growing colonial civil list, might carry the day. What Adams wanted, needed, was an incident — an "outrage" — with which to arouse and inflame a united colonial opposition. Lord North made his one critical mistake when he placed the interests of the British East India Company ahead of those of the Americans.

By 1773 the East India Company was in financial distress. Imports from India rotted in its warehouses while its stocks dropped continually in value. New markets were needed, and quickly, or the Company, the £400,000 a year which the government received from it, as well as the British possessions in India would be endangered. North's solution was to rescue the Company by providing it with new markets in America. When the Company directors suggested to him that the tax on tea imported into America should be repealed, the prime minister declined to take that step. Instead, he allowed the Company to export its tea directly to America without being required as formerly to auction it off to English middlemen who in turn sent it on to the colonies. At the same time the government surrendered, for the moment, the £400,000 yearly payment the Company had made and also gave the Company an emergency loan of £1,400,000. North clung to the tea duty in the colonies not only because he had made it a symbol of Parliamentary supremacy but also because he was intrigued by the thought of the potential increase in the revenues available to the English government in America: "If the East India Company will export tea to America, they will very much increase that duty, and consequently very much facilitate the carrying of Government in that part." [64] In fact North's plan was subtly designed to promote the consumption of tea in America to the benefit both of the Company and of the royal revenues. But North overestimated the naïveté of the colonists. Not only was the duty on tea the one remaining tax left from the hated Townshend program but the entrance of the East India Company into the local markets upset the established patterns of the tea trade, alienating elements of the commercial classes in all the colonial ports. Not the least affected were those who had profited from the smuggling of tea, long a traditional pastime for Americans.

The destruction of the tea sent to America, highlighted by the "party" at Boston, brought a sudden end to the period of watchful waiting. Even had he wished, North could not overlook this insult to the authority of Parliament; to have done so would have been political suicide. Even Pitt proclaimed the action of the Boston radicals as "criminal" and popular opinion swung firmly behind a policy of retaliatory measures.[65] The result was the enactment of the Coercive Acts and the beginning of the end for England's rule in America. So too began the last, humiliating episode in the long history of the colonial customs service. For the Customs Commissioners themselves the Boston Port Act was at first a repetition of their earlier experiences in the aftermath of the *Liberty* seizure and the Massacre. They fled to the shelter of the harbor fort, reporting to the Treasury that as usual they were the special "object of the People's rage." From November 30th to the end of December they were confined to the fort. At the end of December they ventured out to hold a meeting in Boston but confessed frankly to the Treasury Lords that they did not expect to be there long.[66]

The Commissioners were back in Boston from December 30, 1773, until June, 1774. Then they retreated to Salem. To the very end the English authorities displayed a fascinating respect for the letter of the law. With the closing of Boston, and the transfer of all cargoes formerly destined for that port to Salem, that city became the most active port in Massachusetts. Since it was enacted that none of the necessary supplies could be entered into Boston except via the port of Salem (which included Marblehead), the customs officers formerly stationed in Boston could have been put to good use there. Unfortunately, Salem was not legally included in the port of Boston, so the Boston officers went instead to Plymouth, which was legally part of the Boston district, where they sat idly by with hardly a ship entering that minor port while the undermanned staff in Salem and Marblehead struggled with the increased traffic.[67]

Step by step the open conflict between England and the colonies was drawing closer. During these hectic months the major concern of the customs service was to prevent the importation of supplies of war into the colonies, Dutch gunpowder being the greatest item in this trade. When warned to prevent such goods from reaching the colonists, the collector and comptroller in Rhode Island answered that they would do their best but that the inhabitants had already purchased three hundred barrels of Dutch powder and some field pieces as well. They thought the goods were brought from St. Eustatia.[68] Reports from the other colonies told much the same story.

Aside from warning their officers to watch for such shipments, and to carry on their work as best they might, the Commissioners devoted their major energies to the legal problems created by the closing of Boston. From their retreat in Salem they directed the flow of foodstuffs and supplies into Boston. At times their insistence on observing the letter of the law irritated the military officers attempting to implement the blockade of Boston. But by the middle of September, 1774, in spite of Parliament's order that no customs officers should be in Boston, the Commissioners and most of the other customs officers had to flee Salem and take refuge with the army in that city. The countryside was in an uproar and no member of the despised service was safe beyond the immediate protection of the military.[69]

Following the enactment of the Boston Port Act Parliament passed further retaliatory measures. The Massachusetts Government Act (May 20, 1774) brought an end to charter government in that colony. The Quartering Act permitted the forceful quartering of English troops wherever necessary. The British were preparing for war. Nor were the colonists far behind. The First Continental Congress, presenting a united colonial front, assembled in Philadelphia on September 5, 1774. In April of the next year the first clash between the royal forces and the colonists occurred at Lexington and Concord.[70]

The empty authority of the Customs Commissioners lingered on into the fall of 1775. By November of that year Admiral Thomas Graves, commander of the fleet, belatedly informed them that as far as he was concerned their authority had ended with the declaration of martial law.[71] The Commissioners asked the advice of the Treasury but hardly needed to wait for a reply. All over the colonies the English administration had been thrown off with little ceremony. The battle at Lexington and Concord, followed by the fight at Bunker Hill, ended whatever hope the conservatives in America had of obtaining a peaceful settlement of the dispute. Both sides were stirred by the news of the open combats. Symptomatic of the seriousness of the breach was the news from New Hampshire. Governor John Wentworth there had always managed to maintain friendly relations with the inhabitants and was himself a popular and respected figure. On May 18, 1775, the collector and comptroller of Piscataqua informed the Board that they had of necessity taken refuge on a man-of-war in the harbor; the governor had not yet left the province but was fortified in his house and preparing for a siege.[72] If Wentworth in New Hampshire could not maintain his authority, there was little hope that any other royal governor could do so.

By November, 1775, the comptroller of Philadelphia was in London, reporting that events had "put it out of my power of staying in America." Francis Waldo, the collector at Falmouth in Maine and a native of that place, was forced to follow the Philadelphia officers shortly thereafter. One after the other the customs officers fled from their posts to safety under the protection of the British army or to England. When early in 1776 the British were forced to evacuate Boston, the Commissioners themselves left the colonies. Recognizing that, whatever the eventual outcome, for the next few years at least there was little they could do in America, the Commissioners removed first to Halifax. There they discharged all the incidental officers carried on the salary lists and embarked for England.[73]

The departure of the American Commissioners signaled the end of the colonial customs service. Officially the American establishment lingered on until 1783 when the Commissioners and the other officers were finally dismissed. Until that time such as had not been provided with other positions in the English service continued to receive their salaries. Not until the final peace treaty was signed and American independence a recognized fact was all hope abandoned and the one-hundred-and-ten-year history of the colonial service brought to a close. Five more years were required before Charles Steuart managed to complete his accounts of the finances of the American establishment. But in 1789, when the Treasury approved his reports and discharged him from any further responsibilities, the last official action regarding the colonial customs service had been taken. The great experiment which had commenced in 1673 was finished.

XII

Retrospect

FREDERICK LORD NORTH was a man of "habitual diffidence." [1]
While his conciliatory disposition and good-natured indolence made
him an attractive colleague, he was an odd candidate for immortality as
the "minister who lost us America." [2] North himself at times undoubtedly was bewildered by the tides that swept him and the empire he
administered into civil war and disunion. He meant well but lost an
empire, and the causes of his failure must have been obscure even to
him. [3] However, North personally might have taken comfort from the
analysis offered by William Knox, an experienced and perceptive colonial
administrator. Recalling his first experiences in America, Knox observed
that, "it was with no small degree of astonishment, I perceived a total
want of plan or system in the British Government, as well at the time of
their establishment, as in their future management, that the seeds of
disunion were sown in the first plantation in every one of them, and
that a general disposition to independence of this country prevailed
throughout the whole." [4]

Certainly, the history of the colonial customs service conformed to
the pattern described by Knox. The central theme in the story of the
service was its total inadequacy for the assignment with which it was
entrusted. The early years — from 1673 to the rise of Walpole — were
marked by a stubborn and general resistance to the work of the customs
officers. In some colonies opposition reached from the office of the governor down to the smallest of the local courts. In others, the legislatures
were the center of resistance. In all the colonies merchants and business-
men generally were irritated at the restrictions on their activities and
lent their support to efforts to emasculate the trade laws. As Lord Bello-

253

mont wrote in 1699, "a Collectors is the most ungratefull Office in these plantations that can be, if he is Just to his trust in looking into their Trade they hate him mortally." [5] By means of legal harassments, physical violence, and intimidation the colonists successfully prevented the customs officers from enforcing a strict observance of the Acts of Trade and Navigation.

In the face of determined colonial opposition the customs officers found their work nearly impossible. If the Americans would not cooperate voluntarily, the trade laws had to be enforced over their objections. But the distances involved, the isolation of the royal officers, and the weakness of all royal authority in America soon made it apparent that without drastic reforms such an effort was not feasible. As Caleb Heathcote reported in 1716, there was an "abundance of mistakes, in the management of affairs . . . whereby his Majestys Intrest is Greatly Hurt . . . & many of the services . . . neglected & unperformed, & Things are wrong on so many Accounts." [6]

A few years later Heathcote went to the heart of the problem in another report. As long as the colonists had "a power (as they imagine) of making laws separate from the crown, they'll never be wanting to lessen the authority of the King's officers, who by hindering them from a full freedom of illegal trade, are accounted ennemies to the growth and prosperity of their little commonwealths." [7] The fact was that it was impossible to control the economic life of the Americans without also supervising their political and governmental activities in all their aspects. The mercantile system required "the existence of a high degree of both political and social unity as the condition of its success." [8]

Recognizing that the commercial laws could never be implemented effectively until life in the colonies should be made to conform to the dictates of the English government, Heathcote, Archibald Cummings, Sir William Keith, and others suggested that a revenue should be raised in America which could be used to defray the expenses of the various governments, freeing the officials from dependence on the local inhabitants and strengthening the hand of royal government generally. Ironically, during the period from 1715 to 1725 nearly all the measures later enacted under Grenville and Townshend were suggested, from the strengthening of the Admiralty courts to extension of the stamp duties to America and the use of a tax on molasses to raise a revenue. In spite

Retrospect

of warnings that "a neglect therein, may with time, be attended with very ill consequences," the English government failed to act.[9]

Under Walpole and the succeeding Whig ministries the colonies were left to develop in relative freedom. The policy of "salutary neglect" enabled the Whigs to concentrate on England's own internal problems — on the creation of a general prosperity and the support of the Hanoverian monarchy, and later on the renewed rivalry with France. During these years the colonists had little reason to complain. English authority, still theoretically supreme, was not exercised in fact. The royal officers in the colonies, left to their own devices, degenerated "into Creoles" and at length forgot the "Mother Country and her Interests."[10] In many ways these years were the "golden age" of England's relations with her colonies. Compared with the disasters which followed under George III, they have taken on an added luster. But it is worth remembering that this surface harmony was achieved through a partial resignation of authority and responsibility by England. The theories of empire were not altered; they were merely ignored. As George Bancroft remarked, Walpole's policies were "generous and safe," but can "a minister excuse his own acts of despotic legislation by his neglect to enforce them?" Bancroft added, "Woe to the British statesman who should hold it a duty to enforce the British laws."[11] The Molasses Act, in theory a prohibition of trade with the foreign islands but in practice merely one more neglected statute, was a fitting memorial to these years of Whig leadership.

Commencing with the ministry of Grenville, the English government attempted to correct the damage done by the years of neglect. The customs service was reformed and enlarged, the Admiralty courts were strengthened, troops were stationed in America, and steps were taken to raise a colonial revenue to finance these reforms. Unfortunately, the machinery of enforcement in the colonies was rusted from years of disuse and was strained to the breaking point by these radical innovations, which aroused an angry response in America and created an effective, united colonial opposition. Under Townshend, a new and more comprehensive effort was undertaken. New revenues were raised, certain civil officials were taken into the pay of the English government, the customs service was strengthened by the appointment of commissioners to reside in America, and once again the Admiralty courts were

255

reorganized. But the time needed to make this program effective was not available. The colonial opposition shortly caused most of Townshend's plans to be abandoned; and in spite of the cautious approach adopted by Lord North, relations between the colonies and England had become so strained that just one mistake — involving tea — led to an open rupture.

In any list of grievances drawn up by the colonists to explain the reasons for that "open rupture" the operation of the customs service ranked high. An American reading that passage in the Declaration of Independence which denounces the king because he had "erected a multitude of New Offices, and sent hither swarms of Officers to harass our people, and eat out their substance" would understand this reference to the customs officials. More specifically, the complaints in the Declaration that the colonists had been deprived "in many cases, of the benefits of Trial by Jury" and transported "beyond Seas to be tried for pretended offenses" singled out the Admiralty court system, which was a major element in the customs apparatus. And the whole purpose, the basic function, of the customs service was protested in the Declaration when the colonists complained that the king had "combined, with others, to subject us to a jurisdiction foreign to our constitution . . . giving his Assent to their Acts of pretended legislation . . . For cutting off our Trade with all parts of the world."

These were specific grievances, ones Americans could understand, but in a larger sense the customs service played a central role in the coming of the Revolution, as it did in the history of the First British Empire, because its operation was related directly to the procurement of revenue, which in essence was — and is — the key to effective government. Again, William Knox went to the heart of the problem when he explained the American opposition to Grenville's Stamp Act in this way: "The collection of duties would occasion a considerable increase in the number of persons holding office under the Crown, and deriving their appointment from British interest, and would be a severe cheque upon the propagation of antimonarhicall principles within the colonies, and upon illicit connections with foreign countries." [12] Later, at the end of the Revolution, Knox summed up the basis of the dispute more succinctly when he asserted that "it was better to have no colonies at all, than not to have them subservient to the maritime strength and commercial interest of Great Britain." [13]

Benjamin Franklin, in his satirical *Rules for Reducing a Great Empire to a Small One,* observed the same central issue of revenue from an American point of view: "This is another reason for applying part of that revenue in larger salaries to such Governors and Judges, given, as their commissions are, *during your pleasure* only; forbidding them to take any salaries from their provinces; that thus the people may no longer hope any kindness from their governors, or (in crown cases) any justice from their Judges." [14] John Adams put the issue more succinctly still. At the end of his life, reminiscing about the danger inherent in the tax levied under the original Molasses Act, Adams observed that had it been collected it would have provided a "fund amply sufficient . . . to pay all the salaries of all the governors upon the continent, and all the judges of admiralty too." With the steady growth of the molasses and sugar trade, he added, the receipts would have increased until they were "sufficient to bribe any nation less knowing and less virtuous than the people of America, to the voluntary surrender of all their liberties." [15] The issue was control of government, and in revenue lay the key to sovereignty.

The public debate between the Americans and the English over the issue of taxation, in which the customs service was caught up after 1764, centered on the nature of the Old Colonial System. The English, pointing to the theories of the past, claimed complete sovereignty, an inseparable component of which was the right of taxation. The colonists, relying on the practice of the past, asserted that the imperial constitution provided for the protection of their rights and interests. In this dispute between the theory and the practice of the past, the question of right or wrong is irrelevant. The inflexibility of the British theory of empire, its continued hold on the minds of England's leaders, was in opposition to the realities of colonial practices and desires. The result was a conflict which was resolved only by a recourse to arms.

Appendixes

Bibliography

Notes

Index

Appendix A

I. THE CUSTOMS ORGANIZATION IN 1710 *

Colony	Port	Officer	Salary
South Carolina	Charleston	Thomas Broughton, collector	£60
North Carolina	Currituck	Samuel Swann, collector	£40
		Peter Guerard, comptroller	£50
	Roanoke	Nathaniel Chevin, collector	£40
Virginia	South Potomac	John Dansey,† collector	£80
	Accomack	Henry Scarborough, collector	£40
	York River	William Bruckner, collector	£40
	Upper James	Edward Hill, collector	£40
	Lower James	George Luke, collector	£100
	Rappahannock	Richard Chichester, collector	£80
	Cape Charles	Robert Snead, surveyor	£50
	Elizabeth River	Sampson Trevethan, surveyor	£45
Maryland	Patuxent	John Dansey,† collector	£80
	Wicomocco	William Fassit, surveyor	£40
	Williamstad	Thomas Collier, surveyor	£35
	North Potomac	Thomas Seymour, collector	£60
	Pocomoke	Edward Price, collector	£60
	Potomac River	John Phelps, surveyor	£60
	Annapolis	William Bladen, surveyor	£60
	Bahama and Sassafras	Stephen Knight, surveyor	£50
	Delaware Bay	William Dyre, surveyor	£50
Pennsylvania	Philadelphia	John Moore, collector	£160
		William Alexander, comptroller	£80
	Newcastle	Samuel Lowman, collector	£130 (includes boat)

* Audit Office 1: Declared Accounts; Customs, Receivers General and Cashiers (various) Bundles 759–929. See Chapter IV, note 38.

† On Dansey, see Chapter IV.

Appendix A

Colony	Port	Officer	Salary
	Lewis	Henry Brook, collector	£130 (includes boat)
New Jersey	Perth Amboy	Thomas Farmer, collector	£40
	Bridlington	John Rolfe, collector	£40
New York	New York	Thomas Byerley, collector	£55
		William Carter, comp-troller	£55
		William Chambers, waiter	£50
		William Davis, surveyor and searcher	£60
Connecticut	New London	John Stackmaple, collector, surveyor, and searcher	£80
Rhode Island	Rhode Island	Nathaniel Kay, collector, surveyor, and searcher	£100
Massachusetts	Boston	John Jekyll, collector	£100
		Thomas Newton, comp-troller	£70
	Salem and Marblehead	Charles Blechyden, collector, surveyor, and searcher	£100
New Hampshire	Piscataqua	Robert Armstrong, collector and surveyor	£100
Newfoundland	————	Archibald Cummings, preventive officer	£100
Bahama Islands	————	John Graves, collector	£70
Bermuda	————	Thomas Brooke, collector	£50
Surveyor General Northern		Maurice Birchfield	£495
Surveyor General Southern		Robert Quary	£495
		Total	£3,700

II. THE CUSTOMS ORGANIZATION IN 1760 *

Colony	Port	Officer	Salary
Georgia	————	William Spencer, collector	£60
		William Mackenzie, searcher	£30
		William Russell, comp-troller	£50

* Audit Office 1: Declared Accounts; Customs, Receivers General and Cashiers (various) Bundles 759–829. See Chapter IV, note 38.

Colony	Port	Officer	Salary
South Carolina	Port Royal	James Battine, collector	£40
	Wynyaw	Archibald Baird, collector	£40
	Charleston	Hector Beaufin, collector	£60
		John Denton, surveyor and searcher	£30
		George Roupel, surveyor and searcher	£30
North Carolina	Beaufort	Thomas Lovicke, collector	£40
	Currituck	Robert Whitehall, collector	£40
	Roanoke	John Rienset, collector	£40
	Bathtown	William Palmer, collector	£40
	Brunswick	William Dry, collector	£60
Virginia	South Potomac	George Fairfax, collector	£80
	Accomack	John Manby, collector	£40
	Lower James	Carey Mitchell, collector	£100
	Upper James	John Bannister, collector	£40
	York River	John Ambler, collector	£40
	Rappahannock	James Read, collector	£80
	Cape Charles	James Rule, surveyor	£50
	Elizabeth River	Edward Mosely, surveyor	£45
Maryland	Wicomocco	Michael Macnamara, surveyor	£40
	Patuxent	Benedict Calvert, collector	£80
	Williamstad	John Leeds, surveyor	£35
	North Potomac	Daniel Wolstenholme, collector	£60
	Pocomoke	Robert Heron, collector	£60
	Potomac River	Edmund Hough, surveyor	£60
	Bahama and Sassafras	Benjamin Tasker, Jr., surveyor	£50
	Annapolis	Benjamin Tasker, Sr., surveyor	£60
	Chester and Patapsco	James Sterling, collector	£80
	Delaware Bay	Joseph Shippen, surveyor	£50
Pennsylvania	Philadelphia	Grosvenor Bedford, collector	£160 and £80 for a boat
		Alexander Barclay, comptroller	£80
	Newcastle	William Till, collector	£90 and £40 for a boat

Appendix A

Colony	Port	Officer	Salary
	Lewis	Peter Razor, collector	£90 and £40 for a boat
New Jersey	Perth Amboy	John Barberie, collector	£40
	Bridlington	Charles Reid, collector	£30
	Nova Casaria	William Frazer, collector	£40
New York	New York	Archibald Kennedy, collector	£55
		Lambert Moore, comptroller	£55
		Richard Nicholls, waiter	£50
		Alexander Colden, surveyor and searcher	£60
Connecticut	New London	Joseph Hull, collector	£80
Rhode Island	———————	Thomas Clift, collector and surveyor	£100
Massachusetts	Boston	Benjamin Barons, collector	£100
		Nathaniel Ware, comptroller	£70
		Charles Paxton, surveyor and searcher	£100
	Salem and Marblehead	Richard Lechmere, collector	£40
New Hampshire	Piscataqua	James Nevin, collector	£100
(Maine)	Falmouth	Francis Waldo, collector	no salary
Nova Scotia	———————	Henry Newton, collector	£60
		John Newton, surveyor and searcher	£50
Bahama Islands	———————	Jeremy Tinker, collector	£70
Bermuda	———————	John Pigot or Thomas Smith, collector	£70
		Thomas Butterfield, searcher at West End of Island	£30
Surveyor General	Northern	Thomas Lechmere	£495
Surveyor General	Southern	Peter Randolph	£495
		Total	£4,460

Appendix B

THE PROCESS OF ENTERING A SHIP *

"The Practice is, so soon as Ships arrive, the Commanders first wait on the Governor, then go to the Secretaries Office and give Bond and Security as required by the several laws of this Island; after which they go to a Person called the Comptroller of the Customs, whose only Duty as I can find, is to take a Fee of 6s 3d from every Commander; from thence they go and enter with the Naval Officer, and there lodge their Cockets or Manifest (the Collector of the Customs never seeing any of them, nor the Receiver General of His Majesty's Revenue, altho no Ship can land any Goods without a permit from this last Officer); from the Naval Officer the Commanders of Ships receive two Certificates, one directed to the Collector, the other to the Receiver General, in which he sets down what he pleases; with these Certificates the Master goes first to the Collector, with whom he enters and Reports aggreeable to the Commodities specyfyed by the Naval Officer in those Certificates (thus the Naval Officer seems to have His Majesty's Revenues subject to his Comptroul and Management); the Collector keeps one of these Certificates and endorses the other, which the Commanders carries to the Receiver General, who grants a permit and then the Ship is allowed to deliver her Cargo. During this Process (which generally takes three days) no waiter or Custom-house Officer is ever put on board any Ship or Vessel unless she comes from Madeira. Indeed, none of the Officers of the Revenue have any Waiters but the Receiver General, so Your Lordships see how open the door is for fraudulent practices."

* Governor Knowles of Jamaica to Board of Trade, November 18, 1752, C.O. 137/25, foll. 271–280. Unpublished Crown-copyright material, reproduced by permission of the Controller of H.M. Stationery Office.

Appendix C

CUSTOMS REPORT OF 1725 *

Office	Station	Present salary by establishment	Present salary by incidents	Proposed salary
Surveyor and Comptroller	Carolina and Bahamas	£150	—	£150
Collector	Charleston	£60	—	£40
Comptroller	"	—	£30	£30
Collector	Currituck	£40	—	£40
Collector	Roanoke	£40	—	£40
Collector	Bathtown	£40	—	£40
Collector	Upper James	£40	—	£40
Collector	Lower James	£100	—	£40
Surveyor to be sunk	Elizabeth River	£45	—	to be sunk
Collector	York River	£40	—	£40
Collector	Rappahannock	£80	—	£40
Collector	South Potomac	£80	—	£40
Surveyor to be sunk	Cape Charles	£50	—	to be sunk
Collector	Accomack	£40	—	£40
Collector	North Potomac	£60	—	£40
Collector	Patuxent	£80	—	£40
Surveyor	Annapolis	£60	—	—
"The office of Surveyor to be sunk & Benj. Tasker, who at present does that duty to be appointed Collector there at £40 p.a."		£40	—	£40
Collector	Pocomoke	£60	—	£40
Riding Surveyor to be sunk	Both sides of River	£60	—	to be sunk
Surveyor to be sunk	Williamstad	£35	—	to be sunk

* T. 1/254, foll. 31–32.

266

Appendix C

Office	Station	Present salary by establishment	Present salary by incidents	Proposed salary
Surveyor	Bahamas and Sassafras	£50	—	£40

Note: office of Surveyor to be sunk, but if Proprietors make it a legal entry port then Stephen Knight at present Surveyor is to be appointed Collector there at £40 p.a.

Office	Station	Present salary by establishment	Present salary by incidents	Proposed salary
Surveyor to be sunk	Wicomocco and Munni	£40	—	to be sunk
Surveyor to be sunk	Delaware Bay	£50	—	to be sunk
Collector	Philadelphia	£160	—	£40
Collector	Newcastle	£90	£40 to be sunk	£90

Note: to be continued at £90 because fees inconsiderable, but incidents for boat to be stopped.

Office	Station	Present salary by establishment	Present salary by incidents	Proposed salary
Collector	Lewis	£90	£40 to be sunk	£90

Note: as for Newcastle.

Office	Station	Present salary by establishment	Present salary by incidents	Proposed salary
Comptroller to be sunk	Philadelphia	£80	—	to be sunk
Collector	Bahama Islands	£70	—	£70
Surveyor General Southern	—	£495	—	£495
Collector	Perth Amboy	£40	—	£40
Collector	Bridlington to reside at Cohenzey	£40	—	£40
Collector and preventive Officer				

Note: "Jos. Hull Collr & p. warrant 28 July 1725."

Office	Station	Present salary by establishment	Present salary by incidents	Proposed salary
Collector	New York	£55	—	£40
Comptroller to be sunk	"	£55	—	to be sunk
Surveyor and Searcher	"	—	£60	£40
Landwaiter to be sunk	"	—	£50	to be sunk
Collector	Boston	£100	—	£40

Appendix C

Office	Station	Present salary by establishment	Present salary by incidents	Proposed salary
Comptroller	Boston	£70	—	£40
Surveyor and Searcher	"	—	£100	£100
Collector and Surveyor	Piscataqua	£100	—	£40
Collector and Surveyor	Salem and Marblehead	£100	—	£40
Collector and Surveyor	Rhode Island	£100	—	£40
Collector and Preventive Officer	New London	—	£80	£50
Preventive Officer to be "struck off ye Estab."	Newfoundland	"£150 p.s. not to be paid"		to be sunk
Collector and Surveyor	Nova Scotia	—	£60	£60
Collector*	Bermudas	—	—	—
Surveyor General Northern	—	£495	—	£495
	Totals	£3,440	£490	£2,660

Present by Establishment: £3,440
by Incidents: £ 490

£3,930 Total
£2,660 Proposed

£1,270 Reduced

*In 1725 Robert Dinwiddie was acting as collector at Bermuda, but in the relaxed state of English administrative activities he was not put on the establishment until after he petitioned in 1730 for payment for his services for five years past: see Ind. 4624, p. 409. L. K. Koontz in his *Robert Dinwiddie* (Glendale, 1941), 35, reports that Dinwiddie became collector in 1727, which is incorrect. The exact date when he first began to act as collector after coming to Bermuda as agent for the Admiralty in 1721 is not known, but certainly he was performing those duties as early as 1725, as his petition shows.

Appendix D

PORTS OF NORTH AMERICA (1770)*

The District of FALMOUTH (Casco Bay) is bounded on the West by York, and on the East by St. Croix, 80 leagues in length, within this Space are many Islands, Rivers, Creeks and Bays. On the West is Wells, Saco & Scarbrough, and on the East of the Port of Entry is North Yarmouth, Kennebeck, Sheepsgut, Georges River, Penobscot, Mount Desert, Mechias, and Goldsbrough, all very good Harbours and places of trade. . . .

Port of PISCATAQUA includes the Town and River of Newbury to SW, and the Town and River of York, East Northerly, 17 miles to the Entrance of Newbury River, 3 to York, and to the Isle of Shoals is nine miles. The Custom House is kept at Portsmouth . . . Preventive Officers reside at Newbury and York. . . .

Port of SALEM AND MARBLEHEAD. Includes Ipswich, Glocester & Squam. Begins Westward at Nahant Bay, and so Easterly to Cape Ann, and round to Ipswich. The Custom House is kept at Salem 6 miles from Marblehead. . . .

Port of BOSTON. Begins at Lyn northerly, Proceeds Westerly and Southerly along Massachusetts Bay to Cape Cod . . . Round Cape Cod to the Harbour of Dartmouth . . . Also the Island of Nantucket, Marthas Vineyard and Elizabeth Island . . . No Officer but at the Port of Entry except at Plymouth and Nantucket. . . .

Port of RHODE ISLAND. From East to West 30 miles, Includes Newport, Taunton River, Bristol, Warren, Providence, Greenwich, Swanzey . . . The Custom House at Newport and a Preventive Officer at Providence. . . .

NEW LONDON. Extends 48 miles upon the Sound bounded by Guilford on the West and Westerly in Rhode Island Government on the East, New London is the Place where the Custom House is kept . . . Southhold on Long Island is a member of this Port, and the only one where a preventive Officer resides. . . .

Port of NEW HAVEN. Extends from Byram River, which separates the Government of New York & Connecticut on the West, to Hillingsworth

* British Museum, Add. MSS. 15484. Only those parts relating to the boundaries of the districts are reproduced here. Printed with the permission of the British Museum.

Appendix D

exclusive on the East, making a Sea Coast of 85 Miles . . . A Preventive Officer resides at Stamford, authorized to enter and clear coasters. . . .

Port of NEW YORK. Extends thro' the whole Province . . . No Officer but at New York, except at the East End of Long Island. . . .

Port of PERTH AMBOYE. Takes in the Whole Division of the Eastern part of New Jersey. No Officer but at the Port of Entry. . . .

PORT OF BURLINGTON. From its establishment it took on from the head of Navigation on Delaware to Southern Boundary of Glocester County & extended on Delaware about 50 miles Burlington being in the center . . . No Officer but at Port of Entry. . . .

SALEM AND COHENSEY. Takes in Salem County above Cohensey in Cumberland, the Counties of Cumberland & Cape May & 130 miles on Delaware. . . .

PHILADELPHIA. It has been taken for granted that the Limits of this Port begins where a Line divides Pensilvania from New Castle County and Extends on along the River Delaware . . . as far as the River is Navigable above Philadelphia making about 25 miles below and 30 miles above Philadelphia . . . No Officer but at Port of Entry. . . .

Port of NEWCASTLE. This District Comprehends the two upper Counties of Newcastle & Kent, and extends along the River Delaware from Nomans Creek about 21 Miles SW from Philadelphia to Mispellion Creek SW from hence, being about 80 Miles. . . No Officer but at New Castle. . . .

PORT LEWIS. Situated about 3 Miles from Cape Henlopen . . . extends about 30 Miles the North side of Indian River, about 12 Miles to the South of Cape Henlopen . . . The Collector keeps a Deputy in each Creek. . . .

PATUXENT. Comprehends the Ports of Annapolis, Patuxent, & Oxford, includes the Whole of Chesapeak Bay, above the mouth of Potomack River on the west, & Choptank river on the East Side thereof, except the River Chester, which was lopped by the Intercession of Mr. Sterling.

CHESTER. The Collector of Chester & Patapsco and the Collector of Patuxent contending for the Boundaries of the Ports, [it is] proposed that the District should be Limited as in Mr. Sterling's time . . . The Collector resides at Annapolis and acts by Deputy. . . .

NORTH POTOMACK. The Limits are confined to the North side of the River, the South being in . . . Virginia, St. Marys the first port settled & the Office something more than a mile below it . . . Alexandria, Annapolis, & Baltimore have reduced this Town (St. Marys) to two or three houses, No house to be got for the Comptroller, who resides at Annapolis, keeps a clerk in the Office. . . .

POCOMOKE. Extent of this District from Pocomoke to Choptank exclusive is about 30 miles . . . the Collector lives 40 miles from the River, and from thence often clears Vessels, keeps a person also at the Custom House . . . Comptroller lives about 28 Miles from the Collector and keeps his Office there also. . . .

Appendix D

ACCOMACK. This District takes in a Number of Rivers & Creeks which are chiefly Barr'd with sand banks. . . . [no boundaries given]

SOUTH POTOMACK. The Custom House kept for many years past near 5 miles above the Entrance of Machoduck Creek [Machipongo?] . . . The Collector resides up the River within 20 Miles of Alexandria, Carries on the Business by Deputy. . . .

RAPPAHANOCK. The Boundaries of this District is from the Entrance of the River to the Head of it . . . Urbanna 20 Miles from the Entrance on the South side, here the Office is kept. . . .

YORK RIVER. This District in Width about 35 Miles and reaches Inland about 75 Miles . . . How the boundaries of this District were Originally settled not able to say, but from long usage it comprehends to the South a small River Pocosin, York River, Mockjack Bay with 4 small rivers or creeks, which empty themselves into that Bay — To the North the little River Peankatunk . . . Peankatunk is 30 Miles from the Office, 12 only from Urbanna on Rappahanock . . . The principle place is York Town where the Custom House is Established. . . .

JAMES RIVER, Lower Part. Extends from the Capes of Virginia to Lyons Creek where the upper District begins being 35 Miles . . . Hampton the Port of Entry . . . It includes to the South; Elizabeth River . . . On the East near the Mouth is Tanners Creek, five Miles above is Norfolk — to the SW is Nansemond River, on which is the town of Suffolk . . . above that on James River is Smithfield . . . There is a surveyor at Elizabeth River. . . .

JAMES RIVER, Upper Part. From Lyons Creek to the Head of the River which is Navigable for Large Vessels 100 Miles & within 20 Miles of the falls . . . When Vessels arrive in the Upper District they generally Stop at a place called Burrels ferry — Anchor about a Mile from the Shore, the Capt goes 4 Miles by land to Williamsburg and enter what they please and proceed near 55 mile up to Bermuda hundreds where they Discharge in Small craft in the River. . . .

CURRITUCK. Extends from Currituck Inlet on the Virginia line in Latitude 36 . . 20 to Roanoke Inlet in Latutude 35.50 — Includes Powels Point on both sides of Currituck Sound. . . .

ROANOKE. The Boundaries of this Port never Settled — Roanoke Island, Coast of Cranton on the S. Pasquotank River on the North, the whole of Albemarle Sound — the Rivers which fall into it to the Westward of Pasquotank are supposed to belong to this District . . . Edenton is the Port of Entry. . . .

BATH. All Vessels from Sea for the Ports of Beaufort, Bath, and Roanoke enter at Occacock Inlet . . . Vessels bound to Beaufort go near West by North 85 miles distance from the Road — To Bath North by West 65 Miles — To Roanoke or Edenton North East to the Bluff then Various Courses to Edenton 160 Miles — Newburn is 40 Miles from the Mouth of the River — Bath 25 Miles from the Mouth of Pamtico River — the Road Stead above mentioned has been in common with the 3 Ports, hardly any one of them having claimed it as part of their District. . . .

PORT BEAUFORT. Beaufort is situated on the North side of G[*illegible*] Sound . . . No Officer but at Port of Entry. . . .

BRUNSWICK. The Town of Brunswick may be Considered as the Key to Cape Fear River . . . Brunswick 12 Miles from the Bar, 7 Miles above the Town are flatts . . . 8 Miles farther is the town of Wilmington . . . The Officers stationed at Brunswick 15 Miles below . . . No Officer but at the Port of Entry. . . .

SOUTH CAROLINA. The Boundaries of the District of the Several Ports within the Province have never yet been ascertained — Submitted that the Divisions of the Districts within this Province to be made as they are laid down in the Large Map. . . .

WYNYAW. The District Wynyaw and has been interpreted to begin Northerly at Little River, North and South Inlets Form Wynyaw Bay and empty the Large Navigable Rivers of Waccamaw Pee Dea and George Town River — Further South is the two entrances of Santee River . . . No Officer but at Port of Entry. . . .

CHARLESTOWN SOUTH CAROLINA. . . . Charlestown is the Market where the Whole produce of the District Centers Impossible that the Out Door business can be Conducted agreeable to the Instructions by fewer than 10 or 12 waiters and Tidesmen at least from Nov until Jany. . . .

PORT ROYAL. The Office has been most Scandalously Neglected and the Revenue Abused — No Books besides list of Shipping No Records or Vouchers of any kind . . . Pon Pon much Suspected as a place of Smugling on the West and Balls Island on the East of Charlestown. . . .

SUNBURY. Runs NE and SW about 100 Miles — Frederian the Principle Harbour to the Southward. . . .

SAVANNAH. The Situation of the Town a Considerable Distance from the inlet . . . The Ships generally lye at Tybee, which is far below and out of sight of the town. . . .

[Also includes descriptions of St. Augustine and Pensacola, and the Inspector General's recommendations on North Carolina.]

Bibliography

Primary Sources

A. Manuscripts — English*

Bodleian Library, Oxford

Rawlinson Manuscripts
This collection is divided into four sections — A, B, C, and D. Most of the pertinent American items will be found in Section A: see Andrews and Davenport, *Guide . . . British Museum,* 380–410. Library of Congress transcripts.

British Museum

Additional Manuscripts
The various items in this extensive collection are classified according to the date at which they were acquired by the Museum. Numbers 32686 through 33057 comprise the papers of the Duke of Newcastle, the largest single item in the collection. The important Hardwicke Papers include the numbers from 36125 through 36133. Because of the arrangement of this collection, a careful check of every item must be made to find the relevant sources. Most of the documents relating to American affairs are described in Andrews and Davenport, *Guide . . . British Museum,* 72–169.

Egerton Manuscripts
A miscellaneous collection with some American items: Andrews and Davenport, *Guide . . . British Museum,* 28–50.

King's Manuscripts
Once the property of George III, these papers were given to the nation by George IV: Andrews and Davenport, *Guide . . . British Museum,* 25–28.

* Detailed descriptions of the contents of the English archives will be found in the two guides published by the Carnegie Institute: C. M. Andrews and F. G. Davenport, *Guide to the Manuscript Materials for the History of the United States to 1783, in the British Museum, in Minor London Archives, and in the Libraries of Oxford and Cambridge* (Washington, 1908); and C. M. Andrews, *Guide to the Materials for American History, to 1783, in the Public Record Office of Great Britain* (Washington, 1912–1914). Following the entries above, the appropriate pages in these guides are given for further reference.

Bibliography

Lansdowne Manuscripts
Some American items appear here: Andrews and Davenport, *Guide . . .
British Museum,* 8–17.

Stowe Manuscripts
This collection is particularly valuable for items relating to the revenues
raised in America, and includes a group of papers on the Stamp Act:
Andrews and Davenport, *Guide . . . British Museum,* 17–20.

Cambridge University Library

Cholmondeley-Houghton Manuscripts
This collection, deposited at the University Library, is made up of the
papers of Sir Robert Walpole. The items used in this study were given to
me by Stanley N. Katz, to whom I am most grateful.

Customs House, London
As mentioned previously, most of the customs papers were lost in the
Revolution or destroyed in a fire in 1814. Some items have survived, however. In the London Customs House is a volume entitled "Customs Establ.
American Colonies prior to 8th Sept. 1767." There is some disagreement
about the date of this item, but it does provide a detailed list of the customs officers in America and is particularly valuable because it includes
many of the minor or "incidental" officers as well as the established list.
Two other similar but less useful volumes, because they concern only the
established officers, cover the period from 1767 to 1776: Andrews, *Guide
. . . PRO,* II, 118–119.

The most valuable item in the Customs House is Sir William Musgrave's
"Notes and Abstracts from the Minutes and Orders issued by the Commissioners of the Customs." The first three volumes cover the years 1696–
1775. The classification number at the Customs House library is Customs
29/1, 2, and 3. Musgrave's intention in compiling these "Notes" was to
provide the Commissioners with a convenient reference book of precedents
on various recurring problems. Since most of the Commissioners' own
records have been lost, Musgrave's work is especially valuable. There are
two volumes of minutes of the meetings of the Commissioners, covering
the years 1734–1736 and 1767–1768 (Customs 28/1 and 2), but very little
American material appears there. For yet another surviving customs document, see below under the Public Record Office, Customs Papers.

House of Lords

Manuscripts
The papers of the House of Lords have been printed through the year
1714; see below under printed works. The documents of the later period
are described in Andrews and Davenport, *Guide . . . British Museum,*
189–272.

Bibliography

Lincolnshire Archives

Ancaster Manuscripts

These papers belonging to the Ancaster family contain material on the Heathcotes, one of whom was surveyor general of the customs in America. The items I have used from this archive were given to me by Stanley N. Katz. The Ancaster Papers are divided into first and second deposits, etc., and as used in this study, 1 ANC indicates that the item will be found in the first deposit collection, and so forth.

Public Record Office, London

Audit Office Papers

As discussed above (Chapter IV, note 38), the Declared Accounts of this department make it possible to reassemble the statistical data on the regular colonial customs establishment: Andrews, *Guide . . . PRO,* II, 92–93.

Another important financial record is the account of Charles Steuart, covering his years as Cashier and Paymaster of the Board of American Customs Commissioners. His records provide a very valuable and detailed account of the operation and finances of the American Board not available elsewhere. In the Public Record Office his account is classified as A.O.1/844/ 1137.

Of more general interest are the papers and documents relating to the claims of the American loyalists for compensation for their losses and suffering. In some cases these records provide unique information on the earlier period, particularly on the value of the various colonial offices: Andrews, *Guide . . . PRO,* II, 262–263.

Colonial Office Papers

This overwhelming collection of documents relating to the colonies has been partially calendared: see below, under printed works. The printed Journal of the Board of Trade also may be used as an index to some of this collection: see below, under printed works. But so much of the collection is neither calendared nor indexed that a brief guide to the divisions used is helpful:

C.O. class 1: consisting of sixty-eight volumes, covering the years 1574 to 1688. The documents here relate generally to American affairs and cover all the colonies.

C.O. class 5: this series covers the years from 1689 through 1783 in one thousand four hundred and fifty volumes. The first two hundred and eighty-five volumes contain miscellaneous and general papers relating to all the colonies. Starting with volume 286, the collection is divided by colony and concerns only the continental colonies. For example, volumes 751 through 854 are Massachusetts documents, while 924 through 969 cover New Hampshire. In some cases the

Bibliography

series covers more than one colony in a given division, as in volumes 1257 through 1301, which concern proprietary colonies in general and contain information on Connecticut and Pennsylvania and others. Within each of these divisions the papers are generally divided between correspondence between the colonial officials and the Board of Trade on the one hand and the Secretary of State on the other.

The noncontinental colonies are covered in separate classifications. The Bahamas, for example, will be found in C.O. class 23 (28 volumes); Jamaica in C.O. classes 137 and 138. For the rest see Andrews, *Guide . . . PRO*, I, 185–225.

C.O. class 323: this series in thirty-three volumes contains assorted material relating to the plantations in general. Many of the schemes, plans, and suggestions for reform of the colonial system will be found here.

C.O. class 324: this section, like 323, relates to the plantations generally. Much of the material here is of a more routine nature than in 323 (i.e., warrants, royal orders, etc.), but some interesting items do appear, as in the letter from the Duke of Newcastle to Governor Belcher recommending his "neighbor" William Shirley to the governor's "protection": C.O. 324/36, p. 307.

C.O. class 388: a collection of Board of Trade papers relating to trade problems in general rather than to the colonies in particular. The major value of this group lies in the information it provides on the over-all operation of the trade acts and related commercial problems.

Custom Papers

In the Public Record Office is a volume which supplements the items to be found in the Customs House. Customs 21/16 is a copybook of letters outward from the register general of shipping who was associated with the Board of American Commissioners. Covering the years 1768–1775, this volume provides information on the nature and difficulty involved in drawing up the shipping reports from the various collectors, and in some instances the early letters give information on the chaotic situation in the customs service the American Board was faced with on its arrival in 1767.

State Papers, Domestic

This collection consists of documents from the papers of the Secretary of State for the Southern Department, together with some records from other branches of the government. The documents are separated by reigns, i.e., S.P. Dom. William and Mary, S.P. Dom. George I, etc. See Andrews, *Guide . . . PRO*, I, 42–51.

Treasury Papers

The papers in this collection have been partially calendared; see below, under printed works. Andrews, *Guide . . . PRO*, II, 136–265, indexes many but not all the American items for the years not covered by the Calendars. For the most part it is necessary to check each individual bundle or volume of these papers to be sure of catching every important item. The major divisions of the Treasury Papers are as follows:

Ind. 4615–4626: formerly classified as Treasury 4/1–11, these volumes consist of a series of reference books, made at the order of the Treasury, as an index to the papers referred to them by other departments for advice.

Ind. 4633–4650: formerly T. 4/19–36, these volumes comprise a register of the papers read at the Treasury Board. They are useful, like Ind. 4615–4626, as indexes to the Treasury Papers generally.

PRO 30/32: see under Treasury class 11.

Treasury class 1: a series of unbound manuscripts covering the colonial years in six hundred and twenty-three bundles. This collection contains all the surviving incoming correspondence received by the Treasury Lords. Letters from the governors, memorials from private persons, reports from other departments of the government, and many other kinds of documents will be found here. With the Colonial Office Papers class 5, this collection forms the most important series of official documents relating to the administration of the colonies.

Treasury class 11: in thirty-three volumes covering the years 1667–1784. This collection consists of out-letters from the Treasury to the Commissioners of the Customs. Much of the information is routine (i.e., warrants and orders), but for want of any customs departmental records these volumes have great value. Certain of the earlier volumes, once in the possession of the Duke of Leeds, are classified at the Public Record Office as PRO 30/32.

Treasury class 27: thirty-four volumes covering the years 1668–1783, consisting of general out-letters from the Treasury to other departments of the government. Many letters to the customs department, which should properly have been in T. 11, will be found here.

Treasury class 28: three volumes, covering the years 1763–1778, 1778–

1797, 1797–1823. Known as the "American Books," these volumes represent the special attention given to America after 1763. Only volumes one and two are relevant to this study. The "revocation of the Commissioners of the Customs for America," dated October 16, 1783, is in volume two, p. 185.

Treasury class 29: fifty-four volumes covering the years 1667–1783, consisting of minutes of the meetings of the Treasury Lords. Frequently the text of incoming letters as well as the answers of the Treasury appear in part here.

Treasury class 64: a collection of over three hundred volumes of miscellaneous documents relating to general Treasury business. Of particular interest for the history of the customs service are the book of fees taken in the colonies (T. 64/45) and the "Journals" of William Blathwayt, for many years the auditor of the casual revenues (T. 64/88–90).

Treasury class 98: Three volumes, consisting of miscellaneous papers discovered after the other documents had been arranged and the *Calendars* published. Only a few items of interest on colonial affairs appear here.

B. Manuscripts — American

Essex Institute, Salem, Massachusetts

Timothy Orne Manuscripts

These papers of a Salem merchant who lived from 1717 to 1767, offer some of the best material available on illegal trade with the West Indies.

Maryland Historical Society, Baltimore

Gilmore Papers

This collection includes some correspondence between a customs officer, Robert Heron, and the governor, as well as other customs references for the period 1763 to 1774.

Massachusetts Archives, State House, Boston

Of the many volumes on the colonial period found here the following are relevant to this study: volumes II–VI, which contain general colonial documents, 1629–1775; LX through LXVI, maritime papers, 1641–1775; CXIX through CXX, trade papers, 1645–1774. There is a useful subject index located in the Archives.

Massachusetts Historical Society, Boston

Bowdoin–Temple Papers

Bibliography

Particularly useful is the John Temple Letterbook, covering the years 1762–1768.

Charles Henry Frankland, Diary, 1755–1767.

North Carolina Department of Archives and History, Raleigh

Treasurer's and Comptroller's Papers

Includes volumes on Port Bath, Beaufort, Brunswick, and Roanoke, for various years, 1761–1775.

Vice-Admiralty Court Records, 1697–1759.

Historical Society of Pennsylvania, Philadelphia

Customs House Papers

In twelve volumes, covering the years 1750–1774, this is the most complete set of port papers in existence.

South Carolina Archives, Columbia

Public Treasurer's Journal: Duties

Three volumes, covering the years 1735–1776.

Admiralty Court Minutes (on microfilm)

Covers years, 1716–1730, 1736–1748, 1752–1763.

South Carolina Historical Society, Charleston

Henry Laurens Letterbooks

Laurens' letter of September 5, 1767 (Letterbook for 1767–1771, pp. 7–13) gives a long account of his side of the feud with the customs officers.

Virginia Historical Society, Richmond

Lee-Ludwell Papers

Dinwiddie Letterbooks

Virginia State Library, Richmond

Customs House Book for Norfolk, 1764–1775.

C. Printed Works

1. Official Documents

a. Great Britain

Acts and Ordinances of the Interregnum, 1642–1660. Collected by C. H. Firth and R. S. Rait. 3 vols. London, 1911.

Acts of the Privy Council of England. Colonial Series (1613–1783). 6 vols. London, 1908–1912.

Calendar of State Papers. Colonial Series. America and West Indies (1574–1733). 42 vols. London, 1860–1953.

Calendar of Treasury Books (1660–1718). 32 vols. London, 1904–1957.

Bibliography

Calendar of Treasury Books and Papers (1729–1745). 5 vols. London, 1897–1903.

Calendar of Treasury Papers (1557–1728). 6 vols. London, 1868–1889.

Journal of the Commissioners for Trade and Plantations from April 1704 to . . . (May, 1782). 14 vols. London, 1929–1938.

The Manuscripts of the House of Lords (1678–1693). 4 vols. London, 1887–1894.

The Manuscripts of the House of Lords, New Series (1694–1714). London, 1900–1953. This series, now covering the years through 1714 in ten volumes, is still appearing.

The Statutes at Large from Magna Charta to the Twenty-fifth Year of the Reign of King George III, Inclusive. Owen Ruffhead, ed. Revised by Charles Runnington. 10 vols. London, 1786.

b. America

The Acts and Resolves, Public and Private, of the Massachusetts Bay: to which are prefixed the Charters of the Province. 21 vols. Boston, 1869–1922.

The Colonial Records of North Carolina. Collected and edited by William L. Saunders. 10 vols. Raleigh, 1886–1900.

Documents Relative to the Colonial History of the State of New York. Collected and edited by John R. Brodhead and others. 15 vols. Albany, 1853–1887.

Records of the Colony of Rhode Island and Providence Plantation, in New England. John R. Bartlett, ed. 10 vols. Providence, 1856–1865.

Records of the Governor and Company of the Massachusetts Bay in New England. Nathaniel B. Shurtleff, ed. 5 vols. Boston, 1853–1854.

The Records of the Vice Admiralty Court of Rhode Island, 1716–1752. Dorothy S. Towle, ed. Washington, 1936.

Reports of Cases in the Vice Admiralty of the Province of New York and in the Court of Admiralty of the State of New York, 1715–1788. Charles H. Hough, ed. New Haven, 1925.

2. Private Papers

The Barrington-Bernard Correspondence and Illustrative Matter, 1760–1770, drawn from the Papers of Sir Francis Bernard. Edward Channing and Archibald C. Coolidge, eds. (*Harvard Historical Studies*, XVII). Cambridge, Mass., 1912.

The Belcher Papers (Massachusetts Historical Society, *Collections*, 6th series, VI–VII). Boston, 1893–1894.

The Bowdoin and Temple Papers (Massachusetts Historical Society, *Collections*, 6th series, IX; 7th series, VI). Boston, 1897, 1907.

Bibliography

"The Case of William Atwood, Esq., London, 1703" (New-York Historical Society, *Collections*, XIII, 239–319). New York, 1881.

"Colonel Quary's Memorial" (Massachusetts Historical Society, *Collections*, 3d series, VII, 229). Boston, 1838.

Correspondence of William Pitt, Earl of Chatham. 3 vols. London, 1838–1839.

Correspondence of William Shirley, Governor of Massachusetts and Military Commander in America, 1731–1760. Charles H. Lincoln, ed. 2 vols. New York, 1912.

Edward Randolph: Including his Letters and Official Papers . . . 1676–1703. Robert N. Toppan and Alfred T. Goldrick, eds. 7 vols. Boston, 1898–1909.

The Grenville Papers: Being the Correspondence of Richard Grenville Earl Temple, K.G., and the Right Hon. George Grenville, their Friends and Contemporaries. William James Smith, ed. 4 vols. London, 1852–1853.

The Jenkinson Papers, 1760–1765. Ninetta S. Jucker, ed. London, 1949.

Knox, William. *Extra-Official State Papers Addressed to the Right Hon. Lord Rawdon.* 2 vols. London, 1789.

"Mr. Comptroller Weare to the Earl of ———" (Massachusetts Historical Society, *Collections*, 1st series, I). Boston, 1806.

Otis, James. *The Rights of the British Colonies Asserted and Proved.* Boston, 1764 (as reprinted in the University of Missouri, *Studies*, IV, No. 3, Columbia, Missouri, 1929).

Pownall, Thomas. *Administration of the Colonies.* London, 1764.

The Works of John Adams. Charles Francis Adams, ed. 10 vols. Boston, 1856.

The Writings of Benjamin Franklin. Albert H. Smyth, ed. 10 vols. New York, 1907.

The Writings of Samuel Adams. Harry A. Cushing, ed. 4 vols. New York, 1904–1908.

3. Miscellaneous

Legal Papers of John Adams. L. Kinvin Wroth and Hiller B. Zobel, eds. 3 vols. Boston, 1965.

"Plans of Union, 1696–1780," *American History Leaflets*, No. 14 (March 1894). Alfred B. Hart and Edward Channing, eds. New York, 1894.

Tracts and Other Papers Relating Principally to the Origin, Settlement, and Progress of the Colonies in North America, from the Discovery of the Country to the Year 1778. Peter Force, comp. 4 vols. Washington, 1836–1846.

Bibliography

*Secondary Sources**

"The American Revolution: A Symposium," *Canadian Historical Review,* XXIII (March 1942), 1–41.

Andrews, Charles M. *The Colonial Period of American History.* 4 vols. New Haven, 1934–1938.

Ashley, W. J. *Surveys Historic and Economic.* London, 1900.

Bailyn, Bernard. *The New England Merchants in the Seventeenth Century.* Cambridge, Mass., 1955.

Bailyn, Bernard and Lotte. *Massachusetts Shipping 1697–1714. A Statistical Study.* Cambridge, Mass., 1959.

Bancroft, George. *History of the United States, from the Discovery of the American Continent.* 10 vols. Boston, 1834–1874.

Barnes, Viola F. *The Dominion of New England, a Study in British Colonial Policy.* New Haven, 1923.

Barrow, Thomas C. "Archibald Cummings' Plan for a Colonial Revenue, 1722," *New England Quarterly,* XXXVI (September 1963), 383–393.

———. "Background to the Grenville Program, 1757–1763," *William and Mary Quarterly,* 3d series, XXII (January 1965), 93–104.

Basye, Arthur H. *The Lords Commissioners of Trade and Plantations.* New Haven, 1925.

Baxter, W. T. *The House of Hancock: Business in Boston. 1724–1775.* Cambridge, Mass., 1945.

Beer, George L. *British Colonial Policy, 1754–1765.* New York, 1907.

———. *The Old Colonial System, 1660–1754: Part I. The Establishment of the System, 1660–1688.* 2 vols. New York, 1912. Beer intended to follow these volumes with others bringing his study down to 1754 but was distracted from his work by the outbreak of the First World War and never published Part II.

———. *The Origins of the British Colonial System. 1578–1660.* New York, 1908.

Beer, Max. *Early British Economics, from the XIIIth to the Middle of the XVIIIth Century.* London, 1938.

Brooke, John. *The Chatham Administration, 1766–1768.* London, 1956.

Buck, Philip W. *The Politics of Mercantilism.* New York, 1942.

Chamberlain, Mellen. "The Constitutional Relations of the American Colonies to the English Government at the Commencement of the American Revolution," American Historical Society, *Papers,* III (New York, 1889), 52–74.

———. "The Revolution Impending," *Narrative and Critical History of America,* Justin Winsor, ed. VI (Boston, 1887), 1–62.

* Because of the length of the period covered, I have limited this list only to those works which have been particularly useful to me in preparing this study.

Bibliography

Channing, Edward. *A History of the United States.* 6 vols. New York, 1905–1925.

Clark, Dora M. "The American Board of Customs, 1767–1783," *American Historical Review,* XLV (July 1940).

———. *The Rise of the British Treasury. Colonial Administration in the Eighteenth Century.* New Haven, 1960.

Clarke, Mary P. "The Board of Trade at Work," *American Historical Review,* XVII (October, 1911), 17–43.

Dickerson, Oliver M. *American Colonial Government, 1696–1765.* Cleveland, 1912.

———. *The Navigation Acts and the American Revolution.* Philadelphia, 1951.

Donoughue, Bernard. *British Politics and the American Revolution: The Path to War, 1773–75.* London, 1964.

Doty, Joseph D. *The British Admiralty Board as a Factor in Colonial Administration, 1689–1763.* Philadelphia, 1930.

Egerton, Hugh Edward. *The Origin and Growth of the English Colonies and Their System of Government.* Oxford, 1904.

———. *A Short History of British Colonial Policy.* London, 1897.

Foote, Henry W. *Annals of King's Chapel from the Puritan Age of New England to the Present Day.* 3 vols. Boston, 1882–1940.

Fox, Dixon R. *Caleb Heathcote, Gentleman Colonist. The Story of a Career in the Province of New York, 1692–1721.* New York, 1926.

Giesecke, Albert A. *American Commercial Legislation Before 1789.* New York, 1910.

Gipson, Lawrence H. "Aspects of the Beginning of the American Revolution in Massachusetts Bay, 1760–1762," American Antiquarian Society, *Proceedings,* LXVII (Worcester, 1958), 11–32.

———. *The British Empire before the American Revolution.* 12 vols. Caldwell, Idaho, 1936–1965.

Greene, Jack P. "Martin Bladen's Blueprint for a Colonial Union," *William and Mary Quarterly,* 3d series, XVII (October 1960), 516–530.

Guttridge, George H. *The Colonial Policy of William III in America and the West Indies.* Cambridge, Eng., 1922.

Hall, Michael G. *Edward Randolph and the American Colonies, 1676–1703.* Chapel Hill, 1960.

Harper, Lawrence A. *The English Navigation Laws. A Seventeenth Century Experiment in Social Engineering.* New York, 1939.

Heckscher, Eli F. *Mercantilism.* 2 vols. London, 1955.

Hertz, Gerald Berkeley. *The Old Colonial System.* Manchester, 1905.

Hoon, Elizabeth E. *The Organization of the English Customs System, 1696–1786.* New York, 1938.

Jacobsen, Gertrude Ann. *William Blathwayt, a Late Seventeenth Century English Administrator.* New Haven, 1932.

Bibliography

Jarvis, R. C. "The Appointment of Ports," *The Economic History Review,* 2d series, XI, No. 3 (1959), 455–466.

Jensen, Arthur L. *The Maritime Commerce of Colonial Philadelphia.* Madison, 1963.

Johnson, Allen S. "The Passage of the Sugar Act," *William and Mary Quarterly,* 3d series, XVI (October 1959), 507–514.

Keith, Sir A. Berriedale. *Constitutional History of the First British Empire.* Oxford, 1930.

Knollenberg, Bernhard. *Origin of the American Revolution: 1759–1766.* New York, 1960.

Koebner, Richard. *Empire.* Cambridge, Eng., 1961.

Knorr, Klaus E. *British Colonial Theories, 1570–1850.* Toronto, 1944.

Koontz, Louis K. *Robert Dinwiddie.* Glendale, 1941.

Labaree, Benjamin. *The Boston Tea Party.* New York, 1964.

Lokken, Roy N. *David Lloyd, Colonial Lawmaker.* Seattle, 1959.

Lounsberry, Alice. *Sir William Phips, Treasure Fisherman and Governor of the Massachusetts Bay Colony.* New York, 1941.

Malone, Joseph H. *Pine Trees and Politics: The Naval Stores and Forest Policy in Colonial New England, 1691–1775.* Seattle, 1964.

Martin, Alfred S. "The King's Customs: Philadelphia, 1763–1774," *William and Mary Quarterly,* 3d series, V (April 1948), 201–216.

McCormac, Eugene Irving. *Colonial Opposition to Imperial Authority During the French and Indian War* (University of California, *Studies in American History,* I). Berkeley, 1914.

Miller, John C. *Origins of the American Revolution.* Boston, 1943.

Morgan, Edmund S. and Helen M. *The Stamp Act Crisis, Prologue to Revolution.* Chapel Hill, 1953.

Mullett, Charles F. "English Imperial Thinking, 1764–1783," *Political Science Quarterly,* XLV (December 1930).

Namier, Sir Lewis. *Charles Townshend. His Character and Career.* Cambridge, Eng., 1959.

———. *The Structure of Politics at the Accession of George III.* 2d ed. London, 1957.

Nason, Elias, *Sir Charles Henry Frankland.* Albany, 1865.

Osgood, Herbert L. *The American Colonies in the Eighteenth Century.* 4 vols. New York, 1924.

———. *The American Colonies in the Seventeenth Century.* 3 vols. New York, 1904–1907.

Owen, John B. *The Rise of the Pelhams.* London, 1957.

Owings, Donnell MacClure. *His Lordship's Patronage: Offices of Profit in Colonial Maryland.* Baltimore, 1953.

Pares, Richard. *Colonial Blockade and Neutral Rights, 1739–1763.* Oxford, 1938.

———. *King George III and the Politicians.* Oxford, 1959.

Bibliography

————. *Yankees and Creoles*. London, 1956.

————. *War and Trade in the West Indies, 1739–1763*. Oxford, 1936.

Pemberton, William B. *Lord North*. London, 1938.

Pitman, Frank W. *The Development of the British West Indies, 1700–1763*. New Haven, 1917.

Plumb, J. H. *Sir Robert Walpole: The Making of a Statesman*. London, 1956.

Rankin, Hugh F. *Upheaval in Albemarle: The Story of Culpeper's Rebellion, 1675–1689*. Raleigh, 1962.

Rees, J. F. "Mercantilism and the Colonies," *The Cambridge History of the British Empire*, I, 561–602. New York, London, 1929.

Ritcheson, Charles R. *British Politics and the American Revolution*. Norman, 1954.

————. "The Preparation of the Stamp Act," *William and Mary Quarterly*, 3d series, X (October 1953), 543–559.

Russell, Elmer B. *The Review of American Colonial Legislation by the King in Council*. New York, 1915.

Schmoller, Gustav. *The Mercantile System and Its Historical Significance*. New York, 1902.

Schutz, John A. "Succession Politics in Massachusetts, 1730–1741," *William and Mary Quarterly*, 3d series, XV (October 1958), 508–520.

Sherrard, Owen A. *Lord Chatham and America*. London, 1958.

Sibley, John L. *Biographical Sketches of Graduates of Harvard University*. 10 vols. Cambridge, Mass., 1873————.

Spector, Margaret M. *The American Department of the British Government, 1768–1782*. New York, 1940.

Sosin, Jack M. *Agents and Merchants: British Colonial Policy and the Origin of the American Revolution, 1763–1775*. Lincoln, 1965.

Southwick, Albert B. "The Molasses Act — Source of Precedents," *William and Mary Quarterly*, 3d series, IX (July 1951), 389–405.

Turner, Edward R. *The Privy Council of England in the Seventeenth and Eighteenth Centuries, 1603–1784*. 2 vols. Baltimore, 1927–1928.

Walpole, Horace. *Memoirs of the Reign of George III*. 4 vols. London, 1894.

Walsh, Richard. *Charleston's Sons of Liberty*. Columbia, 1959.

Warren, Winslow. *The Colonial Customs Service in Massachusetts in Its Relation to the Revolution* (Massachusetts Historical Society, *Proceedings*, XLVI). Boston, 1913.

Wickwire, Franklin B. "King's Friends, Civil Servants, or Politicians," *American Historical Review*, LXXI (October 1965), 18–42.

Wiggin, Lewis M. *The Faction of Cousins*. New Haven, 1958.

Williams, Basil. *The Whig Supremacy, 1714–1760*. Oxford, 1952.

Wilson, Charles. *Mercantilism*. London, 1960.

————. *Profit and Power*. London, 1957.

Wroth, L. Kinvin. "The Massachusetts Vice Admiralty Court and the Fed-

Bibliography

eral Admiralty Jurisdiction," *The American Journal of Legal History,* VI (July and October 1962), 250–268, 347–367.

Ubbelohde, Carl. *The Vice-Admiralty Courts and the American Revolution.* Chapel Hill, 1960.

Yorke, Philip C. *The Life and Correspondence of Philip Yorke, Earl of Hardwicke, Lord High Chancellor of Great Britain.* 3 vols. Cambridge, Eng., 1913.

Notes

Introduction: A Theory of Empire

1. "Nova Britannia: Offering Most Excellent fruites by Planting in Virginia," London, 1609, in *Tracts and Other Papers,* collected by Peter Force, 4 vols. (Washington, 1836), I, #6, 23.

2. Charles Wilson, *Mercantilism* (London, 1960), 3.

3. Philip W. Buck, *The Politics of Mercantilism* (New York, 1942), 28; Wilson, *Mercantilism,* 10.

4. Hugh Edward Egerton, *A Short History of British Colonial Policy* (London, 1897), 2. Eli Heckscher, discussing the role of the principle of "autarky" or economic self-sufficiency in mercantilist theory, points out that it was of "practical importance really in one context alone, where . . . it was applied only onesidedly . . . That was in the relations between the mother country and her colonies": Eli F. Heckscher, *Mercantilism,* 2 vols. (London, 1955), II, 131.

5. George Bancroft, *History of the United States,* 10 vols. (Boston, 1834–1874), II, 44–46.

6. George Louis Beer, *British Colonial Policy, 1754–1765* (New York, 1907), 195, 244. For Beer, the Revolution was caused primarily by the English failure to solve the problems of imperial defense: "Imperial defence was the rock upon which the Old Empire shattered itself . . .": *Colonial Policy,* 3.

7. Oliver M. Dickerson, *The Navigation Acts and the American Revolution* (Philadelphia, 1951), xiv.

8. Which, of course, could be an explanation for the finding made by Oliver M. Dickerson that "Americans did not oppose the commercial system under which they lived": Symposium on the American Revolution, printed in the *Canadian Historical Review,* XXIII (March 1942), 29.

Chapter I. Origins of the Colonial Service

1. 15 Charles II, c. 7, p. 5.

2. *A.P.C.,* I, #77.

3. Charles M. Andrews, *The Colonial Period of American History,* 4 vols. (New Haven, 1934–1938), IV, 37: Lawrence A. Harper, *The English Navigation Laws* (New York, 1939), 38.

4. 12 Charles II, c. 18.

5. Unless otherwise noted, the term "English" used in reference to the Parliamentary Acts is understood to include colonials as well as natives of England, Wales, and Berwick on Tweed.

6. 15 Charles II, c. 7, p. 6.

7. 25 Charles II, c. 7, p. 2. Sometimes known as the Act of 1672, the bill passed the House of Lords on March 29, 1673.

8. The duties were as follows: one hundred weight of white sugar, five shillings; one hundred weight of brown and muscovado sugar, one shilling six pence; one pound of tobacco, one pence; one pound of cotton-wool, one-half pence; one pound of indigo, two pence; one hundred weight of ginger, one shilling; one hundred weight of logwood, five pounds; one hundred weight of fustic and other dyeing wood, six pence; one pound of cocoa-nuts, one pence. George Louis Beer, *The Old Colonial System, 1660–1754: Part I. The Establishment of the System, 1660–1688*, 2 vols. (New York, 1912), I, 82, note 1, gives the English duties on these same items. The colonial duties were generally slightly higher than the English equivalents.

9. See Customs to Treasury, July 21, 1763, T. 1/426, foll. 269–273.

10. *C.T.B., 1672–1675*, 705.

11. Lords of Trade to Attorney General, January 28, 1675/76, C.O. 1/36, foll. 20–21.

12. Opinion of Attorney General (William Jones), January 28, 1675/76, C.O. 1/36, fol. 21.

13. Andrews, *Colonial Period*, IV, 119.

14. Beer, *Colonial System*, I, 45; II, 233.

15. "Memorial Concerning the Plantation Trade," n.d., Add. MSS. 28079, fol. 84.

16. 25 Charles II, c. 7, p. 2.

17. Treasury to governors, November 12, 1667, T. 11/1, pp. 49–50.

18. Harper, *Navigation Laws*, 78.

19. For such advances see *C.T.B., 1660–1667*, 436, 449; *1669–1672*, 866, 875. On the "farmers" generally, see Elizabeth E. Hoon, *The Organization of the English Customs System, 1696–1786* (New York, 1938), 5–7.

20. 13 and 14 Charles II, c. 11.

21. A. B. Keith, *Constitutional History of the First British Empire* (Oxford, 1930), 76.

22. *Ibid.*, 76.

23. Hoon, *Customs System*, 7. The transfer was complicated and the farm was not ended completely until 1676.

24. Harper, *Navigation Laws*, 51.

25. 12 Charles II, c. 18, p. 1.

26. 15 Charles II, c. 7, p. 8.

27. Privy Council to governors, June 24, 1663, C.O. 5/903, 11–15.

28. Treasury to governors, November 12, 1667, T. 11/1, pp. 45–50.

29. Royal sign manual to governor of Virginia, October 31, 1671, *C.T.B., 1669–1672*, 1126–1127.

30. Treasury minutes of October 26, *C.T.B., 1669–1672*, 948.

31. Harper, *Navigation Laws*, 60.

32. 25 Charles II, c. 7, p. 3.

33. Treasury warrant of December 30, 1673, PRO 30/32/49, p. 96.

34. Instructions to the collectors, December 30, 1673, PRO 30/32/49, pp. 144–149.

35. Instructions to the surveyors, December 30, 1673, PRO 30/32/49, pp. 149–150.

36. Customs to Treasury, May 12, 1675, *C.S.P.C., 1675–1676*, 231.

37. Lord Treasurer (Earl of Danby) to Customs, March 27, 1676, T. 11/3, p. 99.

38. Treasury to Customs, July 17, 1677, T. 11/3, p. 327.

39. Lord Treasurer to Customs, November 16, 1677, T. 11/3, p. 377.

40. Same to same, May 6, 1678, T. 11/4, p. 55.

41. Same to same, June 12, 1678, T. 11/4, p. 71.

42. Harper, *Navigation Laws,* 93–94.

43. *Edward Randolph: Including his Letters and Official Papers . . . 1676–1703,* Robert N. Toppan and Alfred T. S. Goodrick, eds. (Prince Society Publications, XXIV–XXVIII, XXX–XXXI [Boston, 1898–1909]), VII, 159. See also Treasurer to Customs, May 18, 1678, T. 11/4, p. 60.

44. Treasury to Customs, December 18, 1686, T. 11/10, p. 186.

45. Beer, *Colonial System,* I, 281–282. Andrews, *Colonial Period,* IV, 199, mistakenly reports that Dyer never took up his duties. In the records Dyer's name usually appears as Dyre.

46. Treasury to Customs, November 17, 1685, T. 11/10, p. 73. Dyer was recalled probably partly to report on his survey and partly because his unpopularity made him of little further use in the colonies. His previous career in New York had alienated the people there, and as the son of the Quakeress, Mary Dyer (executed in 1660), he was not particularly welcomed in Massachusetts.

47. Keith, *British Empire,* 76. The surveyors' full title was "surveyor and comptroller" but in these early years they were known generally merely as surveyors. Later the word was dropped, and following the English model they were called merely comptrollers. The use of "surveyor" was probably a holdover from the pre-1673 decision to send officers to the colonies to "survey" the workings of the Navigation Acts.

48. Beer, *Colonial System,* I, 176–192.

49. *C.T.B., 1672–1675,* 705; Treasury to Customs, August 17, 1683, T. 11/10, p. 46.

50. A.O. 1, Customs, bundles 820, 822, 823. On these accounts and their use, see below, Chapter IV, note 38.

Chapter II. Early Years in the Colonies

1. Beer, *Colonial System,* I, 4. Clarendon, author of the remark, himself did much to stimulate Charles' interest in the promotion of trade.

2. Herbert L. Osgood, *The American Colonies in the Seventeenth Century,* 3 vols. (New York, 1904–1907), III, 241.

3. A copy of Bland's "Remonstrance" is in C.O. 1/36, fol. 142. All that can be said of the date is that it was written after 1663 and before 1673.

4. The background on Bland's arrival in Virginia and his feud with Ludwell is found in the petition of his mother, Sarah Bland, no date, in C.O. 1/36, fol. 86.

5. Bland to Berkeley, September 16, 1675; Egerton MSS. 2395, fol. 511.

6. Bland to Customs, n.d., Egerton MSS. 2395, fol. 515.

7. Beer, *Colonial System,* I, 290.

8. Lord Treasurer to Customs, August 21, 1676, PRO 30/32/39, p. 202.

9. See the discussion on this point in Chapter I.

10. The warrants for Ludwell and the other new collectors, dated October 3, 1676, are in PRO 30/32/38, pp. 222–223. Two instances will illustrate the continuity of the connection between Virginia families and the customs posts: Edward Digges was the original collector for Virginia; one hundred years later his descendant,

Dudley Digges, was comptroller at York River. Ralph Wormley became collector at Rappahannock River following Bland's removal; in 1698 Christopher Wormley was collector there; from 1764 to 1775 the original collector's namesake, another Ralph Wormley, was collector at the same river.

11. Lord Treasurer to Customs, November 16, 1676, PRO 30/32/38, p. 241.

12. "The Case Between Thomas Miller & Capt. Zachariah Gilliam . . . ," *The Colonial Records of North Carolina,* W. L. Saunders, ed., 10 vols. (Raleigh, 1886–1900), I, 286–289. This report was prepared by the Lord Proprietors and forwarded to William Blathwayt in a letter from Sir Peter Colleton, February 9, 1679/80.

13. *Ibid.*

14. Affidavit of Timothy Biggs, August 15, 1679, *North Carolina Records,* I, 291–293.

15. Affidavit of Thomas Miller, January 31, 1679/80, in *North Carolina Records,* I, 278–293.

16. As above, note 12.

17. "Answer of Capt. Gilliam," n.d. (but read at the Treasury on February 19, 1679/80), *North Carolina Records,* I, 294–295.

18. *Ibid.*

19. As above, note 15.

20. As above, note 12.

21. Proposals of the Customs Commissioners, April 15, 1860, *North Carolina Records,* I, 329–330.

22. "Answer of the Lord Proprietors," n.d. (but read November 20, 1680), *North Carolina Records,* I, 326–328. The emphasis is in the original.

23. Minutes of the Lords of Trade, November 20, 1680, *North Carolina Records,* I, 329–329. One of the proprietors, Seth Southwell, set out for Albemarle as both governor and collector, but he was captured by the "Turks." In his place Robert Holden became collector. Thomas Miller was made collector at Poole, England, became indebted to the crown, and "dyed in prison," with his accounts so "Imbezilled" they could not be audited. See petition of Hannah Larkhan (whose husband was security for Miller), referred to Customs, July 12, 1688, Ind. 4619, p. 297.

24. George Muschamp to Lord Proprietors, April 11, 1687, C.O. 1/62, fol. 90. The *C.S.P.C.* gives this letter as being addressed to the proprietors, but the copy in the Colonial Office Papers does not indicate to whom it was sent.

25. *C.S.P.C., 1681–1685,* 78; Beer, *Colonial System,* II, 170–171. Rousby was appointed in 1676.

26. *C.S.P.C., 1681–1685,* 66, 67, 78–80; Beer, *Colonial System,* I, 98–100, II, 171–172.

27. *C.S.P.C., 1681–1685,* 734, 735; Beer, *Colonial System,* II, 173.

28. Treasurer to Lord Baltimore, May 14, 1685, enclosing an extract from a letter from Captain Allen of the *Quaker,* T. 27/9, p. 75.

29. Blakiston to Customs, April 20, 1685, C.O. 1/57, foll. 226/229.

30. Osgood, *Seventeenth Century,* III, 500–501.

31. *Ibid.,* 172.

32. *Records of the Governor and Company of the Massachusetts Bay in New England, 1628–1686* N. B. Shurtleff, ed., 5 vols. (Boston, 1854), IV, part, 2, p. 210; Osgood, *Seventeenth Century,* III, 185.

33. Michael G. Hall, *Edward Randolph and the American Colonies, 1676–1703* (Chapel Hill, 1960), 2.

34. Lord Treasurer to Customs, June 12, 1678, T. 11/4, p. 71.

35. Toppan, *Randolph,* III, 62.

36. Beer, *Colonial System,* I, 281–282.

37. Randolph to Customs, June 7, 1680, Toppan, *Randolph,* III, 70.

38. Hall, *Randolph,* 57.

39. As above, note 37.

40. *Mass. Records,* IV, part 2, p. 31.

41. *Ibid.,* 73.

42. *Mass. Records,* V, 155.

43. *Ibid.,* 236.

44. *Ibid.,* 337. According to Hall, *Randolph,* 72, note 35, the date February 16, 1681/82 given in the *Mass. Records* is incorrect and should be March 4–7, 1681/82.

45. Randolph's "Reasons of My Protest Against the Law . . . ," n.d., Toppan, *Randolph,* III, 133–140.

46. Osgood, *Seventeenth Century,* III, 310. Bernard Bailyn writes of these years, "Certain of the leading merchants, whose social orientation had shifted from the parochialism of rural and Puritan New England to the cosmopolitanism of commercial Britain, found in the altering political relationship between England and the colonies a long-sought path to political power": Bailyn, *The New England Merchants in the Seventeenth Century* (Cambridge, Mass., 1955), 143.

47. For example, see Randolph's "Articles of High Misdemeanors . . . ," May 28, 1682, in Toppan, *Randolph,* III, 130–132.

48. Randolph to Bishop of London, May 29, 1682, Toppan, *Randolph,* III, 145–149. Osgood, *Seventeenth Century,* III, 385, comments that Dudley "was one among an increasing number of colonists who were ready to strike hands with the agents of the king and share in every respect their obligations and advantages. Outside of New England a career like that of Dudley would not have called for special remark . . . The activities of these men in trade, in the professions, and in public office, preserved the harmonious cooperation of colonies and fatherland."

49. "Representation of the Affairs of N. England," May 8, 1677, Toppan, *Randolph,* II, 265–268.

50. *Ibid.*

51. Osgood, *Seventeenth Century,* III, 319–330; Hall, *Randolph,* 77–78. Randolph returned briefly to England in 1681 after his first few months in Boston, urging again while he was there that New England should be made a royal province. Hall in his *Randolph* (p. 65) finds that Randolph's proposals "were of the worst kind, void of a solution to the impasse between crown and colony and transparent in their selfish inspiration." It is hard to see what basis there is for such a statement. Most of his suggestions made good sense, as pointing out that the reduction of New England would make control of the other colonies easier since the others had been tempted by the independence of their northern neighbors: see Toppan, *Randolph,* VI, 91. Randolph's mistake was in overestimating the potential support immediately available to a royal government in New England. Otherwise the program he offered was remarkably astute, particularly in its recognition of the need to balance the intrusion of English authority with a concurrent development of internal political support within the colonies themselves.

52. Above, note 2.

53. Randolph to Archbishop of Canterbury, October 27, 1686, Toppan, *Randolph,* IV, 131.

54. Randolph to Blathwayt, April 2, 1688, Toppan, *Randolph,* VI, 253.

55. Randolph to Treasurer, August 23, 1686, Toppan, *Randolph,* IV, 114.

56. Randolph to John Samson (one of the Commissioners of the Customs), June 30, 1686, Toppan, *Randolph,* VI, 173–184.

57. See above, Chapter I, note 44.

58. Randolph to Customs, June 30, 1686, Toppan, *Randolph,* VI, 184–185.

59. Randolph to Archbishop of Canterbury, May 28, 1689, Toppan, *Randolph,* IV, 269.

60. Randolph to Lords of Trade, May 29, 1689, Toppan, *Randolph,* IV, 278.

61. Osgood, *Seventeenth Century,* III, 239.

62. Randolph to Bishop of London, October 25, 1689, Toppan, *Randolph,* IV, 307.

63. Andrews, *Colonial Period,* IV, 372.

64. *Ibid.*

Chapter III. A New Policy Defined

1. Randolph to Sir Nicholas Butler, March 29, 1688, Toppan, *Randolph,* VI, 240–247. Butler, one of the Commissioners of the Customs, was a recent convert to Catholicism, and Randolph in his letter offered to "discover to your Honor lands enough to maintain a small convent without any charge to the Crown." Along with Randolph, William Blathwayt, one of Randolph's patrons and a Stuart colonial "specialist," was continued as auditor general of plantation revenues with increased responsibilities.

2. Customs to Treasury, September 16, 1689, T. 1/5, fol. 47.

3. Brenton took office as of December, 1689. The salary continued to be, as it had been for Randolph, £100 per year paid in England. Like Randolph, Brenton had the power to appoint deputies where needed. Phips was a native New Englander who through recovery of a sunken treasure had earned a reputation in England: see Alice Lounsberry, *Sir William Phips, Treasure Fisherman and Governor of the Massachusetts Bay Colony* (New York, 1941). An earlier candidate to replace Randolph was Samuel Wildgos, who originally applied for the office of collector of New York but who noted that the Commissioners felt he was more suited to a post in New England since "he had lived in those parts." However, Wildgos was passed over for Brenton, a man of more experience and better connections: see petition of Wildgos to Treasury, n.d. (forwarded to Customs September 3, 1689), T. 1/5, fol. 51.

4. Brenton to Treasury, May 7, 1691, T. 1/15, foll. 207–208.

5. Customs to Treasury, October 7, 1691, T. 1/15, foll. 203–204.

6. Petition of Brenton, n.d. (enclosed in letter from Customs to Treasury, November 22, 1693), C.O. 5/857, fol. 266.

7. *The Acts and Resolves, Public and Private, of the Massachusetts Bay,* 21 vols. (Boston, 1869–1922), I, 34–35.

8. *C.S.P.C., 1689–1692,* 722.

9. As above, note 7.

10. Deposition of Thomas Cobbit, n.d., C.O. 5/857, fol. 267.

11. Deposition of Henry Grevenraet, August 15, 1692, in Massachusetts State Archives, LXI, 322. Other examples of this contest between the collector and the naval officer will be found in this and other volumes in the Archives at the State House in Boston.

12. Articles offered against Sir William Phips by Jahleel Brenton, n.d. [1694], in *C.S.P.C., 1693–1696*, 398.

13. *Mass. Bay Acts and Resolves*, I, 35.

14. Brenton to Treasury, n.d. (referred to Customs, March 18, 1694/95), in Ind. 4621, p. 80. Brenton asked "to be made the Navall Officer in New England for the better managing his Majestys Service there which hath hitherto suffered by the same Officer." On the reason for not combining the naval office and the collectorship, see below, note 44.

15. Randolph to Customs, June 27, 1693, Toppan, *Randolph*, VII, 356–372. On Meech's trial, see same, 356–357.

16. *Ibid.*, 367.

17. *Ibid.*, 368.

18. *Ibid.*, 368–369, 367.

19. Randolph to Blathwayt, June 28, 1692, Toppan, *Randolph*, VII, 373–375.

20. *Ibid.*, 379.

21. *Ibid.*, 378–379.

22. As above, note 15.

23. *Ibid.;* the quotation is from page 370.

24. Randolph to Blathwayt, April 21, 1692, Toppan, *Randolph*, VII, 351.

25. As above, note 15.

26. Randolph to Blathwayt, August 16, 1692, Toppan, *Randolph*, VII, 398–399.

27. Randolph to Lords of Trade, September 29, 1692, Toppan, *Randolph*, VII, 416. In a more private letter to Blathwayt Randolph reported that "Mr. Brooks the Collector is proud as Lucifer & negligent in his business which upon the arrival of Governor Fletcher will be rectified": see Randolph to Blathwayt, August 16, 1692, Toppan, *Randolph*, VII, 409.

28. Randolph to Lords of Trade, September 29, 1692, Toppan, *Randolph*, VII, 417.

29. *Ibid.*, p. 422.

30. "Action of the Council of Virginia on Randolph's Arrest," April 27, 1693, Toppan, *Randolph*, VII, 440–441.

31. Hall, *Randolph*, 153.

32. Customs to Treasury, November 22, 1692, T. 1/20, foll. 139–143.

33. Same to same, January 26, 1693/94, T. 1/26, foll. 88–91.

34. Andrews, *Colonial Period*, IV, 156. The letter, dated December 25, 1695, was from two Bristol representatives to John Cary.

35. *Ibid.*, 153–154.

36. Randolph to Customs, June 27, 1692, Toppan, *Randolph*, VII, 356, 359.

37. Randolph's "Memorial No. 2" (October 16, 1695), in the *Manuscripts of the House of Lords*, new series (London, 1903), II, 449–451. Another version of this report, found in Toppan, *Randolph*, V, 117, contains an opening paragraph left off in this source. Since that section contained criticism of the customs officers,

Hall, in his *Randolph* (p. 160), credits the omission to censorship by the Commissioners.

38. Randolph's "Memorial No. 1," December 7, 1695, *House of Lords, MSS.*, II, 447–449.

39. Customs to Board of Trade, January 17, 1695/96, *ibid.*, 451–454.

40. Hall, *Randolph*, 161. Randolph's role in the preparation and hearings on the bill are covered more fully in Hall's article, "House of Lords, Edward Randolph, and the Navigation Act of 1696," *William and Mary Quarterly*, 3d series, XIV (October 1957), 494–515. It should be remembered, however, that the surviving records possibly exaggerate the contribution of both Randolph and the House of Lords, as the papers of the House of Commons and the Commissioners have not been preserved.

41. 7 & 8 William III, c. 22.

42. Above, Chapter II, note 2.

43. Above, note 34.

44. As mentioned earlier the collector in New England petitioned to have the naval office combined with his post. The Commissioners of the Customs themselves had written to the Treasury in 1694 that on many occasions they had "recommended the Officers of the Customs as the fittest Persons to be Imployed under the Governors for the Purposes . . . which in fact & practice have been generally executed by the Person called the Naval Officer": (Customs to Treasury, February 16, 1693/94, Add. MSS. 22617, fol. 141). However, in 1697 Governor Nicholson advised that the two offices should be kept distinct so as to provide a check on each other: (Nicholson referred to his earlier report when discussing the same subject in a letter to the Board of Trade, June 10, 1700, C.O. 5/1311, foll. 22–27). Edward Randolph had reported to the same effect. For this reason the two offices were never merged. The Board of Trade testified to the general acceptance of this policy when they wrote in 1696 that "it would be very Expedient that (according to the Constitution of the Customs in England which has provided a Controul upon the Actions of every Officer imployed therein)" the naval officers and the collectors should jointly handle such an important assignment "as that of Signing Certificates for clearing of Ships": (draft of instructions to governors, enclosed in letter from Board to Privy Council, October 27, 1696, T. 1/57, foll. 100–101).

45. 14 Charles II, c. 11. On the writs of assistance see paragraph 5 of 14 Charles II, c. 11.

46. Andrews, *Colonial Period*, IV, 169.

47. *House of Lords MSS.*, II, 234; Andrews, *Colonial Period*, IV, 169. Randolph presumably interpreted the section of the Act of 1660 which stated that seizures made at sea by ships of war should be delivered to the Court of the Admiralty for trial as extending the Admiralty jurisdiction generally in trade violations to the colonies.

48. Above, note 39.

49. Harper, *Navigation Laws*, 183–184 (see particularly, note 11 on page 184). Harper reports that among others Bermuda and New York definitely provided for Exchequer courts.

50. *Ibid.*, 184.

51. Above, note 32.

Chapter IV. The System Takes Shape

1. Andrews, *Colonial Period*, IV, 226.
2. Atwood to Board of Trade, August 15, 1701, *C.S.P.C., 1701*, 415–416.
3. Same to same, October 20, 1701, *C.S.P.C., 1701*, 587–588.
4. Copies of the Admiralty hearings, November 3, 1701, of Payne's petition, and of the action of the colonial Superior Court, are in *C.S.P.C., 1701*, 712–716.
5. Atwood to Board of Trade, December 29, 1701, *C.S.P.C., 1701*, 709–712.
6. On the hearings given Atwood and Weaver after their return to London, see *C.S.P.C., 1702–1703*, 122, 125, 129–131. Atwood's remarks in his defense are worth noting. He observed that if he had connived at illegal trade as charged, "he might have still enjoyed his offices with plenty and outward peace": *ibid.*, 131. Broughton took the opposite side in New York's political feuds and became one of the "instruments" of Lord Cornbury: *ibid.*, 130.
7. Morton to Board of Trade, August 29, 1701, *C.S.P.C., 1701*, 487–488.
8. Quary to Board of Trade, July 25, 1703, *C.S.P.C., 1702–1703*, 570–572; "Colonel Quary's Memorial," June 16, 1703, Massachusetts Historical Society *Collections*, 3d series, VII (Boston, 1838), 229.
9. Quary to Board of Trade, July 25, 1703, *C.S.P.C., 1703–1703*, 570–572. On Mompesson's earlier defense of the common law courts see Andrews, *Colonial Period*, IV, 259–260.
10. Board of Trade to Privy Council, September 7, 1696, C.O. 5/1, fol. 67.
11. Hall, *Randolph*, 169–170.
12. *House of Lords MSS.*, II, 454.
13. Treasury to Customs, November 20, 1696, T. 11/13, pp. 301–302. Two officers included in the twenty-nine on the list were not provided with a salary there: Brenton, the collector in New England, already received £100 from the English revenues; and Brooke, the collector in New York, was listed for no salary, probably because of doubt as to the proper allowance, since he received a substantial sum as collector of the casual revenues also. That question was settled by May 12, 1697, and Brooke was added to the establishment at £50 per year: see Treasury to Customs, May 12, 1697, T. 11/13, p. 343.
14. Petition of William Massey, n.d. (referred to Customs, January 27, 1695–96), Ind. 4621, p. 128.
15. Customs to Committee of the House of Lords, February 22, 1696–97, in *House of Lords MSS.*, II, 445; Hall, *Randolph*, 179.
16. Above, Chapter I, note 34.
17. *House of Lords MSS., II*, 472–481.
18. *Ibid.*, 481–483.
19. When Randolph returned to England in 1700 he presented a "Narrative of his Survey," dated November 5, 1700, which covered in outline his activities since 1697. The information above, as well as the following discussion except where otherwise noted, is from that "Narrative," Toppan, *Randolph*, V, 210–230.
20. Above, Chapter I, note 45; Beer, *Colonial System*, II, 351.
21. The Entry Books of William Blathwayt (T. 64/88–90), Library of Congress transcripts in two volumes, I, 453–471, contains the story of Santen and Governor Dongan. Blathwayt, as auditor of the colonial revenues, was involved in the case.

When Santen returned to England after Dongan had removed him from office, examination of his accounts seemed to support the charges against him. Dongan had reported that Santen was subject to "hypocondriack fitts" and was "wholly unfit for business": see Osgood, *Seventeenth Century*, III, 367. Santen received a salary of £200 from the local revenues as receiver; because of this "extra" income, which was continued for the later officers, the collector of New York was only allowed £50 on the establishment set up in 1696–97.

22. T. 64/88–90, Library of Congress transcripts, I, 434–436, 503, 527. Brooke was appointed receiver in September, 1689, and collector a few months later, at the same salary as Santen and Plowman had received. On Randolph's earlier estimate of Brooke, see above, Chapter III, note 27.

23. Osgood, *Seventeenth Century*, III, 470.

24. Bellomont to Treasury, May 25 and May 27, 1698, T. 1/56, foll. 272–273, 274–275. Hall, *Randolph*, 188, reports that Brooke had originally obtained his post through the patronage of Bellomont, to whom he was related.

25. "Articles Exhibited by the principall Merchants . . . of the Citty of New York . . . against Thomas Weaver . . ." n.d., in Bodleian Library, Rawlinson MSS. A, 272, fol. 286, Library of Congress transcripts.

26. Byerley was suspended by Lord Cornbury, who succeeded Bellomont as governor and who favored the anti-Leislerian faction; the naval officer acted in Byerley's place. For the complicated story of Byerley and Cornbury, see T. 1/90, fol. 148; 94, fol. 389; 95, foll. 31–59; 97, fol. 262; and the *C.T.P.* for the years circa 1707. On Byerley's later troubles, see his petition, n.d. (ca. 1717), T. 1/207, fol. 199.

27. On Connecticut, see Randolph to Board of Trade, November 5, 1700, Toppan, *Randolph*, VI, 233. On the rest, see as above, note 19.

28. On Randolph's last years, see Hall, *Randolph*, 213–223. Fittingly enough, Randolph's last efforts centered on the struggle to break the proprietary governments in America. Randolph, with his long experience, and his memories of the days of the Stuarts, continually appreciated the impossibility of successful English control of the colonies as long as those islands of independence existed. While he was in England, for the last time, in 1700–01, the Board of Trade undertook a campaign to transform the proprietaries into royal colonies. Through indifference and opposition in Parliament, this effort failed: see Andrews, *Colonial Period*, IV, 378–384.

29. On Luke's later career, see Chapter V.

30. Quary's report on the southern colonies is in his letter to the Customs Commissioners, October 15, 1703, *C.S.P.C., 1702–1703*, 737–740.

31. Quary to Board of Trade, January 10, 1707/08, C.O. 323/6, foll. 142–143.

32. On Brenton's willingness to resign and Jekyll's appointment, see Treasury to Customs, January 8, March 28, and May 15, 1706/07, T. 27/18, pp. 275, 292, 308. On Jekyll's background, see below, note 51. On his commission, see Governor Dudley to Treasury, November 10, 1707, T. 1/103, foll. 185–186.

33. Bellomont to Board of Trade, September 8, 1699, Rawlinson MSS. A, 272, foll. 62–63.

34. On Armstrong, see below, note 60.

35. Nathaniel Shannon was the Boston naval officer; Nathaniel Kay and Charles Blechyden were the English officers; see below, note 57.

36. Customs to Treasury, June 25, 1709, T. 11/15, pp. 179–181. At the same

time a surveyor general was established for the four and one-half percent area, covering the rest of the islands.

37. On Birchfield and the Treasury's overruling of the recommendation of the Customs see below, note 60.

38. Audit Office 1: Declared Accounts; Customs, Receivers General and Cashiers (various) Bundles 759–829. These rolls are the official records of salary payments to, and receipts from, the customs officials in England and the colonies. Returns from the colonies, always very irregular, are never complete in the accounts for any one year, making it necessary to examine the rolls for several years preceding and succeeding the desired year. Using these A. O. accounts for the whole period, from 1675 to 1767, I have assembled various charts and indexes, and it is from these personal records that the information for the years 1710 and 1760 has been constructed. See also Appendix A. On the technical, legal definition of an English port in this period, see R. C. Jarvis, "The Appointment of Ports," *The Economic History Review,* 2d series, XI, no. 3 (1959), 455–466.

39. The reasons for the removal, not given at the time, are indicated in a letter from C. Carkesse to the Board of Trade, October 27, 1721, C.O. 323/8, fol. 94.

40. Although not considered in this study, Jamaica was included in the southern surveyor general's district (not being part of the four and one-half percent area). By the end of this period, however, Jamaica had been separated from the continent and was not part of the territory which came under the supervision of the American Board in 1767. A third surveyor general covered the islands included in the four and one-half percent area.

41. These and the following figures have been rounded off to eliminate shillings and pence. And it should be stressed once again that a quick check of the Audit Rolls for the given years will not produce these exact totals, which result from an examination of the Rolls for a long period to obtain a complete yearly listing of the officers and their salaries.

42. Above, Chapter I, note 48.

43. Governor Samuel Shute to Board of Trade, February 17, 1719, C.O. 5/867, foll. 310–317.

44. Grosvenor Bedford, appointed collector of Philadelphia in 1732, was permitted by his patent to act by deputy, and he never left England during his time of office.

45. The best source for information on the duties of the collector is of course the instruction given to him for his guidance. Those in use during this fifty-year period will be found in C.O. 388/46, Ee 43; Andrews, *Colonial Period,* IV, 204–210, gives a compact yet detailed account.

46. Hoon, *English Customs,* 5 ff.

47. Andrews, *Colonial Period,* IV, 211. The surveyor or searcher in Nova Scotia in 1746, along with visiting all the bays and creeks, was required "to rummage all ships and vessels on their first arrival."

48. Hoon, *English Customs,* 182–183.

49. Massachusetts Historical Society, *Proceedings,* LVIII (Boston, 1925), 432–437.

50. C. Carkesse to R. Powys, December 30, 1713, Add. MSS. 22617, fol. 145. For a description of the process of entering a ship, see Appendix B.

51. The information on Sir Joseph Jekyll will be found in the *Dictionary of National Biography.* John Jekyll's connection with Lord Paget and the Imperial

Court is mentioned in the *Boston Weekly Newsletter* for December 28–January 4, 1733/34, the text of which is printed in *Annals of Kings Chapel* (Boston, 1882), 24–26. Jekyll was nominated for the collectorship in January 1706/07 by the Treasurer; but when no favorable action by the Customs Commissioners had been reported by May of that year, the Treasurer wrote to the Board that it was his intention "to grant the said Imploymt. to the said Mr. Jekyll" and ordered "that you forthwith present him": T. 27/18, pp. 275, 292, 308.

52. Moore to the Bishop of London, July 24, 1704, C.O. 5/1262, foll. 291–292.

53. *Journal of the Commissioners for Trade and Plantations* (London, 1920——), I, 57.

54. Customs to Lord Treasurer, May 6, 1710, T. 11/15, pp. 297–298.

55. Petition of G. Muschamp to Lord Treasurer, n.d. (ca. 1703), T. 1/85, foll. 380–381.

56. Petition of M. Birchfield to Irish Commissioners, n.d. (ca. 1697), T. 1/44, fol. 136.

57. The information on both Kay and Blechyden is found in letter, Customs to Lord Treasurer, June 25, 1709, T. 11/15, pp. 179–181.

58. Petition of T. Newton to Treasurer, n.d. (ca. 1706), Ind. 4622, p. 232.

59. R. Quary to Board of Trade, January 10, 1707/08, CO. 323/6, foll. 142–143.

60. Armstrong's own version of the story, written after the event, is found in his petition, n.d. (ca. 1724), C.O. 5/869, fol. 62. Confirmation of his activities as self-appointed adviser to the Commissioners on the matter of administrative changes in 1709 is found in two letters, Customs to Lord Treasurer, June 25 and July 28, 1709, T. 11/15, pp. 179–181, 206–207.

61. On Heathcote, see the discussion in Chapter V.

Chapter V. Reports from the Field

1. The change was made presumably because of Birchfield's unpopularity in his former district. In 1711 it was reported that Birchfield, "tho an extraordinary civill good natured ingenious well bred Gentleman therefore deservedly beloved by almost everybody hath Recd such Treatmt from Govr. Hunter [N.Y.] and his favourites that he finds himself oblieged to return home . . . and Represent things to the Board of Trade and Commissioners of the Customes": P. Sonmans to W. Dockivra, May 30, 1711, Add. MSS. 14034, fol. 135. Birchfield's troubles with Hunter were caused by his favorable attitude toward New Jersey in that colony's struggles to win commercial freedom from New York. On his return to England the Commissioners showed their approval of his conduct by employing him to survey the various colonies, and upon the completion of that survey he was given a new post in the south. On the survey, see Customs to Treasurer, October 21, 1713, T. 1/165, foll. 75–76. Unfortunately Birchfield's report on his observations, which would be of the greatest value, has disappeared, presumably destroyed in the Customs House fire of 1814.

2. Add. MSS. 8832, foll. 260–262. This manuscript and the following number, 8833, comprise a collection of legal cases involving the customs service over the years 1708–1724. Many are the opinions of the English attorney general Northey, as in this 1715 case, when he states that the matter was closed and its revival "very idle."

3. Add. MSS. 8833, foll. 405–408, legal opinion given on March 1717/18. Bladen

was also accused of obstructing investigations in another case: see same, foll. 409–414.

4. All the facts in this case appear in Add. MSS. 8833, foll. 527–530. The legal opinion in England, in fact, was divided on the subject of the fees, with the consensus seeming to be that if fees had been paid in previous crown suits they must be paid this time, in effect leaving the question to be determined by the customary procedure of the colony. The relevant opinions appear under the dates of February 1722/23 and April 1723.

5. Add. MSS. 8833, fol. 418, opinion of April 1718.

6. Section seven allowed suits for recovery of penalties and forfeitures to be heard "in any of his Majesty's Courts at Westminster, or in the Kingdom of Ireland, or in the Court of Admiralty held in His Majesty's Plantations respectively": 7 & 8 William III, c. 22, p. 7. It should be noted, however, that this provision applied only to the recovery of forfeitures and fines and not to original seizure prosecutions.

7. Add. MSS. 8833, foll. 415–418, contains all the information on Kay's troubles, in a legal opinion dated April, 1718.

8. Admiralty to Privy Council, January 3, 1718/19, *C.S.P.C., 1719–20*, 25–26.

9. Smith to Gov. Shute, February 12, 1716/17, *C.S.P.C., 1719–20*, 26–27.

10. J. Menzies to Admiralty, n.d., *C.S.P.C., 1719–20*, 29.

11. J. Smith to J. Burchett, February 18, 1718/19, *C.S.P.C., 1719–20*, 27.

12. Admiralty to Privy Council, January 3, 1718/19, *C.S.P.C., 1719–20*, 26.

13. It is interesting that the evidence concerning the fate of this communication to the Privy Council appears in a document written some forty-eight years later, when the matter of Admiralty jurisdiction was again a pressing issue. On December 18, 1766, Mr. Cooper in a memo to Secretary Conway mentioned the earlier protests and reported that no action had been taken at that time other than the expressing by Mr. West of the opinion that a new act should be passed: Cooper to Conway, December 18, 1766, C.O. 5/67, fol. 175.

14. Customs to Treasury, April 28, 1724, C.O. 5/898, foll. 129–130.

15. Entry of June 9, 1724, Ind. 4637, p. 205.

16. Shute to Privy Council, n.d., Add. MSS. 33057, fol. 435.

17. Entry of June 18, 1724, Ind. 4637, p. 208.

18. Gov. William Burnet to Secretary of State, March 31, 1729, C.O. 5/898, foll. 268–269.

19. Add. MSS. 8833, foll. 415–418, opinion dated April 10, 1718.

20. Gov. Hunter to Customs, May 7, 1711, C.O. 5/1050, foll. 135–138.

21. As above, note 1.

22. Hunter wrote to Walpole on February 13, 1716/17, that Harrison was a "warm friend of ye Right Side" and that there was "not a greater disparity In merit between any two men that I know than between the man he [Heathcote] keeps In and him he would keep out of Employment": T. 1/206, foll. 84–85. Another version of the story was given in a letter from a friend in New York to Heathcote's brother in England: "After the death of one Mr. Davis (an officer of the Customs house here), your brother, put in Mr. Niccol, wo was well beloved by the merchts & on wos fidelity, the Col [Caleb Heathcote was a colonel in the militia] Could depend for information of wt was doing or necessary to be done; But we hear the Commissioners, upon Govr Hunters recommendation, put in

Mr Harrison, wo is a near Relation, of ye Late L'd Bolingbroke, & is now, & has been for above six years past, high sheriff of this City; how much this will affect your brother both wth respect to his interest and character, considering wt sort of men we have among us, may easly be discern'd, & a little time will determine": W. Vesey to Sir G. Heathcote, May 19, 1716, 1 ANC Cl.B.4a, Lincolnshire Archives. As noted in this letter, the governor's success over the surveyor general was not without effect on the latter's prestige, which in turn could only lessen his effectiveness as a customs officer.

23. R. Fitzwilliams to Board of Trade, December 25, 1727, *C.S.P.C., 1726–1727*, 427.

24. Proceedings of the Court of Common Pleas, Philadelphia, November 19, 1724, C.O. 5/1266, foll. 163–164.

25. J. Moore to Lt. Gov. William Keith, October 31, 1724, C.O. 5/1266, fol. 169. The figures on the number of men involved appear in Fitzwilliams to Board of Trade, as above, note 23.

26. Fitzwilliams to Board of Trade, as above, note 23.

27. Keith's activities are taken from his own account as it appears in the Minutes of the Council, Philadelphia, November 12, 1724, C.O. 5/1266, fol. 166. Keith had presented his report to the Council to gain their support. They replied that he had done well in the affair but that it was not something on which they could give advice.

28. W. Keith to Board of Trade, November 25, 1724, *C.S.P.C., 1724–25*, 273.

29. Fitzwilliams to Board of Trade, as above, note 23. The proceedings in the trial are as above, note 24.

30. Minutes of July 19, 1725, T. 29/25, p. 78.

31. Fitzwilliams to Board of Trade, as above, note 23.

32. Lt. Gov. Patrick Gordon to Duke of Newcastle, November 24, 1727, *C.S.P.C., 1726–27*, 405.

33. Anon. letter to Board of Trade, July 10, 1727, *C.S.P.C., 1726–27*, 313.

34. Extracts from a report by the surveyor general southern, dated July 16, 1715, and from a memorial from the surveyor and comptroller of South Carolina, dated October 3, 1715, and from various other customs officers in that colony, T. 1/192, foll. 232–233.

35. Above, note 4.

36. Above, note 31.

37. Add. MSS. 8832, foll. 249–254, legal opinion dated June 3, 1715. In this instance the Virginia act was an old one, passed in 1705, stretched to cover a new situation.

38. As above, note 7.

39. Above, note 10. Compare Menzies' statement made circa 1719 with that of William Shirley some fourteen years later: "In the next place there is at present an Attempt to destroy the Court totally by sinking the perquisites and fees of the Judge from abt thirty pounds a year Sterl to fifteen": Shirley to Newcastle, July 1, 1733, Charles H. Lincoln, ed., *Correspondence of William Shirley*, 2 vols. (New York, 1912), I, 2–4.

40. Gov. Robert Hunter to Customs, May 7, 1711, C.O. 5/1050, foll. 135–138. Hunter, always at odds with the surveyor general, Birchfield, blamed the Council's

attitude on the unpopularity of that officer. In investigating the past history of fees in New York, Hunter discovered that the Assembly in 1693 had established a list of fees which had been printed but never approved by the governor or the Council. The only items he found were an order of the House of Representatives sending a table of fees to the governor and Council on September, 1693, and an order of Council of the same date setting up a committee to look into the matter. No further records appeared, and it is probable that the fees taken after that were the result of a mutual understanding between the parties concerned, possibly arrived at in the committee meeting held in 1693. See Hunter to Board of Trade, May 7, 1711, C.O. 5/1050, foll. 160–161. In 1699 Governor Bellomont prevented the Assembly from passing an act on fees but agreed to a one-third reduction in the fees of the collectors and the naval officer in order to get the legislature to approve the revenue act for that year. See Bellomont to Customs, October 27, 1699, C.O. 5/860, foll. 375–376.

41. Gov. Samuel Cranston to Board of Trade, November 15, 1710, C.O. 5/1264, foll. 211–212.

42. Treasurer to Attorney General, June 17, 1679, T. 27/5, pp. 71–72. 1679 was the year of Danby's impeachment, and perhaps because of the confusion attendant on that event nothing more was done on the question.

43. Gov. Bellomont to Customs, October 27, 1699, C.O. 5/860, foll. 375–376.

44. Carkesse to Board of Trade, November 20, 1716, C.O. 5/866, fol. 308.

45. Above, note 27.

46. Above, note 14.

47. Testimony of R. Wigg, December 13, 1715, T. 1/193, fol. 265.

48. C. Heathcote to Board of Trade, September 7, 1719, in Dixon R. Fox, *Caleb Heathcote* (New York, 1926), 186–189.

49. Blechyden to Board of Trade, April 5, 1721, C.O. 5/868, foll. 49–50.

50. Gov. Hunter to Customs, May 7, 1711, C.O. 5/1050, foll. 135–138. Certainly there was something peculiar about these dealings but whether or not the surveyor general, Birchfield, was as guilty as Hunter avowed is open to question. See above, note 1.

51. J. Smith to J. Burchett, November 8, 1718, *C.S.P.C., 1719–20*, 27–28. It is not indicated in this account what excuse the collector could have had for his actions, but presumably the Frenchman was allowed into the port under claim of necessities of the sea, meaning that his ship was too damaged to proceed further. In such cases, if it seemed the cargo might be ruined through spoilage or such, disposal might be authorized. It is difficult to see just how a cargo of molasses that could be moved from a ship to a warehouse without accident could be so endangered as to require immediate sale, particularly when the owner put to sea again so quickly, all these events having taken place within the period of three months. In any case the captain's later seizure at Canso tends to confirm the truth of this version.

52. Anon. to Board of Trade, July 10, 1727, *C.S.P.C., 1726–27*, 311–312.

53. Representation of Merchants Traders to Virginia to Board of Trade, n.d. (ca. 1717), C.O. 5/1318, foll. 46–47.

54. Customs to Treasury, March 20, 1720, T. 1/236 foll. 92–93. In view of the later difficulties between naval captains and customs officers after the reforms of

1763, it is worth noting that this complaint probably grew out of a contest between the captain and the collector over rights to a seizure rather than from any involvement with pirates.

55. Bellomont to Board of Trade, September 8, 1699, Rawlinson MSS., A, 272, fol. 62.

56. Fox, *Heathcote,* 6.

57. The opening passages of his first letter provide an interesting example of the form such correspondence took: to the Lord Treasurer Heathcote wrote, "I cannot but acknowledge it to be the greatest presumption imaginable for me, who am wholly unknown to your Lordp to take upon me the freedome thus of writing, but when I consider Your Lordp's uncommon zeal for the discharge of that trust which is so happily placed in Your Lordp I cannot but believe that anything offered for the advantage of that Crown Your Lordp so faithfully serves will be very acceptable and plead my pardon": Fox, *Heathcote,* 146–147.

58. Fox, *Heathcote,* 176–177.

59. It is customary today to distinguish between the charter colonies, such as Rhode Island and Connecticut, and the true proprietaries, such as Pennsylvania and the Carolinas, but in the eighteenth century the two were generally discussed as one by the English administrators.

60. Robert Livingston's plan of 1701, *American History Leaflets,* no. 14 (March 1894), 4.

61. Heathcote to Treasury, January 2, 1715/16, *C.T.B., 1714–19,* 185.

62. Heathcote to Treasury, January 28, 1715/16, Fox, *Heathcote,* 180–182.

63. Fox, *Heathcote,* 182–183.

64. Heathcote to Board of Trade, September 7, 1719, Fox, *Heathcote,* 186–189.

65. *Ibid.*

66. Cummings to Board of Trade, August 2, 1716, C.O. 5/866, fol. 304. Heathcote as surveyor general was responsible for the shift of Cummings from Newfoundland to Boston and so took an active part in his settlement there.

67. Carkesse to Board of Trade, October 27, 1721, C.O. 323/8, foll. 94–95.

68. Cummings, "A Short View of Sundry Regulations for the Plantation Trade in America," n.d. (ca. 1720), C.O. 323/8, foll. 1–2.

69. Above, Chapter IV, note 39.

70. Cummings to Board of Trade, September 17, 1717, C.O. 5/866, foll. 369–370.

71. Cummings to Board of Trade, August 2, 1716, C.O. 5/866, fol. 304.

72. Cummings to Board of Trade, January 28, 1717/18, *C.S.P.C., 1717–18,* 163–164.

73. Cummings, "Short View," as above, note 68.

74. Cummings to Popple, June 20, 1722, C.O. 5/868, foll. 296–297.

75. Cummings to Popple, November 3, 1722, C.O. 323/8, foll. 139–141.

76. Cummings' "Scheme" is printed in full in my article, "Archibald Cummings' Plan for a Colonial Revenue, 1722," *New England Quarterly,* XXVI (September 1963), 383–393. Cummings requested that if his scheme were put into effect he might be appointed receiver general of the revenue here "or Commissioner of ye Stamp Duties, or both," indicating that he anticipated the erection of such offices in the colonies and the administration of the fund there.

77. W. Keith, "A Short Discourse on the Present State of the Colonies in

America" (forwarded to the Board of Trade by Lord Townshend on December 12, 1728), C.O. 323/8, foll. 303–314; also in British Museum, Kings MSS., 205, #2.

78. Board of Trade to King, September 8, 1721, *C.S.P.C., 1720–21,* 408–449; also in Kings MSS., 205, #1.

79. Heathcote to Board of Trade, September 7, 1719, Fox, *Heathcote,* 186–189. Heathcote here referred primarily to the proprietaries, but it conforms with his opinions on the general situation as detailed elsewhere.

Chapter VI. The English Scene

1. Customs to Treasury, April 16, 1725, T. 1/254, foll. 29–32.

2. See Appendix C for the details of the proposed alterations.

3. See above, Chapter IV, note 39.

4. Carkesse to Board of Trade, October 27, 1721, C.O. 323/8, foll. 94–95.

5. *C.S.P.C., 1720–1721,* 408–449. This report, so full of details on trade and manufacturing in the various colonies, has not received the attention it deserves. It constituted a major and climactic effort by the Board of Trade at the end of its most active period and provides a valuable picture of the type and extent of information available to the English authorities. In the English records it appears in C.O. 324/10, foll. 296–431.

6. In 1742 the English and Scottish Boards were again separated and thereafter operated as independent bodies.

7. For example, see the discussion of the Sugar Act in Chapter VIII.

8. Hoon, *Customs System,* 60.

9. *Ibid.,* 57, note 4.

10. *Ibid.,* 58, note 5.

11. 7 & 8 William III, c. 27.

12. Hoon, *Customs System,* 58. See also, Franklin B. Wickwire, "King's Friends, Civil Servants, or Politicians," *American Historical Review,* LXXI (October 1965), 25–27.

13. Above, Chapter V, note 31.

14. E. R. Turner, *The Privy Council of England, 1603–1784,* 2 vols. (Baltimore, 1928), II, 358. See also Andrews, *Colonial Period,* IV, 57 ff.

15. C. M. Andrews, *Guide to the Materials . . . in the Public Record Office,* 2 vols. (Washington, 1912), I, 96–97.

16. Above, Chapter V, note 78.

17. See below, Chapter VII, note 94.

18. Andrews, *Guide . . . P.R.O.,* I, 19, note 3.

19. Andrews, *Colonial Period,* IV, 308.

20. Turner, *Privy Council,* II, 345. Andrews reports that in his opinion relations between the Board and the Secretary were harmonious during this period: *Colonial Period,* IV, 309–310. He overlooked the fact that the seemingly peaceful relations were due more to indifference on the part of the Secretary to the work of the Board than to a close working partnership.

21. Above, Chapter V, note 8.

22. J. H. Plumb, *Sir Robert Walpole, the Making of a Statesman* (London, 1956), 367.

23. J. B. Owen, *The Rise of the Pelhams* (London, 1957), throughout. Besides

his comments on the Tories and Whigs as discussed above, and on patronage as discussed below, Owen differs from other authorities in dwelling on the "incoherence of family grouping in this period": *ibid.,* 55.

24. *Ibid.,* 67.

25. *Ibid.,* 69.

26. L. M. Wiggin, *The Faction of Cousins* (New Haven, 1958), throughout; and see particularly pp. 190, 192–193, 211–212.

27. Owen, *Pelhams,* 71. In this connection it is tempting to speculate on the reforms of 1763–64 in relation to the statement that "George Grenville, 'the second of Pitt's party' in Commons, had always been closer to the 'Tory' wing than the rest of his family": Wiggin, *Cousins,* 235. Owen comments that after 1760 "individual Tories began to appear at Court": Owen, *Pelhams,* 71. Tory thought and influence in this period deserve more study.

28. Owen, *Pelhams,* 69–70.

29. Plumb, *Walpole,* 8.

30. *Ibid.,* 20–21.

31. B. Williams, *The Whig Supremacy, 1714–1760* (Oxford, 1952), 180–182.

32. *Ibid.,* 294.

33. As quoted, *ibid.,* 184.

34. No reference to the Customs' reduction scheme appears either in the Treasury minutes or in the outletters. However, the fact that it was not approved by the Treasury is shown by the continuance of the colonial service unchanged after 1725.

35. Memorial of Clerks of the Naval Office, n.d. (ca. 1713), Add. MSS. 22617, fol. 149.

36. J. L. Sibley, *Harvard Graduates,* 10 vols. (Boston, 1873———), VII, 307.

37. Petition of Benjamin Pemberton, n.d., S. P. Dom. Geo. II, bundle 157, fol. 7.

38. J. Belcher to Newcastle, December 3, 1734, C.O. 5/899, foll. 120–123.

39. Pemberton to Newcastle, January 15, 1758, Add. MSS. 32877, fol. 136.

40. J. A. Schutz, "Succession Politics in Massachusetts, 1730–1741," *William and Mary Quarterly,* 3d series, XV (October 1958), 510.

41. Pemberton to Delafaye, November 3, 1733, C.O. 5/899, foll. 48–49.

42. Same to same, October 8, 1733, C.O. 5/899, foll. 46–47.

43. Shirley had come to New England strongly recommended to Belcher's "protection" by the Duke of Newcastle. Belcher offered him the first opening available, the judgeship of the Vice-Admiralty courts, which Shirley declined as ineffectual and underpaid. Shirley did accept the position of advocate general, which he could combine with his own private law practice, and he and Belcher spent the next several years in an unsuccessful attempt to obtain a settled salary for that office. As late as 1736 the two men were cooperating closely in a draft of a bill to be presented to Parliament concerning the king's woods. Belcher's inability to aid Shirley in the salary matter disillusioned Shirley, and by 1738 he had gone over to the opposition. Eventually Belcher's mishandling of the levy of troops for a West Indies expedition in 1740 gave Shirley his opportunity and he became the new governor of Massachusetts. Many of these events may be traced in Shirley's and Belcher's published correspondence, but on Shirley's application for the naval office, see C.O. 5/899, fol. 323.

44. Frances Shirley to Newcastle, July 5, 1741, *Correspondence of William*

Shirley, I, 37–38; Pemberton to Newcastle, January 15, 1758, Add. MSS. 32877, fol. 136.

45. H. McCulloh to Newcastle, February 13, 1753, Add. MSS. 32731, fol. 177. For McCulloh's interest in the post, see same to same, June 22, 1753, Add. MSS. 32732, fol. 86.

46. A. Murray to A. Brett, May 25, 1745, C.O. 5/388, foll. 401–402. This letter is enclosed in another from Brett to Pelham, dated October 11, 1745, which procured the desired letter to the governor. Murray died in 1746 and was replaced by yet another deputy acting for Brett. See Gov. Glen to A. Stone, October 15, 1746, C.O. 5/388, foll. 425–426.

47. Wheatley to Newcastle, n.d., Add. MSS. 32992, fol. 352.

48. In an interesting letter, Gilbert Elliot wrote to Charles Jenkinson, the secretary to the Treasury, on July 30, 1763, reporting that he had heard of the death of Kennedy, the New York collector, and reminding Jenkinson that Newcastle and Bute had previously set that place aside for his brother, "which I know goes for nothing now." However, adjusting to the political changes, Elliot had already spoken to Grenville and asked Jenkinson to second his efforts. His brother took office as collector in New York in 1764. See G. Elliot to Jenkinson, July 30, 1763, Add. MSS. 38201, fol. 45.

49. C. Wager to R. Walpole, March 31, 1722, Cholmondeley-Houghton MSS., Correspondence #944: "There is a deserving young man in So Carolina, whose name is Thomas Gadsden: he was Lieut at Sea, but since the Peace was Master of Marcht Ships, some years but now marry'd and Settled in Carolina. If by a Vacancy of Collector, or Surveyor of the Customs there, he might have your favour to succeed in either of them, it will always be thankfully acknowledged by . . . . . . [C. Wager]."

50. Same to same, December 22 and 24, 1730, Cholmondeley-Houghton MSS., Correspondence #1784 and 1786.

51. Same to same, June 13, 1734, Cholmondeley-Houghton MSS., Correspondence #2214.

52. Minutes of September 13, 1727, T. 29/26, p. 27. Paxton went first to Salem and Marblehead as surveyor and searcher, a post not listed on the establishment but provided for out of incidents. In 1751 Paxton changed places with Jonathan Pue and became surveyor and searcher at Boston. On this exchange of posts see entry of December 19, 1751, T. 11/24, p. 74. Pue had gone to Boston in 1727 to fill the vacancy left by the death of Archibald Cummings: entry of November 22, 1726, T. 11/19, p. 61.

53. Earl of Bath to Newcastle, October 24, 1757, T. 1/372, fol. 223. Even Oxenden, Solly's patron, had to confess the truth of the report on Solly's sanity: same to same, October 28, 1757, T. 1/372, p. 228.

54. Bath to Newcastle, October 24, 1757, T. 1/372, fol. 223.

55. Minutes of May 27, 1756, T. 29/32, p. 389.

56. Treasury to Customs, March 31, 1757, T. 11/25, p. 131.

57. Newcastle to Bath, October 27, 1757, Add. MSS. 32875, fol. 295. Treasury warrant for Waldo, dated October 21, 1757, is in T. 11/25, p. 316. Waldo's £100 salary was to come out of receipts of the port after all other expenses had been paid.

58. J. Mead to J. West, July 14, 1758, T. 1/388, fol. 67. As no detailed description of these districts exists for the period after 1758, the fact that Nevin obtained satisfaction on this point is based on correspondence of a later date which shows that the American Board, created in 1767, considered York and Newbury to be within the Piscataqua district: for example, see letter of January 20, 1775, in Customs 21/16. It is worth noting that the decision on the boundaries in 1757 was made by the Board of Trade at the request of the Treasury: minutes of October 6, 1757, T. 29/32, p. 485.

59. Bath to Newcastle, October 29, 1757, T. 1/372, fol. 225.

60. Below, Chapter IX, note 12.

61. S. Waldo to Newcastle, August 2, 1757, Add. MSS. 32872, fol. 419.

62. Rockingham to Newcastle, August 17, 1757, Add. MSS. 32873, fol. 133.

63. Newcastle to Rockingham, August 23, 1757, Add. MSS. 32873, fol. 244. Newcastle thought that eventually they might be able to fit Quarme into the Stamp Office, but that there might be some delay; hence his inclination towards the "other Scheme."

64. Rockingham to Newcastle, September 5, 1757, Add. MSS. 32873, fol. 480.

65. Newcastle to Rockingham, September 27, 1757, Add. MSS. 32874, fol. 330.

66. Treasury to Customs, March 13, 1749/50, T. 11/23, p. 579.

67. See the discussion on Barons in Chapter VIII.

68. Acklorn to Newcastle, August 28, 1757, Add. MSS. 32873, fol. 332.

69. Above, note 12.

70. Wiggin, *Cousins,* 200.

71. J. White to J. Page, November 20, 1758, Add. MSS. 32885, fol. 451. White desired a position as comptroller in the West Indies which the Commissioners had given to another man considered more suitable.

72. C. Spooner to Newcastle, March 11, 1758, Add. MSS. 32878, fol. 185.

73. "Memorandum relating to South Carolina," n.d., Add. MSS. 33030, fol. 346. The salary was to be raised for Pitt's benefit from £1,900 to £2,400.

74. Owen, *Pelhams,* 62.

75. The most striking of Owen's suggestions in his *Pelhams* is his dictinction between the "favour of the Closet" and the "power of the Closet." In this interpretation the key to politics under the first Georges was the necessity for bringing the powers of the crown and of Parliament into working harmony. The "favour" of one of these branches was not enough alone; consequently the prime minister developed as a bridge between the throne and Parliament, and patronage filled the function of a "lubricant between executive and legislature." Only a man who understood the value and use of patronage could keep the "machine" of government in operation; hence the importance of Newcastle and his like.

76. This quotation from the writings of Ellis Huske is taken from Massachusetts Historical Society, *Collections,* 6th series, VI (Boston, 1893), 3n.

77. Rockingham to Newcastle, August 17, 1757, Add. MSS. 32873, fol. 133. Frankland's payment is inferred from Rockingham's reference to Newcastle's agreement to give the post to Quarme on condition "to continue the Payment" of the £200.

78. Newcastle to Rockingham, August 23, 1757, Add. MSS. 32873. fol. 244.

79. Rockingham to Newcastle, August 17, 1757, Add. MSS. 32873, fol. 133.

80. Newcastle to Rockingham, as above, note 78.

81. Same to same, September 27, 1757, Add. MSS. 32874, fol. 330.

82. William Gage to Newcastle, n.d., Add. MSS. 32699, fol. 606.

83. George Munro to [J. West], July 31, 1756, Add. MSS. 32866, fol. 331. Presumably Munro was unsuccessful in this application, as his name never appears on the receipt rolls, as it would have done even had he operated through a deputy.

84. "Copy of the Answers of Francis Fauquier . . . .," 1763, in Kings MSS., #10. The valuable post was the Lower James. In the following discussion on the value of the various posts, unless otherwise noted the sums mentioned are given in sterling. It is not always possible to tell exactly whether a given source refers to sterling or provincial currency, but in most cases correspondence between a colonial official and the home authorities would use the standard sterling values. It is only in discussions between two colonials that there is a real problem, and then a "wise" guess is the only answer.

85. Belcher to R. Partridge, October 4, 1733, *Belcher Papers* (Massachusetts Historical Society, *Collections,* 6th series, VI–VII [Boston, 1893–1894]), I, 377; Belcher to J. Belcher, junior, November 26, 1734, *Belcher Papers,* II, 163.

86. Pemberton to Delafaye, October 8, 1733, C.O. 5/899, foll. 46–47.

87. Above, note 82.

88. Above, note 80.

89. Since usually the "outdoor" officers, the searchers and tidesmen, would be the ones actually to detect a fraud, they were in the best position to take advantage of bribes; consequently those posts were more important and more desirable than they might appear.

90. Dickerson, *Navigation Acts,* 215, discusses how this was done with regard to coasting vessels and additional fees.

91. Petition of F. Waldo to Treasury, January 10, 1776, C.O. 5/115, fol. 191. Waldo's post had been placed on the establishment at a regular salary after the creation of the American Board.

92. Memorial of R. A. Harrison, February 2, 1784, A.O. 13/83 ("Loyalist Claims").

93. *Ibid.*

94. W. Wood to Jenkinson, November 21, 1763, Add. MSS. 38201, fol. 255. In 1763 Henry McCulloh presented the following estimates of the value of the various posts: New York, upwards of £600 per year; places in Connecticut, from £100 to £250; Boston, the "best" on the continent, but no figures given; New Hampshire and Nova Scotia, little value; Maryland posts, from £100 to £300; Upper James in Virginia, £300; Lower James, £450 to £500; York River, £400; Rappahannock, £200; North Carolina, from £70 to £250; Charleston, upwards of £600; Georgia, inconsiderable; see *The Jenkinson Papers, 1760–1768,* N. S. Jucker, ed. (London, 1949), 229–231.

95. Above, notes 70, 71, 72.

96. Dickerson, *Navigation Acts,* 208–256, comments on the "new race of customs officers" that descended on the colonies after 1767. A check of the officers after that date shows that the large majority had been in the service for many years and if anything was "new" it was the system and not the men that had been changed.

97. See Chapter IV, note 38. These figures represent the net income after the port expenses were deducted.

98. Above, note 86.

99. F. Shirley to Newcastle, July 5, 1741, *Correspondence of William Shirley,* I, 37–38.

100. "Extract of a letter from New England," n.d., Add. MSS. 33029, fol. 322. From internal evidence this letter seems to be the work of Frankland, probably between 1750 and 1754. It is definitely the product of a customs official in New England.

101. For example, see Customs to Treasury, August 13, 1729, T. 11/19, pp. 425–426. The surveyor general had suspended a collector in the Jerseys but was overruled in London.

102. As surveyors general had a great deal of territory to cover, they had to share appointive power with the governors, who were empowered to act in their absence. See instructions to Shirley in *Correspondence of William Shirley,* I, 57–58.

103. Bernard to Shelburne, January 27, 1767, C.O. 5/756, foll. 77–83.

104. Gooch to [Albemarle], Sept. 3, 1739, C.O. 5/1337, foll. 208–209.

Chapter VII. The Fallow Years

1. Cummings to Board of Trade, August 2, 1716, C.O. 5/866, fol. 304.

2. W. Gordon to Board of Trade, August 17, 1720, C.O. 5/867, foll. 344–345.

3. Memorial to the Board of Trade from Thomas Lechmere and the several officers of New England, April 30, 1725, C.O. 5/869, foll. 335/337.

4. Minutes of May 3, 1726, T. 29/25, p. 173.

5. Frank W. Pitman, *The Development of the British West Indies, 1700–1763* (New Haven, 1917), chart facing page 302. The figures cited are approximate.

6. *Ibid.,* 254. The reasons for calling upon Parliament in this affair illustrate one cause for the increasing importance of that body in colonial administration.

7. *Ibid.,* 254–263. The Molasses Act was 6 Geoorge II, c. 13. It was enacted for five years but continued by subsequent Acts until made perpetual in 1764 at reduced rates. Duties under the original Act were five shillings per hundred weight on foreign sugar, nine pence per gallon on rum, and six pence per gallon on molasses. Various drawbacks were added to assist the planters to compete on the European market.

8. The Treasury orders are quoted in a letter from the Customs to Treasury, February 8, 1734/35, T. 1/288, foll. 66–67.

9. *Ibid.* Charles Paxton was the surveyor and searcher appointed at Salem. See above, Chapter VI, note 52. These new officers did not appear on the establishment as they were paid out of incidents at their ports.

10. See Appendix C, Section I.

11. Pitman, *West Indies,* 283.

12. See below, note 92.

13. J. Belcher to Board of Trade, March 2, 1736/37, C.O. 5/879, Cc. 38, as quoted in Pitman, *West Indies,* 281.

14. Edward Channing, *A History of the United States* (New York, 1910), II, 521. The Acts were 12 George II, c. 30, and 15 George II, c. 33.

15. The usual interpretation that Belcher was removed because of agitation by Shirley and other enemies is only partly true. It took a serious mistake to bring about Belcher's fall, and his handling of the levies provided that opening. See W. Bladen to Newcastle, October 8, 1740, C.O. 5/899, foll. 524–526.

16. Customs to Treasury, January 2, 1750/51, C.O. 5/372, fol. 240. This report was forwarded by the Treasury to the Board of Trade.

17. See the discussion on Falmouth in Chapter VI.

18. Treasury minutes of April 29 and May 5, 1752, T. 29/32, pp. 36 and 37; Treasury to Customs, May 12, 1752, T. 11/24, p. 155.

19. American Board of Customs Commissioners to Treasury, September 28, 1772, T. 1/492, foll. 178–179.

20. Cornwallis to Treasury, July 17, 1750, T. 1/340, fol. 124.

21. Customs to Treasury, September 28, 1750, T. 1/340, fol. 126.

22. Frankland to Newcastle, May 19, 1740, Add. MSS. 32693, fol. 289.

23. Elias Nason, *Sir Charles Henry Frankland* (Albany, 1865), throughout.

24. R. Auchmuty to Treasury, December 30, 1742, C.O. 5/883, Ee 90; same to same, November 23, 1743, C.O. 5/884, fol. 12.

25. "Extract of a letter from New England," n.d., Add. MSS. 33029, fol. 322. Salem and Marblehead provided another example of the lax enforcement of regulation in this period. William Bollan had been appointed collector there but was so busy on his other affairs that he never exercised his authority. In his absence the naval officer, Nutting, acted as collector. See Bollan to Newcastle, April 12, 1766, Add. MSS. 32974, fol. 364.

26. Timothy Orne to George Dodge, July 18, 1758, Timothy Orne MSS., Essex Institute, Salem, Massachusetts. Henry Laurens of South Carolina confided to a friend earlier that "Our annual importation of Sugar is very uncertain . . . We believe the major part . . . must be brought in clandestinely": Henry Laurens Letter Book for 1755–1757, pp. 297–299, South Carolina Historical Society, Charleston.

27. Dickerson, *Navigation Acts,* 86.

28. "Evidence before the House of Commons concerning the Molasses Duty 1766," T. 1/434, fol. 56.

29. *Ibid.* One authority told the House that the British islands could provide only three thousand hogsheads of molasses a year. Another estimated that they could satisfy only one-twentieth of the needs of the mainland colonies.

30. Dickerson, *Navigation Acts,* 69.

31. Beer, *Colonial Policy,* 124. Beer was concerned primarily with the war years, hence his reference to the "enemy." Since there were only six years of peace during this period his remarks are applicable generally.

32. Harper, *Navigation Laws,* 268.

33. Dickerson, *Navigation Acts,* 70.

34. Customs to Treasury, January 2, 1750/51, C.O. 5/372, fol. 240.

35. Above, Chapter VI, note 89.

36. Nicholas Brown to Moses Brown, June 13, 1764, as quoted in Richard Pares, *Yankees and Creoles* (London, 1956), 57.

37. Orne to George Dodge, July 18, 1758, Orne MSS., Essex Institute.

38. Testimony of Governor Bernard in support of Cockle, collector at Salem, n.d. (but enclosed in letter of December 7, 1764 to Lord Halifax), C.O. 5/755, foll. 183–187.

39. Palmer to J. West, October 20, 1756, T. 1/368, fol. 29.

40. Treasury to Customs, June 10, 1757, T. 11/25, p. 132. The outcome of this

case is not recorded; but since Palmer remained as collector at Bathtown for many years, presumably it was settled without permanent damage to his career.

41. Edmund and Joseph Quincy to Captain Sinclair, April 10, 1745, C.O. 323/13, foll. 179–180. This collection is made up of extracts from letters which came to light when Sinclair's ship was seized.

42. George Spencer to Pitt, December 14, 1760, C.O. 5/60, foll. 161–164.

43. Governor Glen to Bedford, October 10, 1748, C.O. 5/389, foll. 107–108.

44. De Lancey to Board of Trade, January 5, 1758, C.O. 5/1068, foll. 160–162.

45. Pares, *Yankees and Creoles,* 9. Pares refers to Faneuil's activities circa 1740.

46. *Ibid.,* 10.

47. Dinwiddie to [Board of Trade], June 2, 1736, C.O. 323/10, foll. 61–63.

48. Hardy to Board of Trade, July 15, 1757, C.O. 5/1068, foll. 30–33.

49. Browne to Captain Field, March 6, 1735/36, as quoted in Pares, *Yankees and Creoles,* 56–57.

50. Hancock to Captain Gross, April 12, 1742, as quoted in W. T. Baxter, *The House of Hancock: Business in Boston, 1724-1775* (Cambridge, Mass., 1945), 85–86.

51. Baxter, *Hancock,* 69–72. Baxter's reasons for thinking Hancock's involvement in the schooner *John* in 1738 was not illegal are not valid; stopping at London on the way to Holland hardly answered all the provisions of the Acts of Trade.

52. Clinton to Board of Trade, October 4, 1752, C.O. 5/1064, foll. 144–147.

53. Archibald Kennedy Esq. etc., against the Sloop *Mary and Margaret* Thomas Fowles Reclaimant — in the Court of Admiralty of New York, n.d. (enclosed in letter of 1739), C.O. 5/1059, foll. 132–133.

54. Hardy to Board of Trade, July 15, 1757, C.O. 5/1068, foll. 30–33.

55. See below, Chapter XI, note 68.

56. Dickerson, *Navigation Acts,* 88.

57. Baxter, *Hancock,* 72–73.

58. Orne to George Dodge, July 18, 1758, Orne MSS., Essex Institute.

59. W. Bollan to Board of Trade, February 26, 1742/43, C.O. 5/883, Ee 87.

60. Examination of John Boutin, June 9, 1757, C.O. 5/1068, foll. 22–24.

61. As above, note 58.

62. Hancock to the Hopes, April 12, 1742, Baxter, *Hancock,* 90–91.

63. W. Shobrooke to Newcastle, n.d., Add. MSS. 34729, fol. 348.

64. Dickerson, *Navigation Acts,* 34–42.

65. As above, note 62. Hancock in this leter told the Hopes that the "Letters you send me by way of London Inclose to Francis Wilks Esq. & Co. who will always forward them at the first opportunity."

66. Clinton to Board of Trade, October 4, 1752, C.O. 5/1064, foll. 144–147.

67. R. Auchmuty to Treasury, December 30, 1742, C.O. 5/883, Ee 90.

68. Two memorials from Lockman to Newcastle, n.d., Add. MSS. 33057, foll. 288 and 290. Auchmuty in his letter of 1742 had recommended that the naval officer be assigned from England: see note 67 above.

69. Cholet to J. Nichols, November 7, 1749, C.O. 137/25, foll. 119–120.

70. Shirley to Board of Trade, February 26, 1742/43, C.O. 5/883, Ee 86.

71. Bollan to Board of Trade, February 26, 1742/43, C.O. 5/883, Ee 87.

72. Shirley to Board of Trade, February 6, 1747/48, C.O. 5/886, Gg 3.

73. Clinton to Board of Trade, October 4, 1752, C.O. 5/1064, foll. 144–147.

74. "Copy of the Answers of Jonathan Belcher . . . 1754," Kings MSS. 205, #7.

75. Shirley to Board of Trade, as above, note 70. 15 Charles II, c. 7, p. 6, on the importation of European goods stipulated only that offenses should be heard in "any of his Majesty's Courts" in the colony where the offense took place or "in any Court of Record in England." The argument was that the court of record provision applied to the courts used in the colonies as well as in England. The Admiralty courts were not courts of record.

76. As above, note 71.

77. Auchmuty to Board of Trade, May 31, 1743, C.O. 5/883, Ee 89.

78. See the discussion on Cummings' proposals in Chapter V.

79. Clinton to Newcastle, December 13, 1744, C.O. 5/1094, foll. 374–375.

80. Ways and Means to Raise a Fund to Support Defense, n.d. (ca. 1748), C.O. 5/5, fol. 280.

81. Methods for preventing frauds in the Customs, n.d. (ca. 1748), C.O. 5/5, fol. 276.

82. "Considerations on the Plantations," and "Further Considerations," n.d., C.O. 5/5, fol. 281 and foll. 313–317.

83. F. Fane to Board of Trade, February 26, 1736/37, C.O. 5/365, fol. 195.

84. Minutes of February 28, 1753, T. 29/32, p. 106–107. The question centered on an act of the Assembly of South Carolina.

85. On previous troubles between the navy and the customs officers, see report on the affair between Commodore Knowles and the authorities, November 14, 1744, Add. MSS. 33029, fol. 5.

86. Bollan to Board of Trade, October 24, 1749, C.O. 323/12, foll. 260–262. The fact that customs officers were customarily entitled to be the "informers" in court has misled some writers to conclude that association of the navy in enforcement of the Acts of Trade was a new feature of the reforms of 1764. Actually they were merely given better incentives to participate enthusiastically.

87. Bollan to Board of Trade, June 9, 1755, C.O. 5/887, Hh 51 and 52.

88. For example, see the legal decisions included in Add. MSS. 8832 and 8833. An example of the problem of the relationship between English legal opinion and administrative practice at a later date is the furor around the writs of assistance: after the English authorities had forced recognition of the officers' right to such writs, the granting of the writs by colonial courts was declared invalid by the English attorney general: Bernhard Knollenberg, *Origin of the American Revolution* (New York, 1960), 68.

89. P. Randolph to W. Peters, July 20, 1750, Customs House Papers, I (1750–1761), Historical Society of Pennsylvania, Philadelphia.

90. Order of March 11, 1752, *A.P.C.,* IV, 153–157.

91. Pitman, *West Indies,* 299–300.

92. Testimony at the Board of Trade, 1750, as given in Pitman, *West Indies,* 414–430.

93. Hardwicke to Newcastle, August 13, 1751, Add. MSS. 32725, fol. 59. "Them" referred to the Pelhams, particularly to Newcastle, whom the king never cared for.

94. Newcastle to Halifax, November 7, 1751, Add. MSS. 32725, fol. 378.

95. In 1757 Halifax finally did force his way into the king's Council, but by

then the critical war with France had progressed too far to allow his success to alter the situation of the colonies. In 1761 the Board lost its revived powers, and patronage again became the right of the Secretary of State.

96. Bollan to Board of Trade, February 26, 1742/43, C.O. 5/883, Ee 87.

Chapter VIII. Reform

1. William Bollan to Board of Trade, February 26, 1742/43, C.O. 5/883, Ee 87.

2. Shirley to Board of Trade, February 6, 1747/48, C.O. 5/886, Gg 3. Commissions from the governors served as passes for ships under a "flag of truce." Consequently "popularly-controlled" Rhode Island and Connecticut were ideal centers for this trade.

3. De Lancey to Board of Trade, June 3, 1757, C.O. 5/1068, foll. 5–7.

4. Deposition of Martin Garland, sworn May 31, 1757, C.O. 5/1068, foll. 18–19.

5. Hardy to Board of Trade, June 14, 1757, C.O. 5/1068, foll. 20–21.

6. Beer, *Colonial Policy,* 94–95.

7. *Ibid.,* 99.

8. *Ibid.,* 96–97, note 3.

9. Fauquier to Board of Trade, September 23, 1758, C.O. 5/1329, foll. 82–85. The original French reads, "Nous sommes tous les Jours a la Veille de manquer, sans le Secours de nos Ennemies nous serons obligez de vivre comme vous nous l'annocez avec ce que nous fournit la Colonie. La Condition est dure . . . nous scavons bien qu'il est impossible au Commerce de France de nous secourir." The governor of Pennsylvania during these years did a regular business in flag of truce passes: see Beer, *Colonial Policy,* 91.

10. Colden to Pitt, October 27, 1760, C.O. 5/19, foll. 289–290.

11. Circular letter of August 23, 1760, as outlined in Beer, *Colonial Policy,* 105.

12. Board of Trade, *Journal, 1754–58,* 336–337.

13. Clarke to Board of Trade, December 15, 1739, C.O. 5/1059, fol. 131.

14. Above, Chapter VII, notes 76, 86, and 87.

15. For further discussion of these reports, see Thomas C. Barrow, "Background to the Grenville Program," *William and Mary Quarterly,* 3d series, XXII (January 1965), 93–104.

16. D. M. Clarke, *The Rise of the British Treasury* (New Haven, 1960), 4.

17. Carkesse to Popple, December 1, 9, and 16, 1730, December 17, 1731, July 11, 1737, in T. 1/381, foll. 99–102. At one point the Commissioners showed their annoyance at being asked to consider so many schemes and proposals by having their secretary write "that the Management of the Revenue takes up so much of their time they hope they will be excus'd from examining so many Schemes": letter of December 17, 1731, T. 1/381, foll. 99–102.

18. Customs to Treasury, March 6, 1759, T. 1/392, fol. 34.

19. Board of Trade to Customs, February 24, 1759, T. 1/392, foll. 35–36.

20. Minutes of October 27, 1757, T. 29/32, p. 487.

21. J. West to Customs, January 18, 1758, T. 11/25, p. 329; T. 1/382, fol. 1.

22. W. Wood to West, January 26, 1758, T. 1/382, fol. 3. This investigation was undoubtedly the cause of the changes noted in the letter of the Salem merchant quoted previously.

23. Minutes of February 15, 1758, T. 29/33, p. 16.

24. Treasury to Customs, November 27, 1758, T. 11/25, p. 441.

25. Customs to Treasury, May 10, 1759, T. 1/392, foll. 38–39.

26. Solicitors' report, enclosed in Customs to Treasury, May 10, 1759, T. 1/392, foll. 41–43. The Bollan report referred to was that of February 26, 1742/43, discussed above in Chapter VII.

27. Board of Trade to King in Council, August 31, 1759, T. 1/396, foll. 65–70.

28. Minutes of February 20 and March 18, 1760, T. 29/33, pp. 290 and 304.

29. Minutes of May 6, June 16, and June 22, 1761, T. 29/34, pp. 63, 112, and 122.

30. A. Bradley to Pitt, December 17, 1760, C.O. 5/60, fol. 172; G. Spencer to Pitt, December 14, 1760, C.O. 5/60, foll. 161–162.

31. Governor Thomas Boone to Treasury, August 30, 1761, T. 1/407, fol. 286. The master was given back one-third of the proceeds from the condemnation in return for not contesting the suit.

32. Knollenberg, *American Revolution*, 67–69.

33. Lawrence H. Gipson, "Aspects of the Beginning of the American Revolution in Massachusetts Bay, 1760–1762," American Antiquarian Society, *Proceedings*, LXVII (Worcester, 1958), 11–32. Gipson is primarily interested in the writs of assistance, but he does note the connection between that problem and the preceding struggle over distribution of the profits of seizures.

34. Above, Chapter V, note 14.

35. Above, Chapter VI, note 66.

36. Above, Chapter IV, note 51.

37. "Extract of a letter from New England," n.d., Add. MSS. 33029, fol. 322.

38. Testimony of Governor Bernard, March 16, 1761, T. 1/408, foll. 106–111.

39. Deposition of Charles Paxton, February 18, 1761, T. 1/408, foll. 102–105. The treasurer's demands on the Admiralty court are covered in Bernard's testimony, March 16, 1761, T. 1/408, foll. 106–111.

40. T. 1/408, foll. 106–111.

41. Deposition of E. Richardson, February 27, 1761, T. 1/408, foll. 155–156.

42. Lechmere to Barons, June 24, 1761, T. 1/408, foll. 144–145.

43. Lechmere to Customs, July 8, 1761, T. 1/408, foll. 146–148.

44. Bernard to Board of Trade, August 6, 1761, C.O. 5/891, foll. 87–89. In the case of Erwing v. Cradock, Erwing had admitted the illegal actions of his ship and agreed to pay £500 damages to the Admiralty court. As soon as that was settled, Erwing turned to the common law courts and won a £600 verdict against the collector.

45. Bernard to Board of Trade, August 6, 1761, C.O. 5/891, foll. 87–89.

46. Beer, *Colonial Policy,* 120–121.

47. Temple's action is indicated in the memorial of nine Boston merchants in support of Barons to the Treasury, dated February 18, 1762, T. 1/415, foll. 157–162.

48. The surveyor general would seem to have been correct in his estimate that Barons was not to be trusted with any document. After leaving Boston, Barons went to South Carolina where he again was involved in a most questionable use of a private document: see C.O. 5/390, foll. 101–109, 120–129.

49. Amherst to surveyors general Temple and Randolph, April 24, 1762, C.O. 5/62, foll. 105–106.

50. Beer, *Colonial Policy,* 110, note 2. Only the governors of Georgia and Nova Scotia were not included.

51. Owen A. Sherrard, *Lord Chatham and America* (London, 1958), 10–11.

Bute had been made a privy councilor two days after the accession of George III. He became Secretary of State on March 25, 1761. Bute was a Scottish peer who had not been elected to the House of Lords.

52. See above, Chapter VI, note 75.

53. John Brooke, *The Chatham Administration, 1766–1768* (London, 1956), xi.

54. Duke of Newcastle's minutes of the meeting of the Council, October 2, 1761, as printed in P. C. Yorke, *Life and Correspondence of Philip Yorke, Earl of Hardwicke,* 3 vols. (Cambridge, Eng., 1913), III, 279–280.

55. Sherrard, *Chatham and America,* 17. Leicester House, the residence of the Prince of Wales, under the Hanoverians, was traditionally the center of opposition to the administration. As such, it attracted many Tories to its councils. Bute, as tutor to the Prince of Wales, necessarily was associated with their viewpoints.

56. Richard Pares, *King George III and the Politicians* (Oxford, 1959), 109.

57. John C. Miller, *Origins of the American Revolution* (Boston, 1943), 82.

58. Treasury to Customs, May 21, 1763, T. 11/27, p. 282.

59. Minutes of February 20 and March 18, 1760, T. 29/33, pp. 290, 304.

60. George III to Bute, undated, as quoted in Sir Lewis Namier, *Charles Townshend, His Character and Career* (Cambridge, Eng., 1959), 20.

61. Namier, *Townshend,* 16–17.

62. Knollenberg, *American Revolution,* 35.

63. William Bollan to Josiah Willard (secretary to the province of Massachusetts), March 5, 1758, in Massachusetts Historical Society, *Collections,* 1st series, VI (Boston, 1846), 129–130.

64. Bernard to Barrington, May 23, 1759, *The Barrington-Bernard Correspondence and Illustrative Matter, 1760–1770,* Edward Channing and Archibald C. Coolidge, eds. (*Harvard Historical Studies,* XVIII, Cambridge, Mass., 1912), 4–6.

65. William Knox, *Extra-Official State Papers Addressed to the Right Hon. Lord Rawdon,* 2 vols. (London, 1789), II, 28–29.

66. "Mr. Comptroller Weare to the Earl of ———," Massachusetts Historical Society, *Collections,* 1st series, I (Boston, 1806), 66–84.

67. "Hints Respecting the Settlement of our American Provinces," Add. MSS. 38335, foll. 14–18. On the authorship of this document, see Charles R. Ritcheson, *British Politics and the American Revolution* (Norman, 1954), 10, note 8. My analysis of the text of this document will appear in a forthcoming issue of the *William and Mary Quarterly.*

68. Report of the Board of Trade, 1772, as printed in *The Writings of Benjamin Franklin,* Albert H. Smyth, ed., 10 vols. (Boston, 1907), V, 468. The Currency Act of 1764, while not directly associated with the customs service, is another example of the efforts at centralization in these years: see Knollenberg, *American Revolution,* 181, 204.

69. 3 George III, c. 22.

70. Allen S. Johnson, "The Passage of the Sugar Act," *William and Mary Quarterly,* 3d series, XVI (October 1959), 508.

71. *Ibid.,* 507.

72. Treasury to Customs, May 21 and July 14, 1763, T. 11/26, pp. 282, 303.

73. This point on absent officers has led some writers to serious errors. It is generally presumed that the absentees were "principals" who operated by deputy in the colonies. That was not the case. When an officer went on leave or was absent

for some reason, a person was appointed, with the approval of the surveyor general, to act for him. It was this practice, not the regular use of deputies by English "principals" (which was not permitted in the American customs service generally), that led to the return-to-post orders of this period. Grosvenor Bedford, whose warrant did allow him to operate by deputy, was concerned about his privilege at this time, but he managed to hold it until his death in 1771: see *Jenkinson Papers*, 188–189.

74. Customs to Treasury, July 21, 1763, T. 1/426, foll. 269–273.

75. Minutes of July 22, 1763, T. 29/35, p. 125; Treasury to Customs, July 23, 1763, T. 11/27, p. 304.

76. Minutes of July 29, 1763, T. 29/35, pp. 135–136; Treasury to Customs, August 1, 1763, T. 11/27, p. 284.

77. Customs to Treasury, September 16, 1763, T. 1/426, foll. 289–295.

78. Minutes of September 21, 1763, T. 29/35, p. 164; Treasury to Customs, September 23, 1763, T. 11/27, pp. 319–320.

79. Johnson, "Sugar Act," *William and Mary Quarterly*, XVI, 511.

80. Minutes of September 22, 1763, T. 29/35, p .165.

81. The text quoted here is from House of Lords MSS., #229; but it is available in print in the *A.P.C.*, IV, 569–572.

82. Above, Chapter V, note 8.

83. Johnson, "Sugar Act," *William and Mary Quarterly*, XVI, 512.

84. John Adams to Hezekiah Niles, February 13, 1818, in the *Works of John Adams*, Charles Francis Adams, ed., 10 vols. (Boston, 1856), X, 286.

85. Johnson, "Sugar Act," *William and Mary Quarterly*, XVI, 511.

86. *Ibid.*, 514.

87. 4 George III, c. 15. Along with the lower molasses duty, imposts were placed on certain wines, foreign coffee and indigo, foreign silks and other materials, and British grown coffee and pimento: Dickerson, *Navigation Acts*, 172–179.

88. Knollenberg, *American Revolution*, 93.

89. "Hints Respecting the Military Establishments in the American Colonys," Add. MSS. 38335, foll. 27–33 (see note 67 above).

90. Clark, *Treasury*, 127.

91. Horace Walpole, *Memoirs of the Reign of George the Third*, 4 vols. (London, 1894), II, 51.

92. Grenville to William Knox, September 15, 1768, in Knox, *Extra-Official State Papers*, II, appendix V, 20–21.

93. James Otis, *The Rights of the British Colonies Asserted and Proved* (Boston, 1764), 54 (as reprinted in the University of Missouri *Studies*, IV, no. 3, 84).

Chapter IX. A Time of Troubles

1. There were comptrollers at New York, Georgia, Philadelphia (covering all Pennsylvania including the Lower Counties), South Carolina (including the Bahamas), and at Boston.

2. Above, Chapter VIII, note 77.

3. Comptrollers were placed at York River, Lower and Upper James, South Potomac, Accomack, and Rappahannock in Virginia; at Patuxent, North Potomac, Pocomoke, and Chester in Maryland; at Lewis and Newcastle in the Lower Counties of Pennsylvania; at Roanoke and Brunswick in North Carolina; at Port Royal and Charleston in South Carolina; at Newfoundland and Nova Scotia; at St. Au-

gustine in East Florida; at Falmouth, Piscataqua, New Haven, New London, Salem and Marblehead, and Rhode Island in New England. Canada had been provided with a comptroller in 1762. The comment of D. M. Clark on this period illustrates the lack of accurate information on the customs service: "In spite of increased business, it [the Treasury] agreed to the appointment of only a few additional port officers": *Treasury,* 133.

4. Treasury to Customs, October 10, 1763, T. 11/27, p. 359. Henry Hulton, a former customs officer in the West Indies, was appointed to the new clerkship.

5. Customs to Treasury, October 10, 1764, T. 11/28, pp. 151–153.

6. Treasury to Customs, November 7, 1764, T. 11/28, p. 153. Steuart had recommended himself to the attention of the English government by his efforts to protect some Spaniards who were forced by "necessities of the sea" to stop in Virginia in 1763. It was a delicate moment in relations with Spain and Steuart's part in mitigating the injury done to the Spaniards by local rioters was gratefully acknowledged in London. He received the post of surveyor general as a reward: see Memorial of Steuart, August 26, 1789, A. O. 13/48 ("Loyalist Claims").

7. Treasury to Customs, September 23, 1763, T. 11/27, p. 320. For example of the certificates used, see Customs to Treasury, October 2, 1765, T. 1/441, foll. 388–404.

8. Above, Chapter IV, note 33.

9. Carl Ubbelohde, *The Vice-Admiralty Courts and the American Revolution* (Chapel Hill, 1960), 48–105.

10. Memorial of John Earnshaw, March 7, 1765, T. 1/441, foll. 317–318. Earnshaw was appointed collector at the Upper James in September, 1765.

11. Treasury to Customs, March 20, 1765, T. 11/28, p. 75.

12. Customs to Treasury, August 15, 1765, in T. 11/28, p. 258.

13. 5 George III, c. 45, p. 27.

14. Governor Bernard and R. Hale to Board of Trade, April 8, 1765, in C.O. 5/891, foll. 485–496, 507–508.

15. Customs to Treasury, March 10, 1762, and Treasury to Customs, April 7, 1762, T. 11/27, p. 71.

16. The action of the Commissioners in reducing the salaries is in Customs to Treasury, January 10, 1766, T. 11/28, p. 290. The dispute on fees was still to be argued as late as 1774: see Collector Thomas Ainslie to Governor Guy Carleton, July 4, 1774, T. 1/515, foll. 87–88. The customs officers finally were forced to take such fees as were allowed at Halifax instead of New York.

17. Minutes of October 23, 1764, and November 1, 1765, T. 29/36, p. 111, and T. 29/37, p. 196.

18. Customs to Surveyor General Temple, January 19, 1765, T. 1/441, foll. 299–300.

19. Minutes of May 17, 1765, T. 29/36, p. 343.

20. Proclamation by Governor Bernard, March 15, 1766, in C.O. 5/755, fol. 521.

21. Minutes of November 14, 1766, T. 29/38, p. 191; Bernard to Shelburne, February 28, 1767, C.O. 5/756, foll. 117–119.

22. Edmund S. and Helen M. Morgan, *The Stamp Act Crisis, Prologue to Revolution* (Chapel Hill, 1953), 41.

23. Temple to Customs, May 7, 1765, T. 1/442, foll. 207–210; Morgan, *Stamp Act,* 44–46.

24. Above, Chapter VIII, note 47.

25. The dispute over patronage between Temple and Bernard shows up most clearly in Temple's letter to the Customs Commissioners, June 23, 1766, in the Temple Letter Book, 1762–1768, pp. 157–158, Massachusetts Historical Society.

26. Bernard to Halifax, December 7, 1764, C.O. 5/755, foll. 169–181; Temple to Customs, October 30, 1764, T. 1/429, foll. 335/337.

27. Temple to Customs, November 30, 1764, T. 1/441, foll. 287–290.

28. Bernard to Halifax, as above, note 26.

29. Customs to Treasury, November 18, 1761, in T. 1/408, fol. 101.

30. Bernard to Halifax, December 29, 1764, C.O. 5/755, foll. 205–207.

31. Temple to Customs, May 7, 1765, T. 1/442, foll. 207–210; Bernard to Halifax, May 11, 1765, C. O. 5/755, foll. 229–235; Ubbelohde, *Vice-Admiralty Courts,* 68–69.

32. Entry of September 29, 1764, in the diary of John Rowe, as quoted in Ubbelohde, *Vice-Admiralty Courts,* 59–60.

33. Admiral Alexander Lord Colville to Philip Stephens (secretary to the Admiralty), September 22, 1764, T. 1/442, fol. 331.

34. Bernard to Halifax, December 7, 1764, C.O. 5/755, foll. 169–181.

35. Customs to Temple, January 19, 1765, T. 1/441, foll. 299–300.

36. S. Mather to J. Robinson, April 7, 1773, in T. 1/501, fol. 312; Stephens to Grey Cooper (secretary of the Admiralty to secretary of the Treasury), March 20, 1772, T. 1/495, foll. 330–331.

37. Above, Chapter VII, note 79.

38. 5 George III, c. 12.

39. Morgan, *Stamp Act,* 106–107.

40. Bernard to Richard Jackson, August 24, 1765, as quoted in Morgan, *Stamp Act,* 129–130.

41. Morgan, *Stamp Act,* 130–131.

42. The story of the customs officers and the problem of the stamps is in various letters, House of Lords MSS., #238, pp. 65–107. Temple's letter taking credit for the delaying action will be found on p. 103 of that collection. See also Morgan, *Stamp Act,* 133–139.

43. Morgan, *Stamp Act,* 159–162. The details of the actions of the customs officers in the other colonies will be found in these and the following pages in Morgan.

44. Miller, *American Revolution,* 158.

45. John Robinson and John Nicholl to Customs, October 30, 1766, T. 1/459, foll. 42–49.

46. Andrews to Treasury, September 30, 1766, in T. 1/459, foll. 50–53.

47. Ubbelohde, *Vice-Admiralty Courts,* 96–97.

48. The various papers on the Malcom affair will be found in T. 1/446, foll. 103–133.

49. Minutes of February 6, 1767, T. 29/38, p. 271.

50. Minutes of February 13, 1767, T. 29/38, pp. 282–283.

51. Minutes of March 1766, T. 29/37, p. 374.

52. Affidavit of Edward Davis, n.d. (presented to Treasury, July 13, 1769), T. 1/469, foll. 303–306.

53. Treasury to Customs, October 18, 1766, T. 11/28, p. 127.

54. The story of the fees is covered in the affidavit of Davis, as above, note 51.

55. Extract of a letter from Captain Hawker, dated June 13, 1767, T. 1/459, foll. 170–171.

56. Hawker to governor of South Carolina, May 30, 1767, T. 1/459, foll. 174–175.

57. Extract from a letter from Hawker, as above, note 55.

58. Moore to Customs, August 25, 1767, T. 1/459, foll. 166–173; Hawker to Customs, October 25, 1767, T. 1/461, foll. 252–253.

59. Moore to Customs, as above, note 58.

60. Above, note 45.

61. Laurens to James Habersham, September 5, 1756, Laurens Letter Book 1767–1771, pp. 7–13, South Carolina Historical Society, Charleston.

62. Roupell to Customs, September 16, 1767, T. 1/459, foll. 176–177.

63. Report of Inspector General Williams, December 22, 1768, T. 1/505, foll. 291–292.

64. As above, note 62.

65. Livingston to ———, November 2, 1765, as quoted in Morgan, *Stamp Act,* 107.

66. As quoted in Morgan, *Stamp Act,* 267.

67. Unsigned article in the *London Chronicle,* January 7, 1775, as quoted in Dickerson, *Navigation Acts,* 283. Dickerson naturally puts a different interpretation on this passage than that suggested here.

Chapter X. Fulfillment

1. Sherrard, *Chatham and America,* 271, 258; Namier, *Townshend,* 2–3.

2. Namier, *Townshend,* 29.

3. 6 George III, c. 52. For an indication of American reaction, at least that of New York, to the enactments of the Rockingham administration, see Jack M. Sosin, *Agents and Merchants* (Lincoln, 1965), 97–99.

4. Ritcheson, *British Politics,* 84.

5. William Johnson to William Pitkin, February 12, 1767, Maryland Historical Society, *Collections,* 5th series, IX (1885), 216.

6. Pitt to Shelburne, February 7, 1767, in *Correspondence of William Pitt, Earl of Chatham,* 3 vols. (London, 1838–1839), III, 193.

7. Benjamin Labaree, *The Boston Tea Party* (New York, 1964), 19.

8. 7 George III, c. 46; Miller, *American Revolution,* 243–249.

9. Miller, *American Revolution,* 250.

10. Brooke, *Chatham Administration,* 94–99.

11. Sherrard, *Chatham and America,* 268–269.

12. Namier, *Townshend,* 28–29.

13. 7 George III, c. 46.

14. Miller, *American Revolution,* 247–248.

15. Clark, *Treasury,* 174.

16. Treasury to Customs, April 12, 1765, T. 1/441, foll. 337–338.

17. Customs to Treasury, February 27, 1766, T. 1/453, fol. 298.

18. Minutes of January 9, 1767, T. 29/38, p. 245.

19. Customs to Treasury, April 30, 1767, T. 1/459, foll. 83–86.

20. Minutes of May 1, 1767, T. 29/38, pp. 366–367.

21. "A Plan for an Establishment of a Board of Customs Commissioners in North America," n.d. (read at Treasury July 22, 1767), T. 1/459, foll. 206–207.

22. Minutes of July 29, 1767, T. 29/38, pp. 443–444.

23. Dickerson, *Navigation Acts,* 208–209. Clark, *Treasury,* 182, comments that the appointees were "a rather undistinguished group."

24. Samuel Fitch, a local attorney in Massachusetts, was first used by the American Board as solicitor, until David Lisle was sent out from England at a later date.

25. 7 George III, c. 41.

26. Treasury to American Board, June 29, 1769, T. 28/1, foll. 338–339.

27. See above, Chapter VI, note 100; and Chapter VII, note 25.

28. Ubbelohde, *Vice-Admiralty Courts,* 130–131.

29. See above, Chapter V, note 78.

30. Thomas Pownall, *Administration of the Colonies* (London, 1764), 11–20.

31. Pitt, *Correspondence,* II, 181–183.

32. Margaret M. Spector, *The American Department of the British Government, 1768–1782* (New York, 1940), 12, 17–19.

33. See above, Chapter VII, note 94.

34. Spector, *American Department,* 80.

35. Newcastle to Duke of Portland, September 24, 1768, Add. MSS. 32991, fol. 125.

36. Namier, *Townshend,* 17.

Chapter XI. Collapse

1. Dora Mae Clark, "The American Board of Customs, 1767–1783," *American Historical Review,* XLV (July 1940), 777.

2. Bernard to Shelburne, September 21, 1767, C.O. 5/756, foll. 253–255.

3. Edward Channing, *A History of the United States,* 6 vols. (New York, 1905–1925), III, 86–87; Clark, "American Board," *American Historical Review,* XLV, 785–786.

4. American Board to Treasury, February 12, 1768, C.O. 5/757, foll. 62–65.

5. Bernard to Hillsborough, March 19, 1768, C.O. 5/757, foll. 66–73.

6. Bernard to Secretary of State, March 21, 1768, C.O. 5/757, foll. 76–79; American Board to Treasury, March 28, 1768, C.O. 5/757, foll. 94–95.

7. The incident and its repercussions are covered in the letter of the American Board to the Treasury, May 12, 1768, T. 1/465, foll. 348–349. See also Baxter, *Hancock,* 260–262.

8. American Board to Treasury, March 28, 1768, C.O. 5/757, foll. 94–95.

9. Collector John Swift to Inspector William Wootton, November 2, 1771, in Customs House Papers, XII (1771–1774), item 1, The Historical Society of Pennsylvania, Philadelphia. On Swift generally see Alfred S. Martin, "The King's Customs: Philadelphia, 1761–1774," *William and Mary Quarterly,* 3d series (April 1948), 201–216.

10. Baxter, *Hancock,* 63.

11. Ubbelohde, *Vice-Admiralty Courts,* 121–123.

12. Baxter, *Hancock,* 264–265, prints an eyewitness account of the seizure and the conduct of the crowd.

13. Minutes of July 21 and November 29, 1768, T. 29/39, pp. 170–171, 255.

14. On the attorney general's opinion see C.O. 5/757, foll. 229–232.

15. Ubbelohde, *Vice-Admiralty Courts,* 124–127. Compare Ubbelohde's discussion with the version found in Dickerson, *Navigation Acts,* 240–246. Also, *Legal Papers*

of John Adams, L. K. Wroth and H. Zobel, eds., 3 vols. (Boston, 1965), 173–210.

16. Miller, *American Revolution,* 293–296. The troops had been reduced from four to two regiments before the Massacre took place.

17. Roupell to American Board, July 11, 1768, T. 1/465, foll. 416–418; Ubbelohde, *Vice-Admiralty Courts,* 108–109.

18. Roupell to American Board, July 11, 1768, T. 1/465, foll. 416–418.

19. Ubbelohde, *Vice-Admiralty Courts,* 110–114.

20. Minutes of July 28, 1768, T. 29/39, pp. 172–173.

21. Extract of a letter from the collector and comptroller of Salem and Marblehead, dated June 20, 1768, T. 1/465, fol. 400.

22. Affidavit of Thomas Row, September 9, and John Fisher, September 13, 1768, to American Board, T. 1/465, foll. 402–403, 408–409.

23. There are several revealing exchanges between Temple and Paxton preserved in the Temple Letter Book, 1762–1768, in the Massachusetts Historical Society, such as this one from Temple to Paxton (January 27, 1766): "I shou'd never tho't it worth while to have Enter'd upon particulars in the Manner that I did this morning if you had not Obliged me to it. Ease of mind, and a calm disposition are principal pursuits with me and no consideration shou'd tempt me to the pain that I receive at Recollecting past Insincerity and ingratitude, let it be sufficient that I now coolly tell you, *all that is past I forgive* and desire to forget. I shall always treat you like a Gentleman, but desire no further Intimacy than our offices necessarily Requires."

24. Temple to Grafton, October 25, 1769, T. 1/469, foll. 185–190.

25. Temple to Grenville, November 7, 1768, *The Grenville Papers: Being the Correspondence of Richard Grenville Earl Temple, K.G., and the Right Hon. George Grenville, their Friends and Contemporaries,* William James Smith, ed., 4 vols. (London, 1852–1853), IV, 396–397.

26. Hutchinson to Hillsborough, February 3, 1769, C.O. 5/758, foll. 131–133.

27. American Board to [Treasury], January 12, 1770, T. 1/476, foll. 72–77. Hutchinson secretly had passed on to the Commissioners a copy of an indictment being prepared against them in the colonial courts. He did not want Temple to know of his action for fear that through him the "faction" would learn of his "treachery" and make effective propaganda out of it.

28. Above, Chapter IX, note 26.

29. Temple's certificate in favor of Folger, May 10, 1768, T. 1/465, foll. 248–249; Baxter, *Hancock,* 226–231, 243, 246.

30. Copy of articles #25 and #26 from the report of Inspector Williams, n.d., T. 1/465, foll. 287–289.

31. Charges against Fisher, July 15, 1768, T. 1/465, foll. 326–327.

32. Answer of Fisher, August 31, 1768, T. 1/465, foll. 308–318.

33. American Board to Treasury, October 4, 1768, T. 1/465, foll. 326–327.

34. Cooper (secretary to Treasury) to American Board, December 26, 1768, T. 1/465, foll. 285–286.

35. Treasury to American Board, June 29, 1769, T. 28/1, foll. 338–339.

36. Clark, *Treasury,* 184.

37. Accounts of the Cashier and Paymaster, September 8, 1767, to January 5, 1769, T. 1/461, fol. 250.

38. "Ports of North America," Add. MSS. 15484. Andrews dates this document

"about 1770" and undoubtedly is correct, judging from internal evidence. The document itself seemingly is a summary of various field reports forwarded to the American Board and in turn sent by them to London. See Appendix D.

39. Bernard to Hillsborough, July 11, 1768, C.O. 5/757, foll. 307–308.

40. The text of the circular letter is readily available in *English Historical Documents: American Colonial Documents to 1776,* Merrill Jensen, ed. (New York, 1955), 714–716.

41. Miller, *American Revolution,* 260.

42. Jensen, *American Colonial Documents,* 716–717; Miller, *American Revolution,* 262–264.

43. Ritcheson, *British Politics,* 136–137; William B. Pemberton, *Lord North* (London, 1938), 212–213.

44. Ritcheson, *British Politics,* 136.

45. Pemberton, *North,* 213.

46. Ritcheson, *British Politics,* 138.

47. Bernard Donoughue, *British Politics and the American Revolution: The Path to War, 1773–75* (London, 1964), 7, note 1. In several chapters Donoughue sets out the alternatives to a hard-line policy as they were debated after 1773 (see especially chapters 6, 10, 11).

48. Miller, *American Revolution,* 280–281.

49. *Ibid.,* 267.

50. Steuart's accounts are in A.O. 1/844/1137. The total revenue for the period from September 7, 1767, to January, 1777, was £257,039.

51. American Board to Treasury, December 21, 1770, T. 1/476, foll. 139–140.

52. Deputy Collector Swift to American Board, November 15, 1770, T. 1/476, foll. 91–93; Hatton to same, December 30, 1770, T. 1/482, foll. 157–158.

53. Swift and Barclay to American Board, December 20, 1770, T. 1/482, foll. 185–187.

54. Comptroller General Porter to American Board, June 12, 1770, and O. Richards to the collector and comptroller of Boston, May 21, 1770, T. 1/476, foll. 66–67, 68–69.

55. Hutchinson to [———], August 27 and 29, 1772, as quoted in Miller, *American Revolution,* 327.

56. Pownall to Cooper, August 3, 1774, T. 1/508, foll. 170–177.

57. American Board to Treasury, January 11, 1771, T. 1/482, foll. 194–197.

58. Minutes of July 2, 1771, T. 29/41, p. 206.

59. American Board to Treasury, February 11, 1773, T. 1/501, foll. 350–353. The draft of the proposed new regulations is in T. 1/501, foll. 342–346.

60. Captain Samuel Hood to Treasury, April 19, 1774, T. 1/509, foll. 15–16.

61. Miller, *American Revolution,* 279.

62. Quoted in an enclosure in a letter from Bernard to Hillsborough, February 25, 1769, C.O. 5/758, fol. 147.

63. Adams to Arthur Lee, April 19, 1771, *The Writings of Samuel Adams,* Harry A. Cushing, ed., 4 vols. (New York, 1904–1908), II, 164–167.

64. Labaree, *Boston Tea Party,* 71. The details of the arrangements made with the Company are covered in chapter 4.

65. Miller, *American Revolution,* 355. As North himself noted in his speech on the Boston Port Bill, "we are now to dispute the question whether we have, or

have not any authority in that country": quoted in Donoughue, *British Politics,* 77.

66. American Board to Treasury, January 4, 1774, T. 1/505, fol. 11.

67. Opinion of Attorney General Sewall, May 30, 1774, and American Board to Treasury, June 30, 1774, T. 1/505, foll. 240, 248–249.

68. Charles Dudley and Nicholl to American Board, December 22, 1774, T. 1/505, foll. 69–70.

69. American Board to Treasury, September 20, 1774, T. 1/505, foll. 278–279. On the problems of supplies from Marblehead see same, foll. 251–252, 263–264.

70. For the text of the various Acts, the procedure of the First Congress, and the engagement at Lexington and Concord, see Jensen, *American Colonial Documents,* 781–831.

71. American Board to Treasury, November 30, 1775, T. 1/513, fol. 251.

72. George Meserve and Robert Traill to American Board, May 18, 1775, T. 1/513, foll. 28–29.

73. American Board (now in London) to Treasury, December 5, 1776, T. 1/520, foll. 158–159.

Chapter XII. Retrospect

1. Pemberton, *North,* 21.

2. *Ibid.,* 2.

3. North always hid his sense of failure under a ready and self-depreciating wit, as witness his favorite story of his tutor who told him "You're a blundering blockhead and if you are ever Prime Minister it will always be the same": *ibid.,* 12.

4. Knox, *Extra-Official State Papers,* II, 11.

5. Bellomont to Board of Trade, September 8, 1699, Rawlinson MSS. A, 272, fol. 62.

6. Heathcote to Treasury, January 2, 1715/16, *C.T.B., 1714–19,* 185.

7. Heathcote to Board of Trade, September 7, 1719, Fox, *Heathcote,* 186–189.

8. Osgood, *Seventeenth Century,* III, 241.

9. Heathcote to Board of Trade, September 7, 1719, Fox, *Heathcote,* 186–189.

10. "Extract of a Letter from New England," n.d., Add. MSS. 33029, fol. 322.

11. Bancroft, *History,* IV, 85–86.

12. Knox, *Extra-Official State Papers,* II, 24–26.

13. *Ibid.,* 54.

14. Benjamin Franklin, *Rules for Reducing a Great Empire to a Small One* (London, 1773), in *Writings of Benjamin Franklin,* VI, 134.

15. John Adams to William Tudor, August 16, 1818, in *Works of John Adams,* X, 348. On another occasion, commenting on the use made by the English of the revenues collected between 1765 and 1775, Adams asserted that, "In the course of these ten years, they formed and organized and drilled and disciplined a party in favor of Great Britain, and they seduced and deluded nearly one third of the people of the colonies": Adams to Jedidiah Morse, December 22, 1815, in *Works of John Adams,* X, 193.

Index

Index

Barons *v.* Paxton, 171

Bath, Earl of, 121

Bathtown, N.C., 138, 145, 266; customs staff in *1760,* 263; customs district, boundaries of, 271–272

Battine, James, 263

Baxter, William T., 231, 310n51

Beaufin, Hector Berenger de, 204, 263

Beaufort, N.C., 138; customs staff in *1760,* 263; customs district, boundaries of, 271–272

Bedford, Duke of, 157, 158

Bedford faction (in English politics), 157–158, 224, 225

Bedford, Grosvenor, 131, 141, 263, 297n44, 314–315n73

Beef, trade in, 150, 161

Beer, George L., 2, 143, 287n6, 309n31

Belcher, Jonathan, 117–118, 127, 131, 136–137, 304n43, 308n15

Bellomont, Earl of, 60, 67, 68, 71, 81, 95, 97, 187, 253–254, 300–301n40

Berkeley, Sir William, 21, 22, 23, 29, 37

Bermuda, 14, 18, 56, 66, 72, 74, 221; customs staff in *1710,* 262, in *1760,* 264

Bermuda Hundred, Va., 271

Bernard, Sir Francis, 132, 145, 170, 171, 175, 190, 192–196, 199, 222, 227, 228, 233, 234, 236, 238, 241, 317n25; feud with John Temple, 192–196

Berry, Sir John, 34

Berwick on Tweed, 5, 287n5

Bills of credit, 151–152

Birchfield, Maurice, 72, 80, 85–87, 89, 91, 93, 262, 298n1, 300–301n40, 301n50

Bird, Valentine, 24

Bladen, William, 65–66, 85, 261

Blakiston, Nathaniel, 28

Bland, Giles, 21, 22, 23, 24, 37, 43

Blathwayt, William, 39, 67, 278, 292n1

Blechyden, Charles, 80, 96, 262, 296n35

Board of Trade, 63, 71, 79, 98, 101, 104, 107, 108, 110–111, 112, 113, 116, 124, 134, 155, 156, 157–158, 163–166, 167–168, 175, 176, 177, 184, 225, 294n44, 296n28, 306n58, 311–312n95; report of *1721,* 108, 303n5; function of, 111; revival of (under Halifax), 157–158; Journal of, 163, 275; relations with secretary of state, 303n20

Bollan, William, 150, 151, 153, 154, 156–157, 164, 167, 180, 233, 309n25

Bonds, use of in enforcement of Navigation Acts, 6, 7, 8, 11, 14, 15, 16, 22, 46, 47, 50, 51, 54, 55, 57, 58, 66, 76, 78, 85, 86, 87, 94, 166, 179, 183, 205, 206, 207, 214, 247–248, 265

Boston, Mass., 30, 32, 33, 34, 35, 36, 42, 47, 61, 68, 70, 71, 75, 78, 79, 81, 89, 90, 95, 96, 97, 100, 101, 102, 107, 112, 122, 123, 124, 126, 127, 129, 131, 140, 141, 146, 147, 148, 149, 161, 162, 165, 169, 170, 172, 176, 189, 190, 194, 199, 218, 224, 227, 228, 229, 230, 233, 234, 240, 241, 242, 246, 250, 251, 252, 262, 267, 305n52, 315n1; customs staff in *1710,* 73, 262; value of posts in, 129, 307n94; as site for American Board, 222–223; British troops in, 233–234; customs staff in *1760,* 264; customs district, boundaries of, 269

Boston Massacre, 234, 237, 245, 250, 320n16

Boston Port Act, 250, 251

Boston Tea Party, 249

Bounties, 2, 151

Bowles, James, 79–80

Bradstreet, Simon, **33**

Brandy, trade in, 91, 134, 150

Bread, trade in, 150

Brenton, Jahleel, 40, 41, 42, 43, 47, 48, 54, 61, 68, 70, 71, 81, 292n3, 293n14, 295n13, 296n32

Brett, Apsley, 119, 305n46

Bribes, 96, 130, 190, 194, 230, 231, 307n89

Bricks, trade in, 150

Bridlington, N.J. *see* Burlington, N.J.

Bristol, R.I., 269

Brook, Henry, 262

Brooke, Childley, 67, 68, 293n27, 295n13, 296n22 and n24

Brooke, Thomas, 262

Broughton, Sampson, 60, 295n6

Broughton, Thomas, 261

Broughton Island Packet, the, 207–208, 234

Browne, James, 148

Bruckner, William, 261

Brunswick, N.C., 138, 272, 315n3; customs staff in *1760,* 263; customs district, boundaries of, 272

Bull, William, 204

Bullionism, 2

Bunker Hill, Battle of, 251

Burch, William, 222. *See also* Commissioners of the Customs, American

Burlington (Bridlington), N.J., 7, 267; customs staff in *1710,* 73, 262, in *1760,* 264; customs district, boundaries of, 270

Burnet, William, 132

Bute, Lord, 173–174, 175–176, 177, 225, 305n48, 313–314n51, 314n55

Butler, Sir Nicholas, 292n1

Index

Index

Index

328

Index

Index

Index

Molasses, 97, 101, 102, 134, 135, 137, 142–143, 144, 148, 149, 150, 155, 160, 165, 166, 168, 175, 180, 183, 192, 193, 197, 214, 238, 239, 243, 254, 301n51, 309n29, 315n87

Molasses Act (*1733*), 75, 131, 134–137, 145, 154, 157, 166, 170, 177–178, 179, 182, 255, 257, 308n7; evasion of, 142–143

Mompesson, Roger, 62, 63

Montague, John, 197

Monte Christi, Hispaniola, 161, 162, 167, 168

Moore, Daniel, 204–209

Moore, John, 79, 91, 92–93, 94, 97, 98, 110, 261

Moore, Lambert, 264

Morton, Joseph, 62

Mosely, Edward, 263

Mount Desert, Maine, 269

Munro, George, 127

Murray, Alexander, 119, 305n46

Muschamp, George, 27, 38, 80

Musgrave, Sir William, 274

Mutiny Act, 215, 216–217

Nahant, Mass., 269

Namier, Sir Lewis, 114, 213

Nantasket, Mass., 36

Nantucket, Mass., 78, 129, 238, 241, 269

Naval lists, 12, 78

Naval office, colonial, 35, 43, 44, 46, 47, 50, 58, 60, 68, 69–70, 76, 82, 95, 106, 125, 140, 152, 188, 293n14, 294n44, 310n68; relations with customs officers, 35, 37, 44, 45, 54; duties of, 78; patronage in, 117–119; role in entering ships, 265

Naval stores, 98

Navigation Acts, 2, 3, 4, 7, 9, 10, 11, 12, 13, 15, 17, 18, 20, 21, 22, 23, 27, 31, 32, 34, 36, 37, 38, 42, 45, 48, 52, 53, 54, 55, 56, 57, 58, 60, 61, 62, 63, 68, 72, 76, 78, 84, 85, 87, 93, 94, 95, 103, 106, 107, 108, 112, 138, 146, 147, 152, 154, 159, 160, 165, 167, 168, 169, 170, 171, 177, 182, 184, 186, 187, 190, 192, 196, 197, 198, 201, 202, 206, 207, 209, 211, 222, 237, 243, 245, 247, 248, 253, 254, 256, 310n51, 311n86; Act of *1651*, 4, 5, 11; Act of *1660*, 5, 6, 11, 17, 21, 27, 31, 32, 33, 56, 183, 294n47; Act of *1663*, 4, 6, 11, 12, 21, 31, 32, 33, 45, 311n75; Act of *1673*, 6, 7–9, 10, 13,

14, 21, 24, 28, 30, 32, 54, 106, 177, 178, 182, 288n7; Act of *1696*, 53–59, 60, 65, 69, 76, 87, 102, 112, 196; legal status of Acts, 156–157, 203. *See also* Mercantilism

Navigation laws, *see* Navigation Acts

Navigation system, *see* Navigation Acts; Old Colonial System

Navy, royal, use in colonies, 11, 17, 19, 70, 99–100, 103, 136, 157, 162, 184, 191, 204, 222–223, 227, 232, 245, 247, 248, 294n47, 311n85 and n86; relations with customs service, 35, 156, 196–197, 301–302n54

Nevin, James, 120–122, 264, 306n58

Nevis, 24. *See also* West Indies

New England, 8, 9, 15, 16, 17, 18, 19, 24, 25, 26, 30, 34, 36, 37, 38, 40, 48, 51, 61, 64, 68, 69, 70, 71, 81, 88, 90, 94, 116, 120, 121, 136, 137, 138, 147, 150, 157, 161, 164, 228, 294n44, 295n13, 308n100, 309n25, 315–316n3; customs districts, boundaries of 32, 73, 269–270; *quo warranto* proceedings against the colonies of, 34; customs staff of, memorial on the sugar trade, 134; political groupings in, 291n46. *See also* Dominion of New England; *also individual colonies*

New Hampshire, 30, 60, 62, 68, 71, 82, 90, 95, 99, 121, 164, 251–252; customs staff in *1710*, 73, 262, in *1760*, 264; customs district, boundaries of, 269; value of posts in, 307n94

New Haven, Conn., 124, 241, 315–316n3; boundaries of, 269–270

New Jersey, 18, 19, 47, 51, 60, 72, 74, 91, 99, 120, 153, 161, 163, 168, 186, 241, 245–246, 298n1, 308n101; customs staff in *1710*, 73, 262, in *1760*, 264; customs districts, boundaries of, 138, 270; civil list in, 245

New London, Conn., 61, 81, 120, 262, 268, 315–316n3; boundaries of, 269

New York (city and colony), 17, 18, 31, 47, 51, 56, 60, 61, 62, 66–68, 71, 74, 77, 82, 90, 91, 96, 99, 107, 120, 123–124, 142, 146, 147, 148, 149, 152, 153, 154, 161, 163, 164, 168, 186, 190, 191, 197, 198, 210, 217, 221, 222, 234, 267, 269, 295n6, 298n1, 299n22, 300–301n40, 315n1, 316n16; legislature of, 60, 94, 215; casual revenues of, 66–67, 73, 244n49, 295n21; political groups in (*1690's*), 67–68; customs staff in *1710*, 73, 262, in *1760*, 264; civil list in, 245;

Index

Index

73, 261, in *1760*, 263; courts, used against customs officers, 92, 94; lieutenant governor, feud with collector, 92–93; legislature, 93; customs districts, boundaries of, 270

Penobscot, Maine, 269

Pensacola, Florida, 271

Perth Amboy, N.J., 66, 90, 241, 267; customs staff in *1710*, 73, 262, in *1760*, 264; customs district, boundaries of, 270

Phelps, John, 261

Philadelphia, 47, 74, 78, 79, 91, 92, 95, 97, 107, 110, 131, 141, 161, 163, 200, 221, 222, 224, 240–241, 246, 251, 252, 261, 263, 267, 297n44, 315n1; customs staff in *1710*, 73, 261, in *1760*, 263; customs district, boundaries of, 270

Phips, Sir William, 40, 41, 42, 43, 47, 292n3

Pigot, John, 264

Pimentos, trade in, 183, 315n87

Pintard, John, 146

Pirates, 68, 71, 97. *See also* Privateers

Piscataqua, N.H., 32, 71, 81, 82, 89, 120, 121, 251, 262, 267, 306n58, 315–316n3; customs staff in *1710*, 73, 262, in *1760*, 264; customs district, boundaries of, 269

Pitt, Thomas, 125

Pitt, William, 114, 125, 173, 174, 187, 210, 211, 215–216, 224, 243–244, 249, 304n27; circular letter (*1760*), 163

Plantation clerk, 186, 221, 222

Planters, West Indies, *see* West Indies, British planters

Plater, George, 45

Plowman, Mathew, 67

Plumb, J. H., 115

Plural officeholding, 44

Plymouth, Mass., 78, 241, 250, 269

Pocomoke, Md., 66, 69, 191, 266, 315n3; customs staff in *1710*, 73, 261, in *1760*, 263; customs district, boundaries of, 270

Politics, English, 113–116

Poll tax, colonial, suggestions for, 155

Polly, the, 192, 195

Poole, England, 290n23

Pork, trade in, 150

Port au Prince, 162

Port Dauphin, 161

Port Royal, S.C., 138, 315n3; customs staff in *1760*, 263; customs district, boundaries of, 272

Ports, 297n38; records of, 75, 78, 101; English, 101; free, 162

Portsmouth, N.H., 42, 269

Portugal, 141, 145

Potomac River, 73, 107, 261, 263, 266, 270

"Power of the purse," 210, 226

Pownall, Thomas, 137, 225

Preventive officers, 72, 73, 106; duties of, 78

Price, Edward, 66, 261

Prince of Wales, 314n55

Privateers, 47, 51, 52. *See also* Pirates

Privy Council, 4, 7, 9, 12, 16, 27, 43, 60, 88, 89, 92, 108, 109, 112, 113, 118, 135, 156, 164, 167, 168, 174, 175, 180, 181, 202, 299n13, 311–312n95; function of, in colonial affairs, 110

Prizes, 42, 53, 96, 177

Proclamation Line (*1763*), 176

Prohibitions, use of by colonial courts, 61, 88, 149, 154

Proprietaries, *see* Colonies, proprietary

Providence, R.I., 144, 162, 269

Provisions, trade in, 150, 160, 166–167, 172

Pue, Jonathan, 305n52

Puritans, 291n46

Quakers, 79

Quarantine inspection, 77

Quarme, Mr., 122–124, 126, 306n63 and n77

Quartering Act (*1774*), 251

Quary, Robert, 62, 69, 70, 71, 72, 262

Quebec, 168

Queen Anne's War, 161

Queensberry, Duke of, 146

Quincy family, 146

Randall, William, 187

Randolph, Edward, 16, 17, 30, 31, 32, 33, 34, 35, 36, 37, 38, 39, 40, 43, 44, 47, 48, 49, 50, 52, 53, 54, 55, 56, 57, 63, 65, 66, 67, 68, 71, 291n51, 292n1, 293 n27, 294n40 and n44 and n47, 295n19, 296n28; summary of career of, 69

Randolph, Peter, 187, 264

Rappahannock, Va., 261, 266, 307n94, 315 n3; customs staff in *1710*, 73, 261, in *1760*, 263; customs district, boundaries of, 271

Rappahannock River, Va., 73

Razor, Peter, 264

Read, James, 263

Rebates, 215

"Rebellion Road," S.C., 96

Receiver general, role in entering ships, 265

Registers, *see* Ships, registration of

Registration, *see* Ships, registration of

Reid, Charles, 264

Index

Index

Index